QA 320

Imagining the Internet

Imagining the Internet

Communication, Innovation, and Governance

Robin Mansell

OXFORD
UNIVERSITY PRESS

OXFORD

UNIVERSITY PRESS

Great Clarendon Street, Oxford OX2 6DP
United Kingdom

Oxford University Press is a department of the University of Oxford.
It furthers the University's objective of excellence in research, scholarship,
and education by publishing worldwide. Oxford is a registered trade mark of
Oxford University Press in the UK and in certain other countries

First published 2012
Reprinted 2013

British Library Cataloguing in Publication Data
Data available

Library of Congress Cataloging in Publication Data
Data available

ISBN 978-0-19-969705-2

In memory of
Christopher Freeman and Roger Silverstone

For
Lukas

■ PREFACE

This book is for students of the past, present, and future communication system. It is for people in policy, business, and civil society who want to influence change in this system and also for people who are largely unaware that what they do every day is changing this system. I examine some of the causes and consequences of innovations in the modern digital communication system. These have been at the centre of my interest in social transformation for a long time. Investigations of what has come to be known as the information society normally are conducted within disciplinary boundaries in the humanities, social sciences, or natural and physical sciences. In this book, I cross these boundaries, something I have been encouraged to do throughout my career.

My engagement with changes in information and communication technologies (ICTs) led me on a journey into anthropology, clinical and social psychology, politics, economics, media and communication studies, science and technology policy studies, telecommunication engineering, and sociology in approximately that order and with varying levels of understanding. This was not a journey according to a plan; it was the result of my pursuit of answers to questions about digital technologies and about communication processes. Along the way, remarkable people provided answers to some of my intermediate questions. I have seen how differently people imagine the worlds of technological innovation and social change, depending on their ways of framing questions and the puzzles they want to address.

The idea that mediated communication through time and space is implicated in cultural, social, political, and economic formations was deeply ingrained in my mind through my early exposure to the works of Harold A. Innis and Marshall McLuhan. I was sceptical about their emphasis on technology, so initially I studied clinical, and later, social psychology, seeking answers to questions about the communication process and the genesis of conflict. Some important answers were provided by Professor Hilde Himmelweit, one of the tutors on my master's degree programme at the London School of Economics and Political Science (LSE) in the mid-1970s. She stressed how social practices shape communication systems, identified continuities and disruptive developments in the history of the media, and encouraged her students to explore the value and limitations of efforts to regulate the media and the communication system.

When I returned to Canada, I joined a bank at the time when computers were beginning to replace mechanical machines and transforming banking practice and the skills base required of employees. Bank regulations and 'best practice' manuals seemed to be hindrances to everyday work practice. We had to find ways of sometimes working with, and often subverting, the new information technology applications that we were told to use by senior management and technology system developers, when we wanted to get things done. This experience made me wonder about the ideas of those who hold the power to decide how the communication system develops.

Following this, I began further academic work at Simon Fraser University, and studied with Professors William H. Melody and Dallas W. Smythe, both political economists. One of Smythe's preoccupations was with whether innovations in the communication system might further the interests of the less powerful, becoming an enabler of revolutionary change. One of Melody's was with prospects for the reform of policy and regulatory institutions to help guide innovations in technology in the light of what he and others understood to be the public interest. Their visions of the information society were vastly different as were their ideas about the way power operates within the capitalist system. Yet they managed to conduct research and teaching together and to take common positions in controversial policy debates. I often asked myself how it might be possible to hold such different visions, yet find common cause in the practice of research and policy advocacy.

I worked also with Richard Gabel, an engineer who had helped to build the rural American telephone system before World War II and who knew the contemporary technologies and operator business practices inside out. When Melody and I did a study of the costs of providing telecommunication service in Nova Scotia, Canada, in the early 1980s, Richard Gabel provided consultancy. He encouraged me to think about the coaxial cables buried in muddy trenches in urban streets, in a completely new way, as technologies imbued with social purpose. He connected often conflicting engineering justifications for the design of these and many other components of the communication system with even more often contradictory claims by economists and lawyers about the costs of building and using them. Gabel had a special ability to translate engineering and economic perspectives into insights about power relationships in Western capitalism and democratic goals. He never doubted the links between these domains and he always wanted to question whether changes in the communication system were aligned with values he felt were important in a democratic society.

Those who guided me, from various disciplinary perspectives, in their different ways always had an interest in the politics of technology, all of them resisting claims that digital technologies are simply neutral tools. After joining the Organisation for Economic Co-operation and Development (OECD), I shared a search for effective ICT policy measures just at a time in the mid-1980s when market liberalization and privatization were sweeping through the telecommunication sector. With Hans-Peter Gassmann and Dimitri Ypsilanti, I became involved in exploring the basis for differences in national perspectives on matters of telecommunication equipment and services competition and trade, and privacy and security issues, in response to what had already started to be referred to as ICT convergence.

Professor Christopher Freeman, co-founder of the Science Policy Research Unit (later SPRU—Science and Technology Policy Research) at the University of Sussex, was often cited in OECD reports on the relations between policy and technological innovation and I started to read in the field of science and technology policy studies. A move to SPRU in 1988 gave me the chance to pursue my search for insight into the complicated processes of innovation in the communication system, focusing mainly on political and economic aspects of these changes, but working also with Professor Roger Silverstone— then at Brunel and later at Sussex University, as part of a ten-year UK-funded network of scholars investigating the social and economic aspects of ICTs. His questions about the cultural, the social, and the political, as well as those of many others in our interdisciplinary research programme, were constant reminders to me that the struggle to undertake such an enquiry is hard, but it is always rewarding. In 2001, I joined the Interdisciplinary Programme in Media and Communications at the LSE, led by Roger Silverstone. In 2003, this became the Department of Media and Communications where I now work in an interdisciplinary space with colleagues pursuing questions about the media and about communication technologies, informed by disciplinary backgrounds in economics, law, linguistics, philosophy, politics, social psychology, and sociology.

I want this book to be accessible to those who are seeking to understand processes of social and technological innovation through their respective traditions of practice, policy, and academic study. This involves a certain level of abstraction in the text and, in some cases, a synoptic treatment of debates that are discussed very thoroughly in the academic and policy literatures. I have provided comprehensive notes at the end of the book to guide the reader. In addition to the usual page references for quotations, these notes point to academic works providing in-depth treatments of the concepts I draw upon and to policy, regulatory, and legislative documents that I use in support of my overall argument.

My search for answers to questions about how innovations in the technological and social features of the modern communication system are mediating our lives is not over. This book sets out some of what I have learned so far. It draws on the different ways of seeing the innovation process that I have encountered—each with their sometimes quite radically different views about power and social change and about whether anyone can or should intervene in this process to hold others accountable. I hope this book will provoke readers into thinking about intervention issues because policies and practices are shaping the mediated communication environment in ways that are not always benign.

Robin Mansell
Lewes, East Sussex, 2012

■ ACKNOWLEDGEMENTS

My thanks go to all the master's students in the Department of Media and Communications at the London School of Economics and Political Science (LSE) who, over the last ten years, took my course on new media, information, and knowledge systems; and to students at SPRU—Science and Technology Policy Research, University of Sussex, who took an earlier course on information and communication technology policy. These students have been a constant source of inspiration. I owe a very big debt to my doctoral students at the LSE and SPRU with whom I explored new pathways and who have shaped my thinking in countless ways. Maria Benet, Thomas Cameron-Fawkes, Rhonda Hammer, and Debra Slaco encouraged this project from the beginning; you were always in my mind. Thanks go especially to my colleagues in the LSE Department of Media and Communications—Paolo Dini for his persistent questions; Bart Cammaerts, Shani Orgad, and Margaret Scammell for their constant encouragement; and Sonia Livingstone for her commitment to the project of interdisciplinarity in our field. All of them took the time to comment very helpfully on the penultimate draft. Esra Ercan provided excellent assistance in the early stages of background research on systems theories.

Cynthia Little applied her superb editing skills to the manuscript. My editors at Oxford University Press, David Musson who encouraged this work from its inception, and Emma Booth, were very helpful at every stage in the process. I am very grateful to Peter Morris, artist and friend, for the adaptations to the drawings in Figures 3.1 and 3.2, and for the original drawing in Figure 3.3. I am grateful to Houghton Mifflin Harcourt Publishers for permission to reproduce Richard Brautigan's poem in the opening epigraph ("All Watched Over by Machines of Loving Grace" from *The Pill versus The Springhill Mine Disaster* by Richard Brautigan. Copyright © 1968 by Richard Brautigan. Reprinted by permission of Houghton Mifflin Harcourt Publishing Company. All rights reserved).

I have learned a huge amount from many scholars including Brian Collins, Paul A. David, Nicholas Garnham, William H. Melody, Geoffrey Oldham, Liora Salter, Rohan Samarajiva, and Dallas W. Smythe, as well as other colleagues who I hope will forgive me for not naming individually—many are members of the International Association for Media and Communication Research (IAMCR) or are associated with the Information and Knowledge Management-Emergent (IKM-E) Programme. This book is dedicated to Chris Freeman and Roger Silverstone who saw very different things in my work, but who always and strenuously encouraged me to write, something I have been reluctant to do in monograph form until now. Policy makers, consultants, technology developers, and people who find creative uses of 'new media' helped me enormously over the years. I am grateful to everyone with whom I have discussed aspects of this work. I particularly thank Richard Morgan-Jones for his patience and his persistent idea that I might complete this book. Lastly, Edward Steinmueller, my partner, offered invaluable advice and comment on several drafts and suggested the epigraph which precedes Chapter 1. I am indebted to him for his commitment to this project, for his love and support throughout, and for everything he did to help me cross the finish line. He and others who contributed their insights are blameless for any errors or omissions which remain my responsibility.

■ TABLE OF CONTENTS

■ LIST OF FIGURES

▓ LIST OF TABLES

■ ABBREVIATIONS

3G	Third Generation Mobile Telecommunication Service
4G	Fourth Generation Mobile Telecommunication Service
AACP	Alliance Against Counterfeiting and Piracy
ACTA	Anti-Counterfeiting Trade Agreement
ANT	Actor Network Theory
BBC	British Broadcasting Corporation
BCBS	Basel Committee on Banking Supervision
BIS	Business, Innovation, and Skills, UK Department of
BT	British Telecommunications plc
CDN	Content Distribution Network
CEO	Chief Executive Officer
CERN	European Organization for Nuclear Research
COE	Council of Europe
DBE	Digital Business Ecosystem
DCMS	Department for Culture, Media and Sport, UK
DDOS	Distributed Denial of Service
DNS	Domain Name System
EBU	European Broadcasting Union
EOA	Ecosystem Oriented Architecture
FATF	Financial Action Task Force
FCC	Federal Communications Commission, US
FLOSS	Free/Libre Open Source Software
GAC	Governmental Advisory Committee
GDP	Gross Domestic Product
GEO	Group on Earth Observations
GPS	Global Positioning System
GPT	General Purpose Technology
HADOPI	Haute Autorité pour la diffusion des œuvres et la protection des droits sur internet
HTML	HyperText Markup Language
ICANN	Internet Corporation for Assigned Names and Numbers
ICAO	International Civil Aviation Organization

ICT	Information and Communication Technology
IDN	Internationalized Domain Names
IFPI	International Federation of the Phonographic Industry
IGF	Internet Governance Forum
IIPA	International Intellectual Property Alliance
IMF	International Monetary Fund
INSNA	International Network for Social Network Analysis
IP	Internet Protocol
IPTV	Internet Protocol Television
ISP	Internet Service Provider
ITU	International Telecommunication Union
LDC	Less Developed Country
MIT	Massachusetts Institute of Technology
MPAA	Motion Picture Association of America
NGN	Next Generation Network
NWICO	New World Information and Communication Order
OECD	Organisation for Economic Co-operation and Development
OKS	Open Knowledge Space
OPAALS	Open Philosophies for Associative and Autopoietic Digital Ecosystems
OSS	Open Source Software
P2P	Peer-to-Peer
QdN	La Quadrature du Net
RIAA	Recording Industry Association of America
SBVBR	Semantics of Business Vocabulary and Business Rules
SNA	Social Network Analysis
SOA	Service Oriented Architecture
TCP	Transmission Control Protocol
TRIPS	Trade-Related Aspects of Intellectual Property Rights
UK	United Kingdom
UN	United Nations
UNCITRAL	United Nations Commission on International Trade Law
UNESCO	United Nations Educational, Scientific and Cultural Organization
US	United States
USSR	Union of Soviet Socialist Republics
VoD	Video on Demand
VoIP	Voice over Internet Protocol

W3C   World Wide Web Consortium
WiFi   Wireless Fidelity (network standard)
WiMAX   Worldwide Interoperability for Microwave Access
WIPO   World Intellectual Property Organization
WSIS   World Summit on the Information Society
WWW   World Wide Web
WTO   World Trade Organization
XML   EXtensible Markup Language

I like to think (and
the sooner the better!)
of a cybernetic meadow
where mammals and computers
live together in mutually
programming harmony
like pure water
touching clear sky.

I like to think
    (right now please!)
of a cybernetic forest
filled with pines and electronics
where deer stroll peacefully
past computers
as if they were flowers
with spinning blossoms.

I like to think
    (it has to be!)
of a cybernetic ecology
where we are free of our labors
and joined back to nature,
returned to our mammal
brothers and sisters,
and all watched over
by machines of loving grace.

All Watched Over by Machines of Loving Grace,
Richard Brautigan (1968: 117).

1 Introduction

Richard Brautigan imagines a cybernetic ecology. For some, it is an ecology built on machines that are neither benign nor used gracefully. For others, these machines are instrumental in delivering an information society with the potential to advance us towards the good society. Innovations in digital technologies, including the virtual spaces on the Internet, are accorded near-mystical qualities in societies constructed around this ecology. The technologies may be empowering or disempowering for those who encounter them, but the spread of digital information and communication technologies (ICTs) portends a future in which 'machines of loving grace' bring social transformation that is beyond the control of human beings. This vision is enduring, seductive, and alluring.

While the 'real' for some people in the twenty-first century is being reduced to a shadow in the face of the bright, the new, and the 'virtual', the materiality of life intersects with the virtual in very important ways, including the meanings we give to life. Extending the global reach of networks and selling digital information is creating great wealth for some, but improving material livelihoods and well-being for all remains a challenge, even as investment in digital technologies extends their reach into our lives. There are numerous stories of instances where these technologies are benefiting people and communities, but people cannot live only on a diet of digital bits. There are numerous cautionary tales of inequality and social injustice in the contemporary information society.

The contemporary vision of what the information society is or could be, is of a society in which innovative ICTs, designed by scientists and engineers, encouraged by corporate (and state) investors, and benefiting from the labour of collaborating networked communities, provide easy access to the wealth of human knowledge and to communication capabilities. These capabilities are rendered vastly superior to those previously available through the use of powerful and increasingly cheaper applications of ICTs that enhance the mediated world. The widespread diffusion of ICTs means that everyone will have access to the Internet through a handheld device such as a mobile phone, or through a desktop workstation, or a television in the office, bedroom, or living room. Everyone will be able to produce or consume the information he or she values. Proponents of this vision presume that the outcome of the evolutionary process is a technological system that is 'fit for purpose'—it is equitable and just because it yields the greatest good for all in the information society, which is the good society.

The proponents of this vision diverge in their views about the role of markets in creating incentives for technological innovation and for wealth creation, despite their agreement that technology offers the solution to societal problems. For some, market-imposed information scarcity creates the optimal incentive for the production of digital information that responds to all preferences because information is initially costly to produce. The goal of maximizing creativity and information diversity is believed to benefit from the removal of impediments to the operation of markets and from the enforcement of laws protecting intellectual property. This is the dominant vision. For others, because technological innovation is giving rise to abundant digital information of all kinds and information is virtually costless to reproduce, the optimal motivation for its production and consumption is created when the exchange of information is *not* subject to the constraints of the market; information should be shared freely to maximize its diversity. The proponents of this argument do not provide answers to how economic growth can proceed in a world in which information is freely available. In the face of this *paradox of information scarcity*, every step towards a more sophisticated communication system makes it more difficult to secure the scarcity of information so that it is saleable in the marketplace, and it becomes ever more challenging to stimulate economic growth in economies increasingly dependent on immaterial goods.[1]

In the contemporary vision of the information society, the abundance of digital information is seen as creating a new foundation for the expansion of societies based on improved access to and use of 'knowledge', and digital networks are seen as creating opportunities for participatory forms of democracy on an unprecedented scale. This abundance of information (enabled by efficient use of the radio frequency spectrum, the spread of high-bandwidth networks, cheaper information distribution, near-ubiquitous access to networks, and advances in human representation by digital avatars) is taken as evidence that the evolution of the system is in the public interest. Public policy interventions to guide the development of the system start to be seen by those who are most optimistic about its potential, as an affront to the values of the good society. For them, it is unnecessary to make choices about possible alternatives or to promote diversity through such interventions.

The information society is understood to be arising from an evolutionary process with intrinsic benefits based on the emergent complexity of the technologies of the communication system. This process and its complex adaptive system characteristics are best not interfered with by the state. This despite the fact that the evolution of this system is leading to declining human control and that enhanced control is being sought through the design of hardware and the programming of software in a highly decentralized system. The generative dynamics of a complex adaptive system are such that we should rely on the designers and programmers to ensure that the communication system is consistent with aspirations for the good society. This is the *paradox of complexity* in the Internet Age. It is not a new phenomenon, but it is increasingly important because of the progressive convergence of ICTs. The design of the modern communication system, comprised of ever more complicated components, makes it subject to instability and, therefore, the risks of interventions aimed at guiding the system are seen widely as being greater than in earlier times.

In this book I argue that these accounts misread the implications of the paradoxes of information scarcity and complexity in the Internet Age. This misreading is apparent when the persistent conflicts between a dominant market-led vision of the information society and an increasingly prominent alternative vision of an expanding information commons are examined. My analysis considers whether the evolution of the communication system is mediating our lives in a way that is empowering for people and the choices they can make about their lives *or* whether it is reinforcing power relationships that contribute to persistent poverty and sometimes fear. If the answer to both of these questions is yes, what interventions might foster a society in which people can achieve greater empowerment, freedom, and responsibility in the Internet Age? How is the thinking of different stakeholders related to these questions?

The Internet Age and the Good Society

The questions posed above are important because the communication system of the twenty-first century is mediating most people's lives in increasing numbers of ways. I characterize the contemporary period as the Internet Age to evoke the dreams, hopes, and fears about advances in digital ICTs. This period is characterized also by labels such as the network society, the digital age, and the new media age, all helpful constructions that draw attention to the principal features of the modern era. However, the Internet Age brings to mind contested ideas about opportunities and threats to society in a manner that is reminiscent of the way that the Atomic Age suggests both the benefits and risks of scientific progress in nuclear physics.

The Internet is iconic of our time for young and old. The architecture of the Internet may be a specific technical design, but the Internet label is associated, cynically or not, with 'machines of loving grace'—with a communication system that is increasingly ubiquitous and 'intelligent'. In the academic literature and in everyday speech, *the* Internet may refer to the material or the immaterial, to hardware or software, to the way information is produced and consumed, or to the means by which people communicate for multiple purposes. The term is used so pervasively that it has become imbued with multiple meanings which may be technological, but which also refer to the cultural, social, political, and economic features of most contemporary societies. Like the Atomic Age, there is no single vision, but multiple ones, grounded in the experience of particular uses of the technology and how understandings of these experiences are changing over time.

In this book, I examine how multiple dimensions of the communication system in the Internet Age—personal, institutional, and technological—are implicated in the way people are able to make choices about their lives, individually and collectively. I show why dreams of the realization of a cybernetic ecology—today subsumed within the information society—are in urgent need of assessment. I discuss the feasibility of measures that would guide the evolution of the communication system along a pathway that is more consistent with aspirations for the good society. This requires a critical examination of the implications of the paradoxes of information scarcity and complexity for stakeholders in the information society.

The notion of the good society has a long history in Western philosophy relating to social justice and how it can be achieved. The idea that members of society have a responsibility to attend to the welfare of all has been espoused since Democritus advocated the social compact.[2] For some, the good society is an 'achievable society' in which, according John Kenneth Galbraith, all citizens 'must have personal liberty, basic well-being, racial and ethnic equality, [and] the opportunity for a rewarding life', for example.[3] For others, such as Amartya Sen, the good society is one in which policy choices are not 'indifferent to the lives that people can actually live' or to what people are able to accomplish.[4] There are many problematic aspects of the notion of the good society, as philosopher Martha Nussbaum and many others acknowledge, and I do not attempt to resolve them here. Nussbaum, however, suggests that the idea can be used as a picture to help us 'think creatively about what justice can be in a world', acknowledging that some other picture might be more helpful to articulate people's aspirations for society.[5]

The prevailing visions of the information society, one giving priority to market-led commercial development in the interest of economic growth and the other giving priority to the collaborative production and consumption of information outside the conventions of market exchange, are represented in the scholarly literature and in policy debate as being in conflict with each other. Progress towards the realization of one vision is seen as damaging to the realization of the other. I examine their respective claims in the light of the insights provided by a focus on the paradoxes involved in technological change and transformations in society in the Internet Age. I show that the tensions between adherents to these conflicting visions are symptoms of a false opposition between a vision that privileges the freedom of information and participation and a vision that privileges economic growth. Its resolution lies in presuming that one of these visions must be an incorrect reading, that is, that progress towards the good society requires that one vision be privileged over the other. I want to suggest another reading of this conflict. My reading opens a range of potential means for guiding the evolution of the communication system in a way that enhances the likelihood of outcomes that minimize the dangers associated with 'machines of loving grace'. In order to develop this reading, it is necessary to understand a variety of ways of seeing the processes of social and technological change.

Ways of Seeing and Theorizing Change

British art critic, novelist, and painter, John Berger, emphasizes that 'the relation between what we see and what we know is never settled'.[6] Similarly, the prevailing visions of the information society are never settled. In some visions there is an overemphasis on technological change, knowledge gaps, and the diffusion of technology. Others emphasize symbolic meaning and power relationships that enable active human beings to shape our technological systems. These ways of seeing are associated with different theoretical models of change that have been developed within academic disciplines built up around different purposes and epistemologies. My aim is to critically examine the conflicting visions of the information society and some of the reasons that these conflicts persist. This requires that we make explicit the conventions of these traditions to understand how they become co-mingled in the practices of the Internet Age.

To make sense of these contemporary visions, I employ a strategy of comparison and critical assessment of the social imaginaries of the information society. The notion of the social imaginary has its origins in a number of intellectual traditions. I build my analysis principally around the idea as proposed by political philosopher and commentator on modernity, Charles Taylor. He describes the social imaginary as 'the deeper normative notions and images' invoked by the ways in which we understand 'how things go on' among people[7] (see Chapter 3). Taylor emphasizes that 'the social imaginary is *not* a set of ideas; rather it is what enables, through making sense of, the practices of a society'.[8] For my purpose, it is about the taken-for-granted notions, images, and visions of those engaged with developments in the information society and how they think about and experience the mediated environment, acting upon it in ways that lead to the paradoxes of information scarcity and complexity in the Internet Age.

A paradox involves apparently contradictory criticisms or statements that may be rendered consistent with each other if they are given a 'certain reading'[9] when the nature of power relationships within a complex system is taken into account. In order to perform a re-reading of transformations in the information society, I examine the metacommunications of different stakeholders, that is, their ways of talking or communicating about asymmetrical, contested relationships in the information society (see Chapter 4). This analytical procedure provides a basis for a 'certain reading' of the conflicts that give rise to the two paradoxes. While not new to the Internet Age, we will see that these paradoxes have major implications for whether it is understood to be feasible to guide the progress of the information society towards the good society. My reading suggests broad directions for changes that unsettle received views about what we think we know about changes in the communication system and their consequences.

The prevailing visions of the information society rest in part on distinct ways of understanding or theorizing change in society and on a claim, in the case of the dominant vision, that disengagement from a normative position with respect to values is an appropriate stance for enquiry into the dynamics of change. Taylor observes, however, that if we want to 'grasp what motivates some person or group, how they see the world, and what kinds of things are important to them, disengagement will almost certainly be a self-stultifying strategy'.[10] Roger Silverstone insists that the communication system, through its mediation of our lives, 'constitutes our worldliness, our capacity to be in the world'.[11] The relationship between the communication system and our capacity to be in the world clearly matters for the lives of people everywhere. For this reason, a disinterested stance towards the implications of the contending visions of the information society would be inappropriate for my enquiry.

Studies of the evolution of the information society draw on a variety of incommensurable ways of seeing. This is reflected in disagreements about whether humanistic or mechanistic 'models of man' or social and technological change should guide work in this area.[12] Mechanistic models are thriving despite being regarded by those with an affinity for humanistic models as being 'innocent of matters relating to institutions and power relations'.[13] Mechanistic models are exogenous, that is, these models treat technological change as a shock to a system of pre-existing relationships that requires adjustment to bring the system back to stability. Humanistic models are 'endogenous'; change is attributable to internal 'causes', which are more likely to acknowledge the importance of power relationships and meaning construction. In both models, the alignment or misalignment of technological innovations with a given set of goals such as those of the good society is regarded as being uncertain. However, different assumptions are made about the role of human agency and the capacity of people to shape their environment through their ideas, institutions, and development and use of their artefacts.

This book is intended for readers with different disciplinary backgrounds and from different research traditions. This raises a question about the vocabulary I use to discuss the processes of historical development of the communication system in Internet Age of the information society. I employ three different terms to refer to these historical developments. The most direct is 'change' which is simply the idea that from one time to another there are differences. Change may be an experiential or an observational concept—we experience or observe difference and this is called change. In general, simply noting that change has occurred is not satisfactory. It leaves open the question of why change has occurred and it falls well short of addressing the question presented by 'development'—development towards what, for what, in what direction? To answer these questions requires a theory of what brings about change processes. The most obvious theory of change is that of intentionality—change occurs because someone or some group of people strives to achieve goals, objectives, or a result. However, when it comes to a complex system, such as that discussed in this book, theories predicated upon the idea of intentionality are often inadequate—no single group's intentionality may dominate in bringing about change, or change may happen unintentionally, as the collateral effects of intentional efforts or because of the interaction between the efforts of various actors.

In these cases, two additional terms are appropriate. The first is the concept of evolution. Evolution involves a process of variety generation and a process of selection and inheritance or learning from the past.[14] The coherence of processes of change that are evolutionary need not be obvious. Selection may operate capriciously and variety generation may be limited or biased. Nonetheless, when evolutionary processes are present, it may be possible to explain change in terms of the increased viability of certain institutions, artefacts, or ideas, and the decreased viability of others. The concept of 'fitness' in social life compared to Darwinian or biological evolution is unlikely to have a clear definition, and it is necessary to turn to theories of change predicated upon ideas about human agency.[15] The directionality of evolutionary processes may be discernible. The process or processes of variety generation and selection, processes which may be cultural, social, political, and economic, may favour some directions over others.

The second term is 'emergence' which is drawn from a branch of systems theory called complexity theory. Emergence encompasses evolution, but is less restrictive in that it may also apply to systems in which the elements are stable (i.e. variety is unchanging) and in which selection may be incidental or unimportant. In complex systems with emergent properties, the interaction of a system's elements may be taken to be autopoietic (self-organizing or self-regulating). The presence of autopoiesis provides an explanation of change in two senses. First, autopoietic adjustment implies change from period to period; it is only over a longer period of time that stability may be observed—sometimes referred to as dynamic stability. Second, autopoietic systems may be disturbed by shocks or events that are external. These shocks may disturb the inherent tendency of the system to self-organization or self-regulation, causing changes (previously unobservable) to occur before dynamic stability is restored, or they may be sufficiently disruptive to destroy the autopoietic properties of the system—creating chaos and a lack of stability or order. In this book, the terms evolution and emergence are used to indicate tendencies in historical developments that have 'direction'.[16] In some cases, the underlying processes or mechanisms are analysed in detail in order to tease out the way the paradoxes of information scarcity and complexity can be understood, employing exogenous or endogenous ways of seeking.

The meanings of these terms may be a little obscure for some social scientists, or suggest meanings that are not intended. My aim is not to conflate the epistemological differences between disparate theories of change, especially because theories of evolution and complexity sit uncomfortably alongside discussions about power and ideology in the information society. My intention is not to suggest that evolutionary processes in the social or cultural context are 'natural' or that they are distinct from any of the processes that give rise to technological change. Nevertheless, these terms are increasingly common in research on changes in society in the Internet Age. Many actors, inside and outside the academy, are employing them in the process of making claims that are becoming part of the taken-for-granted legends about the information society.

For those in the social sciences and humanities more familiar with the vocabulary of change, modifying the directions of change will be thought to imply some kind of 'choice' by human agents, with or without a conscious awareness of the consequences of their choices. In this book, I consider the choices available to active agents at the micro-level, for individuals in the information society, and the way these choices appear at the level of institutions. Each of these levels has implications for how power is conceptualized. At the individual level, 'the enterprising self' can be understood to 'shape itself in order to become what it wishes to be',[17] and institutional actions can be understood as being what 'is produced and reproduced in what people do'.[18] My interest in this book is in the social imaginaries—the way people in the information society make sense of their visions and practices and how this is influencing the communication system that is so central to people's lives.

These different models and terminologies depicting 'change' in the information society provide us with disparate ways of seeing the dynamics of change in the communication system. James Carey, a principal contributor to communication theory, suggested that,

> to study communication involves examining the construction, apprehension, and use of models of communication themselves – their construction in common sense, art, and science, their historically specific creation and use.... Behind and within these encounters lie models of human contact and interaction.... Our models of communication, consequently, create what we disingenuously pretend they merely describe.[19]

One model of communication about change, which serves as an example of how such models begin to influence practice in the information society, is the use of exogenous models in economics. Present-day economics finds the multiplicity or 'co-determination' of factors influencing social change, for example, to be a very difficult construct with which to grapple compared to the apparent simplicity of models documenting the cumulative rate and direction of ICT diffusion. It is even more difficult for economists to analyse the way power relationships are involved in processes of technological innovation. For them, change is governed by shocks that are taken to be external to the economic system and then reconciled through a process of equilibration. Problems are stated in univocally rational (or quasi-rational) ways and, thus, are unambiguously solvable through recourse to theoretical models or quantitative simulations of change, constrained by limiting assumptions about the nature of human rationality and choice. The convention in this model is that existing unequal distributions of resources are given; their redistribution is outside the scope of analysis. Wealth is generated by efficiency improvements and is redistributed in the form of increased wages to ever more productive workers, endowed with an ever-expanding stock of tools (capital), with sufficient profit only to stimulate risk-taking rather than a safer and lower return investment.

This model of innovation seems to bear little relation to the 'real' world where frontier-expanding technological change, for instance in ICT, creates wealth by endowing some actors with the power to dominate competitors and re-distributes wealth through the 'creative destruction' of rivals. Models drawn from theories of the dynamics of complex adaptive systems can be integrated with the economists' models by changing assumptions about the way shocks to the system play out in terms of stability or instability and whether the system tends over time towards an equilibrium state. Integrating them with models which embrace a much richer conception of human agency and the way people construct and apprehend the world around them results in the uneasy juxtaposition of incommensurate assumptions about knowing and being in the world.

When the economics model (and systems theories built on metaphors taken from the natural and physical sciences) is taken up outside the academy, it co-mingles with others. Policy makers usually are willing to acknowledge that technological innovation is shaped by political considerations and by social and cultural perceptions and values. In the early phases of the diffusion of digital technologies, for example, the then Secretary General of the OECD, Jean-Claude Paye, said that 'technological change is often equated either with certain hardware, or with specific production processes; this is a mistake. *Technological change is, in its development and application, fundamentally a social process*, not an event, and should be viewed not in static but in dynamic terms'.[20] The idea that innovation is a 'social process' may be obligatory for sociologists, but it sits uncomfortably with the views of economists and many technologists. For many of them, the spread of technology is inexorable and is the result of shocks. It should be accelerated in order to build the information society or, indeed, to achieve any type of progress.

The genesis of paradox is not uncommon in complex systems. Contradictory statements derived from different ways of seeing transformations in the social or technological realms should come as no surprise and they often are valid in the contexts in which they are made. Understanding the genesis of paradox—in this case, the paradoxes of information scarcity and complexity—helps us to see the progressive evolution of the communication system in a different light. This provides a basis for assessing whether or not innovations in the communication system are aligned with the goals of the good society and for beginning to conceive of a more diverse set of interventions than otherwise come to light in debates about information society policy.

Chapter Outline

Convergent ICTs are deeply implicated in many people's lives. There is no doubt that, as Roger Silverstone says, 'mediated connection and interconnection define the dominant infrastructure for the conduct of social, political and economic life across the globe'.[21] Certain ways of seeing make the paradoxes of the Internet Age difficult to examine, but it is essential to do so to answer the questions I address in this book. Without a better understanding of the dynamics of the evolutionary process, we can look forward to a continuing rehearsal of unproductive struggles among the proponents of the contending visions of the information society. In Chapter 2, we 'fast forward' through different ways of seeing the information society, profiling social imaginaries that have become pervasively shared, if contested, in the Internet Age. These features of contemporary social imaginaries are widely seen as opposing visions of the preferred direction of change in the information society.

The book is then structured into two main parts. In the first part (Chapters 3 and 4), I discuss various models that inform the prevailing visions of the information society. These chapters draw upon theories of change, but it is not my intention to suggest that social imaginaries are developed by scholars as scripts that filter into the consciousness of policy makers and those who design and use ICTs and digital information. Following Charles Taylor, the social imaginary should be understood as being shared by large groups of people or even the whole of society, and is not a theory. Some theories developed in scholarly traditions may be exclusive to narrow interpretative communities, without widespread recognition in the wider community, while others play a very prominent role in the social imaginaries of the information society. The imaginaries also emerge out of the interactions of everyday participants in the information society, policy makers, and activists as well as scholars from multiple disciplines. Taken together, these two chapters provide the basis for an analytical framework for assessing the implications of different ways of seeing progress towards the information society and its consequences.

The validity of representations of change in the information society arising from theory and empirical research may not resonate beyond the academy. With a caveat about whether the perceptions and experiences of everyday users, software developers, and other stakeholders in the development of the communication system can be represented by examining the narratives or metacommunications available to the social scientist, the second part of the book (Chapters 5, 6, and 7) examines the social imaginaries of the information society from several different perspectives. This analysis is based partly on findings in the academic literature, on an analysis of the trade and policy literatures, and on my experience of working with technology developers and policy makers over several decades.

In Chapter 3, in the first main part of the book, I focus on the insights provided by theories employed in the social sciences to examine the causes and consequences of technological innovation in the information society. The chapter begins with a short history of the emergence of the 'information society' in the period following World War II and the exogenous models that characterize change as the product of advances in the technologies for information processing. These models are contrasted with insights from endogenous theories of techno-economic change, of the political economy of communication, and of mediation. I consider how what I refer to as the administrative or instrumental and critical traditions of research contribute to the social imaginaries and the different possibilities they imply for policy intervention.

In Chapter 4, I assess what we can learn about the social imaginaries of the information society from system theories that invoke the concepts of evolution and complexity. These models of change will be familiar to those working in the physical and engineering sciences, and many of those who are involved in the design and implementation of the communication system, and in its governance. They are increasingly prominent in the social sciences. A critical assessment of this tradition and the problems it presents for understanding human agency is followed by a discussion of the way this model has been developed to understand paradox and its implications for 'adaptive learning'. At the end of Chapter 4, I outline a critical systems framework to help make sense of the way people, in their different capacities, construct their visions of the information society.

I use this framework in the second part of the book to guide an analysis of the social imaginaries of the information society which seem to characterize the way the communication system is experienced in the everyday lives of its users who encounter it largely from 'in front of the screen' of the computer or other digital device. This is contrasted with imaginaries that are more characteristic of software engineers and scientists whose work takes them 'behind the screen' (Chapter 5). In Chapter 6, social imaginaries of the information society are examined through a consideration of the experiences of a community of developers of a new digital platform for communication and of the representatives of companies and other stakeholders with the strongest interests in maintaining the constructed scarcity of digital information. Chapter 7 turns to an examination of debates about the governance of the communication system in the information society, focusing mainly on the Internet as an exemplary site where the paradoxes of information scarcity and complexity are being played out.

My argument is summarized in Chapter 8. I suggest that the persistent denial of the paradoxes of information scarcity and complexity sequesters debate about possible interventions that might help to reconcile the goals of economic growth with the goals of social justice and the equitable distribution of resources in the information society. Certain interventions are needed to avert the emergence of a runaway technological system. I suggest several interventions that follow from the invocation of a new social imaginary of the information society which resists the excesses of the market without abandoning it, and which encourages experimentation and creativity in mediated environments, with less risk to human beings.

2 Fast Forwarding through the Information Society

Introduction

In the prevailing vision of the information society, a technological revolution gives rise to digital networks and applications that diffuse widely and rapidly throughout society with many disruptive consequences. These disruptions result in the need for adjustments to legal arrangements and policies, to the structure and operation of the economy, and to the norms for social and economic conduct. It is claimed that companies' commercial prospects are damaged each time an innovative technology takes hold. Incumbent companies then seek protection for their economic interests. When solid-state electronics became the 'new art' in the 1950s, for example, it was claimed that this technology was destabilizing the electro-mechanical age and seriously impairing the monopoly telecommunication network providers' abilities to carry out their 'public duty'.[1] Similarly, today's creative industry companies are seeking protection from the disruptive digital technologies that have made the means of copying digital content easily and cheaply available to everyone with the skills to use them.

It is not surprising that there is conflict about what should be done to maximize the benefits and avoid the risks of new technologies and about the interests that should be favoured. For those whose concern is first and foremost with the potential of the huge advances in digital technologies for enabling the production, processing, circulation, and storage of information, these adjustments are needed to support market competition in 'Internet Time'[2] and to enable citizens to manage their lives in an intensely mediated world. Digital networks and applications are bringing all manner of texts and images into our homes. In the Internet Age, the networked abilities of radio frequency identification sensors are leading to the electronic tagging not only of criminals but also of children and pets, and, ultimately, perhaps everyone.[3] These and many other developments are testing our abilities to render dreams of the cyberspace ecology and, more crucially, the technologies and services that actually leave the laboratory, consistent with values of the good society.

This chapter introduces the way the evolution of the communication system in the information society is conceived from the perspectives of science fiction writers, futurologists, and some of those in the policy and scholarly communities. I focus first on prevailing visions of the evolution of 'digital life'. One facet of the predominant vision is a commitment to the idea that the fruits of technological innovation bring disruptions for companies whose profits depend on their ability to maintain some element of control over digital information, that is, its scarcity, so that it can be produced and consumed in the commercial market. The paradox of information scarcity is that digital information is costly to produce initially and is virtually costless to reproduce.

In this vision, the characteristics of increasing returns from positive feedback within complex adaptive systems mean that the technological system is subject to the risk that it will spiral out of human control. Human interventions to guide the system have uncertain consequences. The paradox of complexity is such that the intrinsic benefits of emergent complexity lead to less human control, but enhanced control simultaneously is sought through programming choices. I consider the views of those who foresee the risk of a 'runaway system'. Most debates in policy forums do not focus on the risks associated with declining mastery of the technological system. Instead, they concentrate on the many facets of the digital divide, that is, on how to fill technology or knowledge gaps, which I discuss briefly. The final section explains why there is an urgent need to unmask the false polarization between the prevailing social imaginaries of the information society. This is essential if progress is to be made towards reconciling the goal of economic growth with the goals of social justice and equitable distribution of information resources.

The Evolution of Digital Life

The actions of stakeholders guide both the direction and movement along the technological innovation pathways that influence the evolution of 'digital life'. Along the path towards 'machines of loving grace'—whether welcomed or not—engineers and mathematicians argue that, sooner or later, technological advancement will produce the 'Singularity'. For example, Vernor Vinge, a computer scientist who is also a science fiction writer, argues that a time will come when 'we have the technological means to create superhuman intelligence'.[4] At this point, the end of the human era will have arrived. This kind of post-human vision is a consistent theme in the work of mathematicians, computer scientists, and writers of science fiction. It is a vision of the convergence of the computer and biological sciences and the creation of entities, with runaway consequences beyond the control of humans.[5]

Futurologists take up works of science fiction, embellishing them to offer confusing utopian and dystopian scenarios, invoking visions of the evolution of digital technologies. For example, Ian Pearson, a futurologist, talks about smart bacteria infecting people's minds and controlling them, enslaving them, and turning them into zombies,[6] presenting a vision that echoes Greg Bear's much earlier science fiction story, *Blood Music*. Donna Haraway's widely cited 'Cyborg Manifesto' offers a vision—grounded in the scholarly literature—of a time when the opportunities afforded by new technologies will be seized to cultivate new identities and relationships. This she argues will alter the terms of the political struggle for gender liberation and build on the hybridity of humans and machines.[7]

Each technological advance seems to provoke renewed debate over the possibility of a loss of human control over the technological system. Loss of control is a persistent theme in the history of technological innovation, memorably in the Luddite's resistance to the introduction of mechanized looms in the textiles industry in Britain in the early nineteenth century. That flurry of technological disruption raised concerns about deskilling, job losses, and changes to the rhythm of working life, but the Luddite movement was suppressed by the government of the day.[8] There is enthusiasm for the Internet on the part of the great majority of people. Although some of its applications may be questioned, the entre it provides to rich opportunities of many kinds is being met by little resistance.

Discussion about innovations in ICTs is influenced increasingly by the argument that the best option to advance the benefits and mitigate the risks of a complex technological system is to allow it to evolve, unhindered by human beings. Investment in digital networks and applications in business, government, and all other areas of society is seen as the best way to ensure the optimal adjustments to technological innovations. The priority seems to be to reach the top of the league tables for the diffusion of technology or for literacy in its use, with far less attention to the risks that might be encountered by society as a whole and by groups within society. Governments celebrate success, for example, when the media claim that 'Britain logs on to a world-beating £100bn internet economy', ahead of the United States.[9] When the diffusion of ICTs is linked to threats of cyber war, or actions to restrict the freedom of speech, this is often glossed over as part of the process of adjustment to the evolution of the communication system, which, ultimately, is—or soon will become—consistent with values of the good society.

Timelessness and a context-free way of thinking characterize this vision of the evolution of digital information and ICTs and the adjustments that the diffusion process is assumed to provoke. Any resistance is attributed to a lack of the requisite skills base or to more sinister anti-technology sentiments. Technologies are conceived as autonomous—as independent of the innovation processes in society that give rise to them. Each new generation of technology is presumed, on balance, to be consistent with human well-being, democracy, and freedom.[10] This is the vision prevailing in the imaginations of many of those who promote the benefits of the information society. It embraces particular norms and values about how the world is, or should be, organized. These norms and values are seen as consistent with the supposed benefits of technological progress, the primacy of market exchange as the optimal way to solve the problems of resource allocation, and the perception that it is only a matter of time before everyone benefits from the evolution of the communication system.

The vision portrayed by a study of 'digital life' illustrates this way of thinking. It is suggested that the ubiquity of the 'Internet of Things' (networked sensing of everything and everyone) will automate mundane tasks and gradually recede from human consciousness or awareness.[11] This is a vision offered under the auspices of the International Telecommunication Union, a UN specialist agency with a mandate for governing the communication system in the Internet Age. A European Commission-funded study on ubiquitous computing (an earlier closely related term for the Internet of Things) takes a similar view, but suggests that rather than receding altogether, digital life should be controllable using on/off switches that allow decisions about the level of access people prefer an automated system to have to their private lives.[12]

Developing the means of achieving individual control is seen also as an opportunity for wealth generation from innovations in software technologies to support the pre-filtering of information, software agent-based recommender systems, and other metadata automated systems which operate behind the computer screen. Flexible intelligent systems for information handling, such as smart tagging, the Semantic Web, and online search technologies, are portrayed in the trade literature and in some academic accounts not only as the answers to people's desires to control their communication environments but also as new commercial opportunities. Visions of the ubiquity of these technological solutions are emblematic of their proponents' hopes for an information society built upon a technologically-supported, rational, and calculable life. The claim is that the technological management of abundant digital information presents opportunities that must be taken up because this enables an ever-increasing range of choices for individuals. All these developments are associated with the production and processing of vast quantities of digital information. When technological innovations of these kinds have eliminated information scarcity, it seems to follow that there will be no need for policy intervention to ensure that its production and consumption are in the interests of the public or, indeed, of the good society. Yet, at the same time, those benefitting from the benefits of the abundant information are sorely challenged to develop means of creating profitable business models, consistent with their interests in market-led growth. This is unsurprising in the face of the paradox of information scarcity.

The prevailing vision of the information society is part of a broader vision of how society and the economy should function. For several decades, neoliberalism and the Washington Consensus on the benefits of market-led economic expansion and free trade have dominated debates over policy and regulation, with major implications for public policies affecting the development of the communication system.[13] In line with this policy environment, which typically calls for the withdrawal of the state from governance and the ascendency of market forces, de-regulation of the communication system, and a 'hands-off' stance towards the Internet are widely regarded as being optimal for encouraging the development of societies that depend on digital intangible goods. The less state governance, the better this will be for society—so the narrative goes. Advocates of this position oppose regulation of the Internet, for example, arguing about the dire consequences of intrusive regulations for the evolution of open networks and open access to digital information. Even when there is acknowledgement that there are problems with a policy of non-intervention, for example, the loss of privacy or threats to security, it is argued by some scholars that policy intervention, 'if undertaken, might ruin the very environment it is trying to save'. Instead, it is suggested that the future network environment should be shaped by the generative potential of 'technically skilled people of goodwill',[14] who it is assumed will develop alternatives to a centralized, market-led information society. Recourse to the generative characteristics of a complex technological system is symptomatic of what I call the paradox of complexity.

Since the financial crash in the late 2000s, the neoliberal policy position has been defended less robustly, but the idea that intervention in the governance of the communication system, specifically the Internet, but more broadly the information society, in the name of the public interest, is anathema to many. The dangers of intervention, stemming from uncertainty about the market distorting impacts of interventions or fears of infringement of civil liberties, have a firm grip on the imaginations of many policy makers, companies, and civil society advocates for various reasons. When digital information is no more than a keystroke or tap-on-the-screen away, it would seem to follow that the evolution of the communication system carries very few risks for human beings. When its dangers are acknowledged, for instance, in the event of unwanted intrusions into citizens' lives by software agents, or new forms of cyber warfare, it is assumed that these risks can be managed without restraining or altering the evolution of the new technologies. ICT applications are seen as the answers to political, social, economic, and even environmental risks, with little regard to the way, for example, their energy consumption is creating threats to the global ecosystem.[15]

Thus, a principal component of the prevailing vision of the information society is related to the presumed dangers of policy intervention in the evolving communication system. In this view, the complexity of the system inevitably will defeat any efforts to guide it. This is a seductive argument, perhaps even more so than the neoliberal argument about the benefits of unfettered markets. It is persuasive because many of its proponents are careful to state that their work is not related to the motivations or preferences of human beings. For example, Brian Arthur, a developer of modern theories of increasing returns resulting from positive feedback within complex systems, says 'modern technology organizes itself increasingly into networks of artefacts that sense, configure, and execute appropriately, it displays some degree of cognition.... In fact, not only will these systems in the future be self-configuring, self-optimizing, and cognitive, they will be self-assembling, self-healing, and self-protecting'.[16]

A modern articulation of the super-intelligent system envisaged by those who, like Vinge, dream of the Singularity, is that the communication system is a component of an evolutionary system, the dynamics of which give rise to emergent, indeterminate outcomes. The system is conceived as being self-organizing, that is, it is envisaged as being separate from other components of the system. In this view, consequently, policy interventions are as likely to produce negative as to yield beneficial, outcomes. The best advice is to leave the system to emerge through its own dynamic oscillations. This is the paradox of complexity—the system's very complexity heightens the risks associated with it, but this complexity renders the system interventions that do occur, at least as, if not more, risky.

The outcomes of these oscillations are seen as leading to the end of human beings as we know them in the wake of the emergence of 'machines of loving grace' imagined by Brautigan with more than a hint of cynicism. However, in the prevailing vision of the information society, these same developments are welcomed in policy debates by those who see them as harbingers of a bright future with universal, ICT-supported, personal, and collective empowerment. Optimism about the benefits of ICTs is not misplaced, especially for economically poorer citizens. There are numerous instances of 'clever services', enabled by inexpensive mobile phones, which are providing useful information, for example, about potentially harmful counterfeit drugs, which is of obvious benefit.[17] Unfortunately, though, the availability of digital information, distributed via the Internet using mobile phones or computers or by other means such as compact discs or television, does not necessarily coincide with the greater availability of information that is relevant to people's lives.

The prevailing vision of the information society is that almost all innovative applications of digital technology will be empowering for their users, especially if markets are unhindered by external interventions. However, even when people have access to the new technologies, there is no guarantee that available digital information will be locally relevant or verifiable and trust-worthy. Numerous experiments using real-time data on local developments are providing information that can assist in supporting many types of services, but here, too, there are ethical issues about who can or should collect and make use of such information. In the dominant vision, events such as the Arab Spring or the British riots in 2011 are often cited as resulting from the availability of social media as if this potential for circulating timely information for political or other purposes is 'proof' of the absence of risk associated with the deployment of 'intelligent' ICTs throughout society.

This view of the contribution of digital technologies to political engagement is one that rarely acknowledges that these social media also may be used by authorities to suppress protest movements. Nor does it acknowledge that these technologies are less effective than is commonly believed in creating material wealth (for other than their sponsors) or in encouraging the redistribution of productive activities or wealth within a community.[18] It is seldom noted in discussions about the beneficial impacts of innovations in ICTs, that greater equality and improved social justice do not follow inevitably from the diffusion of ICTs; they cannot, on their own, empower the 'multitude'.[19]

Runaway Systems

In the prevailing vision of the information society, increasingly what seems to matter is the virtual world, not the material or 'real world'.[20] Whether virtual representations in cyberspace are seen as being beneficial or pathological, the vision of a technologically-mediated world seems to have great appeal. It is appealing to science fiction writers and also to those who regard innovations in the communication system as leading to discontinuities in cultural, social, political, and economic organization, not all of which are welcome. Set against the visions of technological progress, there are the reflections of analysts for whom the prevailing information society vision either greatly exaggerates the death of an old order or substantially underestimates the risks associated with the communication system that is being developed.[21]

Some of those who have been deeply involved in developing the technologies of the Internet Age and have been strong advocates of their benefits, seem to be much more pessimistic when they realize that technology does not, on its own, resolve human problems. They argue that if the brakes are not applied, there is a high risk that the communication system will run out of control. For example, in the early 1990s, William Davidow, Intel Corporation's former Vice-President of Marketing and Sales for Semiconductors, and an electrical engineer by training, co-authored an influential book called *The*

Virtual Corporation. This book extolled the enormous benefits associated with the global information and communication system. It anticipated the whole-sale transformation of the structure and organization of companies and markets with innovations in semiconductors and computers, leading to 'formerly well-defined structures... beginning to lose their edges, seemingly permanent things starting to continuously change, and products and services... adapting to match our desires'.[22] Many of these changes in organizational dynamics, in the management of internal and external sources of information, and in the personalization of goods and services, are well in train today.

In his 2011 book, *Overconnected,* Davidow reflects on how his thinking has changed in the light of experience with digital technologies. He argues in this book that the increasing returns associated with positive feedbacks in a complex networked system could yield contagion effects and a system greatly at risk of 'racing out of control'. He wonders whether 'my technologist friends and I weren't every bit as naïve as the missionaries. We brought the world the tools and believed society could only benefit.... Now we find ourselves at the peak of the evolutionary pyramid, facing what H.G. Wells called the "inexorable imperative" to adapt or perish'.[23] Networked information and contagion effects are implicated, for example, in cases of dodgy financial assets which spread like viruses, consigning former 'miracle' economies, such as, Greece, Ireland, or Iceland, to the world financial system's intensive-care wards, and leading to the threat that the global economic system must adapt or perish with thousands of lives affected.

Concerns about the threats accompanying the interpenetration of ICTs and the human or social system are not new. The theme of runaway ICT systems has been discussed widely in the social science literature.[24] Nevertheless, the extent of human dependence in the twenty-first century on the communication system is new. In later chapters, I discuss the problems for society associated with faster speeds of communication, the way immersive virtual worlds alter the way we experience our lives, and whether and how people are able to master or control the technological system. The possibility that the enlightenment supposedly offered by technological innovation might be problematic if it continues along the current pathway, however, is more likely to be entertained when things go wrong than when there is no precipitating crisis. The potentially negative consequences of a world characterized by the increasing intensity of communication between human beings and their virtual proxies may be signalled regularly, but these signals have little effect in 'normal' times.[25] There are, of course, warnings that the speeding up of life in the wake of ICT deployment is outstripping human cognitive capacities and suppressing abilities for reflection. Some observers do claim that, in the absence of intervention to counter the 'inexorable imperative' of the technological system, there is a risk of chaos.[26] In the dominant vision of the information society, however, future technological innovations are expected to provide solutions to mitigate the risks of an 'out of control' system.

The ICT revolution is not the first example of a potentially beneficial, but disruptive, technology being implicated in endangering human beings. Crises of the Atomic Age, such as Chernobyl and Fukushima, highlight risky conditions and sometimes promote an evaluation of alternative policies and standards. While the case is often made for a return to a pre-nuclear power era, in the situation involving ICTs, there is no such reasonable argument for interventions that would suppress the innovation process. For the young, the 'pre-Internet' period is a creation of the imagination; for the old it is a challenge to the memory. Nevertheless, it is unreasonable to ignore the communication system's evolution or to leave its development to chance when some of its features are inconsistent with the values of the good society. As we will see, the direction of evolution is not pre-determined, despite claims about the inevitability of the Singularity.

Closing the Gaps

The risks of the present trajectory of change in the communication system are often sidestepped in policy debates. In most policy forums the focus is on the unevenness of ICT diffusion and on gaps in accessibility to digital information.[27] The initial uneven spread of digital technologies throughout the economies of the wealthy countries and, later, the lower income countries, produces concerns about the implications of the inability to access ICTs and digital information, and about 'the right of the public to take part in this new domain of social power'.[28] These concerns are often depicted mainly as problems that can be addressed by closing the gaps in accessibility to technology, which can be managed through targeted investments in hardware or software.

For example, Nicholas Negroponte (former Director of the Massachusetts Institute of Technology (MIT) Media Lab) adopted a strategy of promoting Internet access for children in low-income countries, claiming that the 'instantaneous and inexpensive transfer of electronic data that move at the speed of light', would lead automatically to beneficial change. The result of supplying schools with one laptop per child in low-income countries, so he claims, is that 'everywhere we go, truancy drops to zero'.[29] But such assertions are not borne out by the experiences of recipient countries unless their governments or other stakeholders are able to put in place accompanying measures (e.g. training, long-term financing, housing, and transport) unrelated to ICTs. Thus, in the dominant vision, the highest priority for information society policy is to close the gaps in access, for instance, to the Internet or a mobile phone. This ambition becomes a proxy for responding to the need for relevant local or distant knowledge and for investment in the other material resources that might enable people to improve their lives. It does little to close the gap between the rich and the poor, except inadvertently.

This way of seeing is typical of the way economic analysis treats the markets for digital information and does not distinguish between information and knowledge. Without such a distinction, any investment in ICT that enhances the capacities to produce, transmit, process, and store information is seen as being equivalent to enhancing the capacity of people to access, produce, and act upon diverse forms of 'knowledge' with beneficial effects. This is the perspective that has influenced the way agencies such as the World Bank and various UN organizations have responded to the challenges and opportunities accompanying advances in digital technologies. The World Bank's *Knowledge for Development 1998* report, which strongly promotes investment in ICTs, for instance, opens with the statement that 'knowledge is like light. Weightless and intangible, it can easily travel the world, enlightening the lives of people everywhere'.[30] Philip Agre, an academic commentator on the information society, argues that the conflation of information and knowledge is 'a utopian idea that stands in the main line of a long millennialist tradition. Its prophets see it levelling hierarchies, dispersing power, and bringing peace to the world'.[31] A kind of 'secularized religion' of technology seems to overtake the imaginations of so many of those who engage in policy advocacy in the information society. Digital technologies and open data initiatives become central to efforts to boost economic growth and to reduce poverty, but without giving sufficient attention to whether such initiatives are helping to level hierarchies or are instrumental in creating new ones that may be no less harmful than the ones they succeed.

If the information society is to be better aligned with values that are consistent with the good society, the vision needs to be articulated in a way that suggests a different social imaginary of the goals of the technological developments. The UN *Human Development Report* provides one alternative in saying that 'the purpose of development is to create an enabling environment for people to enjoy long, healthy and creative lives', by enlarging the choices available to the poor.[32] Too often, and unfortunately, this statement of purpose amounts to lip service in relation to opportunities for all and, in the context of the digital 'revolution', to the assumption that this purpose can be achieved mainly through the diffusion of improvements in ICTs, that is, by filling the gaps. The goals of equality and social justice that are espoused in UN human development reports do not provide remedies for the problems associated with the evolution of the communication system.

One of the greatest puzzles in modern societies is how to *reconcile* the goal of economic growth with the goals of social justice and the equitable distribution of resources, and this puzzle is at the core of many debates about these gaps. For instance, the digital divide agenda, aimed at closing technology gaps and speeding up the transmission of 'knowledge', is symptomatic of the millennialist notion of the 'end of history' or 'end times' in Christian eschatology.[33] Digital divide debates in policy forums often focus on how to distribute existing resources, that is, on the information 'haves' and 'have nots', and what to do about them.[34] This is an important issue. However, the differences in the competing visions of the good society, in this case, an information society underpinned by a complex communication system, are about how to reconcile the goals of economic growth and social justice. In the neoliberal account which is central in the dominant vision of the information society, it is the self-regulating market for ICTs and information that should 'decide' who gets what. What is needed, instead, as Phil Agre suggests, is 'a post-utopian imagination' that emphasizes the 'coevolution of institutions and technologies',[35] and the fact that human agency is always a feature of the economy, even in times when this is ignored. By focusing on the way the paradoxes of information scarcity and complexity are presenting themselves in the Internet Age, it is possible to begin to think about possibilities for intervention that would be consistent with aspirations for the good society.

Critical Reflections on Dreams of Machines

In the contemporary vision of the information society, the evolution of the communication system is conceived as the outcome of disruptive technological innovation that promises benefits for all, but, at the same time, requires adjustments that sometimes are inconsistent with aspirations for the good society. This phenomenon is not specific to ICTs; it is central in the marriage between modernity and modern liberalism. Modernity promises progress, while liberalism promises a meritocratic distribution of the gains from progress, but recognizes that equality of opportunity does not lead to equality of outcome. This is complicit in perpetuating inequality and social injustice and leads to constructs such as the 'deserving poor' and the 'undeserving poor'. In the information society, we could conceive of the deserving and the undeserving 'information poor', an approach characteristic of many digital divide debates. An alternative is to undertake a critical evaluation of how the logics of the paradoxes of information scarcity and complexity are mobilized in the different visions of the information society with the aim of providing a new reading of the possibilities for intervention.

This implies the need to 'unmask' the prevailing visions in the Internet Age to reveal the interests in them and how they influence decisions about policy and governance.[36] Daniel Bell was a close observer of the emergence of the information society in the post-World War II period. He was one of the first sociologists to argue that the evolution of the information society would be aligned with prevailing power relationships, such that certain groups or individuals would come to 'dictate' what information is produced, and for whom, and he challenged researchers to unmask the prevailing ideologies or ways of seeing.[37] In similar vein, Manuel Castells insists that 'the communication process decisively mediates the way in which power relationships are constructed and challenged in every domain of social practice, including political practice'.[38] The need for a critical assessment of the prevailing visions of the information society is as pressing in the Internet Age as it was during the transition from mechanical to electronic means of processing information. I take up the issue of relationships among visions, ideologies, and the social imaginary, as understood by Charles Taylor, in Chapter 3. In the meantime, it is important to signal that the evolution of the communication system in the information society is being guided by the ideas and actions of multiple actors within a complex system of power relationships.

The evolution of the communication system is being guided by the economic power of the largest companies, by the political power of nation states and their institutions, by a host of other actors organized formally into non-governmental organizations, and by individuals in their capacities as consumers and citizens in the information society. Developing a better understanding of how the power relationships guiding the technological innovation process come to be aligned with a vision of an information society that emphasizes private ownership of information and commercial markets is a goal of my analysis of the paradoxes of information scarcity and complexity. Critical examination of the prevailing vision serves as a means to understand possibilities for *reconciling* the goal of economic growth with the goals of social justice and the equitable distribution of resources. The evolution of the communication system is being guided also by a vision that is increasingly prevalent among members of online communities (of scientists, engineers, computer scientists, activists, and everyday users of the Internet) who favour social relationships that privilege the values of online cooperation, non-market information sharing, and common ownership of information.

These two visions usually are represented as requiring a choice between apparently plausible, but contradictory, paths. The path towards cooperation in an information commons is presented typically as consistent with equality and social justice, but it does not resolve the problem of how to monetize information production in the virtual realm in order to pay for the non-virtual essentials of life. The path towards market-led development of the information society seeks better means of monetizing information production, but it does not address the problems of inequality and social injustice that emerge as new technologies and modes of information production become integrated ever more tightly into market-based institutions.

Industrialization and standardized mass production under Fordism instigated the emergence of a technologically progressive approach to market-led growth.[39] In the Internet Age, large positive network externalities and increasing returns, associated with the spread of global connections and faster production of goods and services and shorter time to market, are seen as ushering in the post-Fordist era—what I call the Internet Age. This is creating the conditions for the personalization of goods and services, and for the diversity of information that is seen as being responsive to the preferences of all people,[40] alternately inching and bounding towards the time of 'machines of loving grace'. This vision is widely presumed to be feasible under conditions of constant economic growth and a firm belief that such growth will, eventually and with minimal intervention, foster social inclusion and improvements in people's lives. The dominant vision of the information society is about growth and prosperity, deferring and downplaying the goals of inclusion, equality, social justice, and sustainability of the global system.[41] Thus, technologists, industrialists, policy makers, and civil society members make different assumptions about the *means* to achieve what they understand to be the good society. This happens, for example, in discussions on personal privacy, the security of states, the protection of intellectual property, the prospects for economic growth, and the opportunities for democratic participation in society.

In the light of confusion and uncertainty about the journey towards the information society, it is essential to examine the implications of technological innovation and its outcomes for the lives that people are able to live and for their consistency with values of the good society. In his history of communication technologies, Harold A. Innis suggests that the progress of 'science, technology, and the mechanization of knowledge' tends to emphasize complexity and confusion. If we take the present phase of developments in the digital technologies of the Internet Age as the most recent instance in the history of the 'mechanization of knowledge', then Innis's concern that such technologies come to be associated with 'monopolies of knowledge' that affect conditions for freedom of thought, signals a need for a critical investigation. He says that it is 'extremely important to any civilization, if it is not to succumb to the influence of this monopoly of knowledge, to make some critical survey and report'.[42]

The dominant vision of the information society is a form of 'monopoly of knowledge' insofar as it privileges one vision of society over other visions and practices that also seem to be consistent with values of the good society. The dominant vision that has been discussed so far is hugely influential in the affluent regions of the world and, also, increasingly, in the poorest regions of the world. There are some variations, but the main assumptions—the imperative to secure the relative scarcity of information and to practice non-intervention in the market—are deeply entrenched in the prevailing vision of the information society.

This shapes what it is feasible to discuss within policy debates about the governance of the communication system, as will be demonstrated in later chapters. The contending social imaginaries of the information society usually are seen as oppositional. One or other of them is seen as being a misperception of the dynamics of the evolutionary process.[43] My analytical strategy is to examine why these oppositions persist. I suggest that these misperceptions are illustrations of paradox in the Internet Age. Among the many such paradoxes that could be explored, two stand out as being especially harmful when they go unacknowledged as such—the paradox of information scarcity and the paradox of complexity.

Conclusion

The challenge for my investigation is to see how the taken-for-granted, 'deeper normative notions and images' of these paradoxical ways of seeing come to be influential in guiding the evolution of the communication system. The central questions I set out in Chapter 1 are concerned fundamentally with whether the direction of change is serving human purposes, consistent with the good society. In her book, *Alone Together*, Sherry Turkle asks similar questions, suggesting that 'technologies, in every generation, present opportunities to reflect on our values and direction.... What I call *realtechnik* suggests that we step back and reassess when we hear triumphalist or apocalyptic narratives about how to live with technology'.[44] There is a risk that the communication system is racing out of control and that we are on the cusp of a 'robotic moment' in which human-to-human relationships are devalued. In the face of this risk, it is appropriate to determine whether policy measures might support ameliorative action. This is not to suggest that we should look back with nostalgia to an earlier era. Instead, it is an acknowledgement that the lives of human beings are increasingly mediated by machines with multiple benefits, and that it is important for the research community to study and report on the ways in which they may be harmfully mediated, so as to suggest ameliorative actions.

If the scarcity of digital information or material resources is a problem, in line with the prevailing vision, it can be shelved as temporary, as a problem that will disappear as the self-organizing communication system attends to its survival. Conflicts among proponents of opposing positions with respect to the responses to the paradox of information scarcity frequently are met with the claim that the communication system is too complex to govern. Nothing should be done to guide the evolution of the system because the 'correct' amount of variety and diversity of information in the information society is most likely to emerge if the innovation process is left to the self-regulating market. The system of communication is seen as being immune to human intervention, or human intervention is seen as being liable to pervert the system, resulting in unintended consequences. The best course of action, therefore, is inaction, or perhaps some form of industry self-regulation. Concerns about the risks associated with the evolution of the communication system are deferred to the future. These readings of the evolution of the system lead to non-intervention policies that are frequently responsive to the interests of powerful corporate and state actors. However, they are also consistent with the interests of those who champion a generative process of change from below, claiming that this will maximize the opportunities for creative expression and experimentation in the information society.

An alternative reading requires the invocation of a new social imaginary of the information society in the sense suggested by Charles Taylor. A new social imaginary is needed that is neither utopian nor dystopian, but, instead, enables consideration of whether there is a better direction for a society in which human lives are mediated by machines. A better pathway would be consistent with social desiderata that do not place equality and social justice in opposition to economic growth, and that do not relegate human emotions and experience to a place that is unconnected with our experiences of machines. In the next two chapters (3 and 4), I examine how social imaginaries of the information society are fostered by traditions of work, first, in the social sciences and, then, in the physical and natural sciences. Problematic oppositions between prevailing ways of seeing the information society are shown to be associated with difficulties in understanding the paradox of information scarcity and the paradox of complexity; that is, with a failure accurately to diagnose the conflicts in power relationships that are invoked within a complex, twenty-first century, multi-level information society.

3 Social Imaginaries of the Information Society

Introduction

The evolution of the communication system is giving rise to paradoxes that are rarely discussed explicitly in the scholarly literature on the information society. This creates problems for those who seek to understand the determinants and likely outcomes of the ongoing technological innovation process. The prevailing vision of the information society encourages technological innovation with the promise of benefits for all while, simultaneously, it is facilitating persistence of a social order that is complicit in perpetuating social and economic inequality. Is it possible to choose an alternative pathway in this evolutionary process? Is action required to alter the present path in order to increase the prospects for achieving the aspirations of the good society? Answering these questions presumes an understanding of the interdependence of the processes of innovation and other components of a complex adaptive system, and how this is involved in changes in the communication system.

In this chapter, I introduce selected social science perspectives on the information society, differentiating between those that are consistent with what I will depict as the dominant social imaginary of the information society, and those more compatible with alternative, though still widely held, imaginaries. As indicated in Chapter 1, the uncertain relationship between what we see and what we think we know means that many theoretical perspectives can be used to understand the innovation process and its role in the construction of the information society.[1] In this chapter, I treat insights from theoretical traditions in the social sciences as being provisional or, in Berger's terms, 'unsettled'. No single perspective offers a complete explanation of the evolution of the communication system in the information society. These perspectives co-mingle in the social imaginaries of the information society with different consequences for what we then come to understand as appropriate policy interventions. Roger Silverstone comments that 'the communications we undertake...have consequences for how we see and live in the world'.[2] The aim of this chapter is to draw attention to some of these communications in the social science literature that are integrated within the social imaginaries of the information society.

Following a consideration of the notion of social imaginary, I continue by differentiating between what can be designated as administrative or instrumentalist accounts of features of the information society, contrasting them with accounts that can be designated as critical. I then set out features of the dominant social imaginary of the information society. This discussion draws principally on insights from theories that account for technological innovation as an exogenous shock to society, and on the instrumental traditions of research. This is followed by a discussion of some of the alternative social imaginaries of the information society, in this case drawing on theories in which the innovation process is regarded as being a contributor to the endogenous developments within a complex system, and insights from instrumental and critical theories.

Insights from work in the social sciences (and the humanities) serve as a means of communicating about the evolution of the communication system, providing quite different accounts of how or why change happens. Critical endogenous accounts are more sensitive to asymmetries in power relationships in the information society, amplifying mechanistic models that are characteristic of instrumentalist exogenous accounts. However, even the former do not offer a full picture of the implications of the paradoxes of information scarcity and complexity, which, I have suggested, are a central feature of the information society in the Internet Age. This is taken up in Chapter 4 where I examine what we can learn from systems theories about the dynamics of change in the technological and social realms.

Social Imaginary as Analytical Tool

The social imaginary is an important concept for making sense of the world. Craig Calhoun argues that 'to speak of the social imaginary is to assert that there are no fixed categories of external observation adequate to all history; that ways of thinking and structures of feeling make possible certain social forms, and that such forms are thus products of action and historically variable'. He comments that, 'alternative imaginaries are operative in the constitution of global culture and social relations'.[3] For the sociologist, C. Wright Mills, the 'sociological imagination enables its possessor to understand the larger historical scene in terms of its meaning for the inner life and the external career of a variety of individuals' and the way individuals 'become falsely conscious of their social positions'. It involves a reflexive stance in reaction to 'Science' which he characterizes as 'a set of Science Machines, operated by technicians and controlled by economic and military men who neither embody nor understand science as ethos and orientation',[4] a comment that brings to mind some of the dreams of machines in the Internet Age. The information society often is presented as emerging out of an evolutionary process which is universally applicable. However, common sense suggests that the way people understand the tools of communication, both hardware and software, the way they experience mediated representations, and how they interpret and act (or fail to act) on these representation, is neither fixed nor universally instantiated in a homogeneous way by technology.[5]

Indeed, as many scholars are acknowledging, different social imaginaries are operative in constituting the information society and in guiding the evolution of the communication system. John Thompson, for example, argues that 'the imaginary accounts for the orientation of social institutions, for the constitution of motives and needs, for the existence of symbolism, tradition, and myth',[6] though he challenges views of the imaginary as an 'unceasing and essentially *undetermined* (social-historical and psychical) creation',[7] as in the understanding of the Greek scholar, Cornelius Castoriadis, who worked after World War II in Paris. Thompson argues that, in rejecting a rationalist philosophy of history, Castoriadis leaves no basis for deciding whether we should struggle to achieve any particular imaginary among competing alternatives. For instance, if we were to follow Castoriadis, we would have no basis for concluding whether to favour an information society that is the outcome of an emergent complex system whatever the values it entails, or to favour relations of power within a system dominated by capitalist markets. In other words, we would have no normative basis to guide human choices with respect to the information society.

Others who employ the idea of the social imaginary include Chantal Mouffe, who suggests that 'every hegemonic order is susceptible of being challenged by counterhegemonic practices, i.e. practices which will attempt to disarticulate the existing order so as to install other forms of hegemony'.[8] She argues that there are indeed choices that human beings can make about the pathway that is to be followed. Similarly, Ernest Laclau sees the social imaginary as 'a horizon: it is not one among other objects but an absolute limit which structures a field of intelligibility and is thus the condition of possibility of the emergence of any object'.[9] In our case, the 'object' in question is the systems that are giving shape to the way our lives are mediated by ICTs. Nico Carpentier applies the social imaginary concept in his examination of the feasibility of the emergence of a regime of global governance for the media and communication system. He argues that 'social imaginaries are produced, accepted, and then taken for granted' as people seek some consistency in their experience of the 'reality' of their lives in a world of rapidly changing technologies and cultural and social norms.[10] These treatments of the social imaginary are inflected with a particular interpretation of the power relationships at the heart of processes of social, political, and economic as well as technological change and they are derived from both Marxist and non-Marxist understandings of the ways that power is articulated in capitalist society.

In my analysis, I employ Charles Taylor's definition of the social imaginary. For Taylor, the social imaginary is:

something much broader and deeper than the intellectual schemes people may entertain when they think about social reality in a disengaged mode. I am thinking rather of the ways in which they imagine their social existence, how they fit together with others, how things go on between them and their fellows, the expectations which are normally met, and the deeper normative notions and images which underlie these expectations.[11]

As discussed in Chapter 1, for Taylor, the social imaginary is not a specific set of theoretical ideas that is given from above, but an ethos that enables people to make sense of developments in society. I use this open and flexible concept of the social imaginary because I want to explore competing visions of the information society and what they seem to mean to their respective stakeholders when they adhere to them. When it comes to the framework for the analysis of the experience of these stakeholders and the question of whether there is scope for intervention to guide the evolution of the communication system, it is important to position oneself with respect to matters of human agency, which I do in Chapter 4. Here, my intention is to set out why Taylor's concept is helpful in thinking about the contribution of different traditions of research to an understanding of the evolution of the communication system.

Taylor's concept of the social imaginary is based on a liberal view of moral philosophy that conceives moral order as being similar to the idea of the good society or the social compact that guides the way social actors aspire to maximize human welfare. Taylor explains that the social imaginary should be conceived as ideas that are 'carried in images, stories and legends'.[12] Social imaginaries are widely shared understandings that have achieved general legitimacy. In this sense, the social imaginary is not synonymous with an ideological hegemony insofar as it does not describe a particular dynamic in the distribution of resources in society. Taylor emphasizes that it is important to investigate what is involved when a particular theory or theories penetrate and transform the social imaginary. This is especially important for under-standing how very different theoretical explanations of the emergence of the information society are taking hold and influencing policy and our everyday lives. Taylor suggests that:

for the most part, people take up, improvise, or are inducted into new practices. These practices are made sense of by the new outlook, the one first articulated in the theory; this outlook is the context that gives sense to the practices. And hence the new understanding comes to be accessible to the participants in a way it wasn't before. It begins to define the contours of their world....[13]

The new practices for the design and organization of the hardware and software of the communication system, for its governance, and for everyday life in the information society fit either easily or awkwardly with theories about the dynamics of technological innovation and their implications for society, and with different actors' varying claims to legitimacy. As Taylor says, 'the practice largely carries the understanding. At any given time, we can speak of the "repertory" of collective actions at the disposal of a given sector of society'.[14] Thus, it is the repertory of images, stories, and actions selected by those whose lives are interdependent with the technological system of communication that is central to my investigation. Taylor paid particular attention to the ascendant imaginary in a given historical period. While not neglecting alternatives, he has been particularly interested in how the social imaginary informs all practices in society, practices that include the economic, political, cultural, and social—and in his case, the religious. In my analysis, the aim is to show how conflicts, which are central to an established and to an ascendant social imaginary, can be understood as paradoxes with major consequences for the development of the information society in the Internet Age.

Social imaginaries for Taylor are what make possible a shared sense of the legitimacy of the organization and conduct of society. They define the contours of the social world and influence its governance. They 'can eventually come to count as the taken-for-granted shape of things, too obvious to mention'.[15] Thus, the social imaginaries of the Internet Age influence the way digital technologies are used and the way they permeate and mediate people's lives. They also need not imply a causal relationship from the laboratory to practice. Experience beyond the laboratory can be understood to permeate the experimental world in multiple ways. There is an interpretive and dialectical relationship between what we understand through theory and what we know through practice. As Anthony Giddens says, 'the proper locus for the study of social reproduction is in the immediate process of the constituting of interaction, for all social life is an active accomplishment; and every moment of social life bears the imprint of the totality'. '"The totality", however, is not an inclusive, bounded "society", but a composite of diverse totalizing orders and impulsions'.[16]

In the prevailing vision of the information society as depicted in Chapter 2, however, an 'economic-centred' notion is strongly privileged. For some analysts, this is consistent with the perceived 'natural order of things', and with the emergence in the eighteenth century of a doctrine of the 'harmony of interests', which Taylor traces in detail.[17] This vision is taken up in the dominant social imaginary of the optimal way to encourage the development of the information society, that is, reliance on market forces. This is despite the significance of the information society for polity and culture and despite the availability of an imaginary that is consistent with non-market relations and a sharing culture in an information commons. When these conflicting social imaginaries collide, they do so because the values they embrace are strongly contested. These contestations are attributable to paradoxes which influence understanding of the new technologies and whether they are welcomed or seen as threatening. The genesis of paradox can be brought to light, following Taylor, by providing 'a certain reading'[18] of the contending social imaginaries in a given historical period and their associated practices.

An interrogation of the social imaginaries of the information society in the Internet Age provides a means to account for differences in the way actors understand and make sense of the dynamics of technological innovation and a basis for a critical analysis of their interests in information society developments. It is important to reiterate that the social imaginary is not coterminous with a 'vision' or an 'ideology' and it does not imply—in the abstract—a particular understanding of power. Taylor's is a relatively open concept. This is in keeping with an interdisciplinary approach, with an emphasis on the way stakeholders communicate about their relationships in the information society. Two not always mutually exclusive ways of seeing the information society are present in the scholarly literature in the social sciences on developments in ICTs (and in the media) and their implications for society. These are discussed in the remainder of this chapter to provide an initial basis for the framework that is used later to explore the genesis of paradox and its implications in the information society.

Instrumental and Critical Ways of Seeing

One means of distinguishing between the main ways of seeing the information society and the evolution of the modern (post-World War II) communication system is to consider the prevailing social imaginaries from the perspectives offered by what came to be designated as the administrative or instrumental and critical traditions in social science research.[19] These traditions are present in all academic social science disciplines and they privilege different research questions and assumptions about the values that guide action in the cultural, social, political, and economic world. Following Paul Lazarsfeld, an American sociologist and founder in the 1940s of the Bureau of Applied Social Research at Columbia University, administrative research is that which is 'carried through in the service of some kind of administrative agency of public or private character'.[20] Much of the Bureau's research was funded by corporate or military organizations. This kind of research is instrumental in the sense that those who conduct it normally purport to be agnostic, unbiased, or neutral about the values associated with the ends to be achieved. It is associated with a modernist view of technology in which progressive innovations in technology and in the accompanying social organization are assumed to result in societal improvements that can be controlled or mastered.

Lazarsfeld contrasted administrative and critical research. He understood critical research as 'independent' of the instrumental interests of its funders and, therefore, as more likely to challenge assumptions about the social value of scientific and technical progress. Contemporary critical researchers would likely question the meaning of 'independent' as applied to research, but also would similarly insist that administrative researchers are trapped by the questions they ask and the methodological stances they adopt in undertaking research to support the prevailing status quo.[21] They would argue that interests and power are deeply embedded in the progress of science (and social science), and that this has implications for what is funded, the research questions that are asked, and whether power relationships are the important subjects for investigation.[22]

In the case of the communication system in the information society, administrative research addresses the means by which ICTs might be applied to achieve improvements in control systems. These include controls for targeting missile systems or automated information systems to improve productivity. The administrative researcher tends to examine 'what is' or what is possible, whereas the critical researcher tends to interrogate why things are the way they are, how they happened, and what were or are likely to be their political, social, economic, or other consequences. Thus, critical research is likely to question the implications, for all members of society, of the power relations that emerge with scientific and technological innovation. There are of course departures from these distinctions. For example, in some cases, critical researchers advocate disengagement from normative issues and from suggesting changes in policy so as not to collude or become co-opted by the prevailing power structure. And administrative researchers, in many instances, become advisors to governments, advocating policy actions and reforms, albeit within the constraints of the prevailing power structure and without challenging its fundamental legitimacy to govern. In this chapter, I will be concerned principally with the way these research traditions are informed by, and contribute to, the social imaginaries of the information society, especially with respect to the themes of the potential of human mastery and control of ICTs.

Research that is instrumental in orientation tends to focus on the 'material' components of ICT (the hardware or digital bits) and on mastery of technological and social systems. Critical research is more likely to be concerned with both the material characteristics and the symbolic meaning of technologies and their applications, as well as with the diversity of the information that they enable to be produced and consumed. The questions tend to be about the value of new developments to different interest groups within society. In line with the prevailing social imaginary of the information society, instrumental work mainly emphasizes the innovations in ICTs that support the functions of communication, computation, coordination and control, and memory and record keeping. Critical research is more likely to be interested in the possibility of alternative innovation pathways, that is, in the implications of technological innovation for meaning and identity construction, social or cultural difference, a participatory society, and the well-being of human beings.

It is not easy, as indicated above, to draw clear distinctions between these research traditions. The instrumental concern with technological mastery is evident, for example, in American political scientist and communication scholar Harold Lasswell's question about the 'revolutionary ICT gadgets' of his time—'*How can we effectively master them* so that they can contribute to some result that's worth getting?'[23] Lasswell contributed to the analysis of propaganda and communication during World War II, and was regarded as a very influential social scientist. Despite its administrative orientation, his work was influenced by concerns typical of those working in the critical research tradition. He was interested, for instance, in the relationships between communication, the media, and people's vulnerabilities to the way they are used. As he puts it: 'it is no news that knowledge is power, especially knowledge that is promptly available and includes information about individuals and groups that lays open their vulnerabilities to blackmail or to tactics of positive inducement'.[24]

These distinctions are present in the social sciences that examine various aspects of the information society. In the administrative tradition, the Internet, for example, has been regarded as either a progressive medium contributing to economic growth, providing platforms for advertisers and businesses, or, alternatively, as an inclusive technology that favours democracy. It is more likely to be seen by those working in the critical tradition as being complicit in contributing to the maintenance of unequal power relationships. This is so even when it is also acknowledged that technological innovations are creating opportunities for political contestation, mobilization, and resistance to the prevailing institutions of power.

For researchers in the critical tradition, ICTs have been regarded as providing a basis for political contestation, but not without constraints stemming from the structural features of their production and consumption. Herbert Schiller, an American political economist, differentiated critical from administrative perspectives by observing that the latter are preoccupied with technology because of their belief that 'most, if not all social and economic problems either arise from or can be overcome by *improved technique and instrumentation*, regardless of such institutional questions as ownership, control, and social structure'.[25] Analysis of issues of institutional structure, and of power and its articulation in the material and symbolic realms, differentiates work in the critical tradition from the instrumental tradition. In the critical tradition, attention is drawn to the potential of innovations in technologies to be associated with people's empowerment and their disempowerment, depending on the extent to which they are able to master or control the innovation process.[26] Some of the keywords signalling differences between these research traditions are shown in Table 3.1.

These distinctions are important because understanding the evolution of the communication system and the social imaginaries of information society varies with the analytical tradition that is emphasized. Research in the two traditions differs, in part, because they respond to different questions and embrace incommensurable premises. Thomas Kuhn, American historian and philosopher of science, claims that competing theories arise from different ways of seeing the world and that 'novelty emerges only with difficulty, manifested by resistance, and against a background provided by expectation'.[27] Resistance to new ways of seeing, and expectations about continuities between past and present, account for some of the differences in approaches. However, incommensurability can stem from differences in the values that the technological innovation process is assumed to embrace. This is crucial also for differentiating among the ways that these research traditions contribute to social imaginaries of the information society.

Instrumental approaches advance the project of developing ever more sophisticated technologies. They are concerned with the feasibility of efforts to bring a particular, albeit changing, information society vision into reality by engaging in a purposive innovation process. Alternatives have emerged but the critical research tradition has not achieved the status of a transformational paradigm that has repressed the dominant social imaginary of the information society. Research in the critical tradition has succeeded, however,

Table 3.1. Administrative and Critical Research Traditions

Administrative research	Critical research
Instrumental	Reflexive
Transmission model	Ritual (symbolic) model
Information processing	Material and symbolic
Individual	Individual and collective
Control and mastery	Mediation
Pluralist	Unequal power relations
Finance—corporate and military	Resistance and vulnerability
Productivity and economic growth	Collaborative development
Modernization	Mobilization
Stability	Change

Source: Author.

in provoking reflection on the 'march' towards the information society, and it has contributed to an increasingly widely held repertory of practices embracing resistance to the market-led values of the predominant social imaginary. Key features of the dominant social imaginary of the information society in the post-World War II period are traced in the next section, followed by a discussion of the alternatives.

Prevailing Information Society Imaginary

The designation of wealthy industrialized societies as information societies started to become prominent after World War II. The immediate post-war period saw significant advances in the application of electronic information systems to support the organization and control of information for military and non-military purposes. Many of the key ideas were in circulation long before this, however.[28] For example, in the mid-fifteenth century, the term 'information' was beginning to be used to refer to an instruction or 'fact'. It was in the late 1920s that a physicist, Leó Szliárd, who conceived of devices such as the cyclotron and linear accelerator, invested 'information' with its 'thing-like' character, rendering it available for quantification.[29] By that time, information was being used to describe a mathematically defined quantity. Vannevar Bush, an American engineer, who worked on early analogue computers and on research that would lead ultimately to digital circuitry, proposed the memex in 1945. This was an indexing device that could store different kinds of information and communications, ultimately, as he imagined it, creating associations between all kinds of stored information and infinitely expanding the capacity of available memory systems.[30]

This was not the first such proposal; there had been numerous efforts in the pre-war period to bring technology to bear to construct a society aligned with a vision of a world in which information and control systems would augment the human mind. For example, in 1934, a Belgian entrepreneur and information scientist, Paul Otlet, had the ambition of using the library index card as a means of organizing all the world's information. He described a *Mundaneum* comprised of some 15 million cards, referring to the device as a 'mechanical collective brain',[31] prefiguring the vision of the Internet as facilitating new forms of collective intelligence.[32] Otlet's sketches resemble the modern computer and early conceptions of the relationship between mind and representations of the external world. Figure 3.1 is suggestive of how the features of later information processing devices are prefigured by the features of earlier devices.[33] Figure 3.2 highlights the association between 'intelligence' and information processing and the early idea that media representations of

Figure 3.1. Otlet's 'Web'

reality might be automatically produced, substituting for human (subjective) interpretation.

It was the work of mathematicians, engineers, and economists rather than social scientists from other disciplines, and library scholars, such as Otlet, however, that would become central in the social imaginary of the information society. The research interests of the former groups attracted substantial public and private funding aimed at developing improved means of mastery over the control and processing of information.

After World War II, research in the field of cybernetics became central to the scientific community's search for the development of improved systems in which information feedback would lead to changes in a system and, potentially, improved means of system control. Cybernetics was the label given by Norbert Wiener to the study of the structure of regulatory or control systems within closed system environments, in his book on *Cybernetics: Or Control and Communication in the Animal and Machine*, published towards the end of the 1940s.[34] This research had applications in electronic networks and in many other fields where control is an important feature and where the goal is to regulate a system to achieve stability. Wiener, a mathematician at MIT, characterizes this way of seeing the uses of information systems as involving processes, 'of our adjusting to the contingencies of the outer environment and of our living effectively within that environment. . . . communication and control belong to the essence of man's inner life, even as they

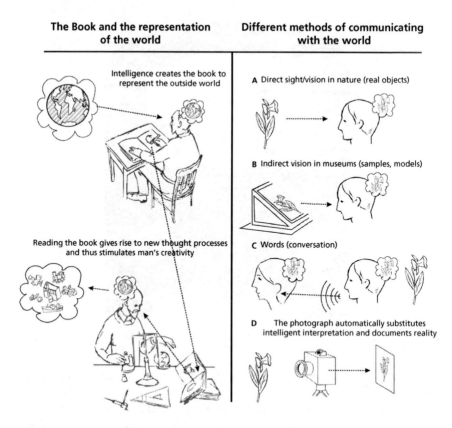

Figure 3.2. Otlet's Mundaneum Vision

belong to his life in society'.[35] Research on control systems was regarded as being about both the physical and biological worlds of human beings.

In 1949, a year after Wiener's book on cybernetics, *A Mathematical Theory of Communication* was published. This was a collaboration between Claude Shannon, an electrical engineer and mathematician at MIT, who had worked with Vannevar Bush, and Warren Weaver, a scientist and Director of Natural Sciences at the Rockefeller Institute.[36] Their aim was to develop new approaches to the automation of information systems. Their model of a sender and receiver in an information and communication system was to become hugely influential, and provided the foundation for technological innovations that eventually led to Internet Age technologies. This model came to be the preferred one and it was consistent with instrumentalist ambitions for technological progress. Researchers in the social sciences were also attracted by simple, 'elegant', ways of theorizing communication systems developed by the mathematicians, physicists, and engineers. The model came to be known as the 'stimulus-response model' of communication. Despite being criticized for its inapplicability to questions about the meaning of information, this model retained its influence, informing the dominant social imaginary of the information society in numerous ways.[37]

By the 1960s, 'information age' terminology was being used in the corporate world as well as by academics. Some sources attribute this label to Richard Leghorn, whose work was in the fields of airborne and space (photographic) reconnaissance and, later, in the broadcast and cable industries.[38] In the social sciences, economists were attracted to the simplicity of mathematical depictions of information systems. They quite easily made the shift from modelling electronic information transmission systems to examining the impact on the economy of information flows. For them, at least, it was only a small step to the assumption that what was being modelled was knowledge. The Nobel Prize winning economist, George Stigler, who received the award for his work on the economics of information, wrote that 'one should hardly have to tell academicians that information is a valuable resource: Knowledge *is* power'.[39]

By the end of the 1960s, the conflation of information with knowledge had become commonplace. Notwithstanding the advances made by Stigler, however, the study of information was to occupy, for some time, what he called a 'slum dwelling' in the economics discipline. The study of information presented difficult problems for economists. They struggled with the challenge of modelling the immaterial characteristics of information (compared to the modelling of material goods such as automobiles or lumber). Theoretical work in economics faced challenges because information has some unusual characteristics compared to other economic resources. The most obvious of these are, first, its non-rivalry (my use of your information does not reduce your holding of it and, because of this, information is often shared), and, second, its expansibility (once someone incurs the often substantial costs of producing the first copy of information, its unlimited reproduction incurs much lower costs and, in the case of digital information, these costs are often negligible).[40] In the conventional economic analysis of markets, buyers and sellers are assumed to perceive that a resource is relatively scarce. In the case of information, with rapid changes in the way digital information can be produced and copied, this condition of scarcity has become increasingly difficult to achieve, a development that challenges the foundation premises of economic theory.

As attention focused increasingly in the early post-war years on the production, circulation, and consumption of digital information in the wealthy economies as a means of growth and employment, information-related research began to proliferate in some branches of economics and in the management field. Fritz Machlup and Peter Drucker in the United States and Yoneji Masuda in Japan were among the early contributors.[41] The questions they investigated were mainly consistent with the administrative tradition. They focused either on measuring the speed of a shift towards greater dependence of economies on information goods supported by the new technologies for information processing and control, or on qualitative assessment of the transformations in the organization of businesses and the structure of industry sectors, in both cases, focusing on the changes accompanying disruptive technologies.

In the social imaginary of the information society that became dominant in the twentieth century, all societies were expected to move through a series of economic stages, from dependence on agricultural production for wealth creation through an industrial revolution with an emphasis on manufacturing, towards growing dependence on immaterial wealth creation, that is, on information processing. This way of seeing the process of technological innovation offers an account of the impact of technological change on society, a technologically deterministic vision, captured in Marshall McLuhan's vision of the 'global village'.[42] By the 1990s, this image of the information society had taken hold in the popular imagination. Its strong emphasis on the materiality of technology was depicted on a cover of a 1993 edition of *Time* magazine which profiled the role of the information highway or infrastructure in bringing 'a revolution in entertainment, news and communication'.[43] This media treatment of technological innovation emphasized the impact of technology on society. As suggested by Figure 3.3, developments in integrated circuits became more and more closely associated with the 'tree of knowledge' that would benefit everyone in society.

In the MIT Media Lab around this time the talk was about 'inventing the future' with digital technologies. The political classes picked up on this message as the information society began to achieve greater prominence in the social imaginary.[44] US Vice-President Al Gore began to promote the information highway in the United States and internationally, and Martin Bangemann, the then European Commissioner for Industry and Telecommunications, did the same in Europe. At around the same time, Japan launched a programme of research on the advanced information infrastructure.[45] Academics were writing about 'promise and peril in the age of networked intelligence',[46] and many influential scholars were providing analyses of progress towards an information society.[47] For those in the administrative tradition, the vision was one of progress towards the ultimate goal of 'perfect' knowledge and of technologies that would help to achieve it. In this view, progress towards this goal was only a matter of time and it would be consistent with aspirations for the good society. Harnessing technological progress in the service of economic growth became the central feature of the dominant social imaginary of the information or 'knowledge' society.

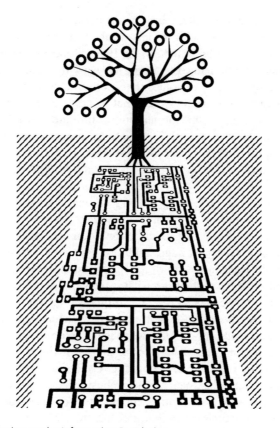

Figure 3.3. Bringing on the Information Revolution

FROM INFORMATION TO KNOWLEDGE SOCIETY

The conflation of information as data or digital bits, information as 'fact', and information as useable knowledge is a feature of the epistemology of the economics discipline. For this reason, the shift from debates about the 'information' to the 'knowledge' society was a slight one for many economists, as well as for others working on instrumental questions about the evolution of the communication system. For economists, there is an important association between knowledge and productivity which fits well with the scientists' and engineers' interest in control systems. The relative intensity of the use of capital and labour resources is understood to influence productivity. Over the long term, capital is replaced, labour skills change, and economic gains are expected from improvements in the knowledge base of the labour force. This is an *exogenous model* of economic growth.

In this model, it is assumed that processes external to the operation of the economic system generate technological progress. Thus, the long run rate of growth is said to be determined *exogenously* because technological change, a fundamental explanatory factor for labour productivity, is modelled as being exogenous to the economic system. In the 1950s, Robert Solow developed this insight further, emphasizing the importance of the rate of technological progress or innovation.[48] He argues that economic growth is accounted for by disembodied technological change, that is, new ways of deploying capital and labour (including organizational innovation) and new knowledge about how to use capital and labour (productivity movements stemming from knowledge improvements). These insights were translated into an emphasis on the importance of investing in innovation and leading-edge technologies such as ICTs.

In the wake of the exogenous model's emphasis on growth and digital information (knowledge), the labels 'knowledge society' and 'knowledge-based economy' were used to describe developments based on the use of ICTs for the acquisition, storage, and processing of information. In the framework of the exogenous economics model, what this means for transformations in society differs little from what is imagined about such transformations in the 'information society'.[49] The emphasis is on analysing the stock of knowledge and the speed of diffusion of the new technologies. An important implication of an emphasis on knowledge is the assumption that an increase in the relative importance of knowledge inputs in the production process implies a changing basis for the competitive success of companies and the need for substantial adjustments to their business strategies and practices. Knowledge comes to be seen as an essential feature of organizations that exist to coordinate the actions of individuals and to maintain some degree of continuity in their collective purposes. As a result, knowledge is embodied in individuals and allows them to earn a return on knowledge investments, giving rise to the idea of human capital and its accumulation (or lack thereof). Human capital came to be seen as a key factor influencing wage and employment opportunities. It is a key factor in whether people are included in or excluded from the imagined benefits of the information society.

The work of those specializing in the organizational adjustments that seem to be needed to accommodate features of the new technologies has complemented the work of economists. The term, knowledge work, was used by management consultant and scholar, Peter Drucker, in his examination of the organizational changes needed to stimulate creativity and efficiency in the workplace when the product is intangible information.[50] When the term 'knowledge economy' entered the popular lexicon in the late 1960s, it did so, not as a scholarly concept, but as a journalistic reference in the *Saturday Review* magazine. From the 1970s, organizations with a considerable influence on the social imaginaries of policy makers, such as the OECD and the World Bank, consistently promoted the idea that 'knowledge is power' and that investment in the communication system is required to drive wealth creation in the knowledge-based economy.[51] By the start of the twenty-first century, *information society* had come to describe societies whose populations were said to aspire towards the wide-scale appropriation of digital ICTs and information to support all aspects of their lives. And the label *knowledge economy* was associated with the privileged role of commercial activity in the marketplace which would give rise to the economic growth of a modern information society and to a wide range of expected social, cultural, and political benefits, consistent with values of the good society.

SPECULATIVE FUTURES

What was understood by 'knowledge' is unclear in most of this literature and it varies depending on the instrumental purposes of research and with the focus of policy debates on the development of the information or knowledge society. In the literature, the word 'knowledge' typically occurs as a singular noun and, as in the case of information, is used in a way that suggests that it is a 'thing' that can be measured.[52] The *Oxford English Dictionary* notes the plural usage of 'knowledges', referring to 'a branch of learning; a science; an art' which it traces to the late sixteenth century. Thus, it seems that historically a conception of multiple knowledges and meanings was prevalent, but with the ascendency of the information processing model and its contribution to the prevailing social imaginary of the information society, treating knowledge as synonymous with information or 'fact' became commonplace. The universality of meaning associated with knowledge became firmly embedded in the social imaginary of the information society. This would have major implications for the representations of people and their values in the information society because it would help to confirm the idea of a hierarchy of universal or factual knowledge about how to organize and govern.

The absence of consistency in the terminology in use has contributed to the speculation about the trajectory of information society development, with many vague and conflicting claims being made about the impact of digital data, information, or knowledge. The enthusiastic take-up of online social media, from an instrumental perspective, for example, might suggest that society has powerful platforms for bringing together the people, skills, and knowledge (facts) needed to tackle many of the world's problems.[53] However, these speculations do not take account of the problems of inequality and exclusion in the everyday world, nor do they explain how the mere existence of these powerful platforms might resolve them. Assumptions are made frequently also about the spread of digital ICTs and changes in people's cognitive abilities, with suggestions, for instance, that 'the linear mind is being pushed aside'.[54] However, discussion about the possibilities for interventions to avert this displacement or to benefit from it, are relatively rare.

The technological enthusiast model presumes that people are buffeted by exogenous technology shocks and inevitably must adjust to the technological system. In this perspective, it is assumed that the innovation process is yielding technologies that are 'fit for purpose', that is, they are consistent with human well-being and the good society.

Pessimism about the outcomes of the interpenetration of these technologies with human experience is similarly affected by speculation. The cynics lament the relatively small amount of attention being given to the way technologies are implicated in people's lives, and the strong emphasis on the 'impact' of technology on the information society and on our post-human lives. When it is claimed, for example, that time spent online is reshaping our brains, and leading to stress and effects on memory,[55] in the instrumental tradition the questions tend to be principally about cause and effect. The focus is on whether online activity is causing changes in cognitive ability or whether differences in cognitive abilities are resulting in new patterns of online activity. It is not usually on whether these 'impacts' of technology are consistent with well-being as is more likely in critical research.

From an exogenous theoretical perspective on the role of technological innovation, the challenge for technologists is to build a better communication system for the good society. The good society here, however, is conceived as one in which individual freedom of choice is the most highly privileged value, and this downplays the importance of collective values and goals. The construction of a communication system, based on digital platforms and modular hardware and software components, is understood to produce shocks that, as discussed earlier, disrupt the structure and organization of production in the ICT industry. This disruption, in turn, is expected to give rise to changes in the way people interact with each other using ICT applications. Questions about the nature of online interactions then become the principal focus of research. For example, how many friends do people have on Facebook? Which new Apps are favoured in the market? How long to the next technology that will embellish the affective experience of networking, such as 3D television? These are the orientations typical of instrumental research that focuses on the 'impact' of technology, on 'shocks' to the social or economic system, and on the need to adjust to these shocks to sustain economic growth and prevailing cultural, social, and political practices.

With the diffusion of multiple means to construct virtual worlds using digital devices and networks, however, and some sixty years after the information processing model became central to the social imaginary of the information society, confusion about how to adjust to the communication system in terms of social, cultural, political, and economic norms is undiminished. This is because the digital features of the communication system that has been built creates the conditions for the genesis of the paradoxes of information scarcity and system complexity that are central to the evolution of the information society. Some of the companies with a strong interest in creating the market and the institutional conditions necessary to maintain the perception that information is relatively scarce are experiencing stress in the form of declining revenues. However, the problems for the economy created by information abundance are either ignored, or treated as a 'problem' variable, in studies focusing mainly on the relationship between the pace and direction of technological innovation and the prospects for economic growth and opportunity.

The social imaginaries of engineers and mathematicians in the post-war period that gave rise to cybernetic theory, persist as witnessed in the search for continuous improvements in digital information systems through miniaturization, modularization, and the greater capacity and reach of networks. The information society imaginary is associated with the challenges involved in constructing a communication system enabling all digital bit streams to be carried within the same transmission system. At the heart of this repertory of images is a vision of ICT convergence. For example, in the 1950s, John Pierce, an engineer associated with Bell Labs, saw that television transmission would be combined with telephony, that mobile phones would fit in a pocket, and that machine-to-machine communication would become fully automated. His vision of electronic information systems involves, 'not only the transmission of digital information, but the use of elaborate computing machinery to sort data, to collate it, to make computations concerning it',[56] that is, to use technology to do things more cheaply and effectively. In this context, communication problems are abstract, and the theory of communication is based on the assumption that 'a bit' is a universal measure of an amount of information. In the twenty-first century, little has changed insofar as it is bit streams that preoccupy company strategists and policy makers who focus on ICT convergence and on broadband speeds for information transmission, consistent with a mathematical theory of the best way of encoding information to reduce uncertainty.

This theory of communication has never been concerned with the meaning of information in the interpretative sense. Pierce argues that the suggestion that a theory of communication should be concerned with matters such as meaning is absurd because, for him, the crucial issue is to understand noise, entropy, and uncertainty and their reduction. However, many engineers and mathematicians have had the ambition to devise a machine that would use language in a meaningful way. The popular press was inspired by the quest for a machine that could 'think'. Computer scientists debated then and, in the computer science discipline continue to do so, whether the Turing test conditions will be met.[57] The field of artificial intelligence has flourished and has contributed to the social imaginary of the information society which embraces a vision of the ultimate convergence of digital technologies.

This is seen as a crucial step in the direction of enabling the extension of virtual worlds into all aspects of people's everyday lives.

THE CONVERGENCE VISION

Technological convergence is the label applied to the fruits of the engineering and mathematical vision of the communication system as a system with increasing capacities to process and store digital bits of information. Ever-higher capacity networks capable of transmitting bit streams of digitally encoded information mean that voice, data, and image signals are integrated or converged. During the 1980s there was speculation in the industry trade press and by Nicholas Negroponte at MIT and John Scully at Apple Computers among others, about whether ICT convergence might lead to the disappearance of existing companies and to the emergence of new ones with strengths in the converged segments of the industry. These imaginaries spawned research on industry convergence, the development of converged digital platforms, and on the pace of innovation required of ICT hardware and software companies to retain leadership in the market.[58] Figure 3.4 includes some older and newer components of the converged digital communication system that constitutes the core of the social imaginaries of the information society.[59]

Technological convergence is associated with a vision of a 'new frontier' where 'virtual community' members have the opportunity to exercise their freedoms. For enthusiasts such as Howard Rheingold, the American author of *Virtual Communities: Homesteading on the Electronic Frontier*, ICT convergence is associated with a transition to the digital age in which the prospect for computers to serve as mind-amplifiers becomes possible, and newly constituted communities have the potential to become 'smart mobs'.[60] In

Figure 3.4. Old and New Components of Converged ICTs

these accounts of convergence, virtual communities wrest control of the communication system from traditional companies and the declining costs of digital technologies lead to radical changes in ICT markets and in society.

The changes in ICT markets due to convergence are seen as signs of adjustments to technological innovation. Many parts of the sector, such as the telecommunication infrastructure, historically were high fixed-cost industries. This made them subject to monopolistic tendencies which had the effect of suppressing competition in the marketplace. In the instrumental tradition, research normally focuses on market performance indicated by various metrics of profit and shareholder value. It focuses also on disputes over how the 'relevant market' should be defined for the purpose of deciding about the fairness of competitive strategies devised by companies in the market.[61] Market power is often examined by modelling the ability of companies to attract data traffic to their digital platforms in the competitive market.[62] Microsoft Windows is an example of a multi-sided platform providing services to applications developers, hardware manufacturers, and end-users. Apple's iPod, in contrast, is integrated vertically so that Apple produces hardware, software, and content either itself or through approved third parties. Research on these developments is mainly concerned with markets rather than their wider consequences, except with respect to the variety and cost of products reaching the market.

The door is open, therefore, to claims about the 'impact' of convergence, such as the idea that convergent ICTs flatten market hierarchies, that information is abundant and there is no need for market regulation, or that all users become content producers. These kinds of impacts are assumed to be consistent with the values of the good society, and the public interest is assumed to be synonymous with market outcomes, whatever they may be. However, there are of course critical perspectives which embrace substantially different ways of seeing the process of convergence. These incorporate a broader range of factors that contribute to the convergence process by relaxing many of the assumptions of the exogenous models. These factors become 'endogenous' within the models that guide research on the information society.[63]

Alternative Information Society Imaginaries

It is important to stress that information and communication have always played a key role in societal organization. The technologies of information and communication did not materialize for the first time in the post-war period, but the move from mechanical to electronic technologies was widely understood as involving major consequences for all aspects of the social, political, and economic order of society. Historical studies confirm that all societies can be designated information societies because of their dependence, in some or other fashion, on information and on the communication process.[64] Fernand Braudel, Richard Duboff, Harold A. Innis, and Armand Mattelart all emphasize how each generation of ICTs comes to be associated with changes in the organization of political control, economic power, and cultural development.[65]

Harold Innis argues that 'civilisation has been profoundly influenced by communication'. He focused on the technologies of communication that have been associated with those influences, comparing these developments with societies where oral traditions (without the use of the mass media) were predominant, concluding that 'oral discussion inherently involves personal contact and a consideration for the feelings of others'.[66] His work has been widely criticized for its technological determinism, but there were many others who, like Fernand Braudel, also emphasized the idea that changes in technologies are often associated with crises—real or imagined—for the societies that are affected by their development. He describes the innovation process as one in which 'the past appears as the result of an accumulation of accidents, breakdowns and distortions'.[67] This view is apparent in the dominant repertory of images of the information society in which technological innovations are regarded as accidental outcomes or shocks that disrupt society and to which society must *adjust*. As noted previously, the theme of adjustment to the exigencies of the technological system is a persistent one—especially in the case of the spread of digital ICTs.

However, for some researchers working in the critical tradition it is important to be sensitive to the ambiguous implications of the technological innovation process. Manuel Castells, for example, emphasizes that the combination of larger quantities of information circulating at ever-greater speeds influences the way we see and experience our lives: 'we are networks connected to a world of networks'.[68] Efforts to understand the ambiguities of mind and behaviour in the information society take us into the domain where the questions are more likely to be about how 'reality' is experienced, whether this is to be welcomed, and whether a social order organized around the new technologies is likely to be both wealth generating *and* inclusive, equitable, and just.

From the perspective of instrumental research and exogenous theories, there is a consensus, often unacknowledged, that technological change is a shock to the societal system, as discussed above. Reasons for departures from this way of seeing include dissatisfaction with the simplistic assumptions of the exogenous approach which do not explain why rapid changes in the technological or social system occur. In the exogenous tradition, there is sometimes consideration of how the rate of technical progress is being influenced by exploiting the unprecedented technological opportunity provided by the miniaturization and modularization of microelectronics technologies. As Adam Osborne says, if aviation technology had advanced at the rate of microelectronics, today's aeroplanes would carry 500,000 passengers, and travel at 20 million miles per hour, for a ticket price of a few pence.[69] This is an example of exogeneity and technological determinism in which the technological opportunity is stumbled upon and generates unprecedented change. It provides no insight, however, into the way human decisions are involved, or into the ways in which the fruits of technical progress are coordinated, accommodated, or resisted, especially when they become pervasive across the economy and society.[70] Endogenous theories and models, in contrast, treat the origins and consequences of these changes as part of a system which requires explanation.

Dissatisfaction with exogenous approaches may be motivated also by a different social imaginary of the role of technology in the good society. In this case, it might be assumed that individualism, consumerism, political liberalism, and democracy (in contrast to various fundamentalisms and dictatorships) are the principal values that should be promoted, and/or that a collective interest in social justice and equality should be valued as much as, or more highly than, market values. Relations of power, which are understood to encompass more than the calculus of 'market power' as in the exogenous approach, then become a focus for research aimed at developing endogenous perspectives.

Endogenous theories explain phenomena such as the dynamics and consequences of the innovation process, through reference to internal causes or origins (in contrast to theories that explain by referring to external shocks).[71] The term 'endogenous theory' evokes the idea that change proceeds from within a system with all its complexity. The concept of an endogenous cause is common to the analytical models employed in the physical and the social sciences. Initially, I consider endogenous accounts of the dynamics of change in the information society that are provided by some economics models which focus on a wider range of factors than is typical of the exogenous models discussed above. These accounts are more amenable to a critical analysis of information society developments because they offer greater opportunity to explore the power relationships that are implicated in the evolutionary process and, therefore, provide a basis for beginning to understand how the paradoxes of information scarcity and complexity are generated, and their implications.[72]

ENDOGENOUS ECONOMICS OF THE KNOWLEDGE ECONOMY

The exogenous model of the economy treats the rate of technological progress as an unexplained residual factor. In the economics discipline, endogenous growth theory was developed in an effort to provide greater insight into how the residual—often assumed to be technological innovation—is associated with changes in the economy.[73] The endogenous economic approach inherits some of the blind spots of its exogenous counterpart, for instance, detouring around the ownership of endowments such as land, and sharing a focus on instrumental ends such as economic growth or the improved management of organizations.[74] However, unlike the exogenous approach, in this model, institutions are permitted to influence the long-run rate of economic growth. It has more to say about the medium-term consequences of policies that may raise the level of investment in technology-related research and development or in education to strengthen human capital.[75]

The proliferation of cheaper and more powerful ICTs, and signs since the 1980s of their destabilizing shocks to the wealthy economies of the world, led work in this area to focus particularly on the relationships between technological innovation and knowledge production, as a key feature of the innovation process. Knowledge-based activities are understood to 'emerge when people, supported by information and communication technologies, interact in concerted efforts to co-produce (i.e. create and exchange) new knowledge'.[76] The emphasis is on accelerating the speed of knowledge creation and accumulation, and on its economic relevance and value.

As indicated earlier, economists usually do not differentiate between knowledge and information. A principal ambition of their work is to measure stocks and flows of 'knowledge' within the economic system. This approach is influential in policy debates on the causes and consequences of the knowledge economy. It is consistent also with the administrative research tradition where the outcomes of investment in knowledge production and consumption are assumed to lead to increased social welfare, that is, progress towards the good society. The endogenous approach goes some way towards dealing with economists' restrictive assumptions about the pre-defined nature of individual preferences. Since modelling efforts have been unable to yield insights into changes in the economy associated with growing dependence on digital information, other approaches have been sought in which the conventional assumptions about isolated individuals have been relaxed. This has enabled economists to consider the implications of social interactions for the coordination of the economic system, and how preferences may change to reflect experience.[77] However, the absence of constructs allowing for a differentiation between information and knowledge means that further experiential aspects of knowledge—that is, meaning—are excluded from consideration. Work in this tradition, therefore, offers a relatively limited vision of the way the economic system functions when the key resource is information. This limitation is acknowledged by economists when they attend to the relationship between what are referred to in the literature as codified information and tacit knowledge, concepts which are helpful in providing a more nuanced account of the contested social imaginaries of the information society, an approach which helps to open up the 'black box' of technology.[78]

As a concept originating outside the framework of economic theory's designation of knowledge, tacit knowledge embraces the observation that 'we can know more than we can tell',[79] that is, knowledge encompasses intuitive, sensory, and other non-explicit aspects. Economists borrowed this designation of knowledge to understand scientific knowledge (characterized by explanatory theory) and technological knowledge (characterized by pragmatic applicability), both of which are codifiable, and a tacit component of knowledge related to being able to predict that certain techniques, methods, or designs will behave in certain ways when guided by explanatory theory. Tacit knowledge is associated with subjective, experiential learning, or craft knowledge, and with cognitive skills related to beliefs, images, perspectives, and mental models. Codification refers to means of expressing knowledge that can be processed as information. Codification is seen as a desirable goal because of the economic properties of information, that is, its low costs of reproduction. One codifies to 'economize' on the more expensive activity of exchanging tacit knowledge, which is more labour intensive and cannot benefit from the low marginal costs of reproduction enabled by ICTs. There are circumstances, however, where investment in codification is not deemed worthwhile, for example, where knowledge is changing rapidly or is highly situated.

The extent to which the conversion of tacit knowledge to codified information is expected to occur is related to the degree of tacitness that is assigned to language. Because the acquisition of knowledge cannot be codified, language can be seen as irreducible tacit knowledge. All language learning is based on the initial acquisition of language through one of the most subtle and mysterious processes in human experience. Proponents of artificial intelligence envisage intelligent machines in the future, but these efforts founder on the inability to codify language acquisition and language production, although there are major advances in codifying language expression. Some tacit knowledge is needed to 'decode' information and advances in digital ICTs are providing new means of producing digital 'facsimiles' and expanding the scope of the information that can be codified.[80] Codification involves cognitive processes for using symbolic information, that is, heuristics (or tacitly agreed rules). As technologies such as the Web, spreadsheets, and computer-supported collaborative tools are applied, the need for such rules increases in order to manage problems of information congestion and filtering. Some palliative approaches include ways to filter information, including documentation about its location, provenance, ownership, and other features by tagging. These developments create incentives for companies to invest in technologies that provide better tools for managing the circulation of increasing quantities of information. Advances in ICTs, consistent with the vision of intelligent machines that augment the human mind (the machines of loving grace) will have to tackle that which cannot be evoked in the imagination through the use of language, accompanied by visual imagery and machine-controlled bio-feedback (e.g. a Wii or Kinect game controller).[81]

The contribution to the social imaginary of the information society of discussions about tacit knowledge and codifiable information is a vision of a cycle of innovation leading to increasing possibilities for reliance on automated information systems, with the prospect of productivity gains in the economy. The economics literature on codification is sometimes misread as promoting codification, but its principal emphasis is on the most desirable balance between investment in codified information and in tacit knowledge. A desirable goal might be, for example, a 'post-literate' world in which inscription (coding) methods, such as electronic blueprints, flight simulators, virtual experiments, or interactive hypertexts and images, become increasingly important. Questions about whether the knowledge needed to engage in coding and decoding algorithms should be the privileged knowledge of the communities that create them, resulting in the exclusion of those who do not have or cannot acquire this knowledge are rarely asked because this tradition does not focus on power asymmetries.[82] A key contribution to the social imaginaries of the information society is insistence on distinguishing between information and knowledge and criticism of the proponents of automated information processing who assume that ultimately it is machines that will make all decisions, rather than human beings.[83] In contrast to some of the visionaries discussed in Chapter 2, it is acknowledged that the application of knowledge is a complex, partly tacit, process. Research on these issues is undertaken at the micro-level of analysis.

Other economists examine the macro-level changes associated with innovations in the communication system employing endogenous perspectives. Although they tend to ascribe changes in society to the impact of revolutionary developments in General Purpose Technologies (GPTs), including ICTs, their insights help to draw attention to discontinuities in the institutional (social, political, and economic) environment that are associated with the diffusion of digital technologies.[84] For instance, the work of Chris Freeman and Carlota Perez, and others researching in this area, has sought to incorporate the analysis of technical and institutional change into the mainstream of economic analysis 'rather than treating it as part of a rag-bag of "residual" or "exogenous" factors'.[85] Their examinations of changes in techno-economic paradigms suggest that some types of technical change have:

such widespread consequences for all sectors of the economy that their diffusion is accompanied by a major structural crisis of adjustment, in which social and institutional changes are necessary to bring about a better 'match' between the new technology and the system of social management of the economy.[86]

This work contributes to a social imaginary of disruptive or revolutionary ICTs in the information society that is sometimes depicted as an exogenous approach. However, in studies of techno-economic paradigms, greater attention is given to the justifications for policy makers to intervene in areas of social and economic organization that go far beyond interventions aimed mainly at speeding up the rate of innovation in ICTs or of increasing stocks of knowledge. This is because as ICTs diffuse widely, they are seen as being accompanied by new types of organization, skills, product mixes, and patterns of investment. Innovations in ICTs are seen as radical or revolutionary because they significantly reduce the cost of storing, processing, communicating, and disseminating information, as we have already seen. But the idea of paradigm change also encourages studies of the patterns of behaviour that give rise to new organizational practices as managers of companies and other institutions seek to adapt to the diffusion of the new technologies and, in some case, to resist these changes.[87] Research shows that there are two main phases in the shift to an ICT paradigm involving the installation of a new infrastructure, followed by its deployment throughout the economy.[88] The length of time between these phases is not without problems, the most significant being that there is likely to be a worsening in income distribution during the process of adjustment. Whether or not this is reversed is regarded as a matter for policy and whether there should be intervention in the market-led innovation process.

Overall, while there is a concern in this tradition with the broader consequences of ICT innovation, it tends to be presumed that, eventually, a beneficial match between technology and the social order will emerge. The technological trajectory, once it is established, is unquestioned in terms of its wider implications for power relationships in society. Specific ICT applications may raise issues for policy, for example, intrusions into people's lives as a result of automated surveillance systems with implications for civil rights, but these are outside the concern of the endogenous model of techno-economic change. Research in this tradition is influential in many national and international policy settings when the focus is on the possible need for intervention to bring stability to the economic system or to reduce the negative impacts of the new paradigm on people's lives.

POWER IN THE INFORMATION SOCIETY

The economics accounts of changes in the ICT techno-economic paradigm generally lack explicit analysis of power relationships. The way the innovation process is implicated in the maintenance of power asymmetries in society is beyond the scope of the models except with respect to analysis of the anti-competitive practices of companies when issues of 'market power' are examined with a view to possible policy intervention to restrain unfair competition in the marketplace. In contrast, in the political economy tradition research focuses explicitly on power relationships and on the unequal distribution of society's resources, asking questions about how these relations are constituted through the production, distribution, and consumption of ICTs and information resources.[89] Political economy research focuses on distributional issues and on actors' 'inducements for acting in a particular way',[90] motivated usually by their economic interests or by their interests in the accumulation of political power. An interest in inducements for the production of ICTs and for their consumption, including their symbolic content, leads to questions about how innovation is influenced by the dynamics of capitalism and how changes in technologies and in social organization are legitimized or resisted through social dissent and struggle.[91] Research often focuses on the organization and structure of markets and on the ownership and the control of information and technologies.[92]

There is another tradition of work that is located in sociological studies and which is similarly critical of the dominant information society imaginary with its emphasis on information processing. This work is often found in studies of the proliferation of collaborating online communities and is associated with the open source software movement. I discuss the political economy tradition first, and then highlight some of the features of work on collaborating communities, emphasizing how they are implicated in the alternative social imaginary.

In the political economy tradition, in contrast to the instrumental tradition, the 'natural' coupling of technological innovation with the values of the good society is likely to challenged.[93] A critical perspective provokes enquiry into the interests of companies in developing markets and into potential alternatives to the dominant social imaginary of the information society. The analysis of economic interests revealed by research in this tradition has been criticized for its persistent, sometimes Marxist, focus on the exploitation of people's labour power, which in some cases does not appear to leave much scope for the observable and, at times, empowering ways in which people do appear to avoid exploitation by capitalist owners of the means of production. As Nicholas Garnham insists, however, relations of power under capitalism provide scope, under certain conditions, for alternatives to such exploitative arrangements to emerge, resulting from resistance on the part of citizens or, in some cases, as a result of policy intervention. As he puts it, there is 'no necessary coincidence between the effects of the capitalist process proper and the ideological needs of the dominant class'.[94]

In this tradition, the mere manifestation of competition among companies engaged in marketing ICTs or digital information in the marketplace is not seen as sufficient evidence of a weakening of the interests of companies in their capacity to manage consumer demand. This is because here 'monopolization refers not to monopoly as such, but to the activities of firms (usually dominant ones) who are seeking to build up, or maintain, a position of market power'.[95] Monopolization refers to a dynamic, ongoing process of change in the wake of technological innovation and changing conditions in the marketplace. Market power, then, is associated with pricing strategies that enable companies to entrench their positions in the market in the face of destabilizing technological change. Incumbent enterprises have incentives to monopolize the market, for instance, by controlling the choke points to information, that is, the gateways in the communication system.[96]

One way to achieve this is to by finding ways to ensure that information is artificially rendered scarce so that this scarcity can be alleviated by monetizing its production and consumption. In the dominant social imaginary of the information society, it is assumed that whatever technologies and applications emerge from the competitive struggle, they are 'fit for purpose', that is, they are the best available to respond to the problem of information scarcity. However, this has no necessary bearing on whether the innovations in technology are consistent with the public interest in a fair distribution of economic resources. Throughout the history of innovation in the communication system, there have been contests over market supremacy among incumbent and new entrant companies, with varying consequences for the users of technology.[97] Arguments about whether technological diversity should be welcomed, to provide choice for users or to acknowledge diverse social or cultural values, are continuous throughout the process of technological innovation, but it is the struggle for market dominance, manifest, for example, in battles between Microsoft and Google, Oracle and SAP,[98] and others, which attract attention.

In the computing industry, the Web browser produced by Netscape was overtaken by Microsoft's Internet Explorer and there are many examples in the telecommunication and broadcasting industries of competitive battles that have edged technologies (using specific standards) out of the market.[99] Whether the corporate winner's technology is perceived as the 'best' from the perspective of users is complicated by factors such as the value of using the same technology at home and at work, sharing experience of use with others, and the availability of instructional and training materials. All of these are reflections of an endogenous process whereby a technology succeeds in winning market share. In the case of Internet browsers, standards co-evolve with the standards for website creation. A current dominant browser may be functionally superior because website designers cater to the browser with the most users. The dominant browser suppliers have an incentive to add new features in order to improve the users' experience, which also raises the costs and barriers to entry for rivals, thereby helping to assure the formers' continued dominance.

Whatever the outcomes of these battles, questions need to be asked about how the public interest is affected and whether the practices of these companies are consistent with empowering people or whether they are exploiting them, with or without their consent. When research focuses on power relationships and inequality, ICT platforms can be seen as creating opportunities to expand the commodity form of immaterial labour, that is, to develop what some have labelled 'immaterial labour 2.0'.[100] Dallas W. Smythe, a political economist who studied the economic features of the communication system, examined the 'audience commodity' at the time when the mass media were predominant. He argues that 'readers and audience members of advertising-supported mass media are a commodity produced and sold to advertisers because they perform a valuable service for the advertisers'.[101] Similarly, whether they contribute their work to online activities on Facebook, or sell their labour using Amazon's Mechanical Turk and other online sites that 'crowdsource' workers, 'audiences' in the Internet Age serve the interests of the capitalist economy through their online labour.

In the Internet Age, people are being encouraged, and sometimes required, to take responsibility for their well-being by working on an unpaid basis, or for low wages, at multiple, globally dispersed online sites on the Internet. In effect, the owners of Facebook and other websites are building their revenues around online participants who are willing to co-produce the service using self-service tools.[102] Self-servicing is a concept that predates the Internet, but which is linked closely to the increasing significance of services and digital information compared to material goods in the economy. The expansion of self-servicing activity with the shift to the ICT techno-economic paradigm is not only associated with the empowering possibilities of choice in the prevailing social imaginary of the information society but it is also associated with the enhanced capacity of companies to find new ways to exploit the labour power of online participants.

The growing capacity of online site owners to exploit the untapped labour power of site visitors is a development which is concealed by the emphasis in the dominant social imaginary on the opportunities to develop new online communities for entertainment or social, rather than for commercial, purposes. Research in the political economy tradition reveals the unequal social and economic conditions under which labour is offered and their consequences for equality and social justice in the information society. If workers' labour power is exploited in online forums, in time, we can expect discontent and active protest against or resistance to the prevailing social imaginary and these practices. In the instrumental research tradition, it is assumed that the winners in the competitive battles among websites simply are more fit-for-purpose and the changes in labour practices are seen as being indicative of a long-run, unalterable trajectory of change. However, the winner may not serve the public interest and the progressive development of online forums for virtual 'work' (whether in the guise of work or leisure activity) is not always being organized in a way that is consistent with values of the good society.

In endogenous models of the information society, especially in the critical tradition which draws on sociological theories, ICT convergence is sometimes understood to be empowering for individuals because of choices that have been made for the configuration of technology. Research in this tradition is critical of the prevailing market-led, neoliberal model of the information society, but it is not always explicit about the power relationships that are responsible for individual empowerment. This is partly because much research which has helped to build an alternative social imaginary of the information society has been conducted outside the social sciences, in some cases, by scholars in the legal profession who have little training in the way power can be theorized. As such, the perspectives developed in this area can appear to be as technology determinist as their counterpart exogenous models which treat technological innovation as a shock to the social system.

The difference is that in this case, governance arrangements for the management of intellectual property rights in information and collaborative decision-making procedures are seen as creating a space for individual empowerment within online communities of various kinds. Empirical research is normally conducted at the micro-level of analysis, focusing on communities of practice, especially communities involved in the development of software, but increasingly also of communities involving political activists or consumers. In this research, the persistence of structural asymmetries on the supply and the demand sides of the market for digital information and ICTs is downplayed. The picture presented is often one of relatively homogeneous communities of empowered information producers and consumers ('prosumers') who engage enthusiastically in blogging, text messaging, social networking, or gaming.

Proponents of this view envisage a pluralist, open information commons. The Internet is seen as providing the tools to enable everyone to access digital platforms, allowing all to participate in society. Thus, in this case, ICT convergence is assumed to be consistent with the values of equality and democracy. It is claimed, for example, that the Internet is transformational because the architectural design of a peer-to-peer (P2P) network favours cooperation and the 'wisdom of crowds'.[103] This vision is characteristic of research on the development of open source software (OSS), for example. In OSS, developers can modify and share software code, in contrast to proprietary software where access is restricted. Software development relies on the activities of distributed participants who work mainly online. Although the code is subject to copyright from the moment it is written, the developer may decide to licence it under provisions including GNU General Public Licenses[104] and licences provided under the Creative Commons initiative.[105] F/LOSS (Free/Libre) is software that is 'free to edit' without incurring the threat of restraint accompanying traditional forms of intellectual property ownership. A variety of licences has been developed without restrictions that prevent the legal distribution of the software over the Internet.

In place of the values of the commercial market, OSS and other forms of online social networking are associated with the values of a gift culture and commons-based peer production.[106] In commons-based peer production, although there may be power struggles over the values that best facilitate online activity, the status and roles of contributors, and the way collaborative values are translated into the 'real' world of experience, there is an emphasis on non-market values because the gift culture is said to embrace altruism and reciprocity. So far, there is little evidence that commons-based peer production will supplant market exchange as the predominant means of exchanging digital information, despite estimates that more than a fifth of global Internet traffic involves copyright-infringing downloading of digital content.[107]

Open source social media platforms are being used to support contests over power among members of civil society, the corporate world, and the state,[108] but these platforms (as well as proprietary ones) are also in use by companies and the state for surveillance. In practice, democracy does not follow automatically from the values associated with new technical arrangements for online information production and sharing. However, supporters of OSS and commons-based peer production generally argue against the intrusion of markets into the public spaces of the Internet and defend the end-to-end architecture of the Internet in the interests of democratic participation in society.[109]

The commons-based model is challenging the sustainability of the market-led model as the dominant model however. In the case of the commons-based model, non-market relationships, and governance from below are advocated as the means to minimize potential harms associated with technological innovation. The strong element of technological determinism that is a feature of the commons-based production model means that much of the research in this area pays scant attention to the asymmetries of power in the wider information society within which this model is developing.[110] Nevertheless, both the practice and the theory of commons-based peer production are influential in an increasingly pervasive social imaginary of the information society, though not one that so far has found an accommodation with the dominant imaginary, despite the fact that there are signs of a blurring of the distinctions between them in practice.

Mediation as a Bridging Concept

Apart from the earlier discussion of the implications of tacit knowledge, the theoretical frameworks considered so far have little to say about the symbolic or experiential aspect of the information society. In addition, the stark oppositions that seem to characterize theories in the instrumental and critical traditions and the way they depict change in the information society are not always helpful in providing a sense of the way human beings experience the dynamics of change in society and the evolution of the communication system.

The concept of mediation can serve as a bridging concept among these disparate ways of seeing the evolution of the communication system. This is because it helps to open up a space for considering the values that are privileged within the conflicting social imaginaries of the information society and, in an admittedly fuzzy way, it helps to reinforce the idea that these theoretical traditions are always provisional and unsettled. I referred in Chapter 1 to Roger Silverstone's view that 'mediated connection and interconnection' are part of the infrastructure of most people's lives in the Internet Age. Many scholars in the social sciences discuss the mediation processes that give rise to social, political, and economic change, emphasizing the role of communication and the media.[111] Research on mediated experience draws attention to the way people engage in meaning construction in their on- and off-line communities, showing that meanings are understood differently depending on cultural, social, political, and economic contexts and on the specific technologies and practices involved. As Silverstone insisted, ICTs are 'doubly articulated' in the economy and in culture.[112]

The underlying technologies of communication, including the Internet Protocol which has come to serve as a focal point in debates about the advantages of the commons-based peer production of information versus proprietary or market-based models, are unseen by people without programming skills or understanding of the design features of the communication system. Everyday users of the Internet normally encounter ICTs as a 'surface' or simply as an entry point to their virtual worlds. As Sherry Turkle puts it, 'when we are at our computers, most of us only deal with surfaces. We summon screen icons to act as agents'.[113] Yet technologies behind the screen, in the 'infrastructure' as Silverstone calls it, are just as important in mediating life in the Internet Age as those technologies which online users are aware of. The majority of Internet users have few reasons to question the values embedded in the communication system. For most people, the communication system is part of their everyday experience, whether of globally dispersed production, socially or politically active online communities, or of computerized systems that may shut down airports, enable online crime including potential harm to children, and out-of-control financial systems.[114]

Mediation may occur through symbolic representation, through the social division of labour, and through the interactions of humans with ICTs.[115] These mediated experiences become part of the social imaginary of the information society and they also become part of the narratives of research in the instrumental and critical traditions. Insofar as mediation is a multi-faceted phenomenon, we need to look beyond the realm of the virtual to the intersections between the virtual and 'real' worlds to understand how power relationships are implicated in the evolution of the communication system.

Mediation is not a new phenomenon, but the intersections of technical systems with everyday life mean that there is a potential for profound changes in power relationships and in perceptions and the experience of mastery of the communication system. The notion of mediation is helpful in providing insight into how the communication system is implicated in conflict—physical and 'virtual'—in the information society because those who apply this concept do so generally from a critical perspective which asks about why conflict emerges and about the dynamics of power.

For example, when the mediation process privileges market values, online experiences, such as those provided by Amazon and many other commercially operated online sites, appear to flourish, but with contradictory outcomes. Amazon, for instance, can be seen as an endogenous development resulting from the specific capacities of the Internet to hold large inventories of virtually represented meta-information about books (and real e-books). Amazon provides more 'shelf space' than a physical bookstore and allows all its 'shelves' to be prominent in its 'shop window'. Mediated experience can involve virtual representations, voices speaking from our computers, and scripts that appear on computer screens. People interact with what might appear to be human beings, but these may be artificially animated constructs. Mediation may be experienced as entertainment or as education and these developments may enter the social imaginary of the information society entirely uncontested. However, they may be promoting loss of memory, disregard for the welfare of others, changes in the values of the workplace, and superficial human relationships associated with a decline in sociability and intimacy.[116] Thus, the notion of mediation, with its concern with power relationships, is helpful in suggesting that indeterminant outcomes are characteristic of the evolution of the communication system.

Critical research on mediated relationships in the twenty-first century information society is also helpful in provoking questions about whether individuals should be expected to assume increasingly greater responsibility for navigating their online worlds through their self-servicing activities without the institutional supports provided by the state. It raises questions about whether alternative arrangements are feasible for ensuring that labour standards are established for online work, encouraging means of curtailing unwanted intrusions in virtual worlds, and developing cultural and social environments that are safe and complement the online worlds that people inhabit. The answers differ from those provided in the instrumental tradition insofar as they do not presume that the existing trajectory of change is 'fit for purpose' simply because it exists.

Furthermore, with an emphasis on the symbolic meaning of information, a consideration of mediation serves as a reminder that information is not a 'thing', the view typical of the exogenous information processing model. When information (or knowledge) is treated as a 'thing', akin to Heidegger's notion of 'essence', then if problems emerge as a result of the communication system, it seems that 'only a god can save us'.[117] The only recourses seem to be to a higher (imaginary) order and to the hope that the communication system will evolve in a benign way. If it is assumed, instead, that technological mediation binds people together and that their actions transform the experience of mediation,[118] it starts to become easier to imagine alternatives to the prevailing power relationships in the information society. Thus, mediation is a concept that helps to amplify insights into the way power relationships are experienced in the information society that are available from studies of the economic features of information, from the political economy of the structural aspects of markets for information production and consumption, and from sociological studies of online communities.

Conclusion

This discussion of the social science research traditions that seek to explain the evolution of the communication system in the information society confirms that it is neither the materiality of technology nor the stocks of digital information that impact on human beings for good or ill. This is a deterministic view, characteristic of the exogenous, instrumental model. Critical perspectives based on endogenous models, such as those concerned with transformations in techno-economic paradigms, changes in the political economy of power relationships, and sociological studies of online communities, make it clear that the empowerment (or disempowerment) of people needs to be understood as the outcome of change in both the symbolic and the material environments. The endogenous models provide understanding of conflicting interests of civil society, states, and corporations in the information society in the process of change, and the concept of mediation serves as a useful reminder of the importance of the symbolic and material aspects of this process.[119]

In their different ways, work in the instrumental and critical traditions shows that each step in the process of technological innovation that provides a basis for the production and consumption of abundant digital information is accompanied by renewed efforts among incumbent companies to impose conditions of information scarcity. These efforts are made in the interests of market development and in the face of resistance from those who seek to liberate digital information from the constraints of scarcity imposed by intellectual property rights. But while copyright protects the rights of the owners of intellectual property, companies are allowing people to copy online information, using business models that seek to generate profit without damping the enthusiasm of Internet users by making it difficult for them to download and share information. The persistence of these conflicting strategies is not well explained by the research traditions I have discussed so far. This is because the technological innovation process is unfolding in a way that is contradictory to the varying interests of the stakeholders in the economic and social value of information. This is associated with the paradox of information scarcity, which I return to later.

In addition, the exogenous models suggest that, as the communication system becomes more complex, it is inappropriate to intervene in the evolution of the system—the system is too complex to govern without uncertain and potentially harmful implications for society. This is the logic in the dominant social imaginary of the information society. Proponents of an information commons bias in the information society claim that resistance to the market-led social imaginary is feasible, but argue also that, because of the system's complexity, non-intervention from the state or companies in the technological system is the best option. On the one hand, the system is too complex to govern. On the other hand, it is claimed that resistance to the persistence of unequal power relationships in the information society and to social injustice depends on the creativity of those who can find a way to challenge the power of the 'programmers' and 'switchers' (large companies that control the communication system, and the state). As Manuel Castells explains, they must seek to preserve 'the commons of communication networks made possible by the Internet, a free creation of freedom lovers'.[120] There is an idea that the evolution of the communication system can indeed be 'steered' towards the values of the good society. This is one facet of the paradox of complexity, which I also address later.

Endogenous perspectives enable us to see that ICT convergence is an evolutionary process that can be altered, abandoned, or subordinated to different cultural, social, political, and economic values. However, they offer a limited basis for analysing these paradoxes because they sequester aspects of the innovation process (effectively rendering them exogenous), which go on 'behind the computer screen', and they are troubled by the implications for human agency that seem to be characteristic of complex adaptive systems. They engender ambiguity in their answers to whether policy intervention with respect to the evolution of the communication system is justified. To make sense of this ambiguity, a framework that gives attention to the features of the technological innovation process that are sequestered in the social sciences, which I discuss in Chapter 4, provides a complementary way of seeing. Social science theory struggles when applied to developments at the interfaces of social and technical systems, a point made frequently by Roger Silverstone in his work on the way digital technologies are mediating our lives.[121] Yet it is exactly at these interfaces that, increasingly, life is lived in the Internet Age. Chapter 4 introduces systems theory and suggests how it can be applied to make sense of the paradoxes of information scarcity and complexity in the Internet Age.

4 Communication, Complexity, and Paradox

Introduction

The social imaginaries of the information society give rise to competing claims about the evolution of the communication system and its consequences for society, as discussed in Chapter 3. Two important paradoxes are located at the heart of these imaginaries. One—the paradox of information scarcity—is the product of an innovation process in which there is pressure both to maintain the intrinsic or constructed scarcity of information and to promote its abundance. The other—the paradox of complexity—concerns the role of human agency in governing a complex system, such as the communication system, in the Internet Age.

The evolution of the communication system can be depicted as being the outcome of exogenous shocks or the interplay of endogenous features. Scholars working within the social sciences often acknowledge that the features of the innovation process operate at multiple levels of individual agency and institutional change and, in the critical research traditions, that power relationships are crucial for the outcomes of the evolutionary process. However, these explanations stop short of developing an understanding of the changes occurring at the interfaces of the components or levels in a complex system.

In the instrumental tradition, the questions are about how the innovation process works, but not why the outcomes matter in relation to the lives that people are able to live. With its instrumental goals, work in this tradition is restricted mainly to analysis of the adjustments made by agents to bring institutional systems into alignment with the 'needs' of the technological system: an alignment that is assumed to be consistent with the values of the good society. Critical research, on the other hand, asks questions about the interests of those agents responsible for building and using the communication system and about unequal power relationships. The paradoxes of information scarcity and complexity that are generated within a complex adaptive system are normally invisible in these ways of seeing and so do not figure in debates about the information society and the practice of governance.

In this chapter I introduce systems theory with the goal of employing it alongside endogenous theories of change in a critical assessment of the evolution of the communication system. I start by differentiating between social science approaches to the complexity of systems, and the systems theoretical approach to the interfaces within complex systems. I then provide a brief discussion of the early development of systems perspectives, illustrating their alignment with the information processing models of communication encountered in Chapter 2, and the renewed interest in them in the social and the physical sciences.[1] This is followed by a discussion of one strand of systems theory that is particularly helpful for understanding the genesis of paradox and its implications for understanding the evolution of the communication system. This perspective is used to suggest repairs or corrections to our ways of seeing the technological innovation process, consistent with Taylor's insistence on the value of providing a 'certain reading' of contradictory statements about developments in society. The penultimate section of this chapter outlines a critical systems framework that is applied in the remaining chapters.

It should be noted that, while certain strands of systems theory are helpful, like Plato's portrayal of Socrates's explanation of the allegory of the cave, theory construction invoking concepts drawn from the social and the natural and physical sciences should be regarded always as temporary and unfinished, a position consistent with my preference for treating theory as provisional and 'unsettled'.[2] The discussion in this chapter should be read in this light—it is provisional. However, I suggest that it does offer a new way of seeing that is helpful in making sense of paradox in the Internet Age.

From Context to Dynamic System Interfaces

In both the social science and natural and physical science traditions, there is agreement that the communication system is complex and that this has profound consequences. In the social sciences, the term 'context' is invoked to signpost the complexity of a system and to delimit components of a system that are not investigated within the boundary of a particular theory or empirical study. Context then serves as the residual explanation for a system's development or evolution. What the context encompasses is usually vaguely implied, conveying an impression that, because a system is complex, it is difficult to say what is guiding the system or who or what might be held accountable. This approach is typical in economics where the simplifying assumptions of exogenous theory are used in order to model the dynamics of change in the market. Technological change, for instance, is often used to describe the unexplained residual (contextual) factor. This can be explained in part by endogenous economic theories as discussed in Chapter 3, but they are limited by assumptions about human behaviour and motivation.

Understanding human behaviour and agency may be central in other social science disciplines, providing greater insight into the situated dynamics and local features of innovation, and shedding greater light on the residual or context. But in these other disciplines, too, even when they are concerned with highly, situated, local features of innovation, explanations of complex phenomena are frequently said to be conditioned by an unspecified context which serves as a limiting assumption for what the theory purports to explain.

Recourse to context as explanation is as common in the instrumental as in the critical traditions of the social sciences. However, there is a tendency towards unifying theories to account for the dynamics of power throughout all the components of a system of relationships in an effort to reduce the 'residual' or unexplained phenomena in a complex system. Despite such ambitions, however, some aspect of a system of relationships is usually privileged with others receding into the background or context. For example, Dan Schiller puts analysis of the labour process at the centre of his exploration of the dynamics of communication practice, although he also calls for the unification of theories of information production and consumption.[3] In this case, the social field in which the labour process occurs is the context or environment for these relationships. Others may argue, for example, that transformations in the market context must be understood by 'grasping the "inside" and the "outside"' of the market sphere to understand political and material processes.[4] Missing is a framework for investigating systems of relationships on the 'inside' and on the 'outside', and yet it is here at the interfaces of systems that paradoxical relationships have their genesis.

Assertions may be made about power relationships to explain communication system developments, but these usually are accompanied by the claim that the context of these relationships needs further analysis. It may then be argued that analysis of the discursive practices of human agents, that is, the ways in which meaning is constituted by individuals, provides a way of understanding complex processes, but invariably 'extra-discursive' features which do not figure in the analysis of social relations are invoked to explain change.[5] In some traditions, the project of analysing a complex system does turn to system boundaries or 'boundary objects' to trace pathways of innovation, but power relationships that generate paradox are not usually discussed.[6] In a theory of 'information worlds', for instance, the boundaries and interactions among members of multiple small worlds in physical and virtual social space are accentuated, but the boundary relationships themselves are not theorized.[7] Some social scientists adopt the language of systems theories and refer to 'first-' or 'second-order' effects in emergent systems, but they give few hints about what this implies for human agency or for the genesis of paradox within a complex system.[8]

In summary, attempts in the social sciences to develop unifying theories of the innovation process have something in common: they call for improved understanding of complex systems, but pay little attention to the implications of systems theories and the limitations of systems thinking in the analysis of the evolution of social and technological systems. I discuss the contributions of systems thinking and cybernetics to the analysis of 'self-organizing systems' and some of the applications of this way of seeing in the next sections.

Systems Thinking and Cybernetics

The social imaginary of systems thinking can be traced to Francois Quesnay (1694–1774), a French economist who was concerned with the circularity of flows in the economy, and to Claude Henri de Saint Simon (1760–1825), who conceived of society as an organic system.[9] Interest in systems theoretical perspectives has waxed and waned in the physical sciences as well as in contributions from social scientists. When systems theories emerged in the study of communication, not surprisingly, they focused on issues of information control. The work of Norbert Weiner and Claude Shannon in the early 1940s, on systems and feedback (see Chapter 2), spawned huge interest in control systems, providing mathematicians and scientists with a basis for exploring the functioning of the human brain and the computer.[10] Despite many scholars arguing that their work had no bearing on meaning construction, their ideas were taken up in a series of discussions sponsored by the Macy Conferences on cybernetics, which were held between 1946 and 1953. These conference attracted social scientists, mathematicians, neurophysiologists, philosophers, and psychiatrists,[11] some of whom had a great interest in the construction of symbolic meaning and in the dynamics of the social system.

This was a period of enthusiasm for interdisciplinary research. One Macy Conference participant argued that the applied aspects of cybernetics 'relate to whatever field of study one cares to name: engineering, or biology, or physics, or sociology'.[12] Anthony Stafford Beer regards all decision-making as being concerned with information, but argues that it is 'logically impossible to use the language of the network's description to comment on its own structure', indicating that were an attempt made to do so, the result would be paradoxical communication.[13] The idea of 'emergence' was present in his thinking insofar as he stressed that an information system is self-regulatory and capable of emergent responses not envisaged by its designers. His conclusion was that information systems are not necessarily subject to human control and are best left to evolve without human intervention.

Nevertheless, many attempts were made to apply cybernetics beyond the realm of electronic signals. These can be traced in the perspectives brought to the Macy Conferences by participants such as Ross Ashby and Frederick Steier. Both thought that cybernetics could be applied in every branch of science, although Steier cautioned that a systems perspective would not help to reveal why things happen, it would inform us only about how they happen.[14] This was because a key concept in cybernetics is 'difference', that is, observation either that two things are recognizably different to start with, or that one has changed over time and can be explained by understanding the system constraints that either enable or preclude change. In this framework it is possible to think about 'freedom of choice' within a system, but this refers to system constraints, not human choices.

In the light of Thomas Kuhn's observations about theory development (see Chapter 3), we would expect theory to develop in response to perceived deficiencies in existing ways of seeing. Systems theory is no exception. Some claim that it developed partly as a response to the reductionism of classical physics, which was found wanting when applied to biological and human systems.[15] Early systems theorists were concerned about cybernetic systems and the issues of control, stability, and instability in systems, but most thought it beyond their remit to make judgements on what might be done about the social or human consequences of these systems. Stafford Beer writes that 'the advance of automation within a country is at once a determinant of economic progress and a threat to the stability of society',[16] but does not call for any action.

Norbert Weiner could foresee no theoretical insight from cybernetics for the social challenges and problems of the immediate post-war period. He sympathizes with those who hope for a better understanding, but says that it would not have 'an appreciable therapeutic effect on the present diseases of society'.[17] For Weiner, problems of indeterminacy and instability in the social system are created by those who 'are compelled by their own cupidity to form coalitions; but these coalitions do not generally establish themselves in any single, determinate way, and usually terminate in a welter of betrayal, turn-coatism, and deception'.[18] Extending natural sciences methods to the social sciences, including economics, was seen as symptomatic of the misunderstanding of scientific achievement. Nevertheless, Wiener was concerned about the trajectory of the information system, observing that, 'it may be used for the benefit of humanity, but only if humanity survives long enough to enter a period in which such a benefit is possible. It may also be used to destroy humanity, and if it is not used intelligently it can go very far in that direction'.[19] To make sense of this, he said that it would be necessary to turn to the narrative methods of historians and those working in the social sciences.

These pioneers of systems theory, for the most part, were pessimistic about the contribution of cybernetics to an understanding of the conduct of human beings, but the ensuing years have seen numerous efforts to apply systems thinking to the analysis of innovation processes, complemented and encouraged by a post-war renewal of faith in the progress of science.[20] In the systems theoretical framework, human agency is deemed to inhere within a system, that is, within self-generating systems, a perception or metaphor that is problematic for most social scientists.

SELF-GENERATING SYSTEMS

Ludwig von Bertalanffy's work on General System Theory provided an attractive theory for researchers searching for an alternative to the linear causality that, at the time, was a central feature of scientific hypothesis testing. Systems theories, when they deal with the dynamics of systems that are open to their environment, suggest that a given final state can be reached from different initial conditions, and that outcomes are indeterminate or unpredictable.[21] This thinking opened up a new way of seeing, and contributed to the information processing model that was so central to the social imaginary of the information society. By the late 1980s, Humberto Maturana and Francisco Varela, in their book, *Tree of Knowledge*, were insisting that organic systems are self-generating since they have the ability to reproduce themselves recursively, delimiting themselves through their dynamic interaction with a boundary. In the case of chemical transformations, for instance, a boundary is essential for a network of transformations. This process is called autopoiesis.[22] They argued that systems behave in ways that are determined by their structure, not by the outcomes of processes of human cognition. Maturana puts it this way:

the identity of a system is constituted and is conserved as a manner of operating as a whole in the system's recursive interactions in the medium that contains it. The constitution and the conservation of the identity of a system, are dynamic systemic phenomena that occur through the recursive interactions of the system with the elements of the medium.[23]

Systems are understood to be 'structurally coupled' through their mutual and symmetrical interdependence.[24] Autopoietic systems are said to reproduce themselves through the dynamics of their network components, and can be open or closed. This characterization is deemed to apply to any living organic system, including the human system. In the human system, the delineation of boundaries within a whole system is of course very problematic since the concepts of metabolism and membrane which are at the core of this theory have no fixed meaning in the social system—social boundaries are humanly constituted, not given by biological features.

In his work on *Self-producing Systems*, John Mingers characterizes Maturana's insights as extending to encompass self-conscious human beings. Thus, he argues, 'we are (as self-conscious beings) constituted through our language, and language is inevitably an intersubjective phenomenon. As Wittgenstein also argued, there can be no such thing as a private language. Thus language is essentially a consensual domain of agreements, of structural coupling that permits the operations of observers'.[25] He (like others before him) did not extend this argument to questions about symbolic meaning or human representations. Nevertheless, systems theory had taken hold in the social sciences, especially in the early work of Talcott Parsons and then later in the work of Niklas Luhmann.

The Social System by the sociologist and economist Talcott Parsons, was published in 1951. Parsons drew upon systems thinking to explain social patterns and the maintenance of social system stability, suggesting that the:

social system consists in a plurality of individual actors interacting with each other in a situation which has at least a physical or environmental aspect, actors who are motivated in terms of a tendency to the 'optimization of gratification' and whose relation to their situations, including each other, is defined and mediated in terms of a system of culturally structured and shared symbols.[26]

His phrasing was a clear response to the then contemporary emergence of the neoclassical economics paradigm in which society is viewed as being governed by the pursuit of gratification through exchange relationships; his work was criticized for its emphasis on the way a system maintains stability and resists change.

Later, the sociologist Niklas Luhmann, whose work was influenced by Parsons, became perhaps the best-known contemporary contributor to systems thinking in the social sciences. He distinguishes among three systems—the organic, the psychical, and the social. His understanding of communication refers to the means by which a social system reproduces itself.[27] Thus, 'communications conclude preceding communications and enable connecting ones. The elements of social systems are recursively produced and reproduced by a network of communications and cannot exist outside of such a network. They organize their own renewal autopoietically'.[28] Human beings are ascribed consciousness, but what matters is the communication processes within the system, where 'understanding' happens only when a receiver acknowledges the information and notices a distinction or difference.[29] When the system has a high degree of complexity—as is the case of the communication—then interventions in the system may lead to outcomes that are deviant (not valued) and what is selected within the system is no more likely to produce change that is valued than change that is not valued. For Luhmann, 'just like life and consciousness, communication is an emergent reality, a state of affairs *sui generis*'.[30]

In the systems theoretical framework, there is an important distinction between the environment of a system as 'it really is' and as 'it [the system] sees it'.[31] How does a system 'see'? As Luhmann indicates:

even in the face of numerous efforts to find ethical foundations, second-order cyber-netics can only ever repeat the question: who is the observer? It can direct this question to every observing system, and therefore also to itself. Every cognitive, normative and moral—and therefore also every ethical—code is thus undermined...It calls for something to be made visible which must remain invisible to itself. It contradicts itself. It executes a performative self-contradiction and thus avoids appearing dogmatic or prescribing cures.[32]

This position suggests that interventions in a system are inherently risky, and it echoes the reluctance of earlier systems theorists to concern themselves with normative issues and the values of society. This thinking about self-organizing systems has contributed to the social imaginary of the information society which envisages it as a complex system that is responsive to its own emergent 'self-organizing' properties. In this view it is difficult to engage in 'prescribing cures' for a social system, should certain norms or ethical practices be found wanting by a group of stakeholders. In the light of emergent complexity, the system is best left to itself rather than being subjected to haphazard interven-tions by policy makers acting hierarchically from above through organs of the state. Autopoiesis (self-organization), as Luhmann acknowledged, is charac-teristic of systems whose evolution may or may not be consistent with particular social norms or values.[33]

SYSTEMS THEORY APPLIED TO HUMAN SYSTEMS

It is one thing to devise theories of system dynamics, but quite another to examine system evolution empirically. Research in the instrumental tradition of the social sciences treats the communication system as a system of rela-tions, leading to many studies on relationships among network nodes.[34] In sociology, network research flourished in the 1930s and 1940s through the work of Georg Simmel and Jacob Moreno who focused on webs of affiliation from a critical perspective.[35] It took off again when low-cost computing power started to become available and researchers began undertaking struc-tural analyses of 'the arrangement of elements in a system and the set of relationships that connect these parts together', bringing this work into line with the instrumental systems theoretical tradition.[36] This work became very widespread towards the end of the 1980s when Everett Rogers concluded that 'our progress has been scientifically imbalanced, atheoretic'.[37] A decade later he observed that cybernetics, as a theory of self-regulating systems, is a theory of communication, 'but communication study has not been much influenced by cybernetic theory', partly because of its mathematical presenta-tion.[38] The strong affinity between this work as it developed through the 1990s and the earlier systems work on information processing is clear.

Cybernetics is about feedback, dynamic processes, and control features within systems, which adjust to feedback and, therefore, are presumed to 'learn'.[39]

With the development of more sophisticated tools for processing network information and storage of large data sets, the mapping (and graphing) of network relationships has blossomed. Barry Wellman, a sociologist who has worked extensively on social networking, urges researchers to regard this field as a broad intellectual approach and 'not as a narrow set of methods', but to little avail.[40] Social Network Analysis research has proliferated, with little grounding in the social sciences instrumental tradition (apart from mathematics), and even less in the critical tradition. One verdict on research on complex adaptive systems is that it has not been helpful in explaining why developments such as the rise of network forms of organization, their structures, and dynamics are emerging in the particular way that they are in modern society.

Because of its mechanistic approach and its absence of a theory of agency, systems theory offers no means of elaborating theories of human self-interest, affinities, or means of exchange.[41] In the absence of any theory of agency, systems theory can appear to be inherently limited when it comes to issues of human intervention in the technological system. In its concern with how society is 'constituted by sets of attractors within the range of possible condition spaces, and ... how changes in controlling variables for the whole system can come to reconstitute the form of that attractor set',[42] it is difficult to find any basis for normative evaluation offered by a knowing subject. Systems theory is a reaction, nevertheless, against the micro-economics focus on the trajectories of isolated individual 'atoms', that is, people bent on maximizing their utility. It renders the relative simplicity of economics extremely problematic because the analysis of complex systems does not provide easy recipes, but, instead, focuses on the 'capacity of systems to *transform themselves*'.[43] From a policy perspective, however, this very complexity suggests that the best option is to wait and see, rather than to act by intervening in the system in an attempt to resolve paradoxes that emerge through the dynamics of the system's oscillations.

The contribution to the social imaginary of the information society has been considerable and has propagated studies on the way network systems appear to organize their self-renewal, the focus of analysis being on recursive self-organizing processes.[44] Insofar as self-renewal is a core concept in economics, systems theory appeals to economists with an interest in the constraints under which rule-bound (autonomous) agents make choices. In this view, 'the elements of an economy, set within an organization structure, are agents. Rules provide the connective dimension of such structure and, as such, rule systems embody and articulate the knowledge contained in the system'.[45] Theory building concerning knowledge, therefore, is understood as being about system constraints. This way of seeing is applied also to the emergent characteristics of organizations within the economic system, where attention focuses on 'meso-rules', which may govern the internal dynamics of systems.[46] The evolution of a complex system is conceived of in terms of the indeterminacy of the formation and re-formation of connections among agents intent on experimenting in ways that do not compromise the viability of the system.

Theoretical work on complex systems draws on the physical science understandings of dissipative structures, evolutionary biology and autopoiesis, and on economic models of learning by doing, the self-organization of markets, emergence (equilibrium), and feedback (price signals and incentives more generally), some of which are derived from the physical and biological sciences in an attempt to explain the co-evolution of technology and society. The result is a story about how '*technology creates itself out of itself*'.[47] For Brian Arthur, a major contributor to 'complexity economics' along with others at the Santa Fe Institute in the United States, the benefit of systems theory, and the analysis of complex adaptive systems in particular, is the awareness it provides about how 'the structures that define the economy continually change and reshape themselves—and therefore constantly need reinterpretation'.[48] He is clear about what his work is *not* about: it is not about the promise or the threat of technology, nor is it about the human side of creating technology. The idea that systems evolve is seen as being consistent with the search for insight into evolutionary processes of emergence that lead to irreversibility. This obviously deflects attention from a study of the outcomes of the process of emergence and whether they are valued or resisted, and by whom.

As I indicated in Chapter 1, in some branches of the social sciences, and in the physical sciences, the notion of evolution is a pervasive one which has been applied in attempts to understand the dynamics of complex human, technical, and natural systems.[49] The analysis that I have presented here is intended to operate on two levels. One of these levels is an outline of how a particular tradition in systems theory tries to explain the dynamics of evolutionary processes in a way that is applicable both to human and physical systems, using the idea of evolution as a metaphor. This is the subject of the next part of this chapter. In the penultimate section of this chapter, the emphasis shifts to another level. On a second level, a critical systems framework is proposed as a way of seeing how the dynamics of a complex adaptive system can be understood to condition actions that are considered to be feasible in the social imaginaries of the information society. These levels are not separable in the world of experience and action. However, for the analytical purpose of explaining a strand of systems theory which is helpful in understanding how paradox is generated by emergent processes within a complex system, they are treated separately here.

Metacommunication and Paradox

Gregory Bateson, who had a keen interest in systems theory and the emerging field of cybernetics, participated in some of the early Macy Conferences. Bateson's formal training was as a biologist and an anthropologist. His eclecticism enabled him to traverse many of the chasms between disciplinary perspectives both within the social sciences, and among the humanities, social sciences, and physical sciences. He began to develop a distinctive perspective on communication processes within complex systems, focusing on the genesis of paradoxical communication and the harms that may be associated with them. By the 1970s, he had developed a theory of mind and nature, a distinctive perspective on communication processes within a complex system.

Bateson put the processes of communication at the core of his work, drawing on systems theoretical insights, but in ways that depart from the framework developed later by Luhmann and discussed in the preceding section. Systems perspectives give prominence to the information processing model and to communication, and Bateson's work is not an exception in this respect. His work has been criticized for its affinity to systems theory and for leaving no scope for human agency or moral values and it has been largely neglected in the social sciences. Nevertheless, it has been applied in the analysis of power relationships within the communication system.[50] Observations in Bateson's work and that of some of his colleagues can be interpreted in a way that is helpful for understanding the genesis of paradox in a complex adaptive system.

In his book, *Steps to an Ecology of the Mind*, Bateson claims that: 'all perception and all response, all behavior and all classes of behavior, all learning and all genetics, all neurophysiology and endocrinology, all organization and all evolution—one entire subject matter—must be regarded as *communicational* in nature'.[51] As already noted, systems thinking was very popular in the 1940s and 1950s and it was this tradition that encouraged a search for generalizations or 'laws' which could apply to all 'communicative phenomena' that occur in systems of all kinds. The work of those who were dreaming of machines that could 'think' was complemented by the work of those who were eager to use the fruits of defence industry research to build a unified theory of systems, applicable across the physical and social sciences.[52] Bateson, Jürgen Ruesch, and others took up this challenge, one of the results being a seminal book, *Communication: A Social Theory of Psychiatry*.[53]

Although this work was couched in the language of science, it can be seen as an instance of political positioning and resistance to the then prevailing social imaginary, inflected by the paradigm of medical and physical sciences which regarded the world through a Newtonian prism as 'the object'. Bateson and

Ruesch's book can be seen also as an effort to counter the simplicity of scientific models, which provided no scope for an investigation of the complexity of systems. In the light of the then recent past, these appeared to give research aimed at improving the welfare of people and their communities, a lower priority than research aimed principally at scientific and technological advancement. The post-war period was a time for reflection on the prevailing scientific paradigm in a period when that paradigm had been used to produce atomic bombs that actually had been used. Alfred Korzybski, the originator of General Semantics Theory, observes that 'the task ahead is gigantic if we are to avoid more personal, national and even international tragedies based on unpredictability, insecurity, fears, anxieties, etc., which are steadily disorganizing the functioning of the human nervous system'.[54]

The concern to avoid the tragedy of more human conflict was evident in the social imaginaries of the scientific community at this time, with many aspiring to put 'science' into the service of a 'saner society'. For some scientists, including social scientists, theoretical research on system dynamics that could embrace natural and human systems, even if metaphorically in the case of the latter, seemed to offer hope for understandings that might avert the tragedies of the past. A means of achieving this seemed to be within reach if the perceptions from the mathematicians' information processing model, that is, communication theory, could be extended into the realm of social or human systems. The problems tackled by Bateson and his colleagues resonate with many current debates about the values and choices that should guide the communication system as it evolves.

DIFFERENCE, PARADOX, AND LEARNING

A key contribution of Bateson's work is his special treatment of information. He builds upon the 'transmission model' of the physicists and engineers of his time, and discusses information as a 'difference which makes a difference'.[55] He coins this phrase to express the way the world appears to an observer, from moment to moment, as change occurs within a system of relationships. Difference is understood as change. The ability for noting and reflecting on difference is seen as having implications for making connections, and remembering over time and under different spatial conditions. Thus, the communication process is seen as time-binding,[56] an idea that also informs the work of Harold Innis and, later, Marshal McLuhan, on communication technologies and the media.

Perceptions of difference (change) are understood to arise out of communication relationships.[57] Bateson condenses this idea in the statement that information can be understood as 'news of difference' or changes which we perceive as maps or patterns that serve as a means of organizing information in a system.[58] For Bateson, composites or collections of perceptions of difference or distinction, and the connections (relationships) among them, are understood as constituting knowledge. Some of these composites are susceptible to consensus, that is, a first-order reality in which 'scientific' verification or refutation is feasible within the bounds of the prevailing scientific paradigm which infuses the social imaginary. However, there is another order, which is normally dismissed in the prevailing way of seeing, that is subject to indeterminacy and uncertainty because of the dynamics of complex systems of relationships.[59]

In my assessment of the social imaginaries of the information society, the challenge is to understand the dynamics of the system and 'the pattern which connects' the various components of that system.[60] In this framework it is important to take account of the way human beings recognize or guess at patterns that emerge, some of which may be 'stable (constant, invariant, similar) and others unstable (inconstant, variable, dissimilar) over time'. This process serves as a set of ideas or rules 'by which and through which a specific structure is organized', resulting in the awareness of a particular pattern,[61] or as Thorstein Veblen might have put it, a particular 'habit of thought'.[62] Thus, the social imaginary can be regarded as a set of rules and norms through which relationships of power are organized and 'evolve'.

In Bateson's model, the communication process is understood as being comprised of messages as in the information processing model of communication, but the messages, in turn, are understood on two levels, rather than simply as a message (or byte of information) that is sent and received. There is the content level, which provides representational information, and the relational level, which provides cues or presentational information. The key to human 'understanding' for Bateson is the emergence of multi-level patterns of information (news of difference), or as he describes them 'ecological wisdom'—basically, 'knowledge of the larger interactive system'.[63] He puts it somewhat cryptically, referring to emergent changes in a system as resulting from 'chance' which 'is tamed within the overall pattern'.[64] Unexpected developments or moves within a system can be revealing of consistent developments, and discrepancies or noise within a system spawn new patterns, that is, new understandings.[65] Thus, system evolution is not about *adjusting* to a consensus (or an equilibrium state). Rather, it is a process in which innovations are selected or rejected, and in which awareness of new or emergent patterns occurs by traversing the boundaries in a multi-level system. This process produces paradox because of contradictions between the content and presentational information emerging through the dynamic process of change.

The idea of multi-level communication is central to Bateson's understanding of the genesis of paradox. Beginning with the level of interpersonal communication, and seeing how perceptions of paradox at this level can be scaled up to address the dynamics at other levels in a system makes this idea easier to understand. Bateson's arguments about the genesis of paradox in a complex, multi-level system of relationships are derived from type theory.[66] Type theory arose from efforts to solve mathematical and logical paradoxes where it was argued that a proposition about a proposition, that is, a proposition which has as its reference at least one proposition, is of a higher order, is of a different logical type, than the proposition to which it refers.[67] If no class can contain itself as a member, then this class must be of a higher logical type than its members. To argue otherwise is to permit contradiction and paradox. For Bateson, this insight provides a way of differentiating among communication relations that occur in systems organized in hierarchies as opposed to 'heterarchies', where communication relations occur in multiple forms, but where power is shared horizontally.[68] What is important here is that complex systems, such as the communication system, are multi-level systems. They are organized in hierarchies and in heterarchies of relationships. This means that hierarchies cannot be claimed to have vanished as the result of the architecture of one component of a complex system, such as the Internet Protocol with its horizontal architecture.

For Bateson, 'metacommunication' refers to 'communication about communication', that is, propositions about the relationships between communications within a system that are presented at a different level.[69] Paradox can emerge when statements are presented at different levels where 'every communication has a content and a relationship aspect such that the latter classifies the former and is therefore a metacommunication'.[70] Thus, metacommunication is a way of 'talking about' relationships, and is especially helpful if those relationships are contested and infused with asymmetric power relationships. When this idea is applied at the individual level to understand communication with psychiatric patients, the notions of 'double bind' and a paradoxical intervention become relevant, concepts that I suggest have implications not only at the level of interpersonal communication but also at the level of institutions and policy.[71] The core idea of the double bind is that 'no matter how one may try, one cannot *not* communicate'.[72] All changes to information, all notice of difference, convey some information about a system.

Insight into the genesis of a 'double bind' was developed initially in work with schizophrenic patients, but Bateson stresses that this phenomenon, which arises out of the dynamic changes within an interpersonal communication system, is also a feature of all communication.[73] His daughter, Mary Catherine Bateson, comments that, 'the double bind is not only a clue to understanding schizophrenia and a wide range of other learned or acquired psychopathologies..., but [also is] part of the fabric of ordinary life'.[74] This approach was developed by Paul Watzlawick, Donald Jackson, and Janet Bevin, who suggest that if hostility or aggression in a communication relationship is unacknowledged, the result may be a denial of contradictory messages.[75] As Watzlawick and his colleagues explain, in a double binding communication relationship:

(1) Two or more persons are involved in an intense relationship that has a high degree of physical and/or psychological survival value for one, several, or all of them.... (2) In such a context, a message is given which is so structured that (a) it asserts something, (b) it asserts something about its own assertion and (c) these two assertions are mutually exclusive. Thus, if the message is an injunction, it must be disobeyed to be obeyed;...(3) Finally, the recipient of the message is prevented from stepping outside the frame set by this message, either by metacommunicating (commenting) about it or by withdrawing.... (4) *Where double-binding is of long-standing, possibly chronic duration, it will turn into a habitual and autonomous expectation regarding the nature of human relationships and the world at large, an expectation that does not require further reinforcement....* (5) The paradoxical behavior imposed by double-binding...is in turn of a double-binding nature, and this leads to a self-perpetuating pattern of communication.[76]

One party in a relationship may find that he or she is unable to comment on a contradictory message, but does so metaphorically to deal with an unequal power relationship. This pathology is recognizable only on a different level, by metacommunicating. Whether any action is taken depends on whether a victim believes that a given relationship is significant for his or her survival. The experience of a double bind can result in an effort to find a change in the experience of paradox, that is, a way of averting a 'self-perpetuating pattern of communication' or, in Taylor's terms, giving statements a 'certain reading'. In the case of the social imaginaries of the communication system, the relevance of this is that metacommunications can be helpful for demonstrating the genesis of paradox, for explaining why these relationships may be persistent, sequestered, and denied, and for revealing new ways of seeing them.

A further insight is the importance of analogue (difference/cooperation) in contrast to digital (distinction/competition) forms of representation. Analogue communication is conceived as nonverbal communication (tone, facial expression, physical gesture) while digital is conceived as relating to content involving complexity, versatility, and abstraction.[77] When these are confounded, the result is perception of paradox. When the digital process of communication starts to be dominant in human relationships, this can be seen as a 'mispunctuation' of the communication relationship into binary oppositions which are presented as either/or alternatives, when in fact they are both/and relationships organized in a hierarchical, rather than a heterarchical, system. This means that it is possible for apparently contradictory statements to be valid, that is, that both/and relationships may be what characterize the dynamics of an evolving system. 'Runaway relationships' can result from mispunctuation and double-binding and can escalate towards aggression, violence, and destruction (at the interpersonal level), and these are patterns of communication that are very difficult to alter.[78] However, there is always a possibility for 'adaptive action',[79] such that a circular, self-referential, communication circuit can be disturbed by metacommunication, and where 'the qualities and characteristics of metacommunication between persons will depend upon the qualities and degree of their mutual awareness of each other's perception'.[80]

Thus, metacommunication, that is, communication about communication, provides a means for interventions aimed at dealing with paradox. Apparent contradictions may be polarized through splitting, conflicting feelings can be projected onto another person (scapegoating), repression or denial can block awareness, or regression can lead to understandings deriving from experience, and reaction may lead to the display of opposite feelings or ambivalence or yield compromise.[81] Identifying paradox and finding means of adaptive action depend on being able to move outside a framework *by metacommunicating about it at a different level.* This, in turn, becomes a strategy for intervention.

In the therapeutic context, for instance, in this view, the therapist is an outsider, 'capable of supplying what the system itself cannot generate: a change of its own rules'.[82] By analogy, insofar as all communication involves both participants and observers within a social system,[83] it is possible to conceive of interventions, even in a complex system that may, after all, be productive. For example, if they expose contradictions between apparently oppositional positions which are better understood as being generated by different positions in a hierarchy of power relationships, it may be feasible for contesting parties to alter their ways of seeing and the nature of their dialogues by relocating them with respect to the power relationships and beginning to pursue a new pathway.[84] Persistent patterns of communication are present not only at the individual level but also within the dynamics of debates among groups and institutions.

If a communication system is regarded as being comprised of both analogue and digital components as defined by Bateson, we can see that insights may emerge from understanding relationships as being both/and as well as being constituted by either/or relationships. In this view, the digital world is the 'domain of opposition and identity as well as difference; it allows for the analytic epistemology of *either/or as well as for the dialectical epistemology of both/and*' relationships.[85] This goes unacknowledged within ways of seeing that do not account for multi-level, systemic relationships and the paradoxes engendered by their dynamic interaction. This view suggests that maintaining an authoritative position at the cost of another's well-being is associated with the perception of threat and vulnerability.[86] It suggests also that decisions may be taken without accounting for the damage they introduce into a system of relationships. Klaus Krippendorf, a scholar of communication in the United States, puts it this way: 'it is the very network of communication that sets the boundaries of what its participants may come to know about the system in which they partake as well as about the network of communication through which this knowledge is revealed'.[87] In other words, what we see 'in reality are the products of the punctuation and the organization of reality by the activities of society in history'.[88] As Krippendorf insists, Bateson's view of communication involves a shift away from individualistic conceptions of power towards a view in which 'power always resides in *social relationships*'.[89]

In this view a paradox or trap is not possible to recognize from a position '*within* a pathological reality construction'.[90] By extension, it is not possible to recognize the paradoxical ways of seeing within the prevailing social imaginaries of the information society using that framework. However, one way to reveal the paradoxes of a social system is to metacommunicate about them, to demonstrate how that 'reality' is replayed recursively within a pattern of relationships. Mispunctuations occur at different levels in a communication system. In this respect, there is little difference between the interactions of nations or of individuals. If discrepant punctuation leads to different views of reality, it is likely to produce apparently irresolvable conflict.[91]

Analysis of system relationships, without reference to power, errs towards self-maintenance of the system, regardless of the values espoused within a given system.[92] Conservatism is a feature of the systems theoretical approach. For many of its proponents it is a means of searching for system stability and maintenance, not change. While it does allow for emergence, the determinants of change derive from a 'within system' dynamic, not from mental processes, practical consciousness, or the choices of human beings. In Bateson's framework, 'causes are not effects'[93] because, although selections are made, human systems are open and the set of possibilities is not pre-given. The set of possibilities is constituted by selections that are remembered, forgotten, and reinvented, and which cannot be predicted from knowing the qualities of the system in which they arise. Emergence and unpredictability do not mean that there is no learning. Just as Michel Foucault argues that 'power must be understood in the first instance as the multiplicity of force relations *imminent in the sphere* in which they operate and in which they constitute their own organization',[94] there is a possibility of learning within complex systems.

In summary, in a systems theoretical framework, learning does occur, with the potential to change habits and redefine the self and the environment, that is, it can lead to changes in the social imaginary and in practices. Learning involves interpretation and higher order cognitive reasoning.[95] And liberation from 'false learning' or the double binds created by paradoxical communication requires acknowledgement of participation in them, contestation of them, and that others are able to contest them too.[96] This liberation offers a means of assessing the evolution of the communication system by explaining how paradox is generated, where it might be visible in the social imaginaries of the communication system, and when policy intervention might help to cope with double-binding (paradoxical) power relationships.[97]

METHODOLOGICAL IMPLICATIONS AND CRITICISMS

A focus on communication within a complex adaptive system, with recognition of multiple hierarchical and heterarchical levels within a system, offers a way of making sense of paradox and the way it gives rise to habitual conflicts between the prevailing social imaginaries of the information society. Asymmetries of power within such multi-level systems are often sequestered or set aside so that chronic patterns in our ways of seeing become legitimized. Bateson argues that, 'without context, words and actions have no meaning at all'.[98] Meaning is emergent. It arises from interactions among individuals, groups, and institutions. Methodologically, this means that if the question we are interested in is about why (not simply how) things happen, then we cannot focus only on the effects or impacts of the communication system. A more productive approach is to examine mispunctuations that generate paradox, especially at the interfaces within a complex system.

In the instrumental ways of seeing, a search for causal relationships and for impacts often suggests that individuals should be blamed for their own misbehaviour (e.g. their failure to learn the skills required to use the Internet) or the misbehaviour of others (e.g. the emotional distress 'caused' by participants in online interaction). In contrast, by focusing on paradox and by punctuating analysis from different positions in a complex system, self-perpetuating and harmful patterns of communication can be brought to light, including those generated by unacknowledged relations of power. In a systems view, understanding is conditioned by where one punctuates the system:

Choosing a causal beginning is arbitrary. The bracketing of a start and a finish creates the illusion of first causes. . . . The illusion is inviting because people use a vocabulary of one-way causality to explain social phenomena. In so doing, they implicitly claim that certain phenomena are 'the causes' and certain phenomena are 'the effects'.[99]

Examining system boundaries or interfaces in this way has implications for judgements about human values and purposes. Bateson said that we live by propositions whose validity is a function of our belief in them.[100] This means that study of the communication system is inseparable from study of human purposes and values. This approach provides a way of understanding the 'out of control' system scenarios in the social imaginaries of the information society. From a systems perspective, the apparently self-destructive features are as much reflections of the dynamics of the system as they are of the cognition of human beings. Equally importantly, the evolution of a complex adaptive system is understood as being always in progress, always being 'regenerated, negotiated and challenged'.[101] Working with a systems framework also means that there is a potential for ruptures to chronic patterns of communication. When a pattern of paradoxical communication persists, there is likely to be 'trouble' of some kind. This may take the form of persistent inequality and social injustice or, indeed, of psychopathology. Intervening means acknowledging paradox, but also devising means of repairing the conditions that are giving rise to it.[102]

A criticism of this way of proceeding is that it entails negation of the agency of self-aware human beings. For instance, some analysts warn that a focus on 'emergent complex systems' represents an attempt 'to reduce human society completely to ordinary complexity', resulting in catastrophic theories and policies.[103] They argue that the use of the language of self-organization, attractor sets, and responses to the 'outside' of a system implies automaticity, which can lead to claims that intervention in a complex adaptive system is pointless (and even dangerous).

Another feature of systems theory that concerns many social scientists is the recursiveness of emergence which suggests the absence of reflexivity, cognition, and learning. For some, this produces anxiety that it is impossible to 'know the dancer from the dance',[104] or, to put it in social science terms, how we can discern meanings, associations, and values if the analytical focus is on control of information or communication (transmission) systems.[105] As sociologist, John Urry, says, there is a danger of ending up with 'social physics'.[106]

However, the systems framework for examining paradox gives us purchase on the dynamics of evolution of a complex adaptive system because it serves as an antidote to would-be simplifications that succeed in endowing paradox with mystery. In reviving an approach that could be characterized as being 'under existential threat'[107] (partly because metaphors of evolutionary systems become associated with Darwinian natural selection), I suggest that a risky move towards theoretical eclecticism is very productive. This is because it disturbs persistent claims about the 'effects' of technologies on individuals and about the 'impacts' of technology which can then lead to apparitions of technological 'folk devils'.[108]

In studies of effects or impacts of the Internet, insights into power relations can be buried beneath the weight of disputes about the reliability or representativeness of empirical results.[109] This is characteristic of studies, for example, on whether the use of the modern communication system leads to increased or decreased social involvement and personal well-being. Widely cited instrumental research from the mid-1990s claimed evidence of an 'Internet Paradox': 'the Internet is a social technology used for communication with individuals and groups, but . . . it is associated with declines in social involvement and the psychological well-being that goes with social involvement'.[110] This led to media warnings that people should moderate their use of the

Internet. By 2002, these negative effects appeared to have dissipated.[111] These conflicting findings were attributed to the passage of time and the diffusion of the technology, without considering why the paradox was experienced in the first place.

Thus, studies of impacts or effects polarize an idyllic future (or past) with an alienated life, without acknowledging that 'communication power is at the heart of the structure and dynamics of society', as Manuel Castells puts it.[112] Research on the effects of the Internet or the information society persists, attracting substantial funding, and is frequently reported in the press. For instance, a news headline claims that 'surfing the web can make you depressed'.[113] The researchers stress that whether the Internet causes mental health problems or whether people with such problems are drawn to the Internet cannot be ascertained using their research design and methods,[114] but the instrumental character of the research questions means that paradoxical power relations involving personality, identity, and changes in sociability that may be implied by the experience of online communication are ignored.[115] An interdisciplinary approach, combining concepts from the system perspective elaborated by Bateson and others, with those from endogenous theories such as those highlighted in Chapter 3, provides a basis for an evaluation of paradoxes common to the Internet Age. It enables investigation not of effects, but of the implications of the interpenetration of technological and human systems and the scope for policy intervention.

A Critical Systems Framework

The communication system historically has been a site of struggle for 'control of the world', with its extension always offering the promise of a better world[116]—the good society. In the prevailing social imaginaries of the information society, a system is promised, emerging out of constant technological innovation, and encouraged by visions of 'thinking machines'. This process gives life not only to opportunities for beneficial change but also to new forms of social, political, and economic inequality and injustice, partly through the genesis of paradox. Even if analysis of these paradoxes reveals 'no obvious avenues along which repair can take place, other than in and through the critique offered in the analysis itself',[117] as sociologist Michael Billig says, I suggest that it is better to examine the evidence than to wait for the 'machines of loving grace'.

Figure 4.1 shows the cluster of concepts that I draw upon to analyse the paradoxes generated by the evolution of the communication system in information society. This cluster brings together—though not harmoniously—

Figure 4.1. Concepts for a Critical Systems Framework

concepts from a systems perspective on the genesis of paradox and from endogenous models of change in technologies within a complex adaptive system.

By punctuating analysis from the perspectives of different stakeholders, discrepant ways of seeing that generate paradox and possibilities for repairing dysfunctional patterns come to light. Analysis of metacommunications (stories about 'what goes on between us') opens up possibilities for examining 'the deeper normative notions' and how these are carried in 'images, stories and legends'[118] of the Internet Age. This analysis is supported empirically by a comprehensive survey of the relevant literatures, analysis of policy documentation from a large number of formal governance institutions, contributions from scholars, policy makers, and practitioners in formal and informal settings relating to policy over several decades, and my direct participation in research aimed at designing digital technology platforms.

Application of this framework enhances the possibility of 'adaptive action', that is, for building a new social imaginary of the information society and for considering governance approaches consistent with values of the good society. It helps to show how the mispunctuation of relationships among the stakeholders involved in the development of the communication system is complicit in the chronic persistence of the dominant and alternative social imaginaries and in the genesis of the paradoxes of information scarcity and complexity discussed in earlier chapters. Some of the differences between these imaginaries are presented in Table 4.1. This table shows that the visions of different stakeholders are aligned with both similar and different components of imaginaries about what is valued in the information society.

Normally, the implications for governance of these social imaginaries are presented as being in opposition, with each 'side' denying the legitimacy of the other side's goals. This is partly a result of the failure to acknowledge the paradoxes that inform these conflicting ways of seeing. When the genesis of paradoxes is explained, different judgements are possible about the need for

Table 4.1. Social Imaginaries of the Information Society

	Dominant social imaginary	Alternative social imaginary
Corporate vision	Market exchange	Commons
	Individual preference	Collective norms
	Technological progress	Technology assessment
	Information processing	Mediation
	Information scarcity	Information abundance
Science and engineering vision	Complex system	Complex system
	Technological mastery	Generative commons
	Emergence	Emergence
	Information processing	Information processing
	Individual agency	Collective action
Political vision	Governance from above	Governance from below
	Multi-stakeholder governance (overseen by governance from above)	Networked coalitions
	Intellectual property rights	Sharing communities
	Security and surveillance	Creativity and experimentation
	Privacy	Anonymity
Civil society vision	Empowerment (in front of the screen)	Empowerment (behind the screen and in front of the screen)
	Risk minimization through individual control	Collective control
	Market-led	Community-led

Source: Author.

intervention to correct the pathway of change, reconciling it with the interests of the stakeholders, but acknowledging that stability and balance are unachievable because the conflicts are enduring.

POWER AND COMPLEXITY

An analysis of paradox in the Internet Age calls for investigation of the complexity of the communication system and it challenges the assumption that technological innovation is inevitably in concert with aspirations for the good society. There is something very important about our relationship with information and its production, circulation, and consumption, beyond matters of quantity, velocity, or circulation—the main problems addressed by the models of information processing. Having more and more information in 'Internet Time' carries risks for human beings. With T. S. Eliot we need to ask, 'where is the wisdom we have lost in knowledge? Where is the knowledge we have lost in information?'[119] Critical endogenous perspectives emphasize that we should neither oversimplify the dynamics of innovation in the communication system nor reduce them to questions about quantities or stocks of 'knowledge'. But they make it difficult to tease out the dynamics that produce the stabilities and instabilities in the complex adaptive system of which the communication system is a part. Systems theory is helpful in this respect.

However, we should not lose sight of human perceptions, motivations, or agency, so we need to be clear about what is understood by power in this critical systems framework. Charles Taylor does not equate the social imaginary with ideology, but ideology is clearly a factor in conflicting social imaginaries. Ideology can be seen as being relatively autonomous in the reproduction of economic relations. For Louis Althusser, for example, ideology takes material and symbolic forms; it 'fixes' people as social subjects, simultaneously, creating the illusion of 'free choice' or agency.[120] Even for Antonio Gramsci, people are said to have 'strangely composite' characters and ideology refers to 'a conception of the world that is implicitly manifest in art, in law, in economic activity and in the manifestations of individual and collective life'.[121] Thus, whatever we take to be the limits of agency and choice within the constraints of the capitalist economy, ideology operates in complicated ways and assumes a certain understanding of power.

Steven Lukes, a political theorist, offers a three-fold classification of power, beginning with a one-dimensional view where power is distributed in a pluralistic way. It is observable, and it is visible in decision-making behaviour in situations where there are conflicting interests. A second dimension takes account of bias with respect to values, beliefs, norms, and procedures and power is as much about non-decision-making as it is about decision-making. The third dimension presumes that conflictual power relations may be covert or latent, and the 'real' interests of stakeholders may be difficult (not impossible) to detect. Lukes insists that 'any view of power rests on some normatively specific conception of interests'.[122]

My interest is in exploring normative conceptions of interests that have become entangled in the paradoxes of information scarcity and complexity. Lukes defines power as 'human agents, separately or together, in groups or in organizations, through action or inaction, significantly affecting the thoughts or actions of others (specifically, in a manner contrary to their interests)'.[123] This is a flexible definition that requires neither the assumption that stakeholders operate in a rational and transparent way nor that agents cannot know their 'real' interests. In addition, Foucault says that biopower is 'what brought life and its mechanisms into the realm of explicit calculations and made knowledge-power an agent of transformation of human life'.[124] Power is developed through technique in the academy, other institutions, and in everyday life. It is partial and temporary, even if in a given moment it seems stable and hegemonic.

Some scholars, such as communication law and policy scholar, Sandra Braman, distinguish a new form of power in the Internet Age—informational power—suggesting that it 'dominates power in other forms, changes how they are exercised, and alters the nature of their effects'.[125] Informational power is related to the collection, processing, and interpretation of digital information for surveillance, cyber warfare, or commercial and social communication purposes. And Manuel Castells identifies 'communication power' as the salient form of power in the network age.[126] I prefer not to privilege a new category of power. In my analysis I retain the flexibility to examine exemplary situations in which power is at work, but focus on changes in information or in the communication system that are not 'authored' or 'sponsored', but, instead, emerge from the intersection of interests of different stakeholders.

COMPLEX SYSTEMS AND POLICY

This discussion of power has a bearing on the way the visions of the information society discussed in Chapter 2 are understood. They are reflections of a complex articulation of power relationships in a multi-level system which is also interpreted in the social imaginaries where multiple, sometimes conflicting, visions come together. Thus, an analysis focusing on the visions alone would provide little guidance for building an equitable and just information society. This is because 'there is nothing about a highly idealized abstraction, a vision, for us to know how to go on together every day, in particular contexts'.[127] The benefit of a framework that draws insight from theories of complex adaptive systems is that, instead of seeing power relationships within a system as tending towards stability and equilibrium as is common in exogenous models in the social sciences, the outcomes of paradoxical communication can be understood to tend towards stability and instability at the same time, albeit, on different levels within a system. Human agents can be understood to act and respond in patterned ways, influenced by power but not in a deterministic way.[128] And paradoxical relationships are such that while a vision may come to dominate, there is a chance that a novel (better) outcome will emerge.[129]

This understanding of the dynamics of power relations in a complex adaptive system has substantial implications for the way we conceive of policy and the policy making process. The instrumental tradition of research on policy making sees decision-making processes as being evidence-based and procedural and focuses on the (quasi)rationality of discourse, persuasion, or argumentation. Policy making is mainly understood to be a matter for institutions established by the state, and the outcomes depend on the information available to various communities of decision-makers.[130] Participants are presumed to have relevant expertise and, in democratic countries, to represent broadly-based interests.[131]

In the prevailing social imaginaries of the information society, this pluralist concept of policy making is invoked when it is assumed that all the stakeholders can exercise their power in shaping policy outcomes in line with deliberative theories of democracy.[132] The new digital platforms are expected to support deliberative forums, which may depart from the Habermasian 'ideal speech situation', but are still presumed to favour political self-efficacy. Thus, for example, some find new potentialities for consensus formation and rational-critical discourse in digital platforms and social media—from Twitter to the BlackBerry Messenger Service. However, decision-making in a multi-level complex system must be expected to involve contraints that limit influence over decision-making by those in authoritative positions, as well as new possibilities for the exercise of power.[133] The idealization of the relation of the new technologies to the public sphere makes it seem as if participants in policy debates are objective and disinterested in their search for the 'truth',[134] consistent with the information processing model.

This view neglects the diversity of identities and the search for justice. As Nancy Fraser points out, 'claims on behalf of "the global poor" are pitted against the claims of citizens of bounded polities'.[135] She argues that policy makers face a 'spectre of *incommensurability*' with respect to the distribution of resources and a misframing of the voices of those who are not integrated within the dominant communities.[136] The result is persistent opposition without apparent solution. A different standard for public deliberation is offered by the notion of agonistic pluralism which acknowledges contested interests and accepts that the terrain of policy making is always vulnerable.[137] This is a view that is easier to work with in a complex adaptive systems framework because vulnerability can spring from the multiple ways in which power is exercised—that is, from the full spectrum of dimensions discussed by Lukes.[138]

Finally, with a focus on paradox, claims that policy intervention is harmful can be seen to have a certain validity just as can claims that policy intervention is needed from either above or below. This is because these perspectives are about the dynamics of change at different levels in a complex adaptive system. Thus, Clay Shirky, an American new media scholar and activist, may be partly right in his claim that the Internet 'lets us design new kinds of participation and sharing', consistent with a utopia organized around scientific and technical reason and the pursuit of freedom, and requiring that all the fruits of techno-logical innovation be allowed to flourish. He agues that those inconsistent with the good society will fail because of the 'natural braking functions of social diffusion'.[139] However, this view, while not entirely invalid, mispunctuates the public interest in the evolution of the communication system.

A systems perspective emphasizes the interfaces between the components in a system, sites where conflict leads to the genesis of paradox rather than the endpoints or outputs of this system which may (sometimes) be subject to selection and, hence, to 'natural braking effects'. Bateson's concern is with how we should 'conduct our civilization' and he warns that 'we should be careful what we pretend because we become what we pretend' and '[w]hat people presume to be "human" is what they will build in as premises of their social arrangements, and what they build in is sure to be *learned*, is sure to become a part of the character of those who participate'.[140] As the learning process takes place, certain social imaginaries become self-reinforcing. They go unquestioned. The systems perspective sensitizes us to the possibility that any system that 'destroys its environment ultimately destroys itself'.[141]

Conclusion

For early proponents of cybernetics and statistical, biological, and computational systems theories, conflating mind and machine, and nature and society were permissible in the effort to formulate a universal theory of complex system dynamics. Meaning and symbolic representation were not at the top of the agendas of most participants in the early Macy Conferences, for instance. As Philip Mirowski points out in his book, *Machine Dreams*: 'If there was one tenet of that era's particular faith in science, it was that logical rigor and the mathematical idiom of expression would produce transparent agreement over the meaning and significance of various models and their implications'.[142]

Much of this work was politically conservative in its search for the determinants of system stability, and it responded to the prevailing post-World War II political climate. In this sense, early systems work can be seen as a critical response to the then prevailing scientific paradigm (physics). Over time, systems theory has experienced a 'rebirth' within the sciences, in work on complex adaptive systems. An affinity to this way of seeing is apparent also in some areas of the social sciences, which can be understood as a reaction to the prevailing 'effects' paradigm.

A one- or, at best, two-dimensional approach to power in policy making, combined with instrumental perspectives on technological innovation and economic, and other changes in society, prevails as the 'scientific' paradigm in the social sciences. These approaches, and especially the information processing model, are very visible in the current social imaginaries of the information society. Critical theories of power have visibility in the academic community in research on the information society and, specifically on the communication system. Critical scholarship provides an understanding of the reasons why policy interventions yield unanticipated consequences, and this can act as a buffer against the search for 'curative' or instrumental policies. Instrumental responses may be welcomed, for instance, as measures to curtail the distribution of child pornography or help citizens to be more aware of the way their activities are monitored in virtual space, but they do not suggest means to repair the harms of the persistent paradoxes.

Advocacy for a 'self-organizing' market to guide the evolutionary process and a justification for non-intervention by policy makers in a complex adaptive system is found in some readings of the systems approach, for example, in claims that a technological system is subject to evolutionary change in response 'not primarily to human need *but to its own needs*'.[143] In this view, there is no alternative to hoping that the evolution of the system will respond to its own 'need' for survival. Some systems analysts in the social sciences locate their hopes for empowering social transformation in 'the realization of practical forces of change that have a potential to rise from the *inside of the systems* in question in order to produce a transcendental outside that becomes a new whole'.[144] The suggestion is that we rely on the emergent potential for transformation.

Theoretical perspectives that focus on power asymmetries often set the 'context' of change on one side, providing some explanation for conflict, but rarely for the genesis of paradox. In contrast, a critical systems framework can be applied to help in achieving liberation from 'false learning' which is associated with the dynamic of paradoxical communication. It offers a basis for a new approach to intervention based on adaptive learning, by focusing attention on the genesis of paradoxes in the Internet Age. The next chapters focus on various sites for the genesis of paradox, first, in the role of the communication system in everyday life (Chapter 5), then in the development of new digital platforms and means of controlling digital information (Chapter 6) and, finally, in policy and governance forums (Chapter 7).

Communication Systems in Everyday Life

Introduction

The communication system mediates every aspect of experience in the information society. Roger Silverstone, in his studies of mediation, insisted that this system, including its infrastructure and content, is increasingly indispensable to the fabric of people's everyday lives and that we must study it in all its complex dimensions—cultural and social, and political and economic. Silverstone included all forms of electronic media in this system, examining them especially with respect to what they mean for the way people value close and distant others, and what motivates people to take action to alleviate suffering, to redress social injustice, and to promote equality. He argued that ICTs are 'doubly articulated' in the economy and in culture because of their status as objects and communication media. For this reason, the communication system needs to be studied not only as a very material object but also as symbolic message.[1] While there may be little disagreement about the importance of mediated communication among scholars and many of the stakeholders in the information society, there is a huge variety of views about its consequences and what, if anything, should be done about them.

The work of social scientists on the way the communication system mediates people's lives is based mainly on their studies of people's interactions from their positions 'in front of the screens' of computers, mobile phones, BlackBerrys, and iPads or their narratives about these interactions. Computer scientists and engineers, in contrast, are also informed by their work on what goes on 'behind' these screens. This research contributes to the prevailing social imaginaries of the information society, as does the work of science fiction writers. William Gibson, for example, introduced the term 'cyberspace' in the mid-1980s, in his science fiction tale, *Neuroromancer*. His vision was stimulated by his observations of young people playing video games and what he surmised they might be imagining about their virtual worlds. He comments that 'everyone I know who works with computers seems to develop a belief that there's some kind of actual space behind the screen, someplace you can't see but you know is there'.[2] The social imaginaries of the Internet surfer or the online game player are differentiated from those of the systems developer by the latter's understanding of what the surfer and games player can only speculate about.

In this chapter, I examine differences among the social imaginaries of the interactions 'in front of' and 'behind' the screen to illustrate how these contribute to the genesis of the paradoxes of information scarcity and complexity in the Internet Age. My purpose is not to suggest that the imaginaries of one group are more 'valid' than those of another in terms of their experience of the virtual world. The critical systems framework developed at the end of Chapter 4 emphasizes the importance of social imaginaries of the communication system punctuated from different vantage points. Different ways of imagining the mediated life of social scientists, computer scientists, and engineers are usually ignored because disciplinary approaches are segregated by their incommensurate epistemologies and methodologies. For example, the imaginaries of engineers are partly based on their understanding of hardware and software components which they are able to map in terms of their functionality and the way they can be organized to form a global view of a system. This is a way of seeing that then becomes familiar and supports meaning construction that can be translated into systems functionality in reassuring ways. The imaginaries of participation in front of the screen in mediated environments generally are not based on these ways of seeing and, in some ways, may be richer as a result. These perspectives are based on different levels of abstraction and they imply power relationships that can give rise to paradoxical outcomes.

These social imaginaries can be treated as metacommunications about the communication system. Their analysis can be punctuated, first by a consideration of those whose experience is mainly in front of the screen, and then by examining the views of those who are developing behind the screen technologies. In contrasting different views, the way the paradoxes of information scarcity and complexity are expressed in prevailing social imaginaries begins to emerge. On the one hand, the social imaginary of the Internet Age is about a new cultural form; one that embraces the economic, the political, and the social; one where innovation in the system is welcomed and explored creatively. On the other, there is a social imaginary where mastery of the communication system is associated with automating virtual relationships, for better or for worse, and for corporate, military, or political purposes.[3] In this case, an intelligent self-organizing system is sought as a solution to nearly all of society's problems. The features of the system from the user's perspective may be described as 'user customizable and *adaptable*', as 'supporting *collaborative* work', or as 'user-*sensitive* displays and features'—all of which are designations consistent with the values of adaptability and flexibility, collaboration, and sensitivity to human emotion. Nevertheless, these labels also signify an increasingly complex system behind the screen, the dynamics and implications of which generally are not part of the social imaginaries of everyday users.

The next section sets the scene for considering these developments in the communication system by highlighting some of the ways it is associated with the challenges of augmenting the human mind through increasingly sophisticated technologies that mediate our lives. I examine some of the social imaginaries revealed by research in the social sciences where 'in front of the screen' developments have been found to have implications for intimacy, identity, authenticity, and creativity; the boundaries between public and private; and what it means to be a participant in mediated everyday life. I then shift to an examination of the perspectives of those with the technical skills required to work 'behind the screen', especially on developments in software agent-based computing that enable, among other things, human interactions with the communication system. For some technologists, the Web is evolving to 'become a giant brain capable of analyzing data and extrapolating new ideas'.[4] One of the attractions of these developments is the capacity to interact with each other through virtual representations.

In some imaginaries of the future, we might be represented, by design or inadvertently, entirely by our avatars. By highlighting the different perspectives as metacommunications, that is, stories about these innovations, differences in what is being assumed about human choice and control over the mediated environment are brought to the fore as are insights into the differing interests of participants in the evolution of the communication system. The dreams of those who hope for a future in which digital technologies are employed to amplify the capacities of the human mind provide a good place to start this account.

Amplifying the Mind

The communication system is becoming more sophisticated in its capacity to process, store, and circulate digital information. There is little disagreement about this. Differences emerge when we enquire into what sophistication actually implies for the mediation of everyday life. The capacities of the system are due to innovations in hardware and software and their information processing capabilities, but it is the developments in software that are of concern in this chapter.[5] The visions (discussed in Chapters 2 and 3) of Paul Otlet and Vannevar Bush, among others, were central to dreams of augmenting human information processing capabilities, of using technologies to enhance human memory, to the ultimate, if contested, goal of devising a system that 'thinks'. In 'As We May Think', Bush described the memex as a machine that can augment human capacities for indexing information, leaving highly valued information trails that 'do not fade', and enhancing scientific memory. The goal of automating human intelligence was consistent with the prevailing social imaginary of a world in which 'man' could 'better review his shady past and analyze more completely and objectively his present problems', in the interests of building the good society.[6] Since Bush's time, developments in software programming and in the protocols for information distribution, such as the Internet, have provided the means for further advances in the automation of information processing.

Howard Rheingold, a keen observer of the information society, described the developments 'behind the screen' as life-affirming because of the way they enable people to interact with them. His hope is that they will reduce loneliness and foster a sense of belonging within the social fabric of society.[7] In his work, he depicts the technological innovations behind the screen as being consistent with a belief in computers as intelligent machines that eventually will be able to mimic our values and preferences, whatever they might be. His imaginary of the information society evokes a self-organizing ecology; a system in which there are nominal fragments of human control behind the screen, but which is beneficial for all those in front of the screen. His is an imaginary in which intelligent software agents are designed to evolve, avoid detection, and pursue all manner of purposes on our behalf.

In one variant of this imaginary, the arrival of the Singularity could see a merging of our biological existence with technology. For Vernor Vinge, the computer scientist and science fiction writer whose ideas were mentioned in Chapter 2, the system's evolution including an exponential increase in scientific output held the promise of artificial intelligence. He expected these developments to feed on one another, driving the potential for the Singularity to 'a point where our old models must be discarded and a new reality rules':[8] a point whose avoidance or confinement is beyond human control. In a tale of science fiction which Vinge refers to, neocytes are implanted with molecular memory and transmitted from generation to generation, embracing and then transcending the 'human' in all its manifestations.[9] Other writers favour a more techno-entrepreneurial approach that puts less emphasis on the progress of science and, like Ray Kurzweil, argue that, 'there will be no distinction, post-Singularity, between human and machine or between physical and virtual reality'.[10] In Kurzweil's view, the primary goal of innovation is to achieve sophisticated computerized pattern recognition and problem-solving capacity that eventually encompasses all human knowledge. For Vinge, however, the post-human era does not necessarily signal loss of knowledge, memory, or reflection even though humans pass from centre-stage. His vision, nevertheless, gives reason for concern about the trajectory of innovation in the communication system and whether there is a need for intervention.

In the early 1990s, Rheingold and others, with great optimism, were trumpeting the benefits of virtual life. They were convinced that the mediated experience of life in virtual communities would be beneficial, despite some worrying developments. A decade later, Rheingold began to see that 'we are changing what it means to be human',[11] and to question how these changes might be controlled so as not to invoke the Singularity, or at least, not accidentally. The mastery of technology in the face of technological innovation has been an ongoing concern for social scientists. How tenuous is our mastery of behind the screen communication system operations? If it is very weak, should we try to repair this by strengthening our understanding and making choices about possible directions for change?

For most people, developments in the field of software automation are very far removed from the experiences of everyday life. Nevertheless, we interact daily with software—online identities are asserting themselves increasingly, expressing *their* hopes and making *their* choices for our lives. These choices may relate to existential questions about the meaning of human life, or searches for fish and chip shops or euthanasia clinics—they involve both the trivial and the profound. The innovation process behind the screen is enabling engineers and computer scientists to launch agents into our world, only a very few of which we control. What began as creatures of our making is becoming a jungle of virtual creatures—some predatory, some parasitical, some cooperative, some competitive, and some feral. In the poem, *The Sorcerer's Apprentice*, the apprentice uses magic to accomplish his tasks, but it soon goes beyond his control. He needs the Sorcerer to put things right, suggesting a conservative return to the wisdom of seniority.[12] However, for those who favour instead an organic solution from below, the issue of control of the communication system must be a concern. One response is to see interventions to 'put things right' as manipulations from above which are both unsafe and authoritarian.

Another response is that more research is needed to enable us to develop a better understanding of these developments before we make decisions about possible action. Rheingold, for example, argues that 'the great lever is still *understanding*—if enough people can understand what is happening, I still believe that we can have an influence'.[13] Manuel Castells comments that these developments occur 'through a specific code of communication, which we must *understand* if we want to change our reality'.[14] Some seek this understanding in the way the immersive environments of the digital world can be said to be augmenting the human mind through the novel connections enabled by hypertext and new forms of electronic media, suggesting that each individual mind remains in control.[15] For most people, most of the time, however, our interactions with the communication system in front of the screen involve calling up information without understanding the values built into the operations that select and present it, or which bring it to our screens, invited or uninvited.

In the next section, I consider what social science research tells us about the social imaginaries of virtuality in everyday life in front of the screen life. This is followed by an examination of these imaginaries from the perspectives of those more familiar with behind the screen developments. In both cases, I treat the results of research in different disciplines as metacommunications that help us to understand different facets of the prevailing social imaginaries of the information society and the paradoxes of information scarcity and complexity. In Chapter 6, I punctuate analysis of the social imaginaries of the information society from the perspectives of the companies in the creative industry and then from the perspectives of the developers of the behind the screen technology platforms.

Virtuality in Everyday Life

Social science research on the experience of virtuality in everyday life often considers processes of identity formation and the way peoples' encounters in the online space created by digital services and social media platforms enable them to augment their participation in the 'real' world. Sherry Turkle writes that, 'computers, with their reactivity and interactivity, stand in a novel and evocative relationship between the living and the inanimate'.[16] It is not surprising that the ways that social scientists approach analysis of the electronic mediations of everyday life differ. In the administrative tradition, research on the way people incorporate virtual worlds into their everyday lives tends to be preoccupied with what Internet users do, how this is influenced by their social and cultural environment, and how online and offline practices become integrated. That is, it examines mainly instrumental concerns about *how* things happen and their *impacts*, while research in the critical tradition is more likely to focus on the meanings people attribute to their online participation and on the power relationships that are invoked.[17]

In both traditions, however, whether the topic is online experience of language development, identity construction, political debate, or religious affiliation, research results invariably find both benefits and risks associated with immersive virtual worlds. Researchers affiliated to these different research traditions tend to be partisan, notwithstanding claims to the contrary. Researchers working in the instrumental tradition report the empowering potential of virtual life and tend to discount the risks associated with online participation (although this is not always the case). Critical researchers, in contrast, are more likely to provide evidence of disempowerment, inequality, alienation, and exploitation although they also find evidence of an empowering potential of online participation to resist the imposition of power from above. They frequently emphasize one set of outcomes and de-emphasize the other. Although researchers in both traditions often focus on procedures to enable the virtual world to be incorporated into people's lives in ways that they value, attention to the power relationships which influence the way the virtual world is experienced is typical of the critical research tradition. The resources available for studies of the impact of life in front of the screen, in the instrumental tradition, are much larger than those available for critical analysis of the power relationships articulated in and outside virtual worlds (supporting cultural, social, business, or political life).

The generalizability of most studies of mediated life is limited by the propensity of researchers to focus on the most popular social media sites, such as the US-based Facebook or sites based in other regions where single providers of particular kinds of sites dominate the market. Also, research published in the English language (or translated into English) relies disproportionately on empirical studies involving online participants based in Europe or North America and, frequently, on questionnaire surveys involving university students acting as respondents, interviewees, or participants in ethnographic research. Cultural difference tends to be overlooked, there are few cross-cultural comparative studies, and the implications of online participation involving both commercial and non-commercial activities tend to be downplayed.[18]

Critical assessment of online interactions from the perspective of what they can tell us about the imaginaries of experience of mastery of the mediated environment is difficult because the main source of data is self-reporting by those engaged in virtual worlds.[19] When people are asked whether this engagement is consistent with well-being, they are invited to reflect on how they are spending their time. This leads to responses that are biased in various ways that are familiar to methodologists, but a positive regard for virtual participation is a frequent response.[20] Ethnographic research is better able to elicit critical reflection on virtual experiences, but this method is much less popular than empirical study of the impact of virtuality using surveys and various kinds of interviews. Nevertheless, social science research does provide insights into some aspects of the social imaginaries, especially concerning the way people accommodate or resist the mediations of everyday life, how they participate and work and how they try to control their mediated lives.

Thorstein Veblen's analysis in the nineteenth century of consumption patterns, mainly in the United States, led him to conclude that our 'habits of thought with respect to the expression of life in any given direction unavoidably affect the habitual view of what is good and right in life in other directions also'.[21] He insisted that people's economic interests were never distinct from their cultural, social, or political interests. The mobile phone is an example of a technology that has become emblematic as a symbol of power in the social imaginary of the information society. Umberto Eco emphasizes the symbolic power of the mobile phone in this way: 'So anyone who flaunts a portable phone as a symbol of power is... announcing to all and sundry his desperate, subaltern position, in which he is obliged to snap to attention, even when making love, if the CEO happens to telephone'.[22] The mobile phone is at the heart of efforts to commercialize virtual space. Of course, innovations in the technologies that support what Veblen calls conspicuous consumption are not new. However, the transformations in socio-cultural constructions of what it means to human beings to conduct their lives online are new. The social imaginary of the virtual that has emerged since Sherry Turkle's book, *The Second Self,* can be understood as a composite of the creative thinking and resourcefulness of human beings who imagine new forms of organization and online practices.[23] This construction is influenced by interactions among virtual communities in the 'real' world, and crossovers between the 'real' and the 'virtual', enabled by the organization of communities around social media platforms which include Facebook, YouTube, and Twitter, among many others.

Divisions within the social sciences persist in undermining our capacity to examine the relationships between the cultural and symbolic worlds and the economic or material aspects of life in the information society. The result is that with the exception of economics and some branches of management studies, most work in the social sciences provides few insights into the relationships between trends in the mediated environment that privilege commercial incentives and those related to social and cultural values. Here, I focus on what can be learned from studies of the socio-cultural experiences of mediation in everyday life in front of the screen.

MEDIATION OF EVERYDAY LIFE

Much instrumental research is devoted to tracking and explaining the diffusion or take-up of technologies that enable the mediation of everyday life.[24] This tradition largely ignores the different symbolic meanings associated with use of the Internet and social media platforms and provides no information about the power relations associated with this use. Its concern mainly is with how rapidly people are accommodating or adjusting to their mediated environments, an approach informed by the information processing model (discussed in Chapter 3). Technology and service diffusion patterns are evidenced by statistics on growth in the take-up of competing social networking sites. Much effort is devoted to measuring the number of 'friends' in online networks. For example, one study indicates that social networkers have an average of 195 'friends'; another shows that membership in social networks is growing at a linear rate; and yet another, that Facebook is enabling more than 25 billion exchanges of information monthly.[25] These sorts of results tell us something about patterns of use, scale of activity, and the centrality of individuals or communities in their networks,[26] but not about the qualities of relationships and whether they are experienced as empowering or disempowering.

The significant issue in these studies is how many online friends one has. There is a frequent assumption that social media participants are intent on maximizing their online networks, and these quantitative approaches are informed by an instrumental agenda. While they may be able to trace the diffusion of new technologies, the assumptions made about the social, psychological, and economic characteristics of 'laggards' and 'lead users' camouflage substantial differences within online populations. The demise of an online application may be explained by its failure to capture the popular imagination or by the idea that a particular application or technology is ahead of its time. But, this yields little insight into why a particular technology and its associated practices become incorporated into people's lives, or the variety of patterns of accommodation and resistance across cultures.

For economists, an eventually successful diffusion process indicates that an initially 'imperfect' design has been perfected through competition in the marketplace, becoming the dominant design. But this perspective does not probe the social imaginary of alternative technology choices that might prioritize different values. Cultural and social values shape how online participants relate to each other and whether they value small- over large-scale communities, for instance. Resistance to what the market offers is one strategy which may sustain the variety of alternatives available to people, but the result is not necessarily desirable. Resistance that leads to a greater variety of social media platforms or online services may lead to inefficiencies in production, and to exclusion, if the price of access becomes higher. From the perspective of the mediation of everyday life, the best outcome may be to wait, and to see what comes later, slowing the take-up of what the virtual world has to offer.

Application of the diffusion model leads to a neglect of the specific contexts for the production and use of virtual environments and ignores the fact that people are active producers and innovators—an observation common in the critical traditions of research in this area. Research in these traditions shows that social interaction, accessing the Internet via a networked computer or a mobile phone, is becoming pervasive, particularly among young people, and is being perceived increasingly as essential for the conduct of all aspects of life.[27] It shows that people of all ages generally are accommodating—and welcoming—the virtual world into their lives. Social networking platforms are mediating the lives of children and adults increasingly intensely, and people are employing their positions in front of the screen to enable multiple information-seeking and communication practices.

Research often measures people's perceptions of their social well-being based on concepts such as integration, acceptance, and actualization, as well as trust, security, and comfort. The use of such social media as Twitter appears, for example, to be encouraging new modes of conversation, new forms of collaboration and information sharing, fostering a sense of connectedness, and providing gratifications associated with social network surfing and the constant updating of online status. However, this work tells us little about the social and cultural values that are being privileged as the virtual world expands, or about the variety or diversity of information production and consumption being encouraged through the mediation of everyday life at numerous online sites. It also contributes little insight into the social imaginaries of the information society that are being privileged as the innovation process behind the screen runs its course.

PARTICIPATING IN MEDIATED VIRTUALITY

In the prevailing social imaginaries of the information society, finally free of the constraints of the mass media that allowed few opportunities to contribute, participants in online social media sites are envisaged as involved creatively in the production of a 'collaborative culture'. This is variously labelled 'mass creativity', 'prosumption', 'co-creation', and even 'produsage', all of which may be associated with some of the features of commons-based peer production (see Chapter 3), although these terms often invoke the value of private intellectual property ownership rather than the value of public domain information which is prominent in information sharing in the information commons.[28]

A P2P model of online interaction is seen as enabling the transparency of online interactions where decision-making power rests increasingly with the person in front of the screen. Several authors, including Don Tapscott in *Wikinomics* and Charles Leadbeater in *We-think*, celebrate the digital collective culture which the virtual mediation of everyday life seems to be fostering.[29] In this version of the social imaginary, social media are facilitating changes in the way people communicate, create, and share information, consistent with the values of cooperation, democracy, and inclusion. This view presumes that behind the screen developments in technology are consistent with these values, encouraging diversity and variety in the mediated communication environment. This view is influential in the metacommunications about transformations in relations of power in the virtual world and, implicitly, in the 'real' world when it is assumed that these favour the empowerment of citizens and consumers.

These social imaginaries of the information society are indicative of a one-dimensional view of power relations associated with these empowering transformations, but there are other perspectives which highlight the potential for disempowerment. Lev Manovich, for instance, argues that user-generated content is produced by participants who 'make their own cultural products that follow the templates established by the professionals and/or rely on professional content'.[30] He suggests that the social imaginary is being colonized by conventions that are designed into the behind the screen technology and that the disempowering implications for the mediation of everyday life are greater than in the mass media era, insofar as they constrain the creative imaginations of participants. Online interactions involve managed forms of activity that constrain the diversity of productive forms of online engagement, something often forgotten in the celebration of the creative potential of digital platforms. Whether these conventions are understood as the product of hegemonic ideology about how to turn virtual environments into spaces for the production and sale of cultural commodities or are understood broadly as the result of emergent social imaginaries which condition widely accepted practices, they become taken-for-granted ways of seeing the possibilities for creativity and experimentation in the information society.[31]

Conventions embedded in the design features of online spaces limit what can be achieved at the sites available to online participants. This is not to say that there is no space for creativity and initiative, such as when young girls invest their identities in their Barbie Dolls, or young boys do the same with their GI Joes or baseball trading cards. The vast majority of cultural expression may well be imitative and ritualitistic, with creativity as we ordinarily understand it being the province of the few. Nevertheless, the conventions built into the behind the screen software (and hardware) are influencing people's tastes and aesthetic values, similar to the conventions in the mass media era. This should not be forgotten in our analysis of information society imaginaries.

Wittgenstein observes that 'what we cannot think, we cannot think: we cannot therefore say what we cannot think'.[32] When the conventions constrain what people are able to think or imagine, they cannot realistically be understood as being empowered in the sense of being *fully* released from the constraints imposed by others in the virtual age. Instrumental accounts often overlook the fact that conventions reflect interests that differ from those of online participants, for instance, in ensuring that participants are put to work directly or indirectly in the service of generating revenue, or to assist in the surveillance of others with little or no transparency. What is downplayed in privileging the consumer and her or his empowerment are the constraints that accompany embodiment within virtual arrangements that are, at least partly or episodically, disempowering.

Comparatively little attention is given to the way that 'places, bodies and selves are unavoidably translated into the conventions of the medium'.[33] For instance, the activities of artists who use online spaces to facilitate the production of art works or to display their performances are constrained by online design features.[34] Research on the visions and practices of artists using online platforms, for example, virtual synchronous production spaces, indicates that few of them have the resources to go behind the screen, or to become mavericks able to challenge the values or conventions that constrain their practice.[35] The result is that the majority of participants in virtual life experience social media according to the conventions laid down by site owners.

Research on conventions of this kind provides us with a rather different vision of online participation compared to the social imaginary of collaborative and democratic online participation. Technological platforms are perceived differently depending on one's mastery and understanding of the conventions embedded in the technology, and one's position with respect to the authority of the state or corporate owners of online sites. In this social imaginary of the information society, everyone is a generator of content, yielding enormous diversity and variety for social, cultural, or political purposes. The potential for participation in social protest movements, political contests such as online deliberation or voting, or artistic creation, is regarded as unbounded.

If we take account of the conventions and constraints embedded in technology, and the variation in participants' skills and propensities to participate, however, a different vision emerges. This raises questions about how 'participatory' the mediation of everyday life really is, and about the experience of both empowerment and disempowerment. Motivations for contributing digital content vary and participants' levels of activity differ. For example, there are reports that only 0.5–1.5 per cent of users of Flickr, YouTube, and Wikipedia were making their own content contributions, based on worldwide estimates in 2007. In the United States, however, it is estimated that some 17 per cent of Americans had posted content in the form of text, feedback at websites or discussion on the Web and that more than half of teenagers who have gone online had created content for the Web by 2005.[36] However, the nature of participation is influenced also by the level and type of skills that teenagers and adults acquire. A relatively small proportion of online participants has the software programming skills to go beyond making basic contributions to content, for example, at sites such as Second Life, where only a small proportion of participants engages in 'modding' using the software tools provided by the site owner.[37] Similarly, collaborative platforms, hosted by the Facebook Developer Platform or Google's OpenSocial platform, report that a small fraction of users accounts for the majority of activity.[38] In addition, there is increasing evidence of what Cass Sunstein calls 'cyberbalkanization', where deliberation among like-minded people may lead not only to the reinforcement of certain views but also to more extreme perspectives.[39]

CROWDSOURCING AND LABOURING IN VIRTUAL SPACE

Research on crowdsourcing provides yet another view of the experience of mediated life.[40] Crowdsourcing refers to soliciting help with tasks from large communities of potential contributors. In the prevailing social imaginaries, online crowdsourcing, an increasingly popular business strategy, is understood to promote opportunities for participation, diversity, and choice. Participants in crowdsourcing are encouraged to contribute to certain websites and to undertake tasks for commercial and non-commercial organizations. This enables the organizations to tap into the creative potential of globally dispersed contributors. Examples include giffgaff, a mobile virtual network operator that invites customers to provide ideas, and Microsoft's Most Valuable Professionals which enables online participants to answer millions of questions annually.[41] In the prevailing social imaginary, these activities are said to be leading to the demise of hierarchical organizations, such that external and internal teams can work to make products and services 'for a better world'.[42]

Apart from the fact that participants at these sites generally have little idea about whether their contributions are valued, this perspective also omits critical assessment of the labour practices and power relationships established among the site owners, those who commission the online work, and the online participants. The social imaginary suggests that participation fosters the values of 'co-creation' and increases opportunities for employment, but the wages and working conditions of virtual workers are rarely examined. When they are, wages are often found to be low and working conditions poor.[43] This type of online contributing also includes voluntary unpaid work for various social organizations.[44] However, these voluntary opportunities do not negate the fact that participation is not always empowering in the Internet Age. The willingness of online participants to visit websites and to produce or consume content in larger or smaller quantities contributes to the social imaginary of the abundance and diversity of information resources.[45] Nevertheless, the development of these and other social media platforms is responsive to the interests of the consumer electronics industry which produces the tools for, and profits from, the 'work' of online participants.

CONTROLLING MEDIATED LIFE

Developments in software programming and in the interactive applications that can be accessed and modified at online sites are providing the means for enhanced automation of information processing. These developments have implications for perceptions of the boundaries between public and private life. Instrumental research is mainly concerned with the implications of automation for in front of the screen experience. Research focuses on facets of 'hyperpersonal' modes of communication,[46] some of which resemble the social imaginary of the 'post-human', and there is interest, for example, in changes in message composing time, editing behaviours, use of language and sentence complexity, and relational tone, as well as awareness of others.[47]

Much attention is given to how emotions are conveyed in online interactions, the depth of the emotion displayed online, and the interactional norms for 'good' behaviour. There are studies of changes in the patterns of who is communicated with, who is avoided, and the consequences for personal stress of being 'always there'.[48] Instrumental research, however, focuses primarily on individual attitudes and behaviours, and this filter level does not indicate changes in the norms governing collective behaviour or the way developments behind the screen in software capabilities are influencing choices about mediated interactions, especially with respect to personal privacy and exposure to risk.[49] This research tradition tends to enquire into whether social media participants are able to tailor their online experience (within the constraints of the platforms they can access) by selecting privacy features, or clicking on 'do not disturb' icons and learning to recognize phantom or other intrusions by spammers. However, while they may be intending to protect their interactions, people upload considerable amounts of personal information. This suggests that while they may claim to understand privacy issues, people do not behave as if they associate personal risk with the provision of such information.[50]

Research from a critical perspective draws attention, in contrast, to social media site owners' control over the boundary between public and private life. For example, owners of sites, such as Facebook, continuously work behind the screen to tweak their sites' privacy conditions to improve their automated systems, claiming this to be in the interests of users. However, if site participants are unhappy with the features available, they have little choice but to continue using a site to maintain connections with other users and they do not seem to leave sites, such as Facebook, with a major market share, even if they are unhappy.[51] In the prevailing social imaginary, responsibility for managing privacy rests with the user. The interests of social media site providers are imagined as being benign except when there is a flurry of media coverage about, for example, ostensibly 'bad behaviour' in the form of an automated system's 'accidental' collection of personal information.[52]

In the political realm, the social imaginary of mediated everyday life conveys a vision of openness and transparency in the public realm of the state, and of empowering participation for those who go online. Social media, including blogs, wikis, social networking sites, and microblogging platforms, are portrayed as means for enhancing government transparency, with accompanying expectations of lower levels of corruption, and new information resources that journalists and citizens can use to hold the state to account.

Virtual platforms that support alternative media, citizen journalism, or political protest movements clearly are empowering, for some users, some of the time.[53] Citizens are using digital platforms to monitor government activities, and 'open government' is acknowledged as important and is welcomed in the wealthy democracies at least,[54] so long as it does not infringe state interests in security or corporate interests in profit.

Critical research portrays a different vision of these developments and addresses such issues as the values informing both human activities and those embedded in the software systems that support online activity.[55] For example, the openness of government may be reduced if digital transparency is revealing too many of the state's 'secrets', as illustrated by the Wikileaks story. Also, online platforms enabling participants to build relationships and access information about government services may be used for malicious attacks against individuals and the state.[56] Finally, states can capitalize on the automated capabilities to respond with force to protest groups.[57] When the techniques of power and control remain hidden, except to those with sophisticated programming skills, it is impossible for people to know what values are embedded in the systems that are mediating their lives. They may be assumed to be values consistent with democracy and social justice until one is subjected to, or is disconnected from, them. If, as Sandra Braman observes, no-one knows who is storing and processing personal information and the stories released by the authorities are misleading or wrong,[58] the social imaginary of control and surveillance and its intrusions into everyday life are likely to gain little traction in the general population as something to be resisted.

CONTESTED IMAGINARIES OF LIFE ONLINE

In summary, these examples illustrate contested claims about the implications of the mediation of everyday life. Research in the social sciences offers us metacommunications mainly about changes in front of the screen, although there are some exceptions. Its main contribution is a better understanding of how online mediation is associated with creativity, and generosity towards others, enabled by an emerging culture of online sharing. I referred in Chapter 4 to Clay Shirky's argument that innovations in the Internet Age will fail if they are not valued by most citizens. He says also that decisions about the mediated environment rest with citizens, since this is the 'only group *who can legitimately decide* how they want to live'.[59] What is valued, however, depends on one's position in a system of power relationships in a society where the online world is only one, albeit an important, component of everyday life. The availability of social media allows social groups to enable their voices to be heard,[60] but there is also a need for procedures to ensure that the voices of those favouring an inclusive society are heard and acted upon. Shirky and others promote a decidedly one-sided view of empowerment that favours a social imaginary of a relatively conflict-free world enabled by progressive innovation in technology.

Sherry Turkle, in *Alone Together*, however, depicts the changes accompanying the experience of virtuality as a 'perfect storm'. Building on more than two decades of detailed analysis of the online experiences of children and adults, she concludes that being:

> overwhelmed, we have been drawn to connections that seem low risk and always at hand: Facebook friends, avatars, IRC chat partners. If convenience and control continue to be our priorities, we shall be tempted by sociable robots, where, like gamblers at their slot machines, we are promised excitement programmed in, just enough to keep us in the game.[61]

Her work yields a different social imaginary of the information society from that offered by Shirky. She suggests, for example, that most people have become so enmeshed in their virtual relations that they neglect others, that elders have not given young people sufficient understanding of empathy for the other, and that insufficient attention is being accorded to 'what is real'. Corrections may be possible, she says, but her work provides few hints about what form these might take.

The prevailing social imaginary of mediated life online is that 'we' are in control and that the virtual environment is a 'natural environment' that we can trust. The presumption, if there is any further consideration of this situation, is that people are aware of what is going on behind the screen or that they can place their trust in others.[62] In the vast majority of these accounts, there are no hints about how the paradoxes of information scarcity and complexity are working themselves out and influencing which experiences of the mediated online world are feasible and which are not. A feature common to experiences of mediated life is automated information processing operations. Some of these are examined next, emphasizing especially those with a bearing on issues related to mastery or control in the virtual world.

Automating Mediation of Everyday Life

The contemporary social imaginaries of the mediation of everyday life suggest that the development of the communication system is consistent with a better life—progress towards the good society, or at least one that is no worse than that of the present. This imaginary is deemed consistent with the goal of automating the communication system, building progressively on its 'self-organizing' potential and on the anticipation of 'machines of loving grace'. However attractive this evocation of machines, the vision is highly individualistic and ultimately may be more compatible with the centrality of individual identity construction and effort, rather than with collective endeavour.

Brautigan, who composed the 'machines of loving grace' poem, arguably was more concerned with people and their relationships. His corpus of work includes a story about a library that receives books, but never lends them out. Authors deposit their work in order for it to be curated or archived, but no one visits the library unless they have something to contribute.[63] The 'machines of loving grace' may be providing us with Internet spaces for creative endeavour that are more like museums than the common characterization of open spaces and virtual online communities as bazaars bustling with transactions—both social and economic.[64] The Internet has created opportunities for many people to self-publish—for an audience of one, themselves—although of course this is not the only purpose of online engagement: contributors to blogs or Facebook may have many objectives.[65] The point is that it cannot be assumed that there is always a correspondence between increased immersion in virtual worlds and the good society, that is, a society in which an appropriate balance between individual pursuits and cooperative and collective action is valued. The design of the Internet may enable us to keep a 'record of all the books we get day by day, week by week, month by month, year by year' to cite Brautigan.[66] But if no one finds them or reads them, the accumulation of knowledge, so often praised by the champions of automated communication systems, will be fruitless, except perhaps for its curators.

This imaginary is evocative of dreams of a computerized communication system that serves as a thinking tool or amplifier of the mind, for the resolution of complex problems in the scientific world, and to support individual human activity.[67] These dreams have always depended on advances in computer programming. In the late 1960s, Joseph Licklider and Robert Taylor presented this computing science vision as one in which people would be active participants, 'not merely passive' senders or receivers of information. In their vision, each person would have an 'OLIVER'—a computer programme residing inside the network which would act as a buffer against the world, bringing enormous benefits.[68] Computer scientists tend to think about mediation as the way negotiations by software agents facilitate transactions that are in line with 'good behaviour'.[69]

This vision of automated life is very consistent with the practices associated with online mediated life in the wealthier countries today. As a citizen of a wealthy country, I can sit in front of my computer terminal and arrange all the transactions required to conduct a satisfactory life. I can sell my labour, and gamble or speculate on my wages to produce more wealth; I can order material goods and procure many human services. Even meeting a prospective partner and marriage can be achieved exclusively through engagement within the virtual world.

Behind the screen automation is reshaping what we remember collectively—the injustices as well as the generous acts of others. Collective memory is now potentially life spanning—what one did and expressed as a young person can survive indefinitely due to the expansion of storage capacity, which allows a whole lifetime of human online communication to be captured, archived, and, potentially, retrieved. The control of intelligent software agents is not exclusive to the online participant. The agents being deployed and relied upon have multiple masters. In an environment that is accepting of these agents, there is a corollary that agents are designed to spy on and supervise, as well as to be subservient to, human beings. The implications of the automation of the communication system go beyond the goals of efficient information processing or new forms of sociability. Software agents become the mediators of our lives in place of human beings.

SOFTWARE AGENTS AS MEDIATORS

Software developers decide on the constraints imposed on the 'choices' of intelligent software agents. Developers engineer protocols that govern these agents, deciding which other agents they can interact with, and how and when. Once operational, a software agent may never encounter a human being, and its designers have no obligation to make their choices explicit, or at least not in a way that is accessible to non-specialists. Only a few of these agents have left the laboratory, but those that have are embedded in the digital applications and services that are encountered daily. These agents are programmed to adopt strategies for making choices. They need realistically to mimic the choices that a human being might be expected to make in a variety of different contexts. Some of these contexts are benign and the agent's choice would be to share the information available to it. Other situations may be risky or untrustworthy and the agent must respond in a way that is less transparent or less cooperative. In the social imaginary, it is these kinds of possibilities that are invoked by references to a system having 'a mind of its own'.[70] Once the agent is designed and implemented, the online participant has little or no control over the programmed choices.

In computer science, efforts to design sophisticated agents usually are presented as efforts to improve the analysis of unstructured information, without regard to social values. The intelligent agent may be designed to gather information, analyse it, and develop clusters based on information tags. For instance, an agent initially may monitor someone's online activity, but if the programming of the agent is sufficiently sophisticated, it will 'learn' how to classify this information to enable the task of information selection by *auto*-categorization.[71] From the online participant's point of view, choices about what to tag and how to organize information are being made behind the screen, and the values and implications for collective memory, for example, are not generally part of the engineering discourse. The highly valued outcome is software agents able to curate our digital photos, emails, and mementos, not to decide how long they should be retained, for example. The specific conventions are developed and employed in popular online sites, but are not imagined by most online participants.

Software agent-based tools of this kind have many beneficial, 'real' world applications, but little attention is given to the potential for their 'misbehaviour' in selecting or failing to select or process information. For example, socially valued developments include archives of photographs relating to HIV/AIDS that are constructed by agent-based searches and can be used for training and information. Disease control and prevention services have been enhanced by the support of software agents that collate vast quantities of information from social media sites.[72] These agents enable electronic commerce, including location-aware, mobile, and networked comparison-shopping, auction bidding, and contract negotiation, for example. However, these programmed agents are subject to a variety of malfunctions, and inappropriately evolving behaviour is not usually signalled to users. In addition, what may be a desirable choice in one context may not be so in another.

SOFTWARE AGENTS AND ONTOLOGIES

The development of intelligent software agents is underway in efforts to employ Semantic Web technology based on formal ontologies.[73] Ontologies involve decisions about meaning. Software developers aspire to create tools for the integration of heterogeneous data on the Web by making the semantics of data explicit using ontologies. Their metacommunications about these developments sometimes suggest the pursuit of 'manifest destiny' in response to the need to make sense of huge volumes of data which otherwise would simply generate noise.[74] Online participants are encouraged to trust in automated reasoning ontologies and there are many beneficial applications of this work in the scientific community and beyond. For instance, ontologies are being used in biomedical networks to analyse disease-causing genes and drug efficacy. They are used in neuroscience, in the study of human anatomy, and in earth and environmental sciences. They are also being developed to link digital content with the aim, for example, of creating 'data gardens' which could enable Web developers to use the information resources of broadcasters in creative ways (assuming some resolution of intellectual property rights issues).[75]

For most online participants, these developments are portrayed as neutral technical solutions that enable them to make sense of their virtual worlds. However, the ontologies of search engines and social media platforms are becoming masters of our mediated world, organizing and categorizing with less and less accountability. Trust is coming to be regarded as relating to the trustworthiness of the software 'system', not the human beings who design and manage it. The conventions of research in this area define trust as 'a belief an agent has that the other party will *do what it says it will* (being honest and reliable) or *reciprocate* (being reciprocal for the common good of both), given an *opportunity to defect* to get higher payoffs'.[76] Consistent with the idea of a self-organizing (metaphorically autopoietic) system, the aim is to design agents such that each develops 'beliefs', often premised upon optimism, about whether the other agents with which it interacts are honest and willing to reciprocate. Agents are said to 'reason' about the reciprocal reliability and honesty of others.

The theme of mastery of the online environment is prominent in the social imaginary of the virtual world, but some critics offer a different view. The schemas that are programmed are not neutral,[77] as there are many different ways of organizing information. Meanings may be contested, and information may be hierarchically ordered, paralleling constructions in the offline world, and unclear to the online participant. These developments are instrumental responses to data overload and confusion. Seen by some as a way of creating holistic knowledge in distributed knowledge communities,[78] they are considered by others to be segmenting communities into exclusive domains whose access is determined by a person's prior training, and knowledge about the choices employed to structure meaning. Automated systems organize information and are becoming the gate-keepers of information and interactions online which the 'average' user believes are 'reliable'.[79] Although there are countermovements aimed at developing bottom-up toolkits for knowledge systems,[80] these are much less pervasive than the developments discussed here which serve as technical mediations that are rendering the bases for human choice increasingly less discernible.

SOFTWARE AGENTS AND SURVEILLANCE

Transparent design of software agent-based systems is an issue because these systems also create opportunities for the control of information by those with malicious intent. Automation requires a micro-recording of what participants are doing online, and sophisticated systems purportedly can ascertain their users' cognitive and emotional states.[81] In the prevailing social imaginary it is presumed that more knowledge invariably is a positive contribution to individual and social welfare. However, the accumulation of facts about a person's search history or email and text communication patterns is only the beginning of the opportunities for analysing the metadata concerning our interactions in the virtual world as well as, increasingly, our movements in the 'real' world. The goal is to develop systems that can analyse keystroke anomalies, word choices, and activity patterns based on knowledge about gender, age, and whatever other personal characteristics can be gleaned in increasingly fine detail by deploying agents that can 'reason'.[82] Thus, surveillance of everyday life online is proliferating in tandem with the development of our 'thinking machines'.[83]

Software agents engage in surveillance to collect metadata in order to extract 'significance' from large amounts of information. The assumption in the prevailing social imaginary is that the origins of data can be traced and verified, but this assumes that both agent designers and the evolving (learning) agents have incentives to behave in trustworthy ways. However, information asymmetries are typical characteristics of commercial markets, and the need for deceit, forgery, or an effective competition strategy may run counter to idealized trusting behaviour. The demise of the *News of the World* in the United Kingdom, owned by Rupert Murdoch's News International, is indicative of how far journalists are alleged to have breached common conceptions of trusted professional production of news stories. The phone hackings that led to the newspaper's closure were possible because of the design of phone systems. The metaphor of trust in 'system to system' relationships is being promoted in research, but at a time when larger and larger mass data storage devices are being brought online, less attention is being given to intrusions into personal privacy and to surveillance.[84] Crime prevention gives rise to demands for identity authentication and strengthens incentives for investment in agents that can collect and analyse larger amounts of data. From an instrumental standpoint, it would be better for people to fail to separate their virtual identities and to conflate the boundaries between their public and private lives, which would make the work of 'agents' engaged in surveillance and data linking more straightforward. This incentive of course stands in stark opposition to the social imaginary of the creative, playful, online participant with multiple identities.

In the case of commercial surveillance (tracking), personalized interactions for transactions require trusting relationships, but there are few limits or bright lights signalling how far companies can breach the implicit trust given to them by customers, who generally have poor awareness of how their data will be used. Information is collected through the active participation of customers registering online, monitoring home pages, and tracking use by 'cookies'.[85] People leave traces in each moment of their mediated lives, and they often provide information in exchange for access, or to complete transactions, leaving open the potential for breaches of trust by the human or software agents receiving it. Cloud computing is being marketed as the latest advance in self-organizing, self-managed 'bioteams'. Clouds could liberate online participants from large commercial vendors, but, at the same time, people are being encouraged to entrust their content to the 'keeping' of the cloud service provider, with few guarantees with respect to the use that might be made of their data.[86]

'Spyware' and other techniques can be installed on personal computers or linked to the use of any Internet facility, exploiting underutilized computational and communication capacity to report to a remote processing site. Internet users do not have a good understanding of the security requirements for a trustworthy online environment.[87] Organized criminal gangs employ people to contact Internet users and offer to install anti-virus software; the software installed harvests credit card details and personal information that sustains these criminals' further efforts. These gangs may be based anywhere in the world,[88] extracting personal information sufficiently successfully to keep their efforts alive. There are an estimated 6.5 million 'botnets' that send spam messages that trick Internet users into providing information that can be used in unlawful ways. In instrumental research, these kinds of compromises of human agency result from the mastery of online mediation by non-human agents, and it is mastery that is the goal of successful software agent development.

In summary, these developments are fostering new relationships between 'virtual' and 'real' reality. Avatar identities presently are believed to be constructions bounded by the imaginations of the person who creates them and by the software designer-provided menu of features and attributes. In the prevailing social imaginary, it is assumed that there is a connection—no matter how tenuous—between a constructed online presence and a 'real' person and that it is the latter who governs the 'virtual' presence.[89] Of course, the 'real' is also the product of the interplay of appearances. Perspectival distortion, to use Slavoj Žižek's term, is always a feature of human experience. As he says,

today, we experience cyberspace as a new transparent artificial life-world whose icons simulate our everyday reality – and this new environment is by definition uncontrollable, it displays an opacity of its own, we never master it, we perceive it as a fragment of a larger universe; our proper attitude toward it is therefore not a programmatic mastery but a bricolage, improvising, finding our way through its impenetrable density.[90]

Software engineers and others with the relevant expertise, however, are making choices that are shielded from most online participants by their very complexity. Those choices may be consistent with the values of the good society or they may discriminate unjustly, exclude, or intrude in ways that are inconsistent with the values of a democratic society. Improvisation is one response, but it is a reactive one. It is consistent with the prevailing social imaginaries which counsel us to adapt to a complex technological system. The volumes of data that need to be searched to find information of interest to law enforcement agencies, to companies, and to other social groups are growing exponentially. But what software agents can and cannot do in terms of auditing information and tracing its origins is not widely debated, at least not as far as most Internet users are concerned.

Conclusion

Studies of the mediation of everyday life in the social sciences focus mainly on features of online participation in front of the screen in relation to such issues as creativity, identity formation, relationship maintenance, intimacy, privacy, and surveillance. When Internet and Web-based tools are used to support choices and decisions, from an instrumental perspective, these choices are assumed to be optimized and consistent with enhancing social welfare. This assumption is contested in critical research which is more likely to examine the implications of asymmetric power relations. However, there is remarkably little work in the social sciences on the implications of the way human agency is compromised by the software agents behind the screen that guide the choices available to online participants, or on the consequences of the pursuit of enhancements to automated information processing systems.

The prevailing social imaginaries of the mediation of everyday life suggest that an empowering communication system consistent with the values of the good society is emerging for users in front of the screen. There are clear benefits from the increasing complexity of automated communication systems. However, the social imaginary of information control in the service of human beings does not negate the potential for disempowerment. Celebrations of empowerment in front of the screen are visions of the information society that are partial, as are dystopian visions of the risks of surveillance and other potential harms. Research is characterized by partisanship with respect to the interests of stakeholders, whether technology developers, investors, or everyday or corporate users of the communication system. Virtual life is associated either with creativity and generosity *or* with loss of intimacy and control. People are depicted either as accommodating and even welcoming computer-mediated interactions, *or* as being hampered in their ability to discern the basis for the choices presented to them by automated systems.

Studies in the critical tradition are more likely to find that online relationships are experienced differently, depending on factors such as ethnicity, gender, socio-economic status, or location, for example. Critical studies also highlight online information processing conventions which are invisible to most online participants, and the ways in which the boundaries between public and private life are being conflated, with implications for the self-management of identities, for political empowerment, and for what 'participation' in society really means. Nick Couldry, a media sociologist in the United Kingdom, reminds us that, 'the apparently free space for new voices that these sites offer may be dominated by norms and strategies that replay, in performance mode, the values and logic of neoliberalism'.[91] Many online 'free spaces' also mirror anarcho-syndicalist views, such as those of the Free Software Foundation advocate, Richard Stallman, who argues that innovations in software agents are translating political discourses into automated virtual spaces, and not always for the good when the discourse is about the benefits of self-organizing markets.

In this chapter, I have explained why it is important to question the adequacy of the guarantors of the consistency of innovations in software and other aspects of the architecture of the communication system, with the values of the good society. If Sherry Turkle is correct that the outcome is mediation of life by 'sociable robots', this issue is crucial. If these robots are operating principally in the interests of information control, efficiency, and profit, then protections are needed against unwanted intrusions into ostensibly private virtual spaces. The construction of computerized intelligence of ever-greater complexity rarely is addressed in depth in the social sciences, which helps to sustain the paradox of complexity. The more our lives are mediated by technology, the more difficult it is to discern whether this outcome is favourable. The drive towards computerized intelligence, impedes access by online participants to—or at least masks—the values and motivations of those who are designing the system. When these developments are seen as the outcomes of a complex self-organizing system, the assumption often is that this is simply the result of an optimizing evolutionary (a 'natural selection' of the fittest) process. And whether adaptation to the system is seen as voluntary or enforced, adaptation becomes the most persistent 'habit of thought'.[92]

The social imaginaries of the engineers and computer scientists who design the behind the screen agents tend to be remote from those who might be able to influence the choices they are making on behalf of human beings, despite efforts to involve people in various user-centred design forums and programmes. Their remoteness from the users in front of the screen does not mean that their imaginaries necessarily differ in terms of what they value, but there is no basis for simply assuming that they are the same.[93] Furthermore, the persistence of the paradox of complexity is such that, in an effort to manage complexity, everyday users of the communication system are encouraged to trust software agents and adapt to their potentially intrusive role in their lives. At the same time, the very use of the agents that augment the human mind disempowers users by removing their volition over what is to be shared and revealed to others. The complexity of the system behind the screen is offered as an argument for non-intervention to address this paradox because of the unknown or detrimental consequences that might result. In the dominant social imaginary it is claimed that the evolution of the complex adaptive communication system is consistent with the goals of companies in generating profits from the production and sale of digital information. Therefore, at least some of the developments in software agent-based computing are biased in this respect—they certainly are not neutral. In the alternative social imaginary, it is assumed that some of these developments are guided by those who value an information commons—a different bias, but one which, nonetheless, is far from transparent to the user.

The paradox of information scarcity means that the development of software agents as mediators and information selectors, automated ontologies for managing information ('knowledge'), and the application of these amplifications of the mind for intrusion via surveillance are challenging the ability of companies to profit from digital information in traditional ways based on their control of information. This control is being weakened by the fact that software agents ultimately may not be fully responsive to their goals. These same developments are challenging the capacity of governments to control the production and circulation of information that is deemed harmful.

In the next chapter (Chapter 6), I examine more closely the social imaginaries of communication system developers and the imaginaries of the company stakeholders who are promoting investment in the technologies in front of and behind the screen.

6 Emergence and Communication Systems

Introduction

The dreams of scientists and the engineers of machines that can 'think', but are controlled by their users in front of the computer screens, are undergoing a transition to dreams of software agent-based machines that are able to 'think' and make 'choices' on behalf of human beings.[1] In the prevailing social imaginaries, this is the result of emergence. It is attributable to the self-organizing properties of a complex adaptive system. In Chapter 4, everyday users of the communication system and its ever-increasing variety of social networking platforms were shown to be linked to enhanced control over the mediated environment in front of the screen.

Online participants are being empowered by these developments to make choices about their lives in an enormous number of ways. They are becoming information creators, information sharers, and information consumers as they exploit the vast array of tools to personalize their environments and to construct online identities. However, the sense of mastery that people are acquiring for cultural, social, political, and economic purposes is being provided by the tools created by a new entrepreneurial class of knowledge workers whose work is conducted largely behind the screen. In addition, there is a conflict between the dominant social imaginary in which all these developments are spurred principally by incentives created in the commercial market and an alternative social imaginary where they are encouraged principally by the ethos of collaboration in an open information commons.

Many of these developments are extensions of behind the screen software or 'wetware' programming, that is, the possibilities of 'intelligent' software agent-based computing discussed in Chapter 5.[2] Information creators and online participants in social networks in front of the screen are constrained by pre-defined scripts and rules that govern their activities, whether these involve leisure activities or unpaid labour, developed by those working behind the screen. In the dominant social imaginary, these developments are welcomed as innovations that are consistent with efforts to augment the human mind and with the interests of companies in profiting from exponential increases in the capacities for producing and processing information. This is seen as consistent with the values of the good society because it enhances the prospects for economic growth through information and knowledge-related activities. Yet the complexity of 'thinking machines' in a complex adaptive system is such that interventions by policy makers or advocacy groups are believed to slow the progress towards the desirable features of the 'machines of loving grace'. In the alternative social imaginary, it is suggested that the direction of evolution in the communication system is favouring an open information commons, consistent with the values of democracy, equality, and social justice. Similarly, proponents of this view insist that the evolution of the communication system is compatible with the values of the good society and that intervention to guide the evolution of system will disturb the generative features of the new 'thinking machines'.

Neither of these social imaginaries takes into account the multi-level character of the communication system, which involves both hierarchical and heterarchical power relationships (see Chapter 4). They also ignore the agency of the actors that are seeking to secure their prospects in the information society. This chapter focuses on the agency of two main groups of stakeholders—the companies seeking to secure profits from the production of digital information in the face of the continuing evolution of a complex communication system, and the system developers who are guided by a commitment to the values of democracy and an open information commons. The aim of this chapter is to illustrate how the prevailing social imaginaries are complicit in a denial of the harmful outcomes, associated with the paradoxes of information scarcity and complexity. These paradoxes are presenting policy makers and advocacy groups with numerous problems, raising questions about whether they can or should seek to guide the evolutionary process to ensure that the communication system is responsive to the public interest. Two cases are discussed in this chapter, both of which dispel the mystique of autonomous, self-organizing systems, a mystique that is firmly embedded in the way people 'imagine their social existence' and 'how things go on between them and their fellows'.[3] The evolution of the communication system may be guided by its own 'needs' when we punctuate the dynamics of the evolutionary process from the perspective of systems theory (as discussed in Chapter 4), but these cases illustrate that this is a very partisan view which helps to camouflage the 'real' interests of stakeholders in the information society.

In the first case, I focus on the actions of the companies that confront the paradox of information scarcity in the Internet Age. The behind the screen technologies are enabling the automation of digital information systems, but these same developments are threatening the capacities of companies to maintain online environments in which digital information is perceived as being relatively scarce. In the face of this threat, notwithstanding claims about the dangers of intervening in a complex adaptive system, governments and large creative industry incumbents are adopting all manner of tactics in their efforts to 'regulate' information through their enforcement of intellectual property rights to enable companies to profit from the sale of information in the marketplace. Denial of the paradox of information scarcity means that both industry and government are complicit in retarding the economic growth of digital information and restricting the chances for the development of an equitable information society that will allow all those who choose to participate to enjoy the benefits of a mediated environment.

In the second case, I punctuate the analysis of the increasingly automated self-organizing complex adaptive system behind the screen, from the perspective of the developers who build components of the communication system. The aim in this case is to show how the values of openness and democracy in the construction of an open Internet-based platform, designed for use by researchers and small businesses, are confronted by the values of the marketplace. The innovation process involves multiple human interventions which 'direct' the evolution of the communication system through choices about practices and design conventions. The social imaginary of an autonomous, emergent, self-organizing system is a very partial view which serves to attract attention away from the implications of the paradox of complexity. Claims that the communication system is involved in its own autonomous self-organization, which renders any intervention—apart from instrumental curative policies—too risky to consider, neglect the fact that power is expressed in numerous ways by human actors through their agency in making choices about the design and operation of the communication system. The arguments about the risks of intervention and the benefits of non-intervention are symptoms of a false opposition. Both ways of seeing have some validity depending on how the analysis of the communication is punctuated. But the combination of commercial interests and an increasingly autonomous communication system is making it less feasible for human agents to direct the evolution of the system in a way that respects the autonomy of human agents and their right to make choices about how they navigate life in their mediated environment.

Controlling Digital Information

Agent-based software developments are offering many possibilities for people to control the production and distribution of digital information in terms of format, timing, and cost, including the option of nearly costless sharing of digital information within online communities. The challenging feature of these technological developments is that they are increasingly feasible without regard to whether or not they infringe intellectual property rights law. Companies in the creative industries are responding to these developments by seeking more effective means of restricting the circulation of digital information to enable them to retain the ability to extract economic value from the online 'publishing' of information, that is, by inducing scarcity.[4] Their efforts to do this are a reflection of a strategy that Paul A. David, economic historian of technical change, observes is 'shaped more by the economics of "publishing" than by the economics of "authorship" ',[5] that is, more by the economic interests of publishing companies than by the creator's interests in royalty payments. The economic value of publishing information in the marketplace is driving the dominant companies especially, to assert their information ownership rights under existing copyright legislation to enhance their control.

The creative industry companies want to restrain online participants from making illegal use of digital information because much of this use threatens their traditional revenue streams. The means of restraint are coming into direct conflict with the aspirations of those who are influenced by the social imaginary of 'free' information, and the interests of online community participants in the cultural and social value of information. This conflict is at the heart of the paradox of information scarcity because the aims of music publishers and other creative industry companies are consistent with the imaginary of the Internet as a marketplace, underpinned by the private ownership of intellectual property.

CONSTRUCTING INFORMATION OWNERSHIP RIGHTS

In the framework of intellectual property protection, copyright law aims to promote invention and authorship, and to safeguard the rights of creators and encourage the dissemination of ideas.[6] The goals of intellectual property rights legislation are to promote invention and authorship of new works, to encourage the dissemination of ideas and the disclosure of inventions, and to protect the rights of authors to receive income from their works.[7] Few would disagree with these goals. However, there are increasingly large numbers of online participants who either disagree with the manner in which these goals are being pursued in the information society or are unaware of the conflict between their ambitions to download and benefit from digital information and the purposes and protections available to authors and publishers provided by existing copyright law.

Copyright grants to the creators of particular types of work an exclusive right to control the making of copies and the broadcasting or other forms of distribution of that work to the public in order to benefit from the sale or rental of this property. Copyright is intended to balance society's interest in the disclosure and dissemination of ideas with the interests of authors in relation to compensation for their efforts. But as Paul A. David argues, 'the legal institutions of copyright as we know them are properly seen as consequences of "industrial policy" actions.'[8]

They are not indicative of a 'natural' balancing of the interests of individual information creators and information consumers.

Proponents of the right to exclusive information ownership take the statutory provisions of copyright legislation as the embodiment of 'natural law', rather than the legal resolution of conflicting interests among the beneficiaries of its enforcement and other members of society.[9] This is in line with the dominant social imaginary of the information society with its emphasis on market-led development. It is based on the rationale that digital information is a commodity whose ownership can and should be transferred under explicit contracts governing the buying and selling of information. The efforts of representatives of the creative industry companies to suppress copyright infringement are aimed at those who seek to benefit through what these companies regard as 'misappropriation' of protected information. These efforts often target online participants who 'misappropriate' information with no expectation of monetary gain from the activity and they spawn a cycle of innovation in technology behind that screen that enables further misappropriation. This is not in the interests of either the companies seeking to enforce copyright protection or many of the participants in virtual worlds.

Protection of copyright comes into conflict with the variety of purposes for which information is created, such as the expression and preservation of language, history, and culture, the promotion of voluntary associations within networks, and the exchange of useful knowledge. With some exceptions, the right of the information creator to legal protection is absolute in law. 'Fair use' or 'fair dealing' provisions that allow access to and reproduction of copyrighted information for education and scientific purposes are exceptions to this form of 'absolute' protection. These provisions are regarded by industry rights holders as concessions that should not be extended to create a significant alternative to their exclusive control over and interest in profiting from the sale of digital information.[10]

Innovations in digital technologies are making it increasingly easy for people to infringe copyright law. Although it is becoming more difficult to enforce the law in the face of these changes—and particularly with the spread of P2P methods of uploading and downloading digital information, copyright legislation is unlikely, in the short or medium term, to be rewritten to alter the present balancing of interests. This is because the creative industry companies continue to favour an approach that is predicated on private ownership of information.[11] This is despite evidence of the way their intransigence is making their existing business models increasingly unsustainable. In some jurisdictions, there are tentative moves to consider how greater emphasis should be given to the interests of non-rights holders, but in general, governments are upholding and seeking to enforce the existing 'balancing' of interests.[12]

Representatives of the creative industries argue that only by enforcing copyright legislation will incentives be created to promote innovation in the digital marketplace. Such is the power of the prevailing social imaginary that enforcement of existing law is seen by most legislators, and the majority of creative industry companies, as the optimal means of stemming declining industry revenues in lucrative markets for music, films, television programmes, and books. The global market for online digital music, for example, is increasing in value, but this has yet to compensate for the losses that the industry claims are due to copyright infringement using the capabilities of contemporary global networks.[13] The industry is demonstrating remarkable resistance to innovative responses to changes in the way online participants engage with digital information in their everyday lives. This is especially evident in the case of responses to the explosion of online P2P file-sharing during the first decade of the 2000s.

SUPPRESSING THE DYNAMICS OF INNOVATION

An increasingly popular means of accessing digital information of all kinds is P2P file-sharing which enables the uploading and downloading of digital content by anyone with an Internet connection.[14] Online participants are experimenting with the innovative features of online platforms that facilitate file-sharing. These practices are being reflected in changing social and cultural norms of moral behaviour online,[15] and these changes are influencing attitudes to the copyright regime and pitting the proponents of the dominant social imaginary of the information society against advocates of the alternative social imaginary associated with an open information commons. This imaginary embraces a commitment to the idea that creativity and altruistic behaviour are fostered best if people face minimal constraints on their ability to engage with digital information.[16]

In this conflict, it is important to distinguish among the interests of the champions of this alternative social imaginary as they by no means uniformly advocate the same solutions. Some would seek to enable the direct appropriation of copyrighted music without the threat of legal sanction; others seek to enable the use—or remix—of copyrighted recordings and other digital content as inputs into other creative works. For example, Lawrence Lessig, a US-based legal scholar, depicts creative online activity as a 'remix culture', and Henry Jenkins sees online experimentation as consistent with a 'collaborationist' culture.[17] This refers to the participatory culture of the Internet Age that we saw operating in Chapter 5 (and which was discussed in Chapter 3), where people are engaging with social media sites on the Internet in numerous creative ways. The voluntary and altruistic ethos that typifies these developments is associated with the notion of a 'free culture' and is giving rise to activism aimed at preserving an open information commons.

In most cases, supporters of a remix culture advocate a more expansive view of 'fair use' or 'fair dealing' provisions under the existing law, and argue for the possibility of reconciliation around the principles of *ex post* compensation. An example would be remixes becoming subject to a royalty if and when they generate revenue. The problem with this solution is that it directly contests the derivative use features of existing copyright law, and infringes the *droit d'auteur* principle, which is intended to assure authors that the integrity of their works will be respected. It may also lead to significant competition even if all parties are involved in producing digital content for profit. In the contested debates over the ways in which the paradox of information scarcity presents itself in an ever-changing technological environment, it is important not simply to elide the interests of participants in the remix culture with those who would prefer to collectivize creative endeavours, without ensuring some direct benefit to the individual creators.

In the alternative social imaginary, notwithstanding differences in the practices and legal regimes being advocated, efforts to suppress creative experimentation are regarded as antithetical to innovation.[18] Lessig says that copyright law is 'captured in a way that undermines some of its most important values and tradition: a tradition that supported innovation and creativity, has supported the new against the old, is now increasingly captured by the old to protect itself against the new'—all this in the wake of technological change.[19] Some efforts to redress what Lessig and others see as an inversion of the original intentions of intellectual property law have been made through the establishment of Creative Commons licences. Creative Commons licences enable creators to retain some part of their rights, about which they decide, while permitting digital content to be copied, distributed, edited, and built upon. This enables universal access and a rebalancing of the relationship with copyright law which requires permissions to be granted in advance for the use of digital information.[20]

For academics such as Yochai Benkler and Martha Nissenbaum, respectively legal scholar and philosopher, the expansion of commons-based peer production, where information is produced with the intention of its being shared on the Internet, indicates a shift in cultural norms. This shift, in their view, is sufficient to warrant a rethinking of the 'natural' balance between the interests of information creators, information owners, and information consumers.[21] The conflicts of interests among these groups are not new,[22] but the force of the collision between conflicting social imaginaries and their associated practices is becoming greater and more pervasive with the spread of the Internet.[23] Publishers regard their efforts to maintain control over digital information as consistent with a 'proper order' because their initiatives are providing profit incentives for both their artist clients and themselves, and are financing many of the costs of generating and promoting the content they publish. This same emphasis on control through copyright enforcement can be seen also, however, as a barrier to the growth of markets and the opportunities for citizens to engage in online activities. This results in negative outcomes in terms of both corporate profit and the benefits for, or welfare of, citizens based on access to digital information.[24]

There is increasing fluidity between 'paid for' and 'free' access (at the point of consumption) to digital information, reflecting industry and user practices that enable the sharing of digital content. Nevertheless, the campaigns mounted by creative industry companies aimed at suppressing currently illegal aspects of these practices, such as the downloading of copyright protected content for personal enjoyment, or non-commercial sharing, or for future monetary gain, are instructive. They illustrate the relatively slow pace at which the larger industrial players seem able to 'adjust' to the technological changes that are implicated in the genesis of the paradox of information scarcity in the Internet Age.

THE CAMPAIGN FOR DIGITAL INFORMATION CONTROL

The variety and intensity of efforts to enforce intellectual property rights on digital information are indicative of the strength of the dominant social imaginary which aligns market-based contractual transactions in information with the good society. These efforts include industry-led initiatives to enact legal measures that intrude increasingly in the everyday lives of online participants, regardless of their guilt or innocence with respect to infringement of existing copyright law.

The creative industry companies, backed by their trade associations, have campaigned in the United States to encourage legislation aimed at curtailing digital 'piracy' of all kinds and, specifically, infringing P2P file-sharing.[25] The first successful legal challenge was against Napster, which operated a free service from 1999 to 2001 to provide an index to sources of downloadable content (much of which was copyright infringing). This has been followed by a succession of efforts to tackle the biggest online sites facilitating illegal file-sharing, either by encouraging their host countries to bring law suits against them or, in the case of China, encouraging the government to suppress this activity.[26]

In the United States, the Recording Industry Association of America (RIAA) and the Motion Picture Association of America (MPAA) have filed thousands of lawsuits against people accused of downloading or uploading copyright-infringing digital content.[27] Cases against those charged with infringing activity continue to make their way through the courts, and a voluntary agreement among the largest Internet Service Providers (ISPs) is set to implement a copyright enforcement programme.[28] The agreement positions ISPs as gatekeepers acting on behalf of the rights holder companies, taking on the problem of infringing-downloading using P2P file-sharing, just as Internet users are moving to streaming services which make it more difficult for creative industry companies to detect infractions.

The International Federation for the Phonographic Industry (IFPI), the International Intellectual Property Alliance (IIPA), and other trade associations in the United States are promoting arrangements in other national jurisdictions that permit them to obtain the names of people accused of infringement. These associations are seeking legislation aimed at implementing a 'graduated response' or a 'three strikes' strategy with ISPs legally mandated to warn their customers that their activities have been monitored and show involvement in suspected infringing downloading. After a certain number of warnings, ISPs are being obligated (albeit in most jurisdictions, subject to the permission of the courts) to disclose the identities of customers suspected of copyright-infringing activity.[29] In some national jurisdictions, such as France, the intermediation of a court is being reduced to an administrative, partly automated, role, and ISPs are being required to suspend or terminate customer accounts on the basis of an accusation which might later prove to be unfounded.[30] Representatives of the creative industry acknowledge that 'there cannot be a one-size-fits-all approach to the problem',[31] but their commitment to implementing an information control regime in line with the dominant social imaginary of the information society is clear.

Similarly clear is the political commitment to the policy consequences of the dominant social imaginary. In the United Kingdom, for example, following a series of reports on the development of the information society, the Digital Economy Act was passed in 2010, providing for a graduated response strategy.[32] Some ISPs claimed that its implementation would harm their business reputations, incur unnecessary costs, and be a disproportionate response to the problems created by P2P file-sharing. Their resistance led to a judicial review of the legislation, but the Court found that the Act should be implemented.[33] The judge in this case concluded that it should be for parliament rather than the courts to decide the appropriate balancing of the interests of the creative industry companies and Internet users. Notwithstanding claims about the implications of changes in digital technologies and social norms, it was argued that 'existing copyright does strike a fair balance' between the respective interests of rights holders and those seeking access to digital content online. The judgement read as follows:

Parliament, through current copyright legislation, has already struck a balance between, on the one hand, the aim of providing incentives to actual and potential creators of audio-visual material, and, on the other, the potential welfare loss to those consumers who would, in the absence of copyright protection, enjoy such material either free of charge or at substantially reduced prices but who, as a result of copyright restrictions, are either deprived of the material or are required to pay higher prices for it. Existing copyright legislation may strike that balance in a way that is controversial or open to criticism. However, in my view, Parliament, when considering measures such as the contested provisions, which could be expected to enhance copyright protection, is entitled to proceed on the basis that existing copyright law *does strike a fair balance between the interests referred to.*[34]

The issues raised by these measures extend beyond rights to access and use the digital information circulating through the Internet. They encroach on the domain of personal privacy protection as ISPs are being authorized to monitor and report on their subscribers' online activity.[35] The ambitions of the creative industry companies normally are privileged, despite contests over the interests that should be accorded the greatest influence by policy makers. There is resistance to these measures, but opponents are not nearly as well-resourced as the creative industry associations and are forced to rely on data related to economic harm that are reported by these associations. Opponents have been ineffective at suppressing the political momentum to introduce new copyright enforcement legislation although they have argued that legislative moves towards stronger copyright enforcement are too harsh and do not respect democratic civil liberties.[36]

In the European Union (EU), for instance, the European Parliament's investigation of copyright enforcement in the light of European goals to foster innovation and competitiveness was summarized in a draft report that included the statement that 'criminalising consumers so as to combat digital piracy is not the right solution',[37] a statement that was subsequently removed from the final report. Among those contesting the imposition of a stronger copyright enforcement regime in Europe, the French activist group 'la Quadrature du Net' (QdN),[38] together with others, brought pressure on members of the European Parliament. The result was an 'Internet freedom' provision calling for a 'prior fair and impartial procedure' to be in place before law suits are brought against those suspected of illegal online file-sharing[39] and concerns have been expressed about the potential for suppression of illegal entertainment content in ways that do not respect the rights and freedoms of citizens.

CHILLING INTERNET USE

The consequences of legal measures aimed at enforcing legislation to reduce the rate of illegal downloading activity reach beyond charging and withdrawing Internet access from infringers, imposing financial penalties, or exacting prison sentences. For example, efforts to trace alleged copyright infringers may affect individuals who are not infringers, or have negative consequences for the organizations providing Internet access because of the threat of actions taken against alleged infringers. Household ISP customers may be notified about the behaviour of household members suspected of infringing acts or individuals who have accessed the Internet via WiFi or local area networks.[40] Schools, libraries, and other public organizations as well as businesses and users in the third sector (charities and other not-for-profit organizations) may need to track and 'log' individual users' Internet connections or disable the usual means of using the Internet in order to limit their liability under the new laws. Everyday users of the Internet may become confused about what constitutes legal and illegal use of the Internet based on conflicting claims in the media. All this might lead to reductions in Internet use—a chilling effect—that would reduce the potential benefits from online activity. These are just some of the possible consequences of the creative industries' graduated response strategy and legislation being introduced to implement it.

There is little evidence on how people will respond to the threats associated with this strategy,[41] but the champions of stronger enforcement undoubtedly will continue their campaign. There is a growing gap between legal and everyday life perspectives on what constitutes good online behaviour. The creative industry companies' campaigns give priority to the rights of the enterprise over those of individuals, encouraging surveillance behind the screen, and leave companies in a position of power over ordinary Internet users.[42] These measures involve ISPs approaching subscribers, who, in their turn, may need to approach other users of their Internet connections (family, friends, or strangers in the case of public access) to discuss their private actions. Encouraging such behaviour on the part of ISP subscribers involves them in the presumption of the wrongdoing of others.

This behaviour can be seen as a form of surveillance by individual or institutional ISP subscribers that is out of step with norms of good behaviour with respect to the privacy of online activities and inconsistent with developing a culture of cooperation and online information sharing. Research on risk perception and trusting behaviour indicates that people's perceptions of a change in the level of risk associated with their activity often are disproportionate to the incidence of the risk. Perceptions of heightened risk may be intensified by media treatments of the issue of online copyright infringement and rumours circulated within online communities. Loss of trust in a formerly trusted entity such as an ISP is difficult to regain.[43]

The chilling effect is potentially strengthened each time the creative industry companies take another step towards curtailing online infringement of copyright law. However, at the same time, new websites spring up providing information about what to do in the case of receipt of an infringement notification. New infringing technologies and websites take over as fast as others are shut down. Information is provided about how to find infringing content such as music and to use direct downloading technology, streaming music and video, and anonymous virtual private networks, making it extremely difficult for authorities to enforce legislation aimed at suppressing these online behaviours that are increasingly common especially among younger Internet users.

CONTRADICTORY INDUSTRY STRATEGIES

All these developments are indicative of the contradictory strategies being adopted by governments and promoted by the creative industries, and they are symptoms of the paradox of information scarcity. While for some groups the open sharing of information is consistent with their interests, for others it is not. The interests of some groups in copyright enforcement are coming into conflict with the interests of those seeking a shift in the balance of copyright protection in favour of others who seek to access and share digital information outside the market system. Internet users are far from homogeneous. Thus, while some social movement organizations lobby for an open information commons and against measures that unduly penalize copyright infringing online participants or which might reduce content diversity,[44] other Internet users have reason to welcome efforts to enforce the protections afforded by intellectual property legislation.

Online users, for example, are becoming increasingly interested in protecting their rights to the virtual objects they create in the virtual worlds of online games, especially if there is the prospect that their virtual money might be exchanged for 'real' money. In the online gaming world, virtual markets are beginning to mimic conventional offline markets.[45] For players of 'gold farming', a popular multiplayer online game, for instance, 'resources are scarce, not abundant; the number of ore veins and bosses is not infinite, and they are rivalrous: whoever gets them denies others. Indeed, gold farming overall exists only because it combines virtual-world scarcity of currency and items with real-world scarcity and unequal distribution of time and money'.[46] The monetization of virtual currencies, combined with the interests of game players in the wage labour provided by players who 'prospect' on behalf of other players, is creating new sites of struggle over ownership rights to digital information.

A further complication is that some creative industry companies are allowing people to copy online information. In some instances, the same companies that are seeking stronger copyright enforcement are also experimenting with business models that will generate profits in a way that does not dampen the enthusiasm of Internet users by making it difficult for them to download and share information. The result is increasing differentiation among information products and the first hints of the novel ways in which creative industry companies can accommodate the changing technological environment. Digital content at some online sites is serving as the advertising content that is used to attract online participants to support services that aggregate, filter, and integrate information, and which generate revenues from those services rather than from access to the content itself. Thus, some companies are acknowledging that market sustainability requires changes that take account of the emerging social norms of online participation (such as P2P file-sharing) and the ways that people prefer to consume digital content.

Apple's launch of its iTunes Music Store in 2003 is a classic illustration of these changes in strategy. Following the launch of iTunes, Apple's sales rose to 70 per cent of the level of infringing downloads by users of Apple MACs. Although initially confining downloading to iTunes subscribers, Apple iTunes soon started offering online music without copy protection. Apple is expected to start offering users the capacity to store their entire music libraries online in the 'cloud' (the global network of Internet servers with immense and growing storage and processing capacity). This service will be provided for a relatively modest annual fee and is not expected to be conditional on whether music is purchased from iTunes or acquired by other means.[47] The new functionalities and services being offered through the packages available with the paid services being offered by other companies include improved reliability, measures to reduce security problems, faster access, extra features such as celebrity playlists, exclusive music tracks, album art, gift certificates, allowances, and audio streaming capabilities.

In addition, some of the creative industry companies are negotiating revenue-sharing arrangements with online communities who want access to their content. Spotify, for instance, has introduced copyright licensing arrangements that allow music to be available online. Activity in the subscription-based and 'free at the point of consumption' markets indicates that there is potential for growth in the variety and scale of these kinds of services. The increasing availability of material where the copyright owner, through various means, has included a Creative Commons licence, indicates that those who copy may not be required to pay in the future and that the industry is belatedly adjusting to what users are coming to understand as good behaviour. In some cases, the industry itself is using P2P file-sharing technologies, such as BitTorrent, to enable access to content as well as other means of downloading. Governments, too, are making use of this technology.[48] These changes are leading to the enhanced attractiveness of the legal offerings provided by companies in the creative industries and to new ways of managing markets in the face of the paradox of information scarcity.

The abundance of digital information, and easier reproduction resulting from innovations in ICTs, raise difficult questions about how creators should be recompensed for their efforts. The present means of achieving monetary reward is to ensure that access to creations is limited. A price is set that is in excess of the reproduction cost, creating an incentive to reimburse creators, but this requires some means of rendering the information creations scarce. Some advocates of a 'free' culture seem to ignore the issue of how creators should make a living. Denying them revenue is inconsistent with equitable treatment. However, when digital information is restricted by a pricing regime that excludes potential creators, the opportunities for innovation and creative production are restricted, and this suppresses the benefits to society.

In addition to their efforts to develop new business strategies and to enforce copyright legislation, companies in the creative industries promote education campaigns to promulgate values consistent with the private ownership of information which then becomes subject to long periods of monopoly control. When education campaigns promoting the value of private ownership are included in digital literacy initiatives, rights holders deem them to be fully justified means of policy intervention.[49] However, when education campaigns recommend alternatives such as Creative Commons licences or downloading copyrighted information for private use, the industry accuses those associated with such campaigns of promoting illegal behaviour.

In summary, as James Boyle, a legal expert in the intellectual property rights field, argues 'an author-centered system has multiple blindnesses'.[50] It has proven very resistant to change because the dominant companies in the creative industries have a huge stake in maintaining the existing copyright regime. Smaller, independent content creators are proposing various means of breaking the pattern of dominance of the large rights holder companies in the digital content industries. The Canadian Songwriters Association, for example, has proposed a small monthly Internet usage fee to provide Canadian consumers with a licence to download unlimited numbers of songs. In this proposal, song writers would receive payment, but the major record label companies would not. Not surprisingly, this proposal generated a new round of protest from the corporate rights holders.[51]

GLOBAL IMPLICATIONS FOR KNOWLEDGE

The implications of the paradox of information scarcity are replicated at the global level where international agreements in trade in information are a persistent feature even in the face of an increasingly ubiquitous information-sharing environment. Economists conflate the terms 'information' and 'knowledge' for the reasons explained in Chapter 3. Analysis of the respective interests of producers and consumers of digital information in the information society as they respond to the paradox of information scarcity usually suggests that there is a contest over the balance between their interests. This interpretation is promoted typically without regard to the location of these information producers and consumers. Disputes are conducted in the light of claims about industry losses and contested estimates of revenues that cannot be verified independently. It is not just the economic value of information that is at stake, however. The social value and meaning of information are also important in assisting people in making choices about how to live their lives.

The enforcement of intellectual property rights, therefore, has implications for the diversity of information and for whether that diversity is consistent with cultural priorities in the virtual (and the 'real') world.

The successes of the creative industry campaigns at the national level have been replicated regionally and internationally. The regions that have introduced copyright enforcement legislation in recent years include the EU through directives on harmonizing copyright and related rights in the information society and on intellectual property rights enforcement. Discussion continues about how to ensure a legislative regime that promotes innovation and boosts creativity in the European marketplace.[52] In addition, a new Anti-Counterfeiting Trade Agreement (ACTA) has been negotiated among national governments.[53] Complementing national initiatives to suppress the growth of infringing P2P file-sharing, the ACTA agreement provides for national authorities,

to order an online service provider to disclose expeditiously to a right holder information sufficient to identify a subscriber whose account was allegedly used for infringement, where that right holder has filed a *legally sufficient claim* of infringement of trademark rights or copyrights or related rights and where such information is being sought for the purpose of protecting or enforcing the right holder's trademark rights or copyright or related rights.[54]

The successful negotiation of ACTA is indicative of the persuasiveness of the creative industry companies' arguments and their insistence on the need for measures to control digital information to protect their interests. ACTA implicates ISPs in monitoring the online activities of their customers and reporting the results on the basis of a 'sufficient claim', leaving considerable scope for interpretation of 'sufficient'. The companies backing ACTA include Google, e-Bay, Dell, News Corporation, Sony Pictures, Time Warner, and Verizon, that is, large companies with an interest in maintaining the relative scarcity of digital information in order to benefit from its exchange in the marketplace. These initiatives are resulting in somewhat different approaches when they are implemented. The differences relate to variations in the permitted technical methods of filtering and blocking, the willingness of creative industry associations to bring charges against individuals, and differences in claims about whether a decrease in file-sharing traffic is likely to follow the implementation of new legal measures. The evidence required by the courts to convict offenders also varies across countries, as do the punishments for those found guilty. There are differences, too, in whether file-sharing of copyrighted content is allowed for non-commercial purposes. Overall, however, the main trend is to employ legislation to ensure that copyright law is respected by Internet users.

Intellectual property rights enforcement, consistent with the prevailing social imaginary of private information ownership, is invoked on behalf of those seeking to protect indigenous or local knowledge in the poor countries of the world. To stem the exploitation of such knowledge by the world's dominant enterprises in the creative industry, these countries are being recruited to the principles of private ownership in an effort to support their local control of this intellectual property. For example, the Bollywood Internet Anti-Piracy Alliance supports the interests of film-producing companies in India, frequently in alliance with the MPAA. This serves the interests of enterprises (and individual creators) in poor countries that are seeking to benefit economically from their indigenous information resources. It is not surprising that efforts are being made to enlist intellectual property owners in lower income countries, given the premise that they have something to gain. However, in these countries the capacities (both technological and political) of individuals to resist enforcement measures may be less well developed and there is a possibility that enforcement actions will be even more severe than thus far in the wealthy countries.

The global contest over the enforcement of intellectual property rights serves to veil the self-interest of companies in the wealthy countries that are seeking to extend and deepen their markets. This is illustrated by debates sponsored by the World Intellectual Property Organization (WIPO), the United Nations agency charged with promoting the effective use and protection of intellectual property worldwide. WIPO is committed to the view that 'development depends on the existence of reliable institutions within which human beings think, interact and carry on business, and that one of the essential elements supporting such institutions is property rights'.[55] Private ownership of information is seen as central to unlocking human potential through access to knowledge.

Within WIPO, the Roundtable on Intellectual Property and Indigenous Peoples provides a forum for debate on the way the global intellectual property regime is influencing access to digital information by developing countries, and the possibilities available to them to protect their indigenous knowledge bases.[56] The intention is that debates should be community-led and benefit-sharing, respecting the interests and value systems identified by the participating countries themselves.[57] This might suggest that measures to foster information diversity would be high on the agenda. However, efforts in this forum to accelerate the move towards internationally agreed instruments for strengthened intellectual property enforcement have been slowed by the diverse views of those involved. Failure to reach agreement in this forum provides an impetus for negotiation of potentially stronger agreements, such as the ACTA (discussed above), which involved only a subset of WIPO member countries. If and when countries sign up to it, it will provide a means of circumventing the United Nations agency.

At its first Roundtable meeting, the existing Agreement on Trade-Related Aspects of Intellectual Property Rights (TRIPS)[58] was depicted as offering 'an opportunity to use intellectual property protection to accelerate economic, social, and cultural development, as well as to increase awareness of intellectual property as a key natural resource in developing nations'.[59] TRIPS was described as encompassing 'the protection of traditional knowledge and indigenous technology and folklore as they relate to the development needs of the LDCs'.[60] Its meetings have focused mainly on the development of technical standards to provide protection for intellectual property, however, not on whether the balance struck among the conflicting parties with interests in the economic value of digital information by TRIPS is appropriate in the wake of social and technological innovation. Other United Nations agencies such as the United Nations Educational, Scientific and Cultural Organization (UNESCO) have been more actively involved in calling for consideration of people's interests in access to information as a freedom and right that should be valued, although it too affirms the importance of intellectual property rights protection for sustaining cultural production.[61]

In summary, some individuals, public institutions, and companies uphold the traditions of private ownership of information and market exchange as optimal to foster economic growth and human development. Others are actively promoting an information commons in which rights to benefit from the creation of digital information are established in a way that is deemed to fairly compensate creators while also respecting rights of access. The scarcity of information, a fundamental requirement for the traditional publishing industry, is being threatened by innovations in the communication system both behind the screen and by changing social and cultural norms in front of the screen. In the light of these changes, alternatives are being considered, and in some cases introduced. This is broadening the range of possibilities for producing and accessing digital information, both 'paid for' and 'free'. However, there is little sign of awareness in policy debates that this is a symptom of the paradox of information scarcity or that the numerous interventions in the marketplace by governments and the creative industry advocates of copyright enforcement are, in fact, interventions in a complex system.

With each move towards greater abundance of digital information, there are countermoves to impose the condition of scarcity through copyright protection. In addition, there are developments behind the screen which promote the further evolution of 'machines of loving grace', encouraged by the social imaginary of the information commons. As we will see in the next section, some of these also are in conflict with the dominant social imaginary of a market-led information society. In this case, the complexity of the communication system is invoked in a bid to secure a space for the emergence of a self-organizing system consistent with the values of the open commons. However, despite claims about the complexity of a self-organizing system, moves to secure this space cannot avoid coming into contact with the values of the dominant social imaginary where the network infrastructure developments and the interests of companies in the commercial world prevail.

Democratizing an Online Digital Platform

The convergence of ICTs has made it feasible to develop many new kinds of digital platforms that are accessible using the Internet and Web-based technologies. A digital platform can be defined broadly as a technical means of accessing a set of distant, interactive, or non-interactive services. These may be broadcast or provided online, and available for a price or for free.[62] These platforms are being developed by companies to support their strategies related to all kinds of electronic commerce and to support the work of many research communities. Most platforms, especially those provided by companies in the entertainment industry, network operators, and online aggregators of services for particular research and business sectors, are based on proprietary systems, aimed at 'locking in' those who access them, thereby generating potential revenue for their owners. The aim is to construct, by whatever means, an information environment in which information is rendered scarce from the point of view of those who have a potential use for it.

These platforms serve as intermediaries providing, for example, information exchange and communication between customers and suppliers, enhanced brand recognition, and direct sales of material products (automobiles, clothing, horticultural products, etc.) or immaterial goods (digital content, insurance, holiday, construction, transport, retail, or other services). For researchers, they provide a growing variety of data processing and storage tools, organized centrally as in developments in cloud computing, or on a decentralized basis. Insofar as they require a fee, they are more attractive to large than to small companies and research organizations. In Europe, smaller companies and research institutions lag in the adoption of digital technologies and platforms that might be expected to enhance their work.[63] Open Source Software (OSS) combined with open, distributed network architectures and platforms are providing alternatives to the available proprietary platforms in an attempt to open up and democratize the market. All of these developments involve the activities of 'knowledge workers' behind the screen.

The discussion in this section focuses on the development of an open digital platform undertaken by a collaborating community of developers (mainly university researchers) specifically for small- and medium-sized businesses and for the research community. It was funded as part of a European Commission digital business ecosystem research initiative.[64] I examine the extent to which the development of this platform and the arguments employed by the developers were able to shape the initiative in line with the values of openness and democracy. I consider how the values of the market compared to those typical of open collaborating research communities became important considerations, and—notwithstanding the extensive use of language referring to complex self-organizing systems—how the decisions that guided this initiative illustrate responses where the implications of the paradoxes of information scarcity and complexity were not acknowledged.

In the course of its development, the platform developers experienced pressure to conform to the values of the competitive marketplace, despite their efforts to design system components aligned with non-market values. Initially, the behind the screen technological components of the platform were discussed using the metaphor of a self-organizing system, but, far from being a system that was responsive 'to its own needs',[65] the system was modified to meet the requirements of communities with conflicting interests. There were differences among the participating research teams in the extent to which perceptions of the development process were consistent with a complex adaptive systems view. The projects were described in this way partly in response to the political project of bidding successfully to the European Commission for funding. At the time, those responsible for the potential line of funding were strongly influenced by the prevailing social imaginary of generative self-organizing systems and their assumed compatibility with the values of the good society.

The choice of an OSS digital platform was driven partly by political momentum in the EU aimed at countering the stronger presence of foreign (mainly American) providers of proprietary digital platforms compared to European-owned companies. It was driven also by the developers' commitment to challenge the intellectual property rights protection discussed in the preceding section. These protections were granting corporate rights holders control of most of the digital platforms on the market in Europe. In line with the social imaginary of the information commons, the developers sought to emphasize information sharing and skills pooling, and to tackle contractual and technological lock in to proprietary systems. This approach was believed to offer a means of reducing online transaction costs for smaller firms (including contract opt out penalties) and creating incentives for collective ownership and sharing of an important component of the digital infrastructure which would support the conduct of business and research.[66]

DIGITAL BUSINESS ECOSYSTEM ASPIRATIONS

The digital business ecosystem projects were undertaken by an interdisciplinary research team that included computer and social scientists, and representatives from public research institutes and universities, mainly in the EU, several large companies representing industry interests, as well as small- and medium-sized enterprises, participating as users of the platform. They were described as aiming to build the foundations for a self-sustaining, self-governing 'digital business ecosystem'. Initially, this ecosystem was envisaged as being 'able to evolve into distributed cognitive systems, engineered to embed mechanisms of evolution and adaptation to local needs and cultures'.[67] In contrast to collaborating OSS communities, which generally work on a project basis and have governance arrangements for negotiating the conflicting requirements of the gift and the commercial economies, the developers found they were having to cultivate norms and practices to foster the values of openness and reciprocity.[68] They were required to do this in an environment in which they needed also to respect the values of limited access and membership, privacy and confidentiality, intellectual property rights, contracting and trading (liability, fair trading, and competition), data and consumer protection, and legal jurisdictional issues.

They tried to separate development of the components of the open platform infrastructure from the service requirements of the competitive market in which the business users would be operating. Their logic was that these could be treated as separable components in a complex system,[69] despite the vision of a self-organizing ecosystem (even if only a metaphor) which would highlight the interdependence of the human actors and technology and their co-evolutionary roles in developing the digital platform.[70] The ambition was to develop the distributed coordination of transactions among Web services which, while not technologically incompatible with proprietary Web-based business services, required a means of enabling cooperation among different machines and the joint development and maintenance of the platform and languages used to run them. The goal was to create possibilities for collaboration among 'peer' institutions (e.g. research institutes), distribution of resources among communities of interested users (e.g. information about municipal services), and the formation of 'ecosystems' of related businesses (e.g. tourist sites in a particular region, or researchers working on a particular problem). The design concept emphasized individual agents exploiting Web services with local autonomy, using customized interfaces and means of accessing services. There was no incompatibility between relying on the distributed coordination of transactions between Web services in 'run time', in the technological infrastructure, and employing proprietary business models and private data for specific services involved in a complex business transaction for the services that would run on this infrastructure. For some, this suggested that this distinction could be maintained throughout the development process.

The developers were concerned with three types of openness—OSS, distributed coordination of the run-time of distributed software to support transactions, and open knowledge for the research community—each implying somewhat different strategies. As far as the transactions were concerned, it was decided that they would be based on P2P interactions rather than on a centralized provider, aggregator, or database.[71] The aim was to develop a platform for reusable and reconfigurable Internet-based services that would meet a variety of business needs requiring automated data exchange outside a company, and satisfy the information-related needs of researchers working in organizations such as universities. The P2P technology, Flypeer, was new, and the developers also wanted to employ a decentralized data storage system,[72] which, however, was only partly implemented due to technical challenges and the different requirements of the potential communities of users.[73]

In summary, the digital business ecosystem development initiative was conceived as being located at the interface of the gift and commercial economies, and as an opportunity to ensure that potentially different interests in the features of the system (e.g. its simplicity versus its complexity, and its open versus proprietary design features) could be resolved. It was positioned between two social imaginaries of the innovation process. The first was an 'associative' vision, in which people were understood to shape democratic arrangements for the development of the communication system. The second was akin to the social imaginary of an evolving, autopoietic or self-organizing system, in which the agency of the developers was assumed not to be a central feature. These features of the imaginary influenced the practices of the developers in a variety of ways and the vision was not fully accepted by all the participants. For instance, some of the developers did not believe that autopoiesis could be realized in practice, and the computer scientists were described as simply working with this social imaginary in order to obtain the financing to pursue their own methods and technical architecture.

Nevertheless, the overarching vision of the digital ecosystem initiative was of a complex system that would be aligned with the values of an open information commons.[74] For example, the new platform was expected to 'help raise awareness of the importance of and lifestyle benefits to be gained by, a more holistic way of living',[75] and the technical system was intended to be open, inclusive, and transparent for all its participants.[76] The decentralized, distributed, technical system was to be designed to incorporate the values of credibility, trust, and security important for business users, alongside the values of openness and transparency important for researchers. To achieve this, the idea of hierarchy was invoked as a means of understanding and, potentially, resolving the contradictions among these values, that is, between openness and decentralization and the need for organizational and technical closure, often achieved using proprietary design features. In line with this ambition, the initiative was described as a nested, hierarchical system where 'the ecosystem-oriented architecture fits inside a digital ecosystem, which fits within one or more cultural contexts, which fit in one or more geographical contexts. Similarly, the different epistemologies fit one inside the other like Russian dolls'.[77] Thus, while the configuration of a networked ecology also suggested the characteristics of the heterarchical networking phenomenon, these hierarchical features of relations within a network were much in evidence.

As the work progressed, the effacement of human agency, which is characteristic of the social imaginary of the systems view of a self-organizing system, even when used as a metaphor, proved extremely challenging. Work on one of the technical components illustrates the problem of reconciling the conflicting values. This was the Open Knowledge Space (OKS).

AN OPEN KNOWLEDGE SPACE

The idea of an OKS was to allow online communities to use collaborative digital tools to organize the production and dissemination of their information. The OKS Desktop was intended to be the access point to the community's knowledge and to include a wiki, files, an issue tracker, Web mail, a blog, and an online forum.[78] The approach was described as:

a process-oriented, community-driven option within a loose and dynamic organizational structure that is directly coupled to the community's governance process and is of greater relevance, value, scalability, and significance to members of the community, particularly those who have participated in its development. Naturally, the outcome of this democratic, collaborative and thus less structured approach is more difficult to predict and will also present some challenges in the visualization and representation of the knowledge, as well as in the mobilization of the community to participate.[79]

It was to be consistent with the values of commons-based peer production. The platform could serve as a host or intermediary for software, scientific outputs, or for business-related information, but its common feature was the use of a distributed network infrastructure and shared hardware and software resources.[80] While it proved possible to work out a 'common language' or sign system for components, such as images, buttons, icons, text, etc., the development of the underlying system of meaning with regard to consistency, integrity, and connections among signs proved to be more difficult and was not addressed despite being at the core of the digital ecosystem idea.[81]

The developers faced problems when the emphasis shifted to researchers as users of the OKS (business users were interested mainly in support for reliable complex Web services) and values became conflicting. There was a need, for example, for visualization tools that would enable the integration of data generated by the developers as part of the research community and by the business activities of small- and medium-sized enterprises. For example, a hotel using the platform might publish on it several different services, such as booking, availability search, or booking cancellation, and all these data need to be visualized, interoperable, and (some of them) retained, in a private domain, for commercial reasons. When the firms were approached, they indicated that they were interested in the support for Web services and had little real interest in the knowledge layer of the initiative. Consistent with the values of the marketplace and competition, a hotel's local needs, for example, would be for a system that would protect sensitive data and ensure anonymity of transactions to competing users of the system.[82] The developers believed that what was needed was 'a clear definition and representation about what the firm is, how it operates and how it can communicate and co-operate with other firms'.[83]

A clear definition was exactly what was lacking. The developers reverted to answers from conventional business models and a global data repository proved impossible to implement because business users needed data that were exploited mainly locally and only some made public. Data ownership issues, and the labour on the part of small user companies involved in resolving them, meant that not all the data could be accessible and there was no means of 'dictating' the use of a common taxonomy or language to agree the meanings of terms employed to specify tasks in different research areas. There was also no consortium-wide recognition of the utility of the tools that the OKS provided. The tools were 'empty' and some lay 'gathering dust'.[84] In addition, some requirements could be met by tools already available on the market. Regardless of the preferences of some developers for an emergent platform open to all and adhering to the democratic principles of data sharing and cooperation, it was necessary to address information ownership, privacy, and security.

It was not feasible to maintain a separation between the, apparently, distinct technological and the other components in this complex system. The social imaginary of a self-organizing system was called into question at the technical level as well. The reliance on the self-organizing properties of software was dependent on 'blue skies' research that had nothing to do with social science components and little to do with the approaches of the computer scientists.[85]

The important issue was how private sector companies would generate and capture economic value through their use of the open resources and capabilities provided by an online platform.[86] Although initially intrigued by the prospect of an OSS platform that would release smaller firms from dependence on proprietary platforms, some companies concluded that closed, proprietary platforms were more consistent with their competitive strategies and business needs. An uncomfortable mix of values and approaches became embedded in the digital ecosystem.

Despite a move towards a platform design supported by digital resources in an open environment, it was necessary to find ways to control information, to enhance its perceived scarcity in line with the interests of the companies. The

OKS developers valued the freedom to benefit from and to use and improve upon other people's ideas, but the businesses wanted to generate revenue from ownership of their accumulated intellectual property with respect to their transactions, by creating the means to ensure its scarcity. The 'self-organizing' digital ecosystem needed to conform to the demands of the participating enterprises or risk being abandoned in favour of the proprietary digital platforms already familiar to many of them.

It may also have been that the traditional proprietary tools were favoured because they were easier to use, more reliable, and already in mass use. It was claimed that the OSS distributed platform had no technical implications for the use of proprietary services running on the platform and no direct implications for the confidentiality and privacy of information or for intellectual property rights. However, a reading of some of the responses of user firms suggests that there was considerable slippage in the social imaginaries of what the digital ecosystem was about. The separation between the domains of business and research was not as clear cut as some of the participants imagined it might be.

IMAGINARIES OF SELF-ORGANIZATION, EMERGENCE, AND CONTROL

The emphasis on the social imaginary of self-organizing systems downplays the significant role of human agency. The people who were expected to become users of the digital platform would have needed to have, or be prepared to acquire, a considerable amount of knowledge about how to configure their access, to provide greater value than was already achievable using pre-defined 'menus' for accessing resources (information or services) or engaging in transactions (such as bookings, purchases, requests). In this respect, the development initiative was more akin to an experiment in 'engineering openness' in response to the need to re-invent the infrastructure for Web-based services that had become established on the market, than an instance of the self-organizing imaginary being put into practice. The P2P infrastructure was partly implemented and tested, and the participants in this digital business ecosystem subsequently set up a non-profit association to enable them to continue their research.[87] However, far from relying on the emergent self-organizing properties of the system to favour a new infrastructure platform, the developers intervened to manage the power relations associated with competition among the, mainly, small- and medium-sized enterprises intending to use the digital platform, and to respond to the requirements of the research community.

This experience was in stark contrast to the social imaginary of a 'digital environment that evolves naturally to support a sustainable economy, where interactions through e-commerce are an integral part of that economy. In a sense the e-infrastructure will become "invisible", or non-intrusive, with regard to the continued development of a sustainable economy that resides within that infrastructure'. In a fully distributed P2P design, there should be 'no dependencies on single organizations, as there is no central authority, and no critical points of failure'.[88] Although in practice the computer science partners did not expect the self-organizing behaviour of the system to achieve this, project partners found themselves writing and talking as if they did, partly in response to the expectations created at the outset of the initiative and the fact that the self-organizing systems model had seeped into the politics inside the European Commission.

The emphasis on the self-organizing features of the digital platform and the attempt to separate the developments in different levels of a complex communication system were fostered by the claim that a 'structural coupling' of the components of the system would somehow yield an environment that could meet the needs of all the human agents involved. This was to be achieved through advances in autonomic computing, that is, further advances in the behind the screen intelligent machine. It was imagined that with advances in interaction computing it would be feasible to specify environments that would generate software services in response to any internal or external stimuli in a constantly changing environment. This science-based aspect of the initiative did not command a large share of the overall budget, and some claims were directed to garnering support from the European Commission. Nevertheless, the use of the language of self-organization served to downplay fundamental conflicts in the interests of the stakeholders in this initiative.

It was acknowledged at times that if the strategy of relying on emergent self-organization should fail to yield the results in terms of an open, distributed platform, then recourse would have to be made to 'brute force' to achieve the goals of the initiative.[89] The turn to scientific theory, although apparently contained within its own domain from a funding point of view, contributed to a legend about the potential of the self-organizing properties of software, which then began to influence claims about the values and properties of the software. In the epistemology of scientific endeavour, ambitious claims for theoretical advance may be made that are neither verifiable nor falsifiable because the aim is theoretical. However, the scientific claims did not remain segregated in the minds of scientists, they started to inform the imaginaries of those concerned with the evolution of this particular component of the communication system.

It was claimed that the technical design of the platform would have no bearing on the potential users whose concerns would be with the economic costs incurred in the adoption and implementation of the new system. Further, even if the new open source technical infrastructure were to be available at lower cost, its failure to take off could be attributed to its incomplete implementation and consequent difficulties related to its use. However, some of the feedback from potential user companies and organizations indicated that, in making their choices, they did not isolate the technical from the non-technical dimensions. Research, commercial, and technical priorities became blended in reference to 'best practice'. For example, an alternative to eBay in which users negotiate with one another for the sale of artefacts rather than using an intermediary (eBay) might appear attractive because it avoids the costs associated with an intermediary. However, such a system requires acceptable substitutes for 'finding' items of interest in a distributed network of individuals offering items for sale, negotiating a commitment to purchase and delivery, and providing recourse in the case of non-delivery. It is relatively easy to describe such a system, but it is much more difficult to enlist a sufficient number of participant-users to make the system a credible alternative to the incumbent form of intermediation.

CREDIBLE ALTERNATIVES AND GOALS

For the developers of the platform, the dominant social imaginary was of a process-oriented, community-driven development consistent with commons-based peer production principles of collaboration. The initiative was intended to be democratic and emergent. In practice, the developers relied on best guesses about user requirements and a high-level technological architecture that was opaque to users. There were attempts to develop a common language in which terms, meanings, and relationships in the development process would become clear, but there was ongoing confusion about the meanings of terms and the values being privileged, as exemplified by the OKS development.[90]

One of the aspirations for the initiative was that control of the network supporting the new platform should be distributed to enhance its transparent and open structure. The P2P Flypeer infrastructure that was developed did respect the local autonomy of participants. The Flypeer platform was partly implemented to support Web-services, but it proved problematic as a platform for porting existing services or developing new ones. The infrastructure enabled companies and researchers to share information should they wish to. However, the influence of the social imaginary of the benefits of open collaboration meant that the resulting system challenged the dominant social imaginary of protecting information, that is, securing its relative scarcity. This was dismissed as a non-technical issue and separated as far as possible from design considerations. Some aspects of the conflict of interests in an open versus a proprietary platform were addressed, but the user companies' evaluation of the prototype suggested that their expectations had not been satisfied and that solutions to their needs were available on the commercial market.[91] Following trials of the platform, it was suggested that the development process had succeeded in reproducing the 'basic regulatory problems and issues that are typical of the Internet in general'.[92]

A problem for the initiative was to define a platform that would be attractive to users, as the immediate appeal of the P2P approach (expressed in the potentially daunting term 'Digital Business Ecosystem') was not strong. Despite recourse to the social imaginary of a complex system's self-organizing potential, the initiative did not depart very far from the functions on offer from proprietary software producers. In the absence of a threshold-sized community, the initiative was faced with the difficulties of establishing a 'brand' and achieving a large enough group of participants to create a viable community. These difficulties became a major stumbling block and the initiative ended with a collection of 'proof of concept' results and an unfunded community interested in their further development.

This interdisciplinary project aimed at reconciling the economic interests in the scarcity of information achieved through proprietary platform implementations, and those of the research community in equality and social justice associated with the values of an open commons. Efforts were made to achieve theoretical integration (not harmonization or unification) among disparate approaches,[93] but the community of developers remained fragmented around its areas of specialism. The technologists focused on the enabling architecture and infrastructure, and the social scientists focused on issues of trust, identity, and information security. Similar to the experience of other application-oriented software projects, the recruitment of user companies based in different regions of Europe, and engagement to use the system for 'productive purposes', proved difficult. After its nearly seven-year span, the technical description of the initiative no longer referred to the potential of an emergent self-organizing system. Systems concepts, such as structural coupling and self-organization, remained in the theoretical description of the initiative and are expected to guide some future scientific endeavours.[94] However, the values of the dominant social imaginary of the information society privileging information scarcity had been injected into a project that had sought to bypass or to modify them, in part or in whole. These values gave precedence to the market and competition (versus sharing), to private information ownership, commercial secrecy, and confidentiality.[95] These values did not *emerge*, they were imposed from above and reflected the prevailing power relationships in the wider system of which this initiative was only a part.

The initial aim was to enable the dynamics of autopoietic computing to foster a sustainable innovation in the communication system—moving from the realm of the social imaginary into the realms of architecture, organization, and norms for the behaviour of companies and researchers. In practice, the key components of this imaginary proved largely unachievable organizationally (and possibly also mathematically). There was a call for further research on the mathematical nature of interaction computing in the interests of achieving the original goals,[96] reminiscent of the dreams of machines which can 'think' on behalf of human beings.

Care was taken to ensure that the potential for advances in self-organizing software was confined to that element of the system and treated only as a means of improving its functional characteristics. It was acknowledged repeatedly that the epistemologies of the technical and social were different. Nevertheless, there was slippage in the discourses employed in this initiative, as indicated by a reading of its outputs. The claims about the separation of these systems receded and, overall, the initiative served to foster the dream of an open system for the production, processing, distribution, and storage of information that would emerge 'naturally'. However, the interests of those in protecting information to secure its scarcity tended to prevail. The values of openness and democracy proved subservient to the power relationships embedded in the wider hierarchical system within which the new digital platform had to operate.

Even a cheaper system from a technical point of view was not compatible with the perceived interests of some of the small- and medium-sized business users or, at the time, with the perceived needs of the research user community. Retrospectively, it might be claimed, perhaps, that the companies did not adopt the open platform largely for functional or technical reasons and that the OSS research community did not grow because insufficient resources were devoted to building it. However, my reading is that the reasons lie in the failure to acknowledge the paradox of complexity in addition to the failure to realize that the paradox of information scarcity was also a problem.

A complex autopoietic system was imagined as being consistent with non-market values and to emerge through advances in interaction computing research. The digital business ecosystem initiative did generate unforeseen, interesting research directions in the natural/physical sciences. But the developers encountered interventions from actors reflecting values instantiated in regulations and laws intended to foster the market-led development of platforms for electronic commerce. The imaginary of the elite class of knowledge workers was superseded by that of another elite class with preferences for the dominant proprietary world market-led online applications. Some of these actors resisted imposition of the values of collaboration and openness when they were seen as interfering with their economic interests. They participated initially as members of a consortium dedicated to an 'open' agenda, requesting modifications, but later, when their concerns were not fully accommodated, they adopted an exit strategy.[97] The premise that the power relations in an open digital platform could be confined to one level in a complex system was apparently unworkable in practice.

Conclusion

This chapter has illustrated many of the ways in which clashes between the competing social imaginaries of the information society are visible in conflicts over the development of the communication system behind the screen. When the analysis was punctuated from the perspective of the interests of the creative industry companies in market-led innovation, these were shown to conflict with the interests of Internet users in the development of the 'thinking' machines that are making it easier for them to imagine that they, rather than system developers, are in control of the communication system. Efforts to enforce private rights of ownership in information are consistent with rewarding information creators, but they suppress the incentives for innovative developments and practices for people who mainly experience the mediated environment in front of the screen. The more forcefully the corporate owners of intellectual property assert their information ownership rights by creating 'choke points' on the Internet and acting as digital information gatekeepers, the more they are called to account for infringements to people's rights to access information or compromises to the public interest in the open circulation of digital information. This is illustrative of the paradox of information scarcity.

The creative industry companies, in some cases, are beginning to reflect the interests of information users in their business strategies, suggesting that there are ways of addressing the paradox of information scarcity. However, proponents of moves to liberate all music downloading sites, for instance, are depicted by representatives of the creative industry as being reckless, while their own interventions in the market to achieve stronger enforcement of copyright are seen as being entirely reasonable. In contrast, making online participants legally liable for copyright infringement detected by the creative industry companies is presented by open information advocacy groups as being equally reckless in stimulating the surveillance of online activity and foreclosing on the open space for the production of digital information. In both of these social imaginaries, there is a strong belief that the self-organizing properties of the communication system are compatible with the good society—this is the paradox of complexity.

In the case of the digital business ecosystem initiative, the social imaginaries of the information society embracing the idea of a generative, self-organizing system behind the screen, played a role in shaping the outcomes insofar as the hope was that the emergence of a new digital platform would be consistent with the values of information sharing, creativity, and democracy. Once incorporated in the technical components, it was expected that these features would be taken up by a broad community of users, eager to be free of the proprietary, externally controlled systems available on the market. In practice, the system developers made choices about the platform in an attempt to reconcile the commercial interests of the user companies in maintaining the scarcity of business-related information with the interests of the research community in sharing information in an open information commons.

When the analysis was punctuated through the eyes of computer scientists and engineers, the evolution of the digital ecosystem system technologies was understood as being neutral with respect to human values, in line with the framing of people (and institutions) as information processors. In this respect, the paradox of complexity was interpreted as benign for human beings. The system was seen as comprising co-evolving sub-systems that give rise to a 'multiplication of possibilities',[98] and power was seen as residing within the system, rather than in the hands of human beings. Despite their belief in a system predicated on openness and the horizontal distribution of power and control, the technical features that were introduced in the digital business ecosystem initiative and the pre-existing experience of user companies with less democratic, but more immediately functional systems, were strong disincentives for the adoption of the digital platform. The solution to the resulting conundrum might have been to intervene to pre-specify user choices to reduce complexity, and to increase their familiarity with the new approach. However, such a move would have contradicted the democratic premise of the initiative. Agency was exercised through the capabilities of the system developers not only from below but also from above through the requirements for the governance of digital information in line with market values.

In the face of major changes in the ease with which everyone can produce, copy, and consume digital information, the proponents of social imaginaries that privilege either private ownership of information or the common ownership of information, devote their efforts to discrediting the arguments of their opponents. The alternative is to consider the possibility that progress towards an information society, consistent with the good society, requires a different reading of the paradoxes of information scarcity and complexity.

In the case of the digital system ecosystem initiative, there were contradictions in the social imaginaries of the various participants in the innovation process. For the developers of the technical system, there was no perceived contradiction in their decisions about the design of the system and their aspirations for the construction of a democratic model for the system and, indeed, they were able to design an open decentralized P2P infrastructure. But there also was very little evidence of their awareness of the contradictions entailed in advocacy of a *self-organizing* system along information commons principles when it is to be employed by users that are subject to the hierarchical rules and norms of the marketplace. In this case these norms took the form of conventional corporate practices for managing information and governance rules put in place by the state to ensure confidentiality and security of electronic commerce.

In the next chapter (Chapter 7), I examine how the conflicting social imaginaries of the information society are playing out in debates about the goals for public policy and governance, especially in relation to the Internet.

7 Political Firestorms in Communication Policy

Introduction

'Internet regulation proposal sets off political firestorm'.[1] This CNN headline captures the outcry that met a new round of proposals for Internet regulation in the United States. And when President Sarkozy broached the subject of tougher Internet regulation at a French government-hosted 'e-G8' summit, there was considerable protest, especially from those keen to defend an open Internet. Sarkozy was calling for internationally coordinated regulation to defend the Internet (and the Web) against monopoly control, copyright breaches, child pornography, intrusions into personal privacy, and security threats associated with malware. Addressing an audience of representatives of companies, including Google, Facebook, Amazon, and eBay, he says, 'the universe you represent is not a parallel universe. Nobody should forget that governments are the only legitimate representatives of the will of the people in our democracies. To forget this is to risk democratic chaos and anarchy'.[2] The United Kingdom government, among others, resisted the French government's initiative.

A communiqué issued later by the OECD, following a high level meeting in South Korea, endorsed 'consensus-based policies' for the Internet devised by diverse groups of government, private sector, and civil society stakeholders. OECD countries were against a move towards an Internet regulatory regime that might dampen incentives for technological innovation and economic growth.[3] Civil society organizations participating in this OECD meeting refused to sign up to the principles in the communiqué because it supported the creative industries' bid to achieve greater protection for copyrighted digital content. The OECD communiqué suggests that many of the requirements for effective Internet governance are in place. Nevertheless, developments in next-generation networks, the shift from personal computer-based to mobile handheld devices, the expansion of sensor-based networks, and the increasing ubiquity of digital content in the virtual world, were all flagged as being likely to present new issues for policy makers.[4]

Developments in these and other areas prompt persistent calls for Internet regulation aimed at curtailing, for instance, online pornography, potential harm to children, or identity theft, all of which are enabled by developments in the hardware and software of the communication system. There are accompanying demands for strong defences against censorship and surveillance in the name of freedom and democracy. Debates about whether and how (much) the Internet should be regulated provoke support both for and against interventions through policy, and formal or informal regulation. Little account is taken of the implications of the paradoxes of information scarcity or complexity in these conflicts about governance issues, but the conflicting positions taken by the stakeholders in these debates often align with the prevailing social imaginaries of the information society.

The stakeholders with an interest in the commodity value of digital information align with the dominant social imaginary insofar as they encourage governance solutions that privilege the market exchange of information. They assume that Internet users will express their preferences in the marketplace and that the role of government is to ensure that governance from above secures the intellectual property rights of rights holders. They also presume that it is the role of government to exercise control over information in the interests of security, surveillance, and privacy. Nevertheless, the extent of governance in the public interest generally is seen as being limited by the complexity of the communication system.

Stakeholders favouring an information commons, in contrast, turn to the generative dynamics of the evolution of the communication system in line with the alternative social imaginary of the information society to secure the interests of the public. They turn to governance from below to empower Internet users, arguing that the sheer complexity of the technological system means that government policy should aim at creating a legislative environment in which information is 'allowed to be free'. In this imaginary there is a strong emphasis on the idea that the dynamics of the innovation process itself will give rise to an emergent, self-organizing, complex system and that it will privilege democratic values, freedom of speech, and content diversity. Thus, while there is convergence in these social imaginaries with regard to the notion that a complex adaptive system will look after its own 'needs', there are marked differences in way the power relationships among the different stakeholders inform their positions on questions of the problems created by the paradox of information scarcity. The colliding social imaginaries are illustrated by some of their metacommunications on the role of policy and regulation with respect to the older and newer components of the communication system in the Internet Age.

This chapter begins by outlining traditional communication policy concerns and goals related to the media and communication sector, showing how interpretations of the public interest in the communication system have changed as the contested social imaginaries of the information society have become prominent. I briefly consider some of the institutions involved in the governance of the modern communication system and the extent to which it is inclusive of a broad range of stakeholder interests. Debates about what has come to be known as 'network neutrality' are then used to exemplify the way stakeholders position themselves in efforts to advance their respective interests in the information society and to marginalize or discredit those of others.

Governing in the Public Interest

Whether regulation by the state is 'fit for purpose' for the media and for the communication networks of the Internet era is a question that is discussed under the rubric of Internet governance. Denis McQuail, media scholar and policy analyst in the media and communication field, defines governance as all the means by which the actors involved are 'limited, directed, encouraged, managed, or called into account, ranging from the most binding laws to the most resistible of pressures and self-chosen disciplines'.[5] Governance, therefore, refers to the institutions and practices that guide the development of the technological and human relationships involved in the innovation process, including the interests of the state, private sector, and civil society and it is generally understood to be a broader concept than regulation. This is because the authority to govern can be derived from laws, regulations, treaties and conventions, business codes of practice, and standards, as well as informal agreements. It is also necessary to bear in mind that governance choices may not lead to action or change in the structure or organization of an industry sector or in the practices of governments because, for many different reasons, decisions often are not implemented for a host of cultural, social, political, or economic reasons.[6]

An important governance question is who is authorized to make decisions? Is it the state through top-down intervention or the private sector through its own self-governance? Should civil society representatives be empowered to make crucial governance decisions? Whether one or the other, or some combination of these, the answers are influenced by the prevailing social imaginaries of the information society. The approaches to governance in the Internet Age are flashpoints for disputes because of the conflicts over the emphasis that should be given to market-led development of the information society and the challenges of governing a complex communication system. Shifts in the scope of media and communication policy, including the Internet, and understanding of the public interest in the evolution of the communication system are accompanied by changes in governance institutions and practices.[7]

The disruptive nature of rapid technological innovation resulting in the convergence of ICTs has promoted increasing emphasis on the participation of representatives of civil society in the governance process. This is attribut- able partly to the fact that the new technological platforms have made feasible their entry into decision-making forums and partly because of the ease with which they can coordinate their participation using online tools and websites. Some claim that the opening up of participation is consistent with outcomes that are more likely to favour governance in line with the social imaginary of an open information commons. Others argue that it attracts attention to developments in only one layer—the Internet Protocol layer—of a complex multi-level system and takes insufficient account of the economic incentives that are needed to drive investment in next-generation networks and applications.

HISTORY OF THE PUBLIC INTEREST IN COMMUNICATION

The idea that there is a public interest in the communication system, under- stood as the means of communication and the content circulating within networks, is deeply embedded in institutions of public policy and regulation in the Western industrialized countries. The notion of *the* 'public interest' in communication has strong economic connotations. The concept originated in the legal treatment of 'businesses affected with a public interest' in the seventeenth century in English common law. By the late 1870s, the idea provided a basis for rulings by the United States judiciary on the public interest in transport, an important activity in the conduct of business. A court in the State of Illinois ruled that it was entitled to regulate the prices charged for rail transport by the private owners of grain elevators, whose monopoly over the transport system was enabling them to set very high prices for use of the system. The court, borrowing from British common law, concluded that certain private property:

does come clothed with a public interest when used in a manner to make it of public consequence, and affect the community at large. When, therefore, one devotes his property to a use in which the public has an interest, he, in effect, grants to the public an interest in that use, and must submit to be controlled by the public for the common good, to the extent of the interest he has thus created.[8]

It was a short step to move from transport as a mode of communication, to the idea that communication networks are also 'businesses affected with a public interest'. This reasoning was applied to justify regulation of the tele- communication industry when services in the United States were provided by the private sector, with the aim of encouraging reasonable prices and better access to services in a market characterized by strong tendencies towards monopoly. Legislation for the communication sector would come to embrace the concept of the public interest through references to the need for policy favouring the 'diversity of media voices, vigorous economic

competition, technological advancement, and promotion of the public interest, convenience, and necessity'.[9]

It was argued that concepts, such as the public interest, should not be
treated as universal principles that are transparent and applicable in every
context, acknowledging that there would be conflicts over the interests of
different parties with a stake in the development of any industrial sector,
subject to public interest legislation. For instance, in the 1930s, Walton
Hamilton, an institutional economist at Yale University, argued that legal
concepts evolve in specific historical and social contexts. He regards legal texts
as the 'henchmen who do valiant service for the overlords of public policy',[10]
suggesting that such texts should be subject to interpretative latitude in the
wake of changing circumstances. The concept of public interest was employed
also in legislation providing for policy and regulation for the media and
telecommunication industries in the United Kingdom and other national
jurisdictions where private suppliers had entered the market—usually after
a period of government ownership.[11]

Hamilton warns that the market within which industries 'affected with
a public interest' operate should not be regarded 'as an automatic, self-
regulating mechanism; like any other human institution it may work poorly,
indifferently, or well'.[12] This was prescient in the light of the neoliberal
prescriptions for regulation that would privilege self-regulating markets
over policy intervention in later decades. As the communication system has
developed, and with ICT convergence, governments and private providers of
media content and communication networks have argued that faith should
be placed in the self-regulating properties of markets or, alternatively, in
the self-regulating properties of the technological system as a means of safe-
guarding the public interest.

CONTESTED PUBLIC INTEREST CRITERIA

Interpretation of the public interest in the telecommunication industry
traditionally emphasizes economic criteria in line with the early history of
the concept. Judgements about the governance of networks and services are
made in the light of assessments of the impact of the industry's capacity to
exploit its monopolistic position in the market by exercising economic
power through pricing strategies. The application of economic criteria
results in a relatively narrow construct of the public interest compared to
that based on criteria such as diversity, fairness, and social justice which are
applied to regulation of the media content industries. For instance, telecommunication is treated as an essential facility or critical economic resource, whereas broadcasting is linked to cultural values, and rights
and responsibilities relating to freedom of speech.[13] The norm for

telecommunication regulation is a focus on investment in infrastructure and (affordable) services for the public. The norm for broadcasting is a focus on the quality of content, freedom of expression, diversity, and plurality, or the role of the state in controlling the content of the media. Thus, the concept of the public interest is broad in the context of media content regulation, and encompasses media plurality and media ownership issues.[14] As markets have been opened to commercial providers of content-related services, the broadcasting industry and increasingly the online entertainment and news content companies are driven by interests in profits, presenting difficult problems for the criteria that should govern the regulation of the public service broadcasting sector.[15]

It is difficult to define what the Internet is for governance purposes. Is it the technical architecture built on the Internet Protocol?[16] Or is it the services that are provided over networks employing this protocol? Where does Internet regulation intersect with the traditional ways in which telecommunication and broadcasting services have been regulated? These are all questions that require answers when the issue of Internet governance is raised and when public interest considerations are discussed. The Internet and what have come to be known as 'new media' services accessed using the Internet do not come under the same regime of governance as the older media and communication networks because of the Internet's origins as an innovative technology at the edge or fringe of what was regarded as the communication infrastructure. Thus, in democratic jurisdictions it is frequently claimed that any attempts to regulate the Internet will infringe civil liberties and human rights or, alternatively, that state control is essential in the name of security. In the discussion on network neutrality later in this chapter, we will find that these claims echo the contending social imaginaries of the information society in the Internet Age.

The public interest might be served, for example, by governance arrangements that allow any actor to pursue his or her conception of public good as long as it does not interfere negatively with the interests of anyone else. Such an understanding of the public interest clearly would go well beyond a market-led social imaginary of the public interest in the information society.[17] If the governance framework were to be aimed at protecting the public interest in a way that is responsive to this broad standard, account would need to be taken of the conflicts and power relationships and their interactions within this multi-level system and the way these give rise to chronic patterns of paradox. There is remarkably little evidence at present of a governance framework that is responsive to a broad standard such as this, as the rest of this chapter shows.

The focus instead in assessing the public interest and appropriate governance measures is normally on the diffusion of technology and, typically, on 'curative' policies supported by instrumental research on communication system developments in front of the screen such as, for instance, voluntary industry codes of practice for consumer protection from online fraud. Little attention is given to evaluating what a particular configuration of market and voluntary activity in the media and communication sector is likely to enable people to accomplish in their lives, and even less to the economic resources and other capabilities they need in order to benefit from access to ICTs and digital information. The emphasis on technology gaps and market-led investment is consistent with the dominant social imaginary of the information society.

When the public interest in the information society is addressed from a critical perspective, issues of equality and social justice are more likely to be privileged. Emphasis is more likely to be given to governance measures aimed at encouraging the diversity of digital content and cultural diversity, the provision of a broad range of cultural, social, and economic information resources that will benefit Internet users, the protection of human rights, and the ways of fostering social equality. This broader approach, compared to the social imaginary of governance for a market-led information society, makes it possible to envisage 'different alternatives for the future, albeit recognizing certain essential traits that characterize our time, underlining the strategic role of information and knowledge'.[18] However, acknowledging diversity in the governance framework for the communication system is especially challenging because of the global reach of the system. This means that the states involved will have different economic and political interests and these, in turn, will be informed by their affinity to the dominant social imaginary of the information society. For the most part, states are less attracted to the alternative imaginary of an open information commons even though it might encourage variety and diversity in the local environments within which information is produced and consumed.[19]

Historically, policies for the media and communication sector were introduced at the international level expressing the interests of the United States and other wealthy Western countries, with some expectation that they would be taken up by the non-Western states (eventually) and in response to various forms of political and economic pressure.[20] In the Internet Age, many states are exercising their autonomy thereby contributing to diversity of the governance arrangements in the information society, but not always favouring democratic values or the ethos of the open information commons. For example, the Egyptian government required the Egyptian division of the mobile communication company, Vodafone, to send text messages on its behalf, and to suspend its services during the political protests in 2011.[21] These and other instances of the exercise of state power are reminders that governance always serves particular interests. There is no homogeneous or universal conception of *the* public interest in the communication system or, as Arturo Escobar puts it, policy 'narratives are always immersed in history and never innocent'.[22] Policy makers representing countries from the global south, from China to Brazil, are becoming more influential as their economies grow stronger. However, it does not follow that challenges to the dominant market-led social imaginary of the information society will be effective in guiding governance outcomes in the direction of the values of the good society. It is also unclear what combinations of governance from below and from above would be consistent with aspirations for the good society.

In summary, some observers seem content to wait for empowerment of their citizens to take advantage of the potential of convergent ICT platforms to challenge the dominant market-led social imaginary without specifying what should take its place. Others are encouraging new forms of Internet governance which have the potential to challenge this imaginary. As discussed in the next sections of this chapter, however, when they become embroiled in debates, especially concerning the governance of the Internet, they mispunctuate the analysis of conflicting interests with the result that measures that might reconcile the concerns of interested parties are not considered. Given the asymmetries in power relationships, the interests of those in the market-led development of the information society generally are prevailing insofar as developments in front of and behind the computer screen are concerned, while policy makers debate means of balancing the conflicting interests of stakeholders. As suggested earlier, this effort to achieve balance misreads the fundamental contradictions created by the paradoxes of information scarcity and complexity. The next section outlines some of the institutional arrangements that are in place for governing the Internet.

Governing the Internet

Turning now to the issues raised specifically about the governance of the Internet since it began to spread beyond the scientific community in the mid-1990s, the focal point for discussions about governance often is characterized as being about whether the Internet is 'ungovernable' because of its global reach. This ungainly term is used frequently by policy makers to suggest that 'in the long run, the endless spiral of connectivity is more powerful than any government edict'.[23] In the prevailing social imaginary of the information society, the suggestion is that the state should not be involved in Internet governance because this will discourage innovation and the creativity needed to sustain a flourishing Internet system.

John Perry Barlow's Declaration for the Independence of Cyberspace articulates a variation of this claim with the assertion that 'you do not know our culture, our ethics, or the unwritten codes that already provide our society more order than could be obtained by any of your impositions'.[24] He refers to those advocating external control over the Internet who either do not share his anarcho-syndicalist or libertarian beliefs or are from a generation that cannot comprehend all the benefits of the cyberworld. For those who see the communication system as a complex adaptive system, its self-organization results in an emergent process in which state intervention is unlikely to benefit anyone who believes in freedom and democracy.

GOVERNANCE ARRANGEMENTS IN PRACTICE

In contrast to this vision of an emergent outcome based on the generative characteristics of the technological system, states do of course attempt in various ways to govern the Internet as part of their broader efforts to control the communication system. In some cases, governance initiatives may be taken to promote investment in broadband infrastructure or to coordinate the technical architecture and operation of the Internet Protocol; in others, initiatives may be taken in the name of security, the protection of children, or, in some states, explicitly in the name of censorship.

The private sector becomes involved in Internet governance through its monitoring and tracking of patterns of Internet use, for reasons that range from efforts to manage traffic efficiently, enforce intellectual property rights, or provide personalized services for Internet users, as we have seen in earlier chapters. Thus, the issue of governance in the Internet Age provokes questions about the moral, political, economic, and social interests of the stakeholders in the information society. Despite the claims about its 'ungovernability', and despite the fact that the Internet is part of a highly complex technological system, it is governed in numerous ways and these are associated with uncertain outcomes.

The Internet is the product of state and corporate governance choices, not solely the result of the choices made by the scientists and engineers who designed it.[25] In one way or another, all states—including democratic and authoritarian ones—are involved in the construction of the Internet whether they privilege the goals of freedom of speech and democracy, of economic growth, or of security. Thus, as Saskia Sassen puts it using the language of sociology, 'power, contestation, inequality, in brief, hierarchy' always inscribe electronic space.[26]

Contestations emerge increasingly as civil society organizations achieve greater prominence in forums hosted by the institutions involved in Internet governance. The political alignment of civil society advocates can range from concerted efforts to push back interventions by the state and private sector, to efforts to achieve a balancing of the interests of all the stakeholders, and in some cases, to support for the continuation of governance from above by the state or the corporate sector.[27] It cannot be assumed, therefore, that multistakeholder approaches to Internet governance (or to policy for the communication sector generally) will be aligned with a social imaginary of an information society that privileges the information commons over the commercial market.

This means that multistakeholder approaches to Internet governance are no more likely, simply as a result of their structure or their decision-making procedures, to be able to repair the problems that emerge as a result of the conditions created by the genesis of the paradoxes of information scarcity and complexity than their predecessors. Changes in the ICT techno-economic paradigm and the growing dependence of economies on digital information have brought Internet governance matters to the attention of a complex matrix of state and private sector institutions, most of which have little or no previous experience of multistakeholder dialogue or decision-making. The actors involved include governments, ISPs, telecommunication network and service suppliers, broadcasters, software companies, hardware manufacturers, trade organizations, the banking sector, and representatives of civil society. The issues, especially at the international level, fall within the remits of a large number of intergovernmental and regional organizations, as indicated by the medley of organizations represented in Table 7.1. For the most part, as the composition of these institutions is state or private sector dominated, their deliberations are well-aligned with the dominant social imaginary of a market-led information society.[28]

Internet governance issues entered the world stage after a lengthy gestation during which efforts were made to give prominence to a broad conception of the public interest in the communication system as discussed earlier. In the 1970s, the Non-Aligned Movement (NAM) and United Nations Educational, Scientific and Cultural Organization (UNESCO) began promoting a New World Information and Communication Order (NWICO), arguing that this was needed to address asymmetries between rich and poor.[29] The *Many Voices, One World* report drew attention to persistent inequalities in the capacity for media production and the need to promote freedom of speech through approaches to governing the communication system.[30] The United States and the United Kingdom responded by withdrawing from UNESCO in protest against NAM criticisms of their lack of reciprocity in trade in services and of their Western-backed approach to media freedom. The positions taken by those from the wealthy countries were seen by representatives of the Non-Aligned countries as promoting a 'one way' flow of information from the wealthy to the poor countries, resulting in suppression of their capacities for developing distinctive information societies.[31]

By the end of the 1990s, the World Bank and several United Nations agencies were promoting a vision of development supported by digital technologies, aimed at addressing knowledge gaps and the digital divide, in order to stimulate market-led growth. States were being encouraged to devise digital technology policies to help them 'leapfrog' the industrialized countries by investing in digital networks and services.[32] Investment was to be encouraged by favouring market-led competition and a governance regime for the

Table 7.1. Institutions with Interests in Internet Governance

Intellectual property rights:

Internet Corporation for Assigned Names and Numbers (ICANN)

United Nations Educational, Scientific and Cultural Organization (UNESCO)

World Intellectual Property Organization (WIPO)

World Trade Organization (WTO)

Security issues:

Council of Europe (COE)

Financial Action Task Force (FATF)

Group on Earth Observations (GEO)

ICANN

Organisation for Economic Co-operation and Development (OECD)

Infrastructure issues:

European Organization for Nuclear Research (CERN)

GEO

ICANN

International Telecommunication Union (ITU)

OECD

UNESCO

World Bank

World Wide Web Consortium (W3C)

WTO

Jurisdiction and sovereignty:

Basel Committee on Banking Supervision (BCBS)

COE

FATF

Hague Conference on Private International Law

ICANN

International Monetary Fund (IMF)

Monetary Authority:

OECD

UNESCO

United Nations Commission on International Trade Law (UNCITRAL)

WTO

Relations between private transacting parties:

Foreign Commercial Relations Committee

GEO

Hague Conference

ITU

OECD

UNCITRAL

WTO

Relations between persons and the state:

International Civil Aviation Organization (ICAO)

GEO

ITU

OECD

WTO

Source: Author, collated from various sources.

Internet (and the media and communication sector generally) borrowed largely from the models developed in the wealthy countries. The then United Nations Secretary-General, Kofi Annan, announced that investment in ICTs should be harnessed to reduce poverty.[33] By 2000, the political momentum driving the prevailing social imaginary of the information society based on the market-led diffusion of digital technologies was attracting high-level diplomatic interest. A World Summit on the Information Society (WSIS) was held in two parts in Geneva in 2003 and in Tunis in 2005 under the auspices of the United Nations General Assembly, organized by the International Telecommunication Union (ITU)[34] with support from UNESCO. This summit provided a novel forum for accredited civil society organizations to highlight the persistent failures to address the relationships between technologies, poverty, and human rights.

The WSIS outcomes advocated some degree of movement away from technology-centred and market-led social imaginary of the information society. Discussion about policy measures and governance arrangements more consistent with the social imaginary of an open information commons were largely dismissed, however, from the mainstream of the WSIS deliberations through careful management of the participation of civil society spokespersons by the Summit's host institution, the ITU. The outcomes of these deliberations contained strong resonances with the dominant imaginary in which 'knowledge is like light'[35]—knowledge in support of development can be delivered through access to digital information. The policy priority was to meet targets for the diffusion of ICTs,[36] and it was argued that a universally applicable information society strategy would benefit all. This strong emphasis on technology and the governance arrangements that will best enable its rapid diffusion is present in most contemporary national jurisdictions. It continues to be in evidence, for example, in the United Nations' *Millennium Development Goals Report 2010*. ICT policy goals for the information society are expressed in terms of progression towards targets for the diffusion of technology using benchmarking indicators measuring Internet connections and mobile telephone subscriptions.[37]

INSTITUTIONAL INNOVATIONS FOR GOVERNANCE

In the shadows of the WSIS and a variety of other forums, however, civil society representatives proposed alternatives to government and corporate-sponsored agendas for the information society. Their voices were reflected in some of the texts that came out the Summit and in some of the actions with respect to governance arrangements that followed.[38] One outcome of the WSIS deliberations was the creation of a new forum within which public interest issues raised by the Internet can be debated. The Internet Governance

Forum (IGF) was established under the auspices of the United Nations General Assembly. It has no formal policy making powers and its mandate is to discuss issues relating to Internet governance in an inclusive and flexible way. It has brought together thousands of representatives of government, business, and civil society.[39]

The IGF is seen by some as being in a good position to address controversial governance issues in such areas as privacy, security, and information diversity, and it has deliberated on issues of freedom from surveillance and censorship. It was sufficiently effective in disturbing metacommunications that were consistent with the dominant social imaginary of the information society that the renewal of its mandate after its first five years was controversial. The governments of both China and the United States expressed concern during the period leading up to the renewal of its initial mandate. Some argue that it is feasible to effectively champion governance outcomes consistent with the alternative social imaginary of an open information commons in this forum. Others argue that it is the interests of companies and states that prevail in the IGF as they do in other formal institutions whose remits bear on issues of Internet governance, but which have fewer possibilities for the voices of civil society to be represented.[40]

Some close observers of debates in this forum argue that the goal of participants representing a broad spectrum of interests in the evolution of the Internet is to adopt governance procedures that enable decision-making through the 'application of shared principles, norms, rules, decision-making procedures, and programs intended to shape actors' expectations and practices and to enhance their collective management capacities'.[41] However, statements like this one about 'collective management capacities' have a strong instrumentalist tone. This is reminiscent of governance approaches where power asymmetries are ignored in the interest of achieving 'shared principles or norms', notwithstanding the underlying conflicts. This is unlikely to foster outcomes aligned with values of the good society. Just how effective this forum for informal multistakeholder governance will prove to be in reconciling conflicting interests is an empirical question.[42] The answer depends partly on whether the stakeholders are able to grapple with the implications of the underlying paradoxes of information scarcity and complexity, and on the degree to which the outcomes of their debates are influential in other formal governance institutions at all levels.

There are other institutions with specific formal mandates for governing the Internet which also attempt to include a range of voices in a multi-stakeholder environment that should, in principle, create opportunities for tackling the challenges created by the paradoxes of information scarcity and complexity. For example, the Internet Corporation for Assigned Names and Numbers (ICANN), founded in California in 1998 as a non-profit, private sector, public benefit corporation, has a decision-making board that is advised by a Governmental Advisory Committee (GAC).[43] ICANN makes decisions about matters of Internet governance that have direct implications for the way the Internet Protocol layer of the multi-level communication system actually operates and in whose interests it operates. Over the years, ICANN has experimented with different procedural models in the attempt to embrace multiple stakeholder interests.

The GAC includes representatives of governments, other public authorities, and some intergovernmental organizations. Despite its advisory status, GAC members try to exert influence, for example, on questions concerning ostensibly technical issues such as whether new top-level domain names in addition to .com, .org, etc., should be permitted. The significance here is that adding new names has implications for companies seeking to boost their brands and, therefore, affects their prospects in the digital economy. ICANN provides a forum for decision-making on contested 'technical' issues, but these issues are also imbued with political and economic connotations. There are polarized views about whether it achieves the democratic goals it espouses in relation to aspirations for the governance of the Internet in line with the alternative social imaginary of the information society.[44] Milton Mueller, political scientist and observer of Internet governance developments, argues that even when it seems to have succeeded in being fully inclusive, 'participation and representation can give people the feeling that they have a stake in the policy making process, even when they are in fact relatively powerless'.[45] Without adequate public accountability for its decisions, ICANN is as likely as any other institution to favour the positions of corporate and government actors in conflicts with civil society representatives. More importantly, debates in this forum are also framed as being about finding ways to reach consensus about shared principles and ways of implementing them. The deeper conflicts between proponents of the dominant and alternative social imaginaries of the information society are presented mainly in terms of oppositions in which the 'winner takes all'.

In the IGF and in other Internet governance-related institutions such as ICANN, the prevailing social imaginaries of the information society in which there is a persistent struggle between those favouring market-led developments and those favouring a wider space for an open information commons is fostered by the framing of many of the issues in instrumental, managerial, or technical terms. The IGF appears to be providing a space for the broadening of the range of perspectives that can be debated. However, without decision-making authority, it seems unlikely to provide networked (multistakeholder) governance that can be effective in reducing the incentives of companies or states to promote innovations in the communication system that result in increasing monitoring and surveillance of Internet user. It has the potential to provide a forum for reflection on the emergence of 'machines of loving grace' that may remove many facets of decision-making from the control of human beings. So far, however, it has shown few signs that it is an institution where the paradoxes of information scarcity and complexity can be confronted.

Finally, even if we were to assume that the presence of civil society advocates within the forums for debate about Internet governance creates a greater likelihood that conflicting interests among governments, the private sector, and civil society might be reconciled, these developments raise additional challenging issues about the *authority to govern*. In principle, civil society organizations should exist to unite otherwise disparate constituencies to constitute a majority and, thus, should have a powerful influence in the Internet governance process assuming they gain access to multistakeholder forums on reasonable terms. However, these organizations may represent vocal minorities whose interests conflict with the mainstream and the positions of democratically elected governments. They may reflect a 'tyranny of the majority' that systematically excludes dissenting voices. Of course, governments and their representatives may be captives of corporate interests, may have been elected undemocratically, or may be unresponsive to the views of their electorates or other social movement organizations.[46] Simply involving representatives of civil society in multistakeholder forums provides only the hope that key problems and controversies might be addressed in ways that are consistent with aspirations for the good society.

The experience of Internet governance in international forums suggests that civil society organizations are more likely to champion positions consistent with a social imaginary of an open information commons in contrast to advocates of a social imaginary of a market-led information society. However, it is not feasible to repair the harms associated with paradox unless their genesis is recognized. If we take the contemporary discussions about the 'neutrality' of the Internet as an illustration of how the interests of the stakeholders are represented in their metacommunications, there is virtually no sign of adaptive action (as discussed in Chapter 4). Such action might go some way to address asymmetrical power relations and succeed in guiding the development of the information society in a direction that is more consistent with the values of the good society. In the next section, deliberations about network neutrality in national and international governance forums are examined to assess the extent to which they show signs of acknowledging the paradoxes of information scarcity and complexity.[47]

Network Neutrality

Newspaper articles carry alarming claims that there is 'no room at the Internet', that the website addresses we are familiar with are about to 'run out'.[48] The implication is a closing down of opportunities for websites with objectives as diverse as commerce and the promotion of free speech and democracy. The press presents this as a technical issue in need of urgent resolution. However, the scarcity (or not) of addresses and, indeed, whether it is a technical problem or a highly charged political issue driven by economic interests, are not apparent to most Web surfers and there are conflicting views also among those with the technical expertise to make assessments.[49] Conflicts over this and many other similar and ostensibly technical issues concerning the future of the Internet are being discussed in governance proceedings focusing on network neutrality. Many of these discussions are conducted within conventional state governance institutions, for example, regulatory agencies or ministries charged with media and communication policy responsibilities. In democratic states, the voices of civil society may be acknowledged in these institutional settings, as interveners or commentators, but this does not mean that the outcomes of debates necessarily favour the values espoused by civil society actors.

MANAGING THE INTERNET BEHIND THE SCREEN

Network neutrality is broadly understood to refer to the design of the Internet as an end-to-end public network which does not discriminate among the types of data that flow through it. Network neutrality is a technologically constituted ideal of the Internet as enabling the indiscriminate flow of all digital information through the communication network. Assuming sufficient capacity, the Internet's technical design—its architecture—makes it possible for every digital bit to be treated equally regardless of its originator's wealth, socio-economic status, or other features. However, these other features can provide clear signals about the nature of the content or bits. Currently, ISPs employ traffic management techniques to balance demand for limited network capacity, arguing that they do so independently of the payments they receive for their services.

ISPs have the technical capability to manage Internet traffic, for instance, by limiting the use of encrypted virtual private networks, restricting the operations of those providing certain kinds of information, and excluding high-bandwidth applications such as Voice-over-Internet-Protocol (VoIP) telephony or P2P file-sharing.[50] ISPs, in principle, have the capability also to monitor third-party content and to suppress copyright-infringing or other 'unwanted' content. These traffic management or traffic shaping methods mean that ISPs are cognisant of the content that flows through the Internet. From an ISP subscriber's perspective, it is difficult to discern whether a reduced ISP service is due to congestion (i.e. measures to manage traffic volumes) or techniques that are responding to corporate or state interests, applied often without public scrutiny.[51]

ISPs claim that without some traffic management, the Internet would be harmed by network congestion. The management of traffic flows involves methods for traffic inspection, such as deep packet inspection (DPI) techniques that are used in ordinary traffic control to manage information flows.[52]

However, DPI techniques have implications for civil liberties, especially when they are used in connection with the detection of copyright-infringing file-sharing or for surveillance.[53] DPI techniques also enable ISPs to give priority to certain content and speed up data transfers for those willing to pay more.[54] The challenge for policy makers, regulators, and the courts is to decide whether the technical interventions of ISPs run counter to the ideal of network neutrality and whether they are in the public interest.

In addition, something more than DPI as presently employed is needed to identify pornography, viruses, and spam, and this is where various techniques for filtering content come into play. The intelligent software agents that are being developed behind the screen (discussed in Chapter 5) increasingly are able to provide the technical means for online 'intelligent' filtering to accomplish the goals which are valued by society and other goals that may be seen as encroaching on human rights. These intelligent software agents can be used to undertake fairly mechanical traffic shaping, governed by the need to, or the possibility of:

1. rationing 'bursty' demand and intense baseload demand periods on the network;

2. choosing priorities among types of traffic, but based on 'level' criteria, for example, constraining all VoIP traffic as opposed to just traffic generated by Skype;

3. introducing more 'intelligent agent' type filtering to produce, perhaps internationally agreed benefits, for example, anti-spam and virus protection, or benefits that are specific to certain national contexts (e.g. anti-pornography or suppression of certain forms of political expression);

4. allowing the extension of 'intelligent agents' to discriminate directly among the traffic on the Internet that gives rise to various forms of 'side payments' (non-transparent business arrangements) to enable some originators of traffic to avoid the actions of the intelligent agents; and

5. establishing full-blown auctioning of priority to be accorded to the traffic generated by both suppliers and customers, by introducing a market.

Which configuration of these possibilities is adopted is what will set a new standard for the practices and social imaginaries of what constitutes network neutrality, such that each step towards the fifth possibility becomes a further one in progress along the road to 'non-neutrality'.

NETWORK NEUTRALITY, PARADOX, AND SOCIAL IMAGINARIES

A strong supporter of the preservation of network neutrality, understood simply as the end-to-end architecture of the Internet ensuring that all content receives the same priority and is treated fairly, is Tim Berners-Lee, credited with co-invention of the World Wide Web, and head of the World Wide Web Consortium (W3C) which promotes standards for the Web. He argues that companies hosting social networking sites are walling off information and that some ISPs are slowing traffic, practices that are inimical to democracy and the principles of universality, decentralization, and open standards that have enabled the Internet to flourish. Distinguishing between 'good' and 'bad' ISPs, he suggests that 'a *good ISP* will often manage traffic so that when bandwidth is short, less crucial traffic is dropped in a transparent way, so users are aware of it.... the goal of the web is to serve humanity. We build it now so that those who come to it later will be able to create things that we cannot ourselves imagine'.[55] His approach relies upon incentives for ISPs to 'behave well' and to ensure that the Internet remains 'neutral' in the sense that its design and operation are consistent with the alternative social imaginary of an open information commons, or at least of 'technological democracy'. As Sandra Braman points out in her analysis of the discourse employed by the designers of the early Internet protocols, however, the aspiration to design a neutral network that could be used with any kind of equipment provided a strong motivation in the early years between 1969 and 1979, but this was one of many, sometimes conflicting aspirations.[56]

In the early days of the Internet in 1990s, service providing companies such as CompuServe, Prodigy, and America Online adopted restrictive policies for accessing digital content, mimicking closed or proprietary network environments for digital information which had provided some means of maintaining control over information, that is, ensuring its apparent scarcity. In the wake of the convergence of ICTs, and as the capacity of broadband networks increased and became more ubiquitously available, these restrictions were lifted. So-called 'walled gardens' became less popular. The interests of some online providers shifted away from models of direct sale of information or of subscription, to revenue generation based on advertising supported models (e.g. Google's 'click through' model). However, advances in technology and the end-to-end design of the Internet, in particular, have meant that the inability to discriminate between different kinds of Internet traffic is encouraging online consumption of both legal and illegal content. This is indicative of the paradox of information scarcity.

Although content delivery networks, such as Akamai, are being used to aggregate content and to contribute to network capacity management and cost reduction,[57] this does not benefit the ISPs because network neutrality principles do not allow them to charge for the large amounts of bandwidth needed to deliver digital content to Internet users. Large content providers are finding ways to avoid having to increase data transmission costs, and using server farms connected by private (high-capacity fibre) networks. This enables them to bypass the public Internet for some of their network requirements. Companies such as Google, Yahoo!, and Microsoft are reported to be adopting this strategy for increasing amounts of traffic, to avoid potential charges levied by the ISPs. These are likely to take the form of metered data transmission charges and caps on bandwidth use. These are being introduced by some ISPs, especially mobile operators, under the guise of requirements for 'efficient network management'. In the face of these developments, retention or not, of the end-to-end technical feature of the Internet architecture is an economically and politically charged issue. ISPs already are involved in interventions in the network related to the third form of traffic management described above. Debates on network neutrality often make it seem as if the technical architecture and operation of the Internet is now, and could remain, free from all forms of intervention.

Network neutrality controversies highlight the complexity of the behind the screen communication system. Stakeholders are confronted with rationales for in front of the screen interventions that are discomfiting to those whose goal is to benefit from the commercial potential of the system. It is unsettling also to those who want to employ it for state security, as well as to those who view the design of the system as best sequestered to secure its emergence, unhindered by politically or economically inspired interventions. The network neutrality debate is actually about whether public policy should sanction a move to the fourth of the elements listed earlier. That is, it is about whether the extension of software agent-based computing should be used to discriminate directly among traffic on the Internet, allowing some originators of traffic to avoid the actions of these agents (whether they are working on behalf of their commercial 'owners' or on behalf of governments).

The social imaginaries of the computer scientists and software engineers suggest that the complexity of the system is such that its evolution is based on its emergent, albeit unpredictable, properties; that the Internet should not be regulated. Companies argue for or against regulation depending on their prospects for generating revenues as either producers of online content, or as carriers of information or, and increasingly, both. ISP strategies aimed at limiting video streaming, putting restrictions on the caching of content, or introducing differential access prices based on the type of traffic, are ways of limiting the network resource by charging customers for the information they transmit, enforcing a condition of market scarcity. This may generate revenues that can be used to construct higher-capacity networks in the future, but it also 'unfairly' discriminates and, therefore, is regarded by proponents of network neutrality to be counter to the public interest in fair access to the Internet.

Issues of the technical or engineering features of traffic management become muddled in these debates with proposals to charge for preferential access to the Internet. The former amounts to a form of technological rationing with the possibility for price discrimination (creating incentives to bypass some aspects of the traffic shaping). The latter involves efforts to create a condition of market scarcity, such that both suppliers and customers must indicate their willingness to pay for preferential access based on price. Eli Noam, analyst of the economics of communication, argues that policy discussion is difficult because:

the rivals in the debate over the treatment of communications networks at times exhibit a messianic fervor and are quick to slay messengers of unwanted news. One side invokes a danger to either the survival of competition, democracy, and the internet; while the other side predicts a grave damage to technology, national competitiveness, and the economy.[58]

The debates about network neutrality are complicated further by the fact that some of the companies have an interest in enforcing their intellectual property rights over digital information in the digital environment. As discussed in Chapter 6, they want ISPs to act as gatekeepers on the Internet to work with them to suppress copyright-infringing practices either by blocking traffic on the Internet or by providing the creative industry companies with the identities of those detected by behind the screen intelligent agents that are used for copyright infringement detection purposes. Other companies that are less directly involved in generating their revenues from the sale of digital information find themselves arguing against network neutrality, but with different revenue models driving their interest.

As the Internet develops, some argue that the preservation of network neutrality (however defined) will require it to be treated, for regulatory purposes, as a 'critical resource',[59] similar to some other components of the telecommunication network as discussed at the beginning of this chapter. The positions of stakeholders also vary with the specific policy and governance arrangements in place in different countries and regions and with differences in the structure of the markets for Internet services. It is interesting, therefore, to look at some of the differences in the way network neutrality is being addressed in the United States and Europe.

Network Neutrality in the United States

Network neutrality has come to serve as an all-embracing term for policy matters relating to Internet regulation. Policy debates in this area became especially prominent in the United States when it became clear that telecommunication network operators and ISPs had incentives that might lead them to block Internet traffic from their competitors, or charge certain service providers to terminate their traffic on their networks while offering preferential treatment to others.[60] If ISPs are permitted to introduce these management practices, the concern is that the Internet, as we presently experience it in democratic countries, might begin to fragment into networks operated by a few dominant companies, with implications for the future use of this open platform for innovation and for the costs of public services. Lawrence Lessig, a legal scholar on intellectual property rights (see Chapter 6), and Robert McChesney, a political economy analyst, in the United States argue that:

Without net neutrality, the Internet would start to look like cable TV. A handful of massive companies would control access and distribution of content, deciding what you get to see and how much it costs. Major industries such as health care, finance, retailing and gambling would face huge tariffs for fast, secure Internet use—all subject to discriminatory and exclusive deal making with telephone and cable giants.[61]

The Federal Communication Commission (FCC) regulates the communication system in the United States. The Internet is treated as an unregulated 'information service', rather than as a 'common carriage' service, subject to regulation to avoid unfair or discriminatory practices, a designation that pre-dates the Internet. As a result, there are disputes about whether the FCC has jurisdiction over the Internet.[62] The FCC's Internet policy statement in 2005 called upon network operators to provide Internet access services in a 'neutral' manner. This statement was seen as creating incentives for industry to invest in broadband networks, but it created no requirement to differentiate the quality of service, something that might have been expected if ISP services had been treated as 'common carriage'. This policy, therefore, may inadvertently have created momentum towards a preference for market prices to discriminate among different types of Internet traffic.

Subsequent FCC deliberations in 2010 concluded also that the end-to-end architecture of the Internet should be preserved and that fixed broadband network providers should not be permitted to discriminate 'unreasonably' among their customers. Claims that the open, public Internet is being threatened are 'not speculative or merely theoretical', the FCC said.[63] This policy did not prevent differential pricing for ISP services based on scale of use of the Internet, but ISPs were not permitted to impose restrictions on the type of use or to discriminate 'unreasonably' among Internet users.

Some of the FCC Commissioners insist that this policy involves the imposition of 'the heavy hand of government into how broadband networks will be managed and operated'.[64] Opponents of the 2010 policy statement say that FCC intervention should require evidence that network operators have been unfairly disadvantaging some Internet traffic by degrading connections, limiting bandwidth, or blocking access to certain services. Without a quality of service measure, however, the operators are at an advantage in disputes over whether their management practices fall within the definition of 'reasonable practice'. In addition, there are other ways to 'buy into' preferential access to the Internet, including acquiring shares in the network operator, affiliating with the content operations of network operators where cross-ownership is permitted, and so forth. At the time of writing, the FCC policy was being contested in the courts where, in addition to the battle between the companies providing Internet access and those producing digital content, public interest advocates are insisting that an open Internet must be preserved in the name of democracy and freedom of expression.[65] Some claim that the policy is a capitulation to ISP interests and that it is not sufficient to guard against discrimination among different kinds of Internet traffic. A 'constitutional' solution proposed by Timothy Wu, a leading legal analyst and public interest advocate, calls for structural separation between the producers of information and the owners of network infrastructure to protect the public interest in an open (neutral) Internet.[66]

Network Neutrality in Europe

Differences in ISP industry structure and governance in Europe compared to the United States mean that the network neutrality contest in Europe is discussed somewhat differently, although its outcomes are similar in many ways since there is a progression towards more overt forms of discrimination among traffic on the Internet in the name of traffic management.[67] As in the United States, in Europe the principle of network neutrality was being upheld at the time of writing. 'Reasonable' network management is permitted to create incentives for investing in a broadband infrastructure (as in the United States),[68] and with a view to protecting civil liberties (in the United States the emphasis is on constitutional speech rights). ISP subscribers must be informed about any traffic management techniques and their impact on service quality, and about other limitations (such as bandwidth caps or available connection speed) applied to their service.[69] Network management, intended to enhance the quality of service, promote the development of new services, secure network stability and resilience, or combat crime, is not regarded as a departure from the principle of network neutrality: 'Exceptions to this principle should be considered with great circumspection and need to be justified by overriding public interests'.[70] But because national regulators in Europe have been slow to take up this issue as a high priority public interest consideration, there is a question about who will grant exceptions.

Europe's Digital Agenda Commissioner, Neelie Kroes, emphasizes the principles of freedom of expression and transparency in network neutrality policy,[71] but the relationship between the issues discussed in network neutrality debates and the paradoxes of scarcity and complexity is barely acknowledged. For instance, a European consultation on network neutrality appears to have yielded 'near consensus' among network operators, ISPs, and manufacturers despite their conflicting interests, and very few respondents expressed any concern about potential threats from network management techniques, or how these might affect freedom of expression, media pluralism, or cultural diversity.[72] However, companies (including ISPs, equipment manufacturers, and pay television operators) are lobbying the European

Commission for the right to self-regulation in this area, arguing that measures that limit their profits will dampen their incentives to build the next generation of high-capacity networks.[73]

Although existing prescriptions for resolving network neutrality controversies offer an inadequate shield against non-neutrality for the reasons outlined above, the controversy may be less intense in Europe than in the United States because the network operators' market dominance (within countries and throughout the European Single Market) is less advanced. They need to court all those who would use their networks to support the distribution of content generated by companies that are American controlled, or that is American in origin, for instance, Google's ownership of YouTube, and Facebook and Twitter-generated traffic.

The issue of whether the market-led or information commons vision of the future of the information society should prevail in debates about network neutrality is likely to re-emerge and promote more overt conflict in Europe. This is likely to happen in due course if a more diverse set of actors recognizes that the freedoms that permit a 're-shaping' of the Internet are being used opportunistically by companies with a stake in the economic benefits of the Internet. It was many years before the European Commission took action to address opportunistic behaviour in the mobile industry for example. After very lengthy debate, it ruled eventually that call termination rates charged by mobile operators across Europe should be based on costs, requiring the elimination of indirect subsidies to mobile operators. These had persisted despite changes in technology and network usage, while national regulators resisted change and conflicts were played out largely behind closed doors.[74] In this, and in other areas of communication policy, monitoring of potential abuses, should ISPs attempt to 'shape' the flow of traffic on the Internet unreasonably, is welcomed as long as it is not coupled with intervention that is regarded as being either too early or too much. Interventions aimed at suppressing these developments are seen as threatening the self-organizing dynamics of the communication system or as threatening civil liberties and rights of access to the Internet. In the latter instance, this claim is based on assumptions about the theoretical non-discriminatory technical architecture of the Internet Protocol, not on the actual practices of companies and governments.

In the United Kingdom, co-regulation, self-regulation, or 'net neutrality lite'[75] are called for to produce voluntary codes of good practice aimed at preserving network neutrality. Because it is difficult to assess actual threats to the Internet's neutrality, it is claimed that non-intervention in this layer of the communication system is the optimal policy.[76] The terminology is slightly different in the United States, but the approach is similar. In the United States, there is a stronger inclination towards litigation among the companies affected by policy pronouncements on network neutrality, but the 'machines of loving grace' are being developed with biases towards the interests of some companies and governments without much scrutiny by any governance authority of the actual practices that are occurring behind the screen.

Conclusion

Skirmishes over network neutrality exemplify features of the paradoxes of information scarcity and complexity. In the dominant social imaginary of the information society, these skirmishes are seen as contests among large corporate stakeholders for dominance in the commercial market, and governments, and civil society representatives, each promoting Internet developments they claim to be in the public interest. Because of the complexity of the communication system, the decision by those who might act to reconcile conflicting interests from within formal governance institutions invariably is to wait to see what happens. Even when conflicts are depicted as a symptom of a broader struggle for power between governments and companies, and individual members of society, a 'light touch' approach to intervention aimed at guiding the evolution of the communication system is seen as the optimal way of ensuring that the outcome is in the public interest.

What has been described as 'networked liberalism'—negotiations among all the stakeholders in their 'flexible and shifting social aggregations'—is expected to yield solutions aligned with the values of the good society.[77] This approach is justified by claiming either that the technological system is simply too complex to govern, or that attempts to do so by the state come with the severe risk that governments will become gatekeepers of the Internet, threatening values such as freedom of speech.[78] Of course, in some countries where interventions to monitor content are commonplace and an explicit part of government policy, governments already are threatening these values. These approaches result in denial of the implications of the paradoxes of information scarcity and complexity in mediated environments serving stakeholders in the information society. The likely outcome of contemporary statements on network neutrality is the emergence of a multi-tier network. A multi-tier network would be comprised of a mix of public networks where traffic is subject to scrutiny for state or corporate monitoring purposes, on the one hand, and private (or bypass) networks that privilege certain Internet traffic and enable it to flow securely for those who can pay, on the other.

These illustrations of information society governance issues raise questions about who has the authority and ability to govern, and in response to what goals. Governance controversies, especially with respect to the Internet, centre on the appropriateness of institutional procedures and structures. Debates about multistakeholder forums and procedures provide a focal point for considering whether the outcomes of deliberations are consistent with the dominant or alternative social imaginaries of the information society, but they downplay the incentives that are favouring an increasingly non-transparent mediated environment. There are few signs that the problems associated with the paradoxes of information scarcity and complexity are being addressed, notwithstanding deliberation within relatively open forums. If, on occasion, the problems generated by these paradoxes are acknowledged, they are met with inaction on the part of policy makers and by the oppositional positions of advocates of network neutrality or departures from it (even when quite different things are meant when this term is used). At the same time, policy assertions by governing authorities are having little influence on the practices of network operators and companies in the creative industries. The ISPs are moving towards market mechanisms for allocating the use of bandwidth, with countermoves from the content producers to minimize the charges for distributing their content. Policy statements about network neutrality are achieving less and less traction as we move incrementally towards a non-neutral Internet era.

When these disputes about the public interest in the Internet Age are punctuated from an instrumental perspective, the governance challenges are perceived to involve a deliberative process of negotiation among stakeholders about what is most likely to benefit Internet users in front of the screen. From a critical systems perspective, however, the challenges for governance involve asymmetrical power relationships among stakeholders located within different levels of a multi-level system, only one part of which is related to the existing features of the Internet Protocol. In the former case, the struggle seems to pit the interests of network operators against those of the large content providers, over measures that will enable them to succeed in the market as they work out how to ensure that information scarcity provides them with opportunities for profiting from the online activities of the users of the communication system. Alternatively, it would seem to pit civil society stakeholders against the state over measures to control the Internet for surveillance and security purposes. However, in both cases, the risks associated with the spread of automated software agents that are being deployed for monitoring and tracking user behaviour and the implications of the use of these agents both for commercial market development and for the rights of everyday users of the Internet are largely ignored. In the prevailing social imaginaries of the information society, the paradox of complexity makes it seem as if it is the communication *system* that has an 'interest' in its self-organized emergence and survival, an interest that is, or ultimately will become, aligned with the values of the good society.

Internet users are becoming locked into bundles of services offered by companies that are asserting control over the communication system including the parts of the system we have come to designate as '*the* Internet'. In the dominant social imaginary, governance issues are depicted as being princi-pally about technical aspects such as traffic flows and routing, domain names, or search engine algorithms. This aligns well with corporate interests in minimizing governance from above by the state, and with civil society inter-ests in minimizing state interference for reasons of surveillance. The denial of asymmetrical power among the stakeholders with respect to the transparency of the behind the screen technologies is facilitated also by the social imaginary of the information commons. This is because these developments are seen as being empowering for them because of the wide range of choices citizens are being enabled to make about how the communication system can best be used to augment their everyday lives.

In these debates about governance of the Internet (and media and the communication system generally), it seems that one group of stakeholders must lose in order for another to win in the battle over network neutrality. The pattern of communication is locked into a chronic opposition of either/or policy alternatives, with the system's very complexity being invoked to prevent measures being taken that would start to address the deeper issues associated with the paradoxes of information scarcity and complexity. The outcome is a communication system that is, in practice, largely ungoverned with respect to the behind the screen developments from the perspective of citizen interests and transparency, notwithstanding the wealth of discussion in governance institutions at all levels and the persistent political firestorms over whether and how the Internet's architecture should be retained, with respect to the Internet Protocol. As the system continues to evolve, increas-ingly intrusive 'machines of loving grace' are coming to be taken for granted by all the participants in the information society.

All technologies are transformed in their journey from invention to wide-spread use. They are neither completely prefigured to the preferences of stakeholders nor are they fully malleable. Encouraging each actor to pursue his, her, or 'its' own conception of the 'good' in the absence of a wider range of policy alternatives in the Internet Age may seem initially to be consistent with empowering people because of the wealth of new opportunities in front of the screen. However, the contemporary social imaginaries of the information society are instrumental in denying the capacities of the state and dominant private sector companies to decide through their practices which technologi-cal innovations should be encouraged and which should be discouraged.

In the next and final chapter, I argue that these persistent patterns in the debates about the evolution of the communication system are the result of a mispunctuation of the conflicts around the power relationships within a multi-level system in which both hierarchical and heterarchical dynamics are in play. The result is that potential policy measures that could guide the system along a different pathway are sequestered. I suggest also that the public interest in the information society is such that it is crucially important to work towards the development of a new social imaginary of the information society, one that is consistent with policy interventions that guide the evolution of the system in a way that is better aligned with the values of the good society.

8 Conclusion

We were born for something better!
And what the inner voice speaks
will not mislead the soul that hopes.

(von Schiller, 1797)[*]

Introduction

I began this book with questions about how and why people imagine the changes to the 'machines of loving grace' in the ways that they do. How are choices about the evolution of the communication system influencing the way people live their lives in the mediated environment of the Internet Age? The new cyberspace ecology is mediating people's lives in ways that extend the range of their choices, but is also reinforcing unequal power relationships in society. If, as Roger Silverstone insists, the communication system constitutes our 'very capacity to be in the world', then clearly this matters.[1] Few would wish to return to a time before the Internet and the software and hardware tools that are providing opportunities for young and old. My critical assessment of the social imaginaries of the information society is not inspired by neo-Luddite yearnings, but by the hope that the communication system can be integrated into people's lives in a way that maximizes benefits and minimizes harms.

In *Media and Morality*, Silverstone argues that the dynamics of mediation are taken for granted in most media and communication policy and regulatory discussions. His concern was with ethics and the values that should guide the professionalization of media producers in a period of rapid technological change. My analysis, although it gives greater emphasis to changes in the technological system, is addressed similarly to the values that should guide those who influence the way the communication system is mediating people's lives. Contemporary approaches to the governance of the media and the communication system are characterized by persistent clashes among stakeholders whose visions of the information society are influenced by very different social imaginaries. In this book I have shown why governance measures aimed at reconciling their disparate interests are often blind to the implications of the paradoxes of information scarcity and complexity as they present themselves in the Internet Age. This form of blindness is not a new phenomenon as Rosalind Williams, historian of technological change, suggests, 'the role of subterranean technologies is commonly neglected because the artefacts themselves are hidden from view'.[2] This has serious consequences because it leaves the direction of communication system evolution to the preferences of stakeholders whose interests are not necessarily well-aligned with the values of the good society.

In this chapter I suggest how it might be possible to begin to foster a new social imaginary of the information society, one that amplifies the chances that our 'machines of loving grace' operate in a way that contributes to a mediated environment in which people can achieve greater empowerment, freedom, and responsibility. My analysis of the implications of the paradoxes of information scarcity and complexity should be seen as a beginning, as setting the stage for further development through research that seeks a better understanding of what these paradoxes mean for communication system governance, and how we think about the public interest in information society developments.

Social Imaginaries and Paradox in the Internet Age

Social imaginaries are what enable people to make sense of the practices of a given society. The practices of many different stakeholders in the information society with respect to the development of ICTs and their governance constitute the social imaginaries of the information society. Two social imaginaries are prominent in the Internet Age: one is principally about the relationship between economic growth and technological change and the other is principally about the relationship between technological change and human agency. In each of these relationships, there are dominant and alternative imaginaries, which are assumed by their proponents to be consistent with the values of the good society. I have suggested that these imaginaries are the products of false learning in the sense that they do not acknowledge the implications of the paradoxes of information scarcity and complexity in the Internet Age. Scholarly work, aimed at modelling the process of technological change in society, although by no means the only source of learning, plays an important role in constituting these social imaginaries. One branch of this work favours an exogenous model of change, the other favours a variety of endogenous models of change, as discussed in Chapter 3.

In the *exogenous model*, technological change is treated as an exogenous shock to the cultural, social, political, or economic system. Change is depicted by employing mechanistic models, and questions are asked about adjustment to these shocks. The assessment of outcomes involves measurements to calibrate the impacts or effects of shocks on economic growth, productivity, or stocks of knowledge in the case of economic analysis, and other measurable changes in perception or behaviour in the case of other branches of the social sciences that adhere to the premises of this model. In the Internet Age, technological shocks come from massive changes in the capacities to produce, process, distribute, and store digital information. The exogenous model is strongly influenced by the cybernetics information processing model with its emphasis on the way innovations in technology augment the speed and complexity of human information processing.

In this model, advances in technology are regarded as autonomous of the social system. The policy response is to rely on efficient markets and individual choice to guide the evolution of the communication system. Market demand for ICTs and digital information is believed to maximize individual choice in the information society and to spur technological innovation that will lead to intelligent machines that will be responsive to human needs. However, the need to adapt to these changes constitutes the only choice in many cases. The exogenous model is a deterministic model, and it leaves unexplained many factors that contribute to technological change; these become the unexplained residual, which progressive improvements in technology ultimately, it is assumed, will provide solutions to economic or social problems.

In *endogenous* models, however, it is acknowledged that social transformation is only partly about tools and machines. In endogenous models, efforts are made to take account of the complex interfaces between the material and symbolic worlds. Lewis Mumford, an American philosopher and science and technology historian, preferred the term *technics* to technology, to express this. For Mumford, *technics* encompass people's wishes, ideas, goals, and habits, as well as the tools and machines.[3] He argues that 'to understand the dominating role played by technics in modern civilization, . . . one must explain the culture that was ready to use them and profit by them so extensively'.[4] He was convinced that 'the problem of integrating the machine in society is not merely a matter . . . of making social institutions keep in step with the machine: the problem is equally one of *altering the nature and the rhythm of the machine to fit the actual needs of the community*',[5] a view echoed in Sherry Turkle's comment that 'we become the objects we look upon but *they become what we make of them*'.[6]

My examination of the social imaginaries of the information society shows that what we make of our communication machines differs depending on the assumptions we make about human agency. In the case of endogenous models, the boundary to the components of the system that gives rise to technological change is often fuzzy, allowing it to encompass the technological and the social systems. Instead of exogenous shocks, the main interest is in the interactions within a complex system. In the social sciences, the concept of mediation, and theories of political and economic power and changes in techno-economic paradigms, for instance, are employed to explain aspects of these relationships. These relationships are described empirically and are understood as involving human agency and dynamically changing power relationships. In the physical and natural sciences, these relationships are depicted increasingly more frequently as comprising a complex adaptive system. The couplings within this system are understood metaphorically to be the result of adaptive learning whose outcomes produce stability or instability within the system. Analysis of the system is framed by the information processing model which ignores the meaning of information and human agency. These distinctive interpretations of the dynamics of technological change make their presence felt in conflicts between the two predominant social imaginaries of the information society.

Interpreted within the *dominant social imaginary* of the information society, technological change is understood as an emergent and unpredictable process within a complex adaptive system. It follows that nothing should be done to intervene in the evolution of the system because it would heighten the risk of unpredictable outcomes and produce greater instability within the system. It would seem to follow that an unfettered or unregulated market system would create optimal incentives for the production of ICTs and digital information, assuming private intellectual property ownership rights are in place and are enforced. An *alternative social imaginary* interprets the endogenous model of system complexity differently. In this imaginary it is assumed also that the process of technological change is emergent, but that a complex system gives rise to innovations and incentives for the production of ICTs and digital information when human agency is deployed to create the best conditions for the decentralized sharing of information within a commons-based peer production model.

Proponents of these two imaginaries are pitted against each other in policy and regulatory debates; one group advocating reliance on the emergent properties of a complex system underpinned by intellectual property rights, the other, reliance on the emergent properties of a complex system underpinned by the generative activities of communities of online participants. In these social imaginaries, individual choice is valued differently, although in both it is claimed that outcomes are consistent with democracy and the values of the good society. In the dominant social imaginary, the good society is achievable if individual choice is maximized, for example, when improved access to digital technologies or information is shown to empower individuals. In the alternative social imaginary, empowering individuals to make choices is valued, but is achieved through decentralized collective action.

Throughout this book, I have demonstrated how, in both of these social imaginaries, the implications of the paradoxes of information scarcity and complexity are ignored. A paradox occurs when two correct statements are contradictory. When the nature of paradox is not acknowledged, this creates discomfort and efforts to cope with unacknowledged paradox can be harmful for the actors involved. The paradox of information scarcity in the Internet Age can be stated as follows:

- information is initially costly to produce and intellectual property rights create the optimal incentives for creativity, diversity, and growth;
- information is virtually costless to reproduce and the optimal incentives for creativity, diversity, and growth occur when it is freely distributed.

In the face of the information scarcity paradox, the challenge is how to create incentives for the production of diverse information. For cultural, political, social, and economic reasons, diversity is highly valued in the information society, along with the freedom of individuals and responsibility. The conflicts among stakeholders in the light of the social imaginaries lead to several possible outcomes. The first is continuation of the frictions between and resistance to the views of the opposing group. The second is emergence of new ways to legitimize the free circulation of digital information. The third is new ways to garner the economic returns from digital information. Some combination of these outcomes is likely, with the relative strengths of each influencing the way contested values are combined.

A statement of the paradox of complexity in the Internet Age is that:

- there are intrinsic benefits from the emergent complexity in the technological system behind the screen, which are leading to loss of control;
- there are intrinsic benefits from the emergent complexity in the technological system behind the screen, which are leading to greater control achieved through programming within a decentralized system.

Again, the conflicts between proponents of the conflicting social imaginaries can produce a number of possible outcomes. The first is friction between those who advocate withdrawal of the attempts to regulate the communication system because of the risks of intervening in a complex adaptive system, and those who argue that intervention is needed, in the name of the public interest. The second is an increasingly complex technological system that maximizes the interests of companies profiting from digital information. The third is an increasingly complex technological system that maximizes the interests of the state in surveillance. A fourth is an increasingly complex technological system that favours the interests of decentralized online communities, whatever their values. All these outcomes are likely, the issue being how they are combined. In this paradox, there is presently no answer to the question of how various stakeholders can be held accountable for their actions.

In contemporary debates about governance in the information society, the conditions that give rise to the paradoxes of information scarcity and complexity are imagined as opposing claims, and the argument is polarized around the efforts of those privileging one set of claims to discredit the efforts of those privileging another set of claims. Paradox, however, cannot be resolved simply by rebalancing the outcomes within a complex adaptive system so that stakeholder interests are accommodated in the light of a solution to these competing claims. When the paradoxical nature of these claims is recognized, it is clear that conflict among stakeholders with different interests is inevitable and that the asymmetric power relations among contending groups will persist. The challenge, therefore, is how to reconcile stakeholder interests in the face of paradox. This is a problem that requires a different approach to those being pursued in contemporary governance debates.

In the prevailing social imaginaries of the information society, there is a particularly problematic feature which complicates the search for reconciliation. Despite insisting that emergence within a complex adaptive system should be the optimal guide for the evolution of the communication system, in practice, there is significant intervention by human actors. In the dominant social imaginary, this intervention takes the form of intellectual property rights legislation, the effect of which is to suppress the potential for the circulation of information that is virtually costless to reproduce. In the alternative social imaginary, intervention is constituted by the actions of hardware developers and software programmers, whose ostensibly neutral actions, in reality, variously favour the interests of companies in profiting from digital information, of the state in surveillance, or of virtual community participants. Both proponents of strong intellectual property rights and the developers behind the screen are assumed to be acting in ways that are consistent with general social welfare. Within the frameworks of these social imaginaries these kinds of interventions in the communication system's evolution are not presumed to be problematic and the proponents of the practices pertaining to these conflicting social imaginaries are not accountable. In the case of proponents of the dominant social imaginary, it is assumed that, at the time it was enacted, intellectual property rights legislation achieved the 'correct' balance between conflicting stakeholder interests and that there is nothing to suggest that social welfare would benefit from a re-examination of that assumption. In the case of the proponents of reliance on the generative activities of hardware developers and software programmers, it is assumed that their values will be aligned with those of society. The result is an unaccountable information society based on a bias favouring the commodity production of information and the progressive 'augmentation of the mind' through greater complexity of the communication system behind the screen.

Harold A. Innis warned that progressive 'mechanization of knowledge' is associated with increasing complexity and that major changes in the mediated environment historically have led to confusion especially about how communication technologies should be governed.[7] He claimed that new generations of technology (such as the automation of information production, processing, circulation, and consumption) are often associated with knowledge mono-polies as discussed in Chapter 2. As he puts it, 'use of a medium of communication over a long period will to some extent determine the character of knowledge to be communicated, and suggest that its pervasive influence will eventually create a civilization in which life and flexibility will become exceedingly difficult to maintain'.[8] In the dominant social imaginary, it is claimed that the state has decided on the optimal balance between the interests of information creators and general social welfare. In the alternative information society social imaginary, the claim is that we should rely on the 'wisdom' of an elite community of hardware developers and software programmers. As William Melody, scholar of the political economy of the information society, suggests, 'electronic monks' are being charged with establishing the values that guide people through the digital world and they are constituting a new knowledge monopoly.[9]

To assist in focusing attention on the implications of paradoxes that lead to the conflicts between the proponents of the different social imaginaries, the critical systems framework presented in Chapter 4 integrates analysis of the factors giving rise to these paradoxes in the Internet Age with analysis of changing power relations among the stakeholders in the information society. This framework facilitates a re-reading of these paradoxes which is neither utopian nor dystopian, but is aimed at understanding whether there is a better pathway for society and whether adaptive action can serve to repair outcomes associated with conflict that is generated by paradox.

In the contemporary social imaginaries of the information society, technological progress is taken for granted as something to be welcomed and the idea that it may be either benign or harmful is 'too obvious to mention' in debates over how best to govern the communication system.[10] The policy interventions that are introduced are curative measures intended to cope with those results of technological progress flagged as being inconsistent with the values of the good society. At the same time, they constitute tinkering within the constraints of a self-organizing complex adaptive system in which the equilibrium state or basic trajectory of change and any power asymmetries are assumed to be unalterable at least insofar as development of the communication system is concerned. Curative policies include, for instance, efforts to develop ways to support children deemed vulnerable to risks associated with the Internet. These policies are often formulated without examining the power relationships that give rise to potential harms, the variability in children's resources to cope with the threat of harm, or the broad range of interventions that would be needed to address this complex issue.[11]

In these social imaginaries of the information society, the evolutionary process is seen as being either wholly or largely beyond human control; it is ungovernable by authoritative government measures from above because the system is emergent and indeterminate. This message eschews normative judgements about inequality and social injustice and how they are influenced by choices about the evolution of the communication system. The self-organizing complex communication system may absorb information from its environment, but is itself agnostic about value preferences. For optimists, the emergence of 'machines of loving grace' heralds the dawning of the Singularity. For pessimists, network contagion effects and increasing returns signal the risk that the system will spin out of control with dark implications.

Policy and regulatory interventions to guide the system are deemed irresponsible in the face of complexity and an unknowable future. The optimal pathway is withdrawal of the state. This serves some companies well because it frees them to pursue their interests in monetizing digital information, employing the complex communication system to achieve their goals. State withdrawal also resonates positively with the interests of those advocating an open commons decentralized approach since this appears to be a way of curtailing state surveillance and fostering democratic values.

Re-reading Paradox

The critical systems framework encourages a re-reading of the implications of the paradoxes of information scarcity and complexity. In this framework, the idea of mediation emphasizes the fact that the communication system is 'doubly articulated' in the economy and in culture. Changes in power relationships are coupled with the material characteristics of hardware and software and with the symbolic meaning of tools, machines, and digital content. Whatever the power relationships and their outcomes, they are related to changes at different levels within a complex adaptive system. Understanding developments at the interfaces between these levels helps to explain the paradoxes of the Internet Age.

As discussed in Chapter 4, tackling the problem of paradox requires an understanding that the evolution of the communication system is subject to the dynamics of power relationships in a multi-level complex adaptive system comprised of hierarchical *and* heterarchical relationships. For instance, the architecture of the Internet on one level in the system may suggest heterarchy, but this does not eliminate hierarchical relationships among other components of the communication system. As a result, the problems for stakeholders with different interests are not about whether competition in a hierarchical information marketplace should be privileged *or* whether cooperation in a heterarchical open commons should be encouraged. Instead, they are about how to facilitate reconciliation between both kinds of relationships. Similarly, the issue is not whether the dynamics of technological change behind the screen should be ungoverned *or* whether elite programmers should make choices about which technologies to deploy. Instead, it is about how the evolution of the system can be governed in ways that respect the emergent characteristics of the system and acknowledge that, in practice, interest-driven interventions are occurring all the time, with outcomes that are inconsistent with the values of the good society some of the time. These either/or ways of seeing the challenges of the Internet Age are examples of persistent patterns of double-binding communication which need to be disrupted by a both/and perspective. This is more likely when the nature of paradox is acknowledged and efforts are made to disturb persistent patterns of thought that reinforce denial of the implications of paradox.

Paradox, as Bateson's work suggests, is generated by self-referential communication 'circuits'. These circuits can be disturbed by metacommunications—information that makes a difference—enabling the insight that conflict arises in paradoxical situations as a result of efforts to secure survival (e.g. companies pursuing strategies to maintain their dominance in the marketplace, or citizens resisting surveillance by automated software agents to secure their autonomy). Adaptive action aims at destabilizing patterns of dysfunctional either/or communications—metacommunications about the 'way things are'—potentially generating a new social imaginary that acknowledges the reality of paradox and the harms that it creates, and seeks repairs to alleviate those harms.

Disturbing patterns of communication that deny paradox makes it possible to accept the validity of respective stakeholder visions for the information society, in the light of their respective positions within a complex adaptive system, *and* to encourage a transition that relocates and redirects debate on another gradient allowing paradoxes to be addressed through adaptive action.[12] Repunctuating the analysis of paradoxical conflict in the context of this new way of seeing could enable governance interventions responding to the harms created by paradox to be debated and adopted as appropriate. There are many examples of victims of paradox in the information society involved in chronic battles to secure their survival. These include conflicts over the enforcement of traditional rights of information ownership and over the regulation of the Internet, as in the case of network neutrality debates. The analysis in the preceding chapters shows that it is possible to consider the implications of the paradoxes of information scarcity and complexity in a new light if dysfunctional patterns of communication are disturbed by new information about the way paradoxical relationships of power are implicated in the dynamics of the mediation process in the Internet Age.

One step towards interrupting dysfunctional patterns of communication is to disrupt the habit of thought that insists there is something natural about the 'braking functions of social diffusion' to quote Clay Shirky. It is human beings, not a self-organizing system, who need to make corrections to reconcile stakeholder interests within a complex adaptive system characterized by paradoxical phenomena. This requires more than critical reflexivity to acknowledge that stakeholders in the information society have partisan interests. I have suggested that it requires adaptive action aimed ultimately at empowering all those with partisan interests to give birth to a new social imaginary of the information society. This approach differs substantially from the 'adaptations' and curative policies envisaged when the genesis and implications of paradox are denied.

Oppositional ways of seeing can be maintained only when the hierarchical and heterarchical relationships within the complex multi-level communication system are ignored. When there is no effort to repunctuate the analysis to account for the way paradox is experienced on these different levels, it is impossible for stakeholders to gain insights into why their actions yield outcomes that result in chronic conflict and harm. A line in a poem by W. B. Yeats asks 'how can we know the dancer from the dance?'[13] In similar vein, Bateson asked 'how can you hear the music if you are one of the notes?'[14] Both refer indirectly to the way paradox is generated when those involved are caught within two mutually contradictory realities, both of which may be valid reflections of their experience of those realities. Harmful outcomes are likely to result from their strategies to secure their respective positions—enforcement of intellectual property rights or augmentation of the human mind behind the screen in unaccountable ways. Without a repunctuation of the relationships that are generating the paradoxes of information scarcity and complexity, it is impossible for the stakeholders to imagine how their respective interests might be reconciled because their patterns of debate do not enable them to distinguish their parochial interests from those of society. Following Charles Taylor, a re-reading of paradox is possible when the dichotomous either/or ways of thinking are substituted by both/and ways of seeing which are responsive to the experience of paradox.

Adaptive actions that respond to the experience of paradox differ from the adaptations evoked by the contemporary social imaginaries. Adaptive action aims to rupture persistent habits of thought by bringing the conflicts engendered by the paradoxes of scarcity and complexity to the foreground. Adaptive action can foster opportunities for liberation from the false learning that occurs when paradox is denied. It creates the means of encouraging a new social imaginary with more diverse choices involving neither the excesses of hegemonic governance from above with its neoliberal ideology of the market nor naive trust in the generative power of dispersed online communities as a means of governance from below.

Adaptive actions cannot resolve or eliminate the experience of paradox, nor can they achieve a better equilibrium or balance among stakeholders with conflicting interests. However, they can suggest ways in which reconciliation leading to new pathways can begin to be imagined and ultimately acted upon. I have provided some of the conceptual tools for thinking about this. The next section outlines several crucial actions that would encourage corrections in the presently circular debates about governance of the communication system in the information society.

Adaptive Action and Policy Corrections

Several opportunities for adaptive action emerge from my re-rereading of the paradoxes of information scarcity and complexity. These suggest policy corrections aimed at fostering a new social imaginary of the information society that would guide the evolution of the communication system in a way that resists the excesses of the market and encourages experimentation with less risk to human beings. This was the goal I set at the beginning of this work. Three areas of adaptive action that would be desirable and can be considered urgent are: (*a*) action to diffuse monopolies of knowledge; (*b*) action to foster online creativity; and (*c*) action to govern decisions about augmenting the human mind.

MONOPOLIES OF KNOWLEDGE

A crucial arena for adaptive action is related to the intrinsic value of the emergent properties of a complex adaptive system. This is leading to the increasing complexity of the communication system and to reduced human control over the system. In the dominant social imaginary the response is to forbear from governance that interferes with the emergent process. In the alternative social imaginary, efforts to guide the evolution of the system rely on an elite group of programmers introducing local adjustments through their decentralized activities in the information commons.

Harold Innis's work is often read as a deterministic account of the impact of communication technology on society. Such a reading might suggest that it is the Internet—however defined—that establishes the conditions for the production, circulation, and use of knowledge. However, the history of change in the use of ICTs of all kinds confirms that there is nothing straightforward about the relationship between advances in technology and social transformation. From the end of World War II to the 1970s, the model of social and economic growth relied heavily upon capital-intensive, physical technologies. After that, there was a substantial move towards reliance on immaterial goods and digital information, but little acknowledgement of the implications of the paradoxes of information scarcity and complexity. In the dominant social imaginary, developments in technology, information, and knowledge are conflated. Strengthening consumer demand for digital information is the greatest priority, together with curative policies to meet the needs of the 'deserving' information poor by filling gaps in access to information or technology. In the alternative social imaginary, the approach is similar, but the priority is to strengthen the conditions for experimentation in an open information commons.

Adaptive action is needed to encourage correction such that investment in hardware and software is not treated as a proxy for the capacities of people to make sense of their mediated environment. The notion that there is a global knowledge base that can be employed to alleviate social and economic disadvantage and is accessible through ICTs, but without capacities to evaluate digital information critically in the light of other sources of knowledge, would come to be seen as a profound misunderstanding of the mediated world. A shift towards emphasizing multiple forms of digital information and the importance of tacit knowledge would take precedence over measures of stocks of information and points of network access in the digital world. The belief that investment in hardware and software is the highest priority for stimulating economic growth and for supporting democratic values would be challenged by distinguishing among tools, information, and knowledge. Public and private investment in ICTs would be scrutinized in the light of competing claims over scarce resources. For example, policies and private sector initiatives aimed at broadband expansion, a home computer for every child, or a rural kiosk in every village would be evaluated in the light of other urgent social goals.

The idea that the automation of the communication system always is consistent with productivity improvements and the growth of the economy would be critically evaluated, acknowledging that there may be limits to the extent to which 'intelligent machines' can or should be tasked with making choices. Greater attention would be given to the relationship between codified information and tacit knowledge, to unequal power relationships that influence who has the knowledge necessary to decode algorithms of codified information, and to what people need to do in order to acquire knowledge that is meaningful to them. This would encourage attention to the meaning of information and to the importance of its variety. Valuing information diversity outside the framework of the commercial market would start to encourage a new social imaginary of the information society in which information is understood, not as a 'thing', but as a component of the multiple knowledges that are essential for learning.

FACILITATING ONLINE CREATIVITY

A further adaptive action would encourage a correction in the direction of the evolution of the communication system so that the values of the good society would be served by both the market exchange model for digital information and the information commons model. The priority in the dominant social imaginary of the knowledge economy is to secure the scarcity of digital information by enforcing intellectual property rights to foster economic growth. In the alternative social imaginary, 'information wants to be free' to be 'mashed-up' in creative ways in a commons-based peer production environment. The conflict between copyright holders and everyday online participants would be addressed initially by recognizing that attempts to control digital information through the imposition of rights of ownership and the suppression of creative online activity have lost credibility in the Internet Age. This would weaken the argument that online methods to detect copyright infringers, such as methods of deep packet inspection, are justified. This, in turn, would provide an opportunity for a debate about the other interests these methods serve, including those of the state and the science and engineering communities, and whether they are consistent with standards of social justice.

In a new social imaginary the acceptability of targeting individuals engaged in online file-sharing and other means of sharing information would begin to wane, shifting debate towards ways of broadening the scope for a flourishing collaborative and sharing culture. The impasse between those claiming that a radical curtailment of creative output would result from lowering existing legislative barriers to information exchange and those claiming that an information commons would stimulate improvisation and creativity would be broken. Stakeholders would begin to debate the arrangements that would create market incentives for the production of digital information *and* incentives for the sharing of information.

This correction is needed to encourage means of empowering citizens through their participation in online environments, while remaining consistent with the values of economic growth, the security of the state, and the protection of individuals from potential harms. Few would support measures that favour the empowerment of people to watch hours of pornography, which might provoke them into acting out what is portrayed. Any such measures must be concerned with value choices about economic opportunity and ethics. The outcomes of the debate could influence education campaigns explaining the full range of possibilities available to digital information producers, consumers, and citizens. Other changes that might be considered include modifications to the way digital information producers, including artists, are compensated for their efforts such as a tax applied to the use of the Internet or an allocation from general taxation accompanied by mechanisms to distribute the resulting pool of resources to information creators.[15] As a new social imaginary begins to take hold, consideration could be given to rolling back expansionist intellectual property rights legislation so as to minimize the creation of new monopolies of knowledge and to facilitate the opening of the digital commons to creativity.

AUGMENTING THE HUMAN MIND

Adaptive action is needed to address the question of whether investment in the communication system should be guided by human beings or by the choices of our 'machines of loving grace' and how the human beings should be held accountable. The fascination with intelligent machines aimed at augmenting the human mind in immersive environments is deeply embedded in the prevailing social imaginaries of the information society. Claims by computer scientists and online marketing specialists, that software agent-based computer systems should set (or should be designed to set) their own priorities, must be challenged if the public interest in minimizing unwanted intrusions is to be protected. The volumes of data that need to be searched to find information of interest to law enforcement agencies, to companies, and to other social groups are growing exponentially. However, what software agents can or cannot do in terms of auditing information and tracing its origins is not easily visible on the governance agenda.

Measures are needed to protect citizens from unwanted intrusions into the virtual spaces they deem to be private and to ensure that the state's interests in security are met, but these must be handled in a transparent way and be subjected to ethical scrutiny. The absence of public debate about such measures is due partly to the claim that the communication system is too complex to govern and that it responds to its own 'needs'. Adaptive action would encourage attention to the progressive automation of the communication system that is allowing choices about people's lives to be delegated to software agents. Instead of seeing the boundary between public and private information as the outcome of a given trajectory of technological innovation, questions would be raised about whether the companies claiming to depend on intrusive software agents really need this information to support advertising-based online commerce models and about what alternative models are available.

Questions would also be raised about the extent to which governments depend on the use of these agents for monitoring to generate information about illegal activity. Legislation designed to provide privacy safeguards is coming to be seen by the state as shielding those engaged in activities that are disapproved of or condemned, and by companies as limiting their commercial prospects. In a new social imaginary, consideration of the way these developments infringe human rights would increase and the refrain would no longer be simply that little if anything can be done to curtail the excesses of monitoring practice because the communication system is global and complex.

Self-regulatory codes of practice offer some safeguards, but cannot prevent the processing of data that have been rendered 'non-personal'. These codes of practice would come to be regarded as curative policies that ignore the fact that digital platform owners have incentives to exceed commonly accepted norms of behaviour, as do governments. In a new social imaginary it would be acknowledged that the processes leading to the automation of everyday life are cumulative and adaptive (in the evolutionary sense), and surveillance, privacy intrusions, agent misbehaviour, and lack of transparency are predominating. What is possible today may become excessive in the future. The right to be free from surveillance would not be seen as an unaffordable luxury in the face of an emergent complex adaptive system. Questions would be asked about whether the market is likely to curtail excesses and whether hacker and other online communities should be presumed always to be acting in the interests of citizens.

In a new social imaginary there would be reasons to question whether surveillance by the 'machines of loving grace' should be the taken-for-granted as the norm in the information society. It could be that software agents should be used to perform ever more revelatory and comprehensive surveillance if justified by commercial, policing, or security reasons. They could also be tasked to facilitate surveillance by charities seeking donors, or cults seeking new recruits. It would be a choice to extend the limits to surveillance using intelligent software agents. However, the response instead might be to limit such developments inasmuch as they are motivated by opportunities for commercial gain and by state interests in security more than by benefits to consumers and citizens. Were a new social imaginary to begin to take hold, it might be possible to consider measures that would limit the excesses of surveillance while allowing the benefits of a communication system that augments the human mind. In a new social imaginary, it might become reasonable to ask questions about the interests guiding the choices of the 'electronic monks' and their authority to decide about the technologies behind the screen.

In the contemporary alternative social imaginary, it is assumed that we should rely on a new knowledge elite—the software programmers and hardware developers—to decide the features of the communication system behind the screen, and on self-organizing civil society groups to galvanize change in support of a more equitable and just world in front of the screen. For example, political philosophers, Michael Hardt and Antonio Negri, acknowledge that 'control over linguistic sense and meaning and the networks of communication' is a core issue in political struggle.[16] However, they look to the impact of the tools of the Internet Age to create the conditions where 'self-organization' reaches a threshold that provokes fundamental societal change that they assume will be aligned with the values of the good society.[17] This model is reminiscent of the shocks envisaged by technology on society in the exogenous model and it is assumed that the meaning of information is consistent with values of the good society. Manuel Castells suggests that 'networks... process the goals they are programmed to perform',[18] appearing to assume that self-organizing social movements will programme the goals for the tools and machines for mass self-communication[19] in a way that is consistent with the values of the good society. The questions are why we should assume that these groups represent the majority and whether some form of accountability for the new leaders is necessary. The evidence from empirical studies of self-organizing online communities is that they create new norms and hierarchies that are not always based on the values of meritocracy.

The false oppositions resulting from the denial of the paradoxes of information scarcity and complexity are visible in formal settings for governance of the communication system. The persistent contest over the Internet's architecture in disputes about network neutrality is indicative of this. These debates are around whether the end-to-end architecture of the Internet Protocol is sustainable in the face of interests in controlling digital information for economic gain and interests in liberating digital information for creative purposes. However, when the paradoxes are acknowledged, it is possible to see that state and corporate practices are already well down the path to a *non-neutral network*. In a new social imaginary, debate would focus on the reality of the mediated world behind the screen, whether there is a need to restrain intelligent software agents, and on whose authority such restraint should be considered.

A Final Reading

Adaptive action is a response to the paradoxes of information scarcity and complexity in the Internet Age. Adaptive action differs substantially from the idea of adapting to the shocks of technological change. It differs also from the idea that these technologies are malleable in the hands of their unspecified designers, users, or audiences. This is because such action becomes feasible only with effort to repunctuate debates that are otherwise locked into oppositions between the contemporary social imaginaries of the information society. Responses to paradox have an ethical dimension which can be debated only when the potential harms associated with a failure to respond to paradox are acknowledged. Opening up governance forums with a remit to address the conflicts that occur in the course of constructing the information society (e.g., regulatory proceedings, intergovernmental organizations, etc.), to a wide range of stakeholders, may help to disrupt dysfunctional patterns of communication that are sustaining the prevailing social imaginaries. However, a procedural response alone is unlikely to empower those who could give birth to a new social imaginary of the information society.[20]

What is needed is improved knowledge of the interactions within a multi-level communication system which lead to the genesis of the paradoxes of information scarcity and complexity. We must hope that unexpected developments within the complex adaptive system will reveal discrepancies in presently taken-for-granted ways of seeing and that this recognition will spawn new patterns of communication that will produce a new understanding of these paradoxes. Unexpected developments are more likely to emerge from the scholarly community and become part of a new social imaginary when researchers cross conventional academic boundaries that serve to sequester discussion of these paradoxes. Interdisciplinary research is helpful in creating opportunities for critical assessment of the paradoxes of the Internet Age because it encourages the development of critical systems frameworks such as the one I employed in my analysis. Researchers are enabled to practise reflexive research, but also to be open to surprises that disturb their conventional ways of seeing the dynamics of the evolution of the communication system—that is, they are more likely to be cognizant of news of difference.

Mumford observes that 'the instrument only in part determines the character of the symphony or the response of the audience: the composer and the musicians and the audience have also to be considered . . . *we will have to re-write the music in the act of playing it*.'[21] It is not possible to stand apart from the evolution of the communication system to evaluate its impacts because for most of our lives we are immersed in the mediated world. The music can be re-written in the act of playing it in the hope of creating a new social imaginary of the information society. A new social imaginary would be alert to paradox and stakeholders might start seeking to reconcile their conflicting interests in a way that acknowledges the harms that otherwise would occur—that is, the excesses of the market, of unrestrained experimentation, and unaccountable developments in front of and behind the screen.

My analysis of the contemporary social imaginaries reveals how the experience of paradox in the information society is being systematically denied. The results illustrate the value of an interdisciplinary approach, suggesting what further interdisciplinary studies that cross the boundaries of disciplinary enquiry might accomplish.[22] This kind of approach is met with scepticism in some quarters. For instance, Paul Streeten, an economist closely associated with the human development agenda, argues that 'the only forum where interdisciplinary studies *in depth* can be conducted successfully is under one skull'.[23] My aim is not to sacrifice in-depth analysis on the altar of a transdisciplinary research agenda: it is for this reason that I restrict my analysis to two important paradoxes of the Internet Age and do not offer detailed recommendations for policy. It could be argued that this is an idealist approach because I have not said to whom those making the choices about the evolution of the communication system should be accountable. One response to this is that this will depend on the particular configuration of institutions and power relations in specific places, which it does. Another is that in the twenty-first century mediated environment, this is an open question which needs urgently to be addressed through future research and by society as a whole. Research provides at least a starting point.

An interdisciplinary framework facilitates engagement among scholars who work within their respective specialisms and with those engaged in debates in governance forums who are proponents of the prevailing social imaginaries of the information society. The analysis of paradox, and proposals for adaptive action, create the possibility for dialogue about a new social imaginary. It is essential, however, to acknowledge that incommensurable epistemologies and languages, for example in the ways that terms such as change, evolution, and self-organization are used, make such debate a daunting prospect. Accounts of complex adaptive systems do not embrace a theory of human agency and so clashes occur when this theory is juxtaposed with theories from the humanities and social sciences.[24] In addition, the so-called 'laws' that seem 'deep' enough in the natural and physical sciences cannot be imported to the social sciences without artificially replanting them. As a consequence, there is a lack of reciprocal understanding among those working in the humanities, social, and natural sciences about the evolutionary process that is giving rise to a complex communication system.[25]

My response has been to highlight differences in the visions of the information society and the broader social imaginaries that embrace them. These can be traced to different ways of seeing. I have sought to illustrate why they matter, not to smooth over the differences. Encounters with the 'other' can be evocative. In this book, such encounters have yielded the beginnings of a social imaginary of the information society in which the virtual world would not be enclosed to the degree that the rights holders to digital information advocate, and people would not experience their mediated lives as being scrutinized by unknown others. Plato said that 'just as the eye was unable to turn from darkness to light without the whole body, so too the instrument of knowledge can only by the movement of the whole soul be turned from the world of becoming into that of being'.[26] Being in the world of the information society requires that we find ways to cope with the paradoxes of the Internet Age. My analysis of the paradoxes of information scarcity and complexity demonstrates that it is in no-one's interest to preserve the status quo. If Charles Taylor is correct, a new social imaginary will start to influence practice and to generate movement to a new gradient of power relationships in the information society.

Evaluations of progress towards the information society in the instrumental research tradition often do not offer normative conclusions or, when they do, these are disconnected from the theories that ostensibly underpin them. Critical evaluations are more likely to consider the implications of power relationships for individual agency or for the exercise of institutional authority. Critical researchers, however, are not willing necessarily to become involved in policy advocacy. Some argue that disengagement is the only way to avoid co-option by those with political or economic power and collusion with them in sustaining unequal power relations. In my experience, nevertheless, scholarly engagement with policy reform from within, and resistance to governance from the 'outside', tend to comingle, albeit at different times in the career of a researcher. The analysis of Internet Age visions and power relations in this book is disengaged insofar as it is not about details of decision-making in particular institutions or countries or about tactics for mobilizing resistance to inequality and social injustice using the tools of social media. It is normative, nevertheless, because I advocate a novel way of seeing the evolution of the communication system and adaptive actions aimed at coping with the harms associated with the paradoxes of information scarcity and complexity in the Internet Age.

My re-reading of these paradoxes brings a broader range of options for action into play. People are entitled to a world in which the benefits of both digital technologies and commercial and freely circulated information are not outweighed by the harms of intrusive and non-disclosed incursions into their virtual and 'real' lives. There is a high risk that the latter will outweigh the former if nothing is done to cope with the paradoxes of information scarcity and complexity in the Internet Age. The soul may hope for an empowering communication system, but my analysis shows that there is a need to guide the evolution of the system along a pathway that is not 'indifferent to the lives that people can actually live'.[27] It is very difficult to distinguish between the dancer and the dance in policy debates that deny or ignore the implications of these paradoxes. This makes it hard to confront asymmetrical power relations among stakeholders, and values that are being accorded high priority in the governance process, when they are inconsistent with those of the good society. The critical systems framework focuses attention on the causes and consequences of paradox, increasing the possibilities for governance aimed at reconciling diverse interests and guiding the evolution of the communication system in a direction that is aligned with aspirations for the good society.

Governance should not entail a choice between an emergent self-organizing system where 'learning' machines take precedence over human values, and an information commons in which a new elite makes our choices for us. The judgement of a self-organizing multitude may prove in the long run to be vindicated as the optimal way of organizing society. But in the near- and medium-term, analysis of the 'whole body' makes a useful contribution because it provokes questions about accountability for the choices being made. Leaving outcomes in the information society to the emergent self-organization of any unaccountable group means adapting to 'machines of loving grace', benign or otherwise. Re-writing the music in the act of playing it requires evaluation of dreams of 'machines of loving grace' and deeper and continuing critical investigation of the values and actions of stakeholders in order to make a difference in the trajectory of change in the communication system. It requires governance measures from below and above to secure the public interest in a communication system that is fit for economic growth *and* for limiting unwanted intrusions into people's lives.

■ NOTES

Chapter 1

1. Paradoxical features of innovation also are investigated in the management field (e.g. Handy, 1994) and by some economists (e.g. Layard, 2005; Stiglitz et al., 2010).

2. See Chroust (1946) on the 'origin and meaning of the social compact doctrine'. Democritus argued in favour of private ownership as the means to deliver the goals of the social compact, a concept developed by Locke, Hobbes, Rousseau, and others.

3. Galbraith (1996: 4).

4. Sen (2009: 18) in *The Idea of Justice*.

5. Nussbaum (2006: 415, 414) in *Frontiers of Justice*. See also Nussbaum's (2000) *Woman and Human Development*, Sen's (1985) 'Rights and Goals', and Etzioni's (2002) 'The Good Society'.

6. Berger et al. (1972: 7). In sociology, the social construction of reality is frequently taken-for-granted (Berger and Luckmann, 1966). In the management field, 'strategy' may be understood as the 'collective mind' (e.g. Mintzberg, 1989; Weick, 2001). Charles Taylor's (2002*a*) concept of the social imaginary is more open to embracing different ways of seeing and refers not only to specific actors but also to a moral order of society that embraces the market economy and the public sphere, however defined. As Taylor (2004: 4) puts it, 'the underlying idea of moral order stresses the rights and obligations we have as individuals in regard to each other, even prior to or outside of the political bond'. He borrows directly from Thompson (1971) and acknowledges the work of Anderson (1983), Habermas (1962/ 1989), and Warner (2002).

7. Taylor (2007: 171) in *A Secular Age*.

8. Taylor (2002*a*: 91, emphasis added). Scientists may find the social imaginary easier to understand as a socially constructed ontology.

9. Taylor (2007: 624).

10. Taylor (2007: 286).

11. Silverstone (2007: 26).

12. OECD (1988: 11).

13. Melody (1999: 376).

14. Theories of evolution are often implicated in discussions of changes in technology and in the social system, see Beinhocker (2007), Dawkins (1982, 1989), Trivers (1985), and Wilson (2008).

15. A common bowdlerization of Darwinian evolution is to employ the term 'survival of the fittest' to mean that one can state unequivocally what constitutes fitness or conclude that evolution produces generalized improvement. In the biological world, evolutionary change can and does result in 'dead ends' or other results that are ultimately inimical to viability (Gould, 2007).

16. See Stirling (2008).

17. Rose (1999: 154) in *Governing the Soul*.
18. Giddens and Piersin (1998: 77) in 'conversations'.
19. Carey (1989/1992: 32). Carey was developing Raymond Williams's (1966: 19–20) observation: 'Communication begins in the struggle to learn and to describe.... many of our communication models become, in themselves, social institutions.... arguable assumptions are often embodied in solid, practical institutions which then teach the models from which they start'.
20. OECD (1988: 11, emphasis added). This text comes from a report that drew on the works of Norman Clark, Giovani Dosi, Chris Freeman, Richard Nelson, Luc Soete, Sydney Winter, and others, all of whom have been influential contributors to research in the fields of the economics of technological innovation and science and technology policy research. They are economists. However, most, if not all of them, would have been aware of research on the 'social shaping of technology' which was becoming increasingly prominent at the time, see Mackenzie and Wajcman (1985), Bijker et al. (1987), and Latour and Woolgar (1986).
21. Silverstone (2007: 26).

Chapter 2

1. This was a persistent claim during the anti-trust dispute between Western Electric and American Telephone and Telegraph (AT&T), see US (1958: 3986–7).
2. See Cusumano and Yoffie (1998) who used this term in reference to competitive battles to achieve market dominance.
3. See BBC (2009), Giusto et al. (2010), and Lyon (2009) on electronic tagging.
4. Vinge (1993: np) in 'Technological Singularity'.
5. Bear's (1985) science fiction work, *Blood Music*, imagines a 'noösphere' which frees itself from Earth.
6. See Pearson's (2010) website for examples of futuristic visions.
7. Haraway (1991: 150) in *A Cyborg Manifesto*.
8. See Graham (1999), a moral philosopher, for a critique of the neo-Luddite perspective on the Internet where he acknowledges that an 'ideology of technology' has been implicated in large historical errors and that technology is not neutral for the social order. His argument addresses the question, 'how new is the Internet?'
9. *The Guardian* (2010: 35).
10. This assumption persists notwithstanding works on the politics of technology which have been reasonably widely discussed beyond the academic world, see, for example, Ellul (1990) and Winner (1977).
11. See ITU (2006). Santucci is said to have first used the term 'Internet of Things' in 1999. The European Commission has a Head of Unit for the 'Internet of Things', aimed at understanding the Internet as 'thing-centric' rather than 'people-centric' (Santucci, 2011).
12. Ducatel et al. (2001: 15–16).
13. See Mansell (2011) on the implications of neoliberalism for ICT policy and regulation of the media and communication sector, and Stiglitz's (2010) discussion of neoliberalism. The 'Washington Consensus' was the term coined by Williamson (1990) to describe the cluster of policy prescriptions for poor countries promoted by the World Bank and the International Monetary Fund in areas including the treatment of fiscal deficits, public expenditure,

tax reform, interest and exchange rates, trade policy and foreign direct investment, privatization, deregulation, and property rights. The phrase is closely associated with 'market fundamentalism' or 'neoliberalism', that is, the withdrawal of the state from governance and the ascendency of the market.

14. Zittrain (2008: 35, 246) in *The Future of the Internet*.

15. See Maxwell and Miller (2011) on ICTs and the environment, and Touré's (2008) position on climate change and ICTs for the ITU. This view is found in many reports on the contribution of digital information and ICTs to economic growth (OECD, 2010).

16. Arthur (2009: 207) in *The Nature of Technology*.

17. *The Economist* (2011).

18. Howard's (2010) work is an example where the cause and effect relationship between social media and social impacts is examined critically, noting that theories of social change should not be linked to specific ICT applications.

19. Measures of disparity in income show that among the world's wealthy countries, the gap between rich and poor is widest in the United States, despite it being one of the countries with the deepest ICT penetration. In the United States, the Gini index of household income inequality rose from 0.458 to 0.468 from 1999 to 2009 according to the US Census Bureau, far in excess of countries like Denmark and Norway, and ahead of the United Kingdom and New Zealand, see http://en.wikipedia.org/wiki/List_of_countries_by_income_equality, accessed 28/07/2011.

20. Lahlou (2008) discusses the importance of cognitive technologies in enabling organizational change.

21. Webster (2006) and Winston (1998) both argue that the idea of disruptive technologies in the information society underplays the importance of continuity.

22. Davidow and Malone (1992: 5) in *The Virtual Corporation*.

23. Davidow (2011: 213) in *Overconnected*.

24. See Shapiro (1999) on individual empowerment and Beniger (1986) and Winner (1977) on the idea that technology is, or may become, 'out of control'.

25. Meier's (1962) work is an early discussion of the importance of the types of media that are used in urban environments for the intensity of communication, using a 'sender–receiver' model. As a regional planning systems scholar, he warned of potential social problems arising with the saturation of communication in urban areas, but little note was taken.

26. Hassan's (2008) argument is a critical and pessimistic view of the information society.

27. See Mansell (2011) for an analysis based on a ten-year survey of UN agency and World Bank reports.

28. Juneau (1980: 4–5), the then Deputy Minister of Communications in Canada, making a relatively early statement on the right to communicate. The growth rates for the diffusion of ICTs and especially the Internet are not in question. In the period between 2000 and 2011, world Internet use grew by 480.4 per cent (2,527.4% in Africa and 151.7% in North America) (Internet World Stats, 2011), but there are major differences in the rates of diffusion as documented in UNCTAD (2010b).

29. Negroponte (1995: 183) in *Being Digital* and OLPC//News (2010). One account of this initiative in Peru reports the low-cost laptops being returned to their boxes because the

Ministry of Education had provided no support for teachers or children to use them (OLPC//News, 2011).

30. World Bank (1999: 1). In the uncited original by Thomas Jefferson (1813: 1291): 'He who receives ideas from me, receives instruction himself without lessening mine; as he who lights his taper at mine receives light without darkening me. That ideas should freely spread over the globe, for the moral and mutual instruction of man, and improvement of his condition, seems to have been peculiarly and benevolently designed by nature, when she made them like fire, expansible over all space, without lessening their density in any points and like the air in which we breathe, move, and have our physical being, incapable of refinement or exclusive appropriation. Inventions then cannot, in nature, be a subject of property'.

31. Agre (1998: 3), citing Noble (1998) on the religion of technology.

32. UNDP (1990: 1). 'Human development is the process of enlarging people's choices—not just choices among different detergents, television channels or car models but the choices that are created by expanding human capabilities and functionings—what people do and can do in their lives' (UNDP, 1999: 16). See also Sen (1999) and Streeten (1982) who were contributors to this report.

33. The 'end of history' is a central theme in Fukuyama's (1992) work.

34. In the academic literature there are many critical perspectives on this approach: Couldry (2003), Golding and Murdock (2001), Gunkel (2003), Hargittai (2003, 2004), Murdock and Golding (2004), Norris (2001), van Dijk (2006a), Wade (2002), and Warschauer (2003). For an economic analysis, see Antonelli (2003). UNESCO's (2005b) report on *Knowledge Societies* is much more closely aligned with the critical scholarly literature than other reports on this topic produced by UN agencies.

35. Agre (1998: 4) in 'yesterday's tomorrow'. Karl Polanyi (1944/2001) argued in *The Great Transformation* that people (or nature) should not be treated as objects whose price is calculable in the market.

36. In *The End of Ideology*, Bell (1962) discusses the need to unmask ideologies. Unmasking claims about the benefits of globalization and the overemphasis on the market-led development of networks is discussed in Mansell (1994).

37. See Bell's (1973) *The Coming of Post-Industrial Society*.

38. Castells (2009: 4) in *Communication Power*.

39. Amin (1994) and Coriat et al. (2006) provide critical appraisals of these developments.

40. See Cusumano and Yoffie's (1998) *Competing on Internet Time* and Shapiro and Varian's (1998) *Information Rules*.

41. UNDP (1999: 16).

42. Innis (1951/1991: 190) in *The Bias of Communication*.

43. Elinor Ostrom (2005) makes an argument in support of 'both-and' frameworks, for example, preservation of an open commons and private property ownership, or bottom-up local and top-down state governance, and see Andersson and Ostrom (2008).

44. Turkle (2011: np e-book edition) in *Alone Together*.

Chapter 3

1. Berger et al. (1972: 7) in *Ways of Seeing*.

2. Silverstone (1999: 16) in *Why Study the Media?*

3. Calhoun (2002: 170) on 'imagining solidarity'.

4. Mills (1959/2000: 1, 4).

5. Chouliaraki (2006) discusses the analysis of media discourses as a way of understanding mediation processes, taking account of the embeddedness of media texts in technological artefacts and in social relationships.

6. Thompson (1982: 664) on 'ideology and the social imaginary'.

7. Castoriadis (1987: 3 emphasis in original) in *The Imaginary Institution of Society*. The quote continues, '... of figures/forms/images, on the basis of which alone there can ever be a question *of* "something". What we call "reality" and "rationality" are its works'. The social imaginary is not the gaze of the 'other' or an image in a mirror reflecting material conditions. Gaonkar (2002) argues that Castoriadis's understanding of the social imaginary does not address how change emerges locally. Theoretical debates about the scope for autonomy from hegemonic ideologies and the way historical practice inflects the present raise important issues that are not addressed here. I assume that ideologies are pervasive, but changeable, and that they are not determining of outcomes in the classical Marxian interpretation of class relations. See also Patrice Flichy (2007) on *The Internet Imaginaire*.

8. Mouffe (2005: 18) in *On the Political*.

9. Laclau (1990: 64) in *New Reflections on the Revolution of Our Time*.

10. Carpentier (2011a, 2011b: 116) invokes Lacan (1994) in his discussion of fantasy.

11. Taylor (2007: 171). For a favourable critical appraisal of Taylor's work, see Abbey (2004). For a critique of the concept, see Fraser (2007), especially Chapter 6.

12. Taylor (2002a: 106).

13. Taylor (2002a: 111).

14. Taylor (2002a: 107).

15. Taylor (2007: 176). Taylor follows Hans-Joerg Gadamer, insisting that his argument is not a relativist one, but that understanding varies with the object studied and with the student of the object (Taylor, 2002b), see also *Modern Social Imaginaries* (Taylor, 2004). Taylor differentiates his argument from Marxist conceptions of ideology, arguing that there are multiple modern social imaginaries in contestation with one another.

16. This is the 'double hermeneutic' in the social sciences (Giddens, 1993: 8).

17. Taylor (2002a).

18. Taylor (2007: 624) differentiates between paradox and contradiction.

19. This terminology has been used in the field of media and communication studies, see *Journal of Communication* 1983, 33(3), 1993, 43(3), and 2008, 58(4). A similar term in other areas of the social sciences is 'instrumental'.

20. Lazarsfeld (1941/2004: 169).

21. Melody and Mansell (1983) on administrative and critical research.

22. For instance, as Nico Carpentier (2011a: 357) puts it in *Media and Participation*, 'media technologies are not neutral, in the sense that they are embedded within a series of material and discursive practices that structure the use of technology'.

23. Lasswell (1951: 1, emphasis added) on practitioners as social scientists.

24. Lasswell (1972: 307) on communication research and public policy.

25. Schiller (1974: 18, emphasis added) in *Waiting for Orders*.

26. Garnham's (1979) 'Contribution to a Political Economy of Mass Communication' is a comprehensive statement of this tradition. Graham (2007) argues for the inclusion of a cultural perspective. See also Mosco's (2009) *The Political Economy of Communication*.

27. Kuhn (1962: 64). His *The Structure of Scientific Revolutions* explained how dramatic shifts in scientific explanation come about after lengthy periods of consensus, resulting in incommensurability. Fuller (2000) argued that Kuhn neglected disputes within paradigms, but Kuhn (2000) replied that incommensurability does not make comparison between theories impossible.

28. See Beniger's (1986) *The Control Revolution*.

29. See Mirowski's (2002) *Machine Dreams* for an historical account of the emergence of 'cyborg' science.

30. Bush's (1945) 'As We May Think' proposed an electro-mechanical hypertext system for storing, accessing, and editing information, and linking it together.

31. Wright (2003: np). Otlet envisaged 'a moving desk-shaped like wheel, powered by a network of hinged spokes beneath a series of moving surfaces. The machine would let users search, read and write their way through a vast mechanical database stored on millions of 3x5 index cards' (Rayward, 1990: 1, citing Otlet) and see Otlet's (1934) *Traite de documentation*.

32. Lévy (1997) is among those who associate digital networks with collective intelligence. John Lilly began working on biocomputing in the 1940s focusing on meta-programming (learning to learn, symbols, metaphors, and models), developing models for 'the enhancement of the very human depths of communication with other minds' (Lilly, 1972: xviii).

33. This is the process of remediation (Bolter and Grusin, 1999) and pre-mediation (Grusin, 2010). For an account of these processes in the mobile telecommunication industry from the systems perspective, see Ibrus (2010).

34. See Wiener's (1948/1961) *Cybernetics*.

35. See Wiener's (1950: 17–18) *The Human Use of Human Beings*.

36. See Shannon and Weaver's (1949) *Mathematical Theory of Communication*.

37. The stimulus-response model is still taught to social scientists, see Heath and Bryant (2000) for the communication field. It is pervasive also in marketing and management research (Möller and Wilson, 1995), despite recent shifts to relational and network approaches, see Johansen (2009).

38. Leghorn (2011) contributed funding for the establishment of research and teaching programmes in the management of technological innovation at MIT's Sloan School of Management.

39. Stigler (1961: 213). The assertion that 'knowledge is power' may be attributed to Bacon's (1597/1924) statement 'Nam et ipsa scientia potentia est', but the idea originates in the Old Testament—'A man of knowledge increaseth strength', Proverbs 24:5, King James Version (Titelman, 1996).

40. For works on the economics of information, see Arrow (1984), Jussawalla and Edenfield (1984), Lamberton (1971), and Macdonald (1998).

41. See Drucker (1969), Machlup (1962), and Masuda (1980).

42. See McLuhan's (1964) *Understanding Media* which drew on Innis's earlier work, albeit with different emphases and interpretations.

43. *Time Magazine* (1993).

44. See Brand's (1987) 'The Media Lab: Inventing the Future at MIT'. For an edited collection of republished works on the information society covering most of the period discussed here, see Mansell (2009).

45. See European Commission (1994), Gore (1993), and Ministry of International Trade and Industry (MITI) (1994). Later 'A Green Knowledge Society: An ICT Policy Agenda to 2015 for Europe's Future Knowledge Society' (Forge et al., 2009) linked innovations in ICTs to the sustainability of the economy. More recently, the European Commission stated that 'the overall aim of the Digital Agenda is to deliver sustainable economic and social benefits from a digital single market based on fast and ultra fast internet and interoperable applications' (European Commission, 2010*b*: 1, 2010*c*).

46. See Tapscott's (1995) *The Digital Economy: Promise and Peril in the Age of Networked Intelligence.*

47. See Castells's (1996, 1997, 1998) *The Information Age* and van Dijk's (2006*b*) *The Network Society.*

48. See Solow's (1956) 'a contribution to the theory of economic growth'.

49. Braman (1995) reviews the use of the term 'information economy'. Some focused on the share of information activities in the economy (Bell, 1973; Ito, 1991; Machlup, 1962; Porat and Rubin, 1977), on information in its commodity form (Mosco, 1996; Schiller, 1981), and on information and the coordination of the economy (Bressand et al., 1989, David and Bunn, 1988; Lundgren, 1995).

50. See Drucker (1959) on a 'post-modern world'.

51. See Mansell (2011) on 'power and interests' in ICTs.

52. The *Oxford English Dictionary* defines knowledge as 'the fact or condition of being instructed, or of having information acquired by study or research; acquaintance with ascertained truths, facts, or principles; information acquired by study; learning; erudition'.

53. See Tapscott's (2010) blog 'ClimateSpark'.

54. Carr (2010: 10) in *The Shallows*. de Kerckhove's (2010) work on the *Augmented Mind* would be an exception in this regard.

55. These Stanford University researchers do not claim that being online is the cause of these effects, only that it is associated with a distinct approach to information processing (Ophir et al., 2009).

56. Pierce (1956: 306) in *Electrons, Waves and Messages.*

57. Turing (1950) proposed an imitation test such that a human interrogator would be able to detect whether answers were being provided by a human or a machine. He also said that 'I believe that at the end of the century the use of words and public opinion will have altered so much that one will be able to speak of machines thinking without expecting to be contradicted'. Oppy and Dowe (2011) discuss the issues and objections related to Turing's arguments. See Roszak (1994) and Boden (1996: xvii) on the progress of Artificial Intelligence—as Boden observes, this is an interdisciplinary field of study drawing on science (biology, ethnology, psychology, neuroscience, physics, and computer science) and on the humanities (philosophy, linguistics, and the history of art and science). Russell and Norvig (2010) highlight the progress of research in this area.

58. See Cusumano's (2010) *Staying Power.* Another important feature is the progressive miniaturization and modularity of ICT system components, especially semiconductors. This influences the organization and management of digital information and has implications for whether ICT applications are interoperable and whether they are open or closed to their

users, see Arthur (2009). Beinhocker (2007: 175) argues that modularity leads to webs of technology and emergent patterns of technological, social, and economic organization. Research on modularity focuses on the success or failure of firms in adapting to innovations in the components of technology, see Gawer and Henderson (2007), Henderson and Clark (1990), and Steinmueller (2006), and on ICT systems integration, see Brusoni and Prencipe (2001), Hobday (1998), and Langlois (2002).

59. The reader's basic familiarity with the scale of the ICT industry in terms of its significance in the economy is assumed. For reference, see IDATE (2010) and UNCTAD (2010a).

60. See Rheingold's (1993/2000, 2002) *The Virtual Community* and *Smart Mobs*.

61. For example, the European Commission's Competition Commission found that Microsoft had abused its dominant position in the personal computer operating system market by refusing to disclose interoperability information that would have enabled competitors to fully interoperate with Windows PCs and servers and by tying Windows Media Player with its dominant Windows PC operating system (European Commission, 2007). The Commission is investigating allegations that Google Inc. is abusing its dominant position in online search, focusing on whether Google lowers the ranking of unpaid search results of competing services that specialize in providing online content. Microsoft claims that Google gives preferential treatment to its own search products (Couts, 2011, European Commission, 2010a).

62. See Albarran (2002), Brock (1994), Doyle (2002), Maniadaki (2011), and Picard (1996) for analysis of the economics of the media and communication industries. Melody (1973) discusses how technological determinism is linked to the institutional structure of the media industries. In the EU, Title VII of the Treaty on the Functioning of the European Union (TFEU) deals with rules on competition, and Articles 101 and 102 specifically refer to restriction or distortion of competition and dominant position (European Commission, 2008). A multi-sided ICT platform 'serves two or more distinct types of customers who depend on each other in some important way, and whose joint participation makes the platform valuable to each' (Evans et al., 2005: 190). See also Economides and Katsamakas (2006) and Hagiu and Yoffie (2009).

63. Ciborra (2004), Orlikowski (1992), Star and Ruhleder (1994), and Swanson and Ramiller (1997) discuss why the relationship between technological innovation and societal goals are always uncertain without recourse to analogies to non-human systems.

64. See Melody (1985) on the information society.

65. See Braudel (1979/1992), DuBoff (1983), Innis (1950), and Mattelart (1996/2000).

66. Innis (1951: 191) in *The Bias of Communication*.

67. Braudel (1979/1992: 85) in *Civilization and Capitalism*.

68. Castells (2009: 139) cites those who argue that the cells in the brain do not hold meaning, but that it is feasible to understand relationships between 'what we see and what we do' (Damasio, 2003; Damasio and Meyer, 2008: 168).

69. See Osborne's (1979) *Running Wild: The Next Industrial Revolution*.

70. Prencipe et al. (2003) discuss the coordination of complex product systems; the role of standardization is discussed in Mansell's (1995) 'Standards, Industrial Policy and Innovation'.

71. In statistics, an endogenous relationship exists if an independent variable is correlated with an error term in a regression model, for instance.

72. There are many other endogenous perspectives on the innovation process. One of these is Actor Network Theory (ANT) which provides a framework and methodology for tracing relationships among actors (and 'actants' or technologies). Negotiations over the design and application of technologies are traced indicating periods of disruption, followed by stability and subsequent closure, revealing why some pathways are adhered to and others, which may be favourable for some groups, are abandoned. See Callon (2001), Latour (2005), and Law (1999) in *Four Models for the Dynamics of Science, Reassembling the Social*, and 'After ANT', respectively. Research in the field of information systems is concerned with innovation and socio-technical systems employing terminology such as translation, enactment, and congealing, see, for example, Avgerou (2002*b*), Bijker and Law (1992), Katz and Aakhus (2002), Latour (1994), and Whitley (1997). In the case of ICT use in higher education, for example, the challenge may be to discover why certain online learning configurations are privileged by developers and adopters for reasons that may be cultural, political, or economic (Darking, 2004). Or the focus may be on contestation over the development of electronic identity cards, tracing actor interests through fine-grained, micro-level analysis (Whitley and Hosein, 2009). Relatively little attention is given to the actors' economic, political, social, or cultural interests as they are embedded in institutions (Avgerou, 2002*a*). Avgerou explains that socio-technical theories of information systems drawing on Bloomfield et al. (1997), Hirschheim et al. (1996), Introna (1997), Orlikowski (1992), and Walsham (1993) grew out of action research at the Tavistock Institute of Human Relations, following the work of Mumford (2000) and challenging the engineering view of systems through the development of interpretivism in the analysis of social systems (Checkland, 1981).

73. See Arrow (1962), Romer (1990), and Rosenberg (1982*a*). Perhaps more tellingly, Abramovitz (1956: 11) called the residual 'a measure of our ignorance' about the causes of productivity increases, and see Griliches (1996) for a brief history of this issue in economics.

74. Endogenous theories of technological innovation are common in the management of technological innovation and the economics literatures, see Rooney and Schneider (2005) and Zack (1999).

75. See Aghion et al. (2009), Foray (2004, 2009), Mowery (2009), and Universities-National Bureau Staff (1962).

76. David and Foray (2003: 27) in 'economic fundamentals of the knowledge society'.

77. Metcalfe and Ramlogan (2005: 670) in 'limits to the economy of knowledge and knowledge of the economy', and see Bowles (1998: 75), an American economist, who examines endogenous preferences reflecting experience acquired through individual learning which influences framing and situational construal, intrinsic and extrinsic motivations, norms, task performance, and cultural 'transmission'. As Bowles says, 'markets and other economic institutions do more than allocate goods and services . . . economists have long assumed otherwise'.

78. See Rosenberg's (1982*a*, 1994) *Inside the Black Box* and *Exploring the Black Box*.

79. Polanyi (1966: 4) in *The Tacit Dimension*. For discussions of tacit knowledge, see Leonard-Barton (1992), Nelson and Winter (1977), Papert (1980), and Wagner and Sternberg (1985).

80. See Cowan and Foray (1997: 596), Johnson et al. (2002), Lundvall and Johnson (1994), and Steinmueller (2000) for debates on this issue.

81. See Foray and Steinmueller (2003) on the 'economics of knowledge inscription'. Kinect is the interface for the Xbox 360, introduced by Microsoft in 2010, which uses a sensor device

to detect motion and face and voice recognition. Similar to Nintendo's Wii, people use their bodies to react to games, but they do not have to use a wireless handheld controller.

82. See Kahin (2004) on the privileging of some knowledge communities over others which raises questions about power.

83. See Brown and Duguid (1998, 2000) and Wenger (1998) on communities of practice.

84. For GPTs, see Bresnahan and Trajtenberg (1995) and for work on the history of technological systems, see David (1975, 1990), Nelson and Winter (1982), Nelson (1994), and Rosenberg (1976, 1982a, 1994).

85. Freeman (1988: 1) and Perez (1983). See also Freeman and Louçã's (2001) *As Time Goes By*. Their work contributed to a diverse tradition in historical studies influenced by a systems perspective which includes the works of Beniger (1986), Davies (1996), Hughes (1987), Klang (2006), Mayntz and Hughes (1988), Nightingale et al. (2003), and Summerton (1994). There is, in addition, in the tradition of science and technology studies with its root in sociology, a strong tradition of research on large technical systems, see Bowker (1996), Ellul (1990), Gras (1993), MacKenzie (1996), and Williams (1990).

86. Freeman and Perez (1988: 38). Joseph Schumpeter (1934/1961) argued that periodically certain enabling technologies emerge that challenge older modes of social and economic organization.

87. See Freeman's (2007) short discussion on the ICT paradigm. Freeman (1995), Lundvall (1992), and Nelson (1993) review the history of ICT innovation and Dosi's (1982) work focuses on technological trajectories.

88. See Perez's (2002) *Technological Revolution and Financial Capital*.

89. Political economy emerged out of moral philosophy in the eighteenth century as the study of the economies of states and markets in the works of Adam Smith, David Ricardo, and Karl Marx. In 1615, Antoine de Montchrétien published *Traité de l'economie politique* in France.

90. Mill (1829/1874/2000: 114) in 'Essays on Some Unsettled Questions of Political Economy'.

91. There are traditions of institutional and Marxist political economy, see Comor (1994), Henten et al. (2003), and Melody (2003) for the former and Bettig and Schiller (1997), Calabrese and Sparks (2004), Garnham (1990), McChesney (2008), Mosco (2009), Smythe (1981), Wasko et al. (2011) for the latter.

92. Halloran (1974: 5) said '... we are interested in the factors that govern or influence what the media make available, as well as the factors that govern or influence what use is made of what is made available... We must ask questions about organization and structure, and about ownership, control, resources and technology...'.

93. In the administrative research tradition, existing distributions of power are assumed to be given or they are assumed to be unalterable (Melody, 1985).

94. Garnham (1986: 23, emphasis added) in 'contribution to a political economy of mass-communication'. Breen (2011) makes a similar point when he argues that the relationships between innovations in Internet-related technology, content, representation, and power in society are never closed.

95. Clark (1961: 21) in *Competition as a Dynamic Process*, see also Bauer (2005) and Melody (1985) on market power.

96. See Mansell (1996) on controls on the 'information highway' and Anderson (2010) for a debate in *Wired Magazine* on this issue.

97. See Mansell and Steinmueller's (2000) *Mobilizing the Information Society.*

98. Microsoft's history begins in 1975 with the development of BASIC language software for the ALTAIR 8800 computer by Bill Gates and Paul Allen. Google's history officially begins in 1997 when Larry Page and Sergey Brin filed for incorporation of the company. Oracle was founded by Larry Ellison and others in the United States in 1977 as Software Development Laboratories to commercialize relational database software. Founded in 1972, SAP AG (Systems, Applications, and Products in Data Processing) is based in Germany.

99. See Cusumano and Yoffie (1998) on the battle between Netscape and Microsoft.

100. See McKercher and Mosco's (2008) *Knowledge Workers in the Information Society* and Mosco's (2008) 'Knowledge workers of the world! Unite?' and Coté and Pybus (2007) who build on Lazzarato (1996) referring to the imaginary and arguing that labour in the virtual world must include 'cultural and artistic norms, fashions, tastes, consumer standards and, more strategically, public opinion' (Lazzarato, 2004: np). Hardt and Negri (2001) argue that labour is cerebral, affective, and computerized.

101. See Smythe (1977, 1981: 8) on the 'blindspot of Western Marxism' and *Dependency Road.* This argument led to an extended debate on a 'blind-spot' in Western Marxism (Murdock, 1978).

102. Cohen (2008) and see Gershuny (1978) on 'self-servicing' in earlier ICT innovation phases.

103. The link between democratization and technology is attributed to the distributed P2P architecture of the Internet. The network protocol enables all types of data, applications, and services to be transported, which explains its designation as an end-to-end network. The World Wide Web is the result of efforts to define a standard for accessing and retrieving the information hosted on computers that access the Internet. A proposal by Tim Berners-Lee was launched in 1991 (Berners-Lee and with Fischetti, 1999). After the Mosaic Web browser was deployed in the market in 1993, a global information network began to spread. See Benkler (2006), Feenberg (1999, 2010*a*), Lessig (1999, 2006, 2008), and Surowiecki (2004) for discussions of the values embedded in ICT architectures and networks.

104. See Stallman (2009) who pioneered the idea of copyleft and is a main author of the GNU Public License, a widely used free software licence. He began working on the GNU Operating System in 1983, a UNIX like operating system, and launched the Free Software Foundation in 1985.

105. See Rosen (2004) for differences between open and free software and their licensing regimes.

106. The gift economy concept is derived from the anthropologist, Marcel Mauss's (1954/1969) work on the implicit obligation to 'repay' a gift in some cultures. On 'commons-based peer production', see Benkler and Nissenbaum (2006). Berdou (2011), Bergquist and Ljungberg (2001), Dalle et al. (2005), Kollock (1999), Raymond (1999), and Weber (2004) discuss the attributes of the gift economy and online contributions. Empirical studies demonstrate that a mix of volunteer and paid work and open source and proprietary approaches is common, and that altruism which favours sharing and collaboration can coexist with conflict. See Healy and Schussman (2003), Kettell (2008), Lakhani and von Hippel (2003), Lerner and Tirole (2000), Ljundgberg (2000), Mateos-Garcia and Steinmueller (2008*a*), Moon and Sproull (2002), O'Mahony and Ferraro (2003), Sadowski et al. (2008), von Hippel (2002), and Weber (2004).

107. As of 2011, approximately 23.8 per cent of global Internet traffic has been classified as copyright infringing. BitTorrent is said to account for 11.4 per cent of this infringing

activity. This study, undertaken for NBC Universal, estimated the amount of non-pornographic traffic associated with films, television programme episodes, computer games, and software, as well as cyberlocker traffic (downloads from sites such as MegaUpload, Rapidshare, or HotFile) and video-streaming. In the United States, 17.5 per cent of traffic is estimated to be infringing (excluding pornography). A reasonably detailed account of the methodology is provided with reviews of other studies, with the usual caveats about the quality and accuracy of the results (Price, 2011).

108. See Beckett and Mansell (2008), Bennett (2003), and Van de Donk et al. (2004), for instance.

109. Hassan (2008: 223) in *The Information Society*.

110. Many researchers in the critical tradition question these values, see Braman (2006), McKercher and Mosco (2008), Mosco (2008), Robins and Webster (1999), Schiller (2007), and Webster (1999).

111. Silverstone (2007: 26). Other terms for mediation are mediality, mediatization, mediazation, and remediation, premediation, and transmediation. Livingstone (2009: 5, 13) says that 'we need media and communication research to understand how the media mediate, for the same reason that we need linguistics to understand how language mediates, economics to understand how money mediates, literature to understand how narratives and myths mediate, and consumption studies to understand how material goods mediate', arguing that the breadth of application of the concept can result in references to the 'mediation of everything'. Krotz (2007) prefers 'mediatization' which he uses in arguing that long-term processes of change in the media of communication and socio-cultural developments need to be examined comparatively in Western and non-Western cultures. See also Bolter and Grusin (1999), Grusin (2010), Lievrouw (2009), Martin-Barbero (1993), Meyrowitz (1985), Silverstone (1999), and Thompson (1995) for variations in usage of terms with a common reference to 'mediation'. 'Mediation' is understood across scholarly boundaries and it is helpful in this regard. Further, while the term seems to refer to 'everything', when it is applied in specific contexts where research questions serve to bound the meaning of mediation, it is helpful when it is used in a complementary way with other concepts.

112. See Silverstone's *Television and Everyday Life* (1994), *Why Study the Media* (1999), and *Media and Morality* (2007) and Silverstone and Hirsch (1992).

113. Turkle (2011: np e-book edition) in *Alone Together*.

114. Neogi and Cordell (2010) discuss these opposing perspectives.

115. See Garnham (1979).

116. Sennett (2006: 188) in *The Culture of the New Capitalism*.

117. Feenberg (2010a: 194) in *Between Reason and Experience*, citing Heidegger's (1993: 107, 105) last interview conducted in 1966, published posthumously in 1976. Heidegger was asked whether the individual can influence technology development. He responded: 'technology is in its essence something which man cannot master by himself'.

118. Feenberg (2010b: 10) in 'Ten Paradoxes of Technology', but there are few treatments of the way paradox emerges in the information society. See also Feenberg (2000, 1992).

119. DiMaggio et al. (2001) suggest the integration of sociological and political economy and a similar suggestion was made by Mansell (2004).

120. Castells (2009: 431–2) in *Communication Power*.

121. See Silverstone (2002) in 'Complicity and Collusion'.

Chapter 4

1. See Goergen et al.'s (2010) work supported by the UK Economic and Social Research Council, the former Department for Trade and Industry, and the Advanced Institute of Management Research. See also Antonelli (2011), Delorme (2010), Frenken (2006), and Rosser (2009).

2. Unfinished also is debate about the role of agency and the determinants of techno-social pathways, diversity, and agency, see Geels and Schot (2007). Geels's (2002) work on technological transitions employs a multi-level perspective to focus on these processes drawing from economics, sociology, and cultural theory. Although it addresses complexity, it does not tackle the genesis of paradox in hierarchical and heterarchical systems.

3. See Schiller's (1996) *Theorizing Communication*.

4. See Barry and Slater's (2005) introduction to *The Technological Economy*.

5. Discursive practices constitute subjective meaning for human beings and discursive meanings, following Foucault, depend on historically developed rules that render statements discursively meaningful or not. Jessop (2005) takes this approach in 'Cultural Political Economy'.

6. See Star and Griesemer (1989) for the more general sociological approach to boundary objects which refer to abstract or concrete objects that are ascribed meaning by different communities of actors, see also Bowker and Star (1999).

7. Jaeger and Burnett (2010: 31) refer to these as 'a boundary object, lifeworld information exists both apart from individual small worlds and also within individual worlds, where it is instantiated and experienced according to the constraints, expectations, and norms of the localized worlds themselves'.

8. Küng et al.'s (2008) *The Internet and the Mass Media* refers to these concepts without discussing the implications of their emergent systems framework.

9. See Mattelart and Mattelart (1998).

10. The term Cybernetics was selected by Weiner from the Greek word $Kυβερνήτης$ (*kybernetes*) meaning 'steersman' or 'governor' (Rogers, 1994/1997: 396; Shannon, 1948; Shannon and Weaver, 1949).

11. The first conference was called 'Feedback Mechanisms and Circular Causal Systems in Biological and Social Systems'; the conferences were seen as experiments in multidisciplinary science. Some of the participants and their themes are documented at http://www.asc-cybernetics.org/foundations/history/MacySummary.htm accessed 28/07/2011.

12. Beer (1959/1964: 7) in *Cybernetics and Management*.

13. Beer (1966: 208) in *Decision and Control*.

14. See Ashby (1956: v), Mirowski (2002), and Steier (2005).

15. This is not to suggest that modern physics, for example, particle physics is any less reductionist. Research on biological systems as discussed by Rosen (1991) distinguishes between 'relational biology' (interacting with live organisms) and reductionist analysis of organisms (killing an organism to discover what its components are made of).

16. Beer (1959/1964: 458).

17. Wiener (1948/1961: 24).

18. Wiener (1948/1961: 159).

19. Wiener (1950: 162).

20. See Heylighen and Joslyn's (2001) *Cybernetics and Second-Order Cybernetics*.
21. See von Bertalanffy's (1950, 1956, 1968) work on General System Theory.
22. See Maturana and Varela's (1987) *Tree of Knowledge*.
23. Maturana (1997: np) on 'metadesign'.
24. These ideas were developed in the Cybersyn project organized partly by Beer which aimed to establish a real-time computer-controlled and planned economy in Chile in the early 1970s, before the military coup (Medina, 2005), see also Beer (1994).
25. Mingers (1995: 110) in *Self-producing Systems*.
26. Parsons (1951/1991: 3) in *The Social System*.
27. See Luhmann's (1995) *Social Systems*.
28. Vanderstraeten (2000: 587) following Luhmann.
29. See Luhmann (1995), Mingers (1995), and Zeleny and Hufford (1992) for criticisms of this argument.
30. Luhmann (1992: 252) on autopoiesis.
31. Luhmann (1996/2000: 92) in *The Reality of the Mass Media*.
32. Luhmann (1996/2000: 120–1).
33. See Luhmann (1985, 1992) *A Sociological Theory of Law* and on autopoiesis.
34. Network analysis built on work by members of the International Network for Social Network Analysis (INSNA) founded in 1977, see http://www.insna.org/ accessed 28/07/2011.
35. See Moreno's (1934) and Simmel's (1946) *Who Shall Survive?* and *The Web of Group-Affiliations*, respectively.
36. Rogers (1987: 291) in 'progress, problems and prospects for network research'.
37. Rogers (1987: 285).
38. Rogers (1994/1997: 386, 405) in *A History of Communication Study*.
39. Rogers (1994/1997: 406).
40. Wellman (1983: 156) in 'network analysis'.
41. See Monge and Contractor's (2003) *Theories of Communication Networks*.
42. Byrne (1998: 71) in *Complexity Theory and the Social Sciences*. See also Marion's (1999) *The Edge of Organization*.
43. Allen and Torrens (2005: 583, emphasis added) in 'knowledge and complexity'.
44. Vanderstraeten (2000: 581) in 'autopoiesis and socialization' draws on Walter Buckley's (1967, 1968) work on society as a complex adaptive system which emphasizes feedback loops.
45. Metcalfe and Foster (2004: xi) in *Evolution and Economic Complexity*.
46. Dopfer and Potts (2004: 5) on 'evolutionary foundations of economics'.
47. Arthur (2009: 168, emphasis added) in *The Nature of Technology*. Arthur argues that it was not until the publication of his article on 'positive feedbacks in the economy' in 1990 that this approach started to be widely accepted as a way of understanding the evolution of technological systems.
48. Arthur (2005: 28) on 'complexity and the economy'.
49. Hodgson (2006) provides an analysis of the way evolution has been treated in the social sciences and especially in economics.

50. See Wilden's (1972/2001) *System and Structure* and Eicher-Catt and Catt's (2010) *Communicology.*

51. Bateson (1972: 282–3, emphasis added) in *Steps to an Ecology of Mind.*

52. See Mirowski's (2002) *Machine Dreams.*

53. Ruesch and Bateson (1951: 64) in *Communication, The Social Matrix of Psychiatry.* Ramage and Shipp (2009) summarize contributions to this debate. Mathur (2003: 64) notes that they retained this argument in the preface to the 1968 edition of the book, stating that a unified theory 'could adequately represent the person, the group and society all within one system'.

54. Korzybski (1933/1994: author's preface to 1948 edition) in *Science and Sanity.*

55. See Bateson (1972: 480) in *Steps to an Ecology of Mind.*

56. McWhinney (2005: 22) on Bateson's typology of learning. Time-binding comes from Korzybski (1933/1994) and resonates with the later work of both Innis and McLuhan.

57. See Bateson's (1979) *Mind and Nature.*

58. Bateson (1979: 37). Or as Klaus Krippendorf (1984: 25) says, 'knowledge arises in the alternating sequence of distinction and relation'.

59. Watzlawick et al. (1967: 141) in *Pragmatics of Human Communication.*

60. See Bateson (1951*b*) in 'Information and Codification'.

61. Wilden and Hammer (1987: 1). Bateson drew on Peirce's (1931/1935) concept of abduction. See Charlton's (2008) *Understanding Gregory Bateson.*

62. See Veblen (1899/2008) in *The Theory of the Leisure Class.*

63. Bateson (1972: 433).

64. Bateson (1979: 354).

65. 'All that is not information, not redundancy, not form and not restraints—is noise, the only possible source of *new* patterns' (Bateson, 1972: 416). See also Harries-Jones (2004).

66. Developed by Alfred Whitehead and Bertrand Russell (1910). This theory rules out self-reference to prevent the emergence of antinomies and paradoxes in logic. It states that no class can contain itself as a member. For example, the statement that propositions can be either true or false is a proposition and should be either true or false. But because it can only be true it is seen as a proposition about propositions, and is not to be confused with the propositions to which it refers, see http://pespmc1.vub.ac.be/ASC/THEORY_TYPES.html, accessed 28/07/2011.

67. See Mitchell (1991). The theory seeks to rule out paradox and finds that notions informed by self-reference are meaningless. 'A language describes an object language and in turn is described by a metalanguage, which is in turn described by a metametalanguage and so forth ad infinitum' (Whitehead and Russell, 1910: 72).

68. See Bateson (1951*b*, 1972). Heterarchy is discussed by McCulloch (1945) in the context of biology and neural networks and is metaphorically implied in the notion of rhizome developed by Deleuze and Guattari (1980/1987).

69. Bateson (1951*b*: 209).

70. Watzlawick et al. (1967: 54).

71. See Fein (1992) for the application of these ideas at the institutional level of analysis.

72. Watzlawick et al. (1967: 49).

73. See Bateson (1972).

74. Bateson (2005: 15).
75. See Holmes (1998).
76. See Watzlawick et al. (1967: 212, 215, emphasis added).
77. Watzlawick et al. (1967: 66–7). 'Human beings communicate both digitally and analogically. Digital language has a highly complex and powerful logical syntax but lacks adequate semantics in the field of relationship, while analogic language possesses the semantics but has no adequate syntax for the unambiguous definition of the nature of relationships'.
78. Bateson (1972: 61–71).
79. Bateson (1951a: 212) on 'conventions and communication'.
80. Bateson (1951b: 210).
81. See Argyris and Schon (1996), Cohen (2001), and Lewis (2000) on theories of organizational change, denial, and paradox resolution.
82. Watzlawick et al. (1967: 235).
83. Harries-Jones (2004: 150).
84. See Arnett (1986) for a discussion of Buber's concept of dialogue.
85. Wilden (1972/2001: 174, emphasis added) in *System and Structure*. This view is different from that espoused by Luhmann (1992: 251–2): 'Self-reference (or reflexiveness) is not a property peculiar to thought or consciousness but instead a general principle of system formation with special consequences for the structure of complexity and evolution... One must not begin with the concept of action but with the concept of communication'.
86. See Holmes (1998: 106) on the therapeutic process.
87. Krippendorff (1984: 34) on 'an epistemological foundation for communication'.
88. Wilden (1972/2001: xlviii) in *System and Structure*.
89. Krippendorff (1989: 186) who also warned that this tradition was responsible for holding back productive lines of research in the field of human cognition.
90. Krippendorff (1989: 180, emphasis in original) on 'the power of communication'.
91. Watzlawick et al. (1967: 96–7).
92. See Krippendorff (1995) in 'Undoing Power'.
93. See Bateson (1972, 1979).
94. Foucault (1978: 92, emphasis added) in *The History of Sexuality*.
95. Rapport (1999: 194) in context as an act of personal externalization.
96. See Krippendorff (1995).
97. Wilden (1972/2001: xix–xx).
98. Bateson (1979: 15).
99. See Bateson (1972).
100. Bateson (1951a: 212) in 'conventions and communication'.
101. Grant (2003: 100) on 'destabilizing social communication theory'.
102. Rieber and Green (1989: 88, emphasis added) in *The Individual, Communication and Society*. This notion is central in therapeutic intervention and may be scaled up to the institutional level where people make their choices within the constraints of the rules and norms of institutions, see Bailey and Burgoon (1992), Chenail and Morris (1995), Conville and Rogers (1998), and Watts (1961) on therapeutic discourses and relational transitions.
103. Functowicz and Ravetz (1994: 570) on criticism of the concept of emergent complex systems.

104. The text of Yeats's (1926/1989: 221) poem 'Among School Children' reads, 'O chestnut tree, great rooted blossomer, Are you the leaf, the blossom or the bole? O body swayed to music, O brightening glance, How can we know the dancer from the dance?'

105. See Carey's (1989/1992) 'A Cultural Approach to Communication'. Giddens (1991: 20) insists that 'the susceptibility of most aspects of social activity, and material relations with nature, to chronic revision in the light of new information or knowledge' is the key to reflexivity, a quality that system analysis does not address.

106. Urry (2004: 110) on social physics, citing complexity research by Byrne (1998), Capra (2002), Hayles (1991), Kelly (1995), Krugman (1996), Mingers (1995), Prigogine (1997), Rihani (2002), Rycroft and Kash (1999), White (1992), and Zohar and Marshall (1994), as examples.

107. Poteete et al. (2010: 11) in *Working Together.*

108. See Cohen (1980) and Wall (2001) in *Folk Devils and Moral Panics* and crime and the Internet, respectively.

109. See, for example, Livingstone (1996) on the problems of effects studies.

110. Kraut et al. (1998: 1029) in 'Internet Paradox'.

111. See Kraut et al.'s (2002) 'Internet Paradox Revisited'.

112. See Castells (2001) in *The Internet Galaxy* and Castells (2009: 3) in *Communication Power.* He says, 'why, how, and by whom power relationships are constructed and exercised through the management of communication processes, and how these power relationships can be altered by social actors aiming for social change by influencing the public mind', is an appropriate goal for research.

113. See Sinclair (2010) reporting a study of more than 1,000 young people conducted by the University of Leeds Institute of Psychological Sciences, exploring the relation between excessive Internet use and mental health.

114. See Morrison and Gore (2010) on excessive Internet use and depression.

115. Aboujaoude's (2011) *Virtually You* provides a reasonably even-handed treatment of the evidence for and against 'Internet Addiction' and considers some of the wider implications of difficulties in discerning differences between the 'real' and the 'virtual'. Guimón and Zac de Filc (2001) assess the significance of the virtual for psychotherapeutic theory and intervention. Orgad (2005) examines the way the Internet facilitates storytelling.

116. See Mattelart's (1996/2000) *Networking the World.*

117. Billig et al. (1990: 15, 16) in *Ideological Dilemmas.*

118. Taylor (2002a: 106) in 'modern social imaginaries'.

119. Eliot (1936: 179) in 'Choruses from the Rock'.

120. See Althusser (1971) in 'ideology and ideological state apparatuses'.

121. Gramsci (1971: 328) in *Selections From the Prison Notebooks.*

122. Lukes (1974/2005: 38) on 'Power: a radical view'.

123. Lukes (1974/2005: 38) on 'Power: a radical view'.

124. Foucault (1978: 143), and see Rose and Miller (1992).

125. Braman (2006: 26) in *Change of State.*

126. See Castells's (2009) *Communication Power.*

127. Mowles (2011: 257) in *Rethinking Management.*

128. Mowles (2011) sets this out drawing on work in the management field and especially Stacey et al. (2000).

129. A complex adaptive system, 'as modelled by a computer program, consists of a large number of interacting entities called agents which operate according to a set of rules guiding their interactions with other agents . . . local variations in responses between agents can escalate into large population-wide changes which destroy some forms and create others' (Stacey et al., 2000: 60–1).

130. These communities may be designated as policy communities, actor networks, or epistemic communities, for example, Atkinson and Coleman (1992), Haas (1992), and Kenis and Schneider (1991).

131. This is the public sphere depicted in Habermas's (1997) approach, albeit with various caveats with respect to the privileges of entry into this sphere. Epistemic communities in the policy sphere are seen as 'a network of professionals with recognized expertise and competence in a particular domain and an authoritative claim to policy-relevant knowledge within that domain or issue-area' (Haas, 1992: 3).

132. Calhoun (1992: 2), and see Guttman (2010) and Habermas (1962/1989) on the public sphere and the deliberative process.

133. See Cammaerts (2008b), Cammaerts and Van Audenhove (2005), and Coleman (2005) for discussions of the limitations of online deliberation.

134. See Calhoun's (1992) and Fraser's (2010) *Habermas and the Public Sphere* and *Scales of Justice*, respectively.

135. Fraser (2010: 2), see Dean (2003), Fraser (1990), Keane (1995), and Thompson (1993) for criticisms of Habermas's notion of the public sphere.

136. Fraser's (2010: 3) use of misframing seems similar to my use of mispunctuation, a term that seems to resonate more with languages employed outside the humanities and the social sciences.

137. See Laclau and Mouffe's (1985) *Hegemony and Socialist Strategy* and Mouffe's (1999) *Deliberative Democracy or Agonistic Pluralism?* There are other conceptions of the 'public' and public discourse and publicity, following, for example, Arendt and developing the notion of theatricality as well as the legitimacy of forums for dialogue in the democratic sphere (Barnett, 2003), and the role of rationality, objectivity, and subjectivity as well as personal or private boundaries of decision-making (Ferree et al., 2002; Warner, 2002), but these are not developed here.

138. It is also consistent with Castells's (2009: 3) view that 'the most fundamental form of power lies in the ability to shape the human mind. . . . coercion alone cannot stabilize domination' and Silverstone's (1999: 143) observation that communication (and media) policy 'is all about power'.

139. Shirky (2010: 27, 120) in *Cognitive Surplus*. This seems to echo Edward Bellamy's (1887/1960) *Looking Backward* (from the year 2000), written in 1887 envisaging a world that had emerged.

140. Bateson and Bateson (1987: 178, emphasis added).

141. Wilden and Hammer's (1987: 309) *The Rules are No Game*.

142. Mirowski (2002: 19) in *Machine Dreams*.

143. Arthur (2009: 214, emphasis added).

144. Fuchs (2009: 71, emphasis added) on the political economy of the Internet.

Chapter 5

1. See Silverstone's *Television and Everyday Life* (1994), *Why Study the Media?* (1999), *Media and Morality* (2007), and Silverstone and Hirsch (1992).

2. McCaffery (2000: np emphasis added), interviewing William Gibson, author of *Neuromancer* (1984).

3. Napoli (2011) reviews developments in the media audience ratings industry using computerized techniques.

4. Strickland (2011: np) on 'How Web 3.0 Will Work'.

5. The CPU or Central Processing Unit of a computer, mobile handset, etc., such as the Intel Pentium or AMD Athlon semiconductor chip based on integrated circuitry, is the digital device that determines how fast a computer can process information. The popular interpretation of Moore's Law describes the number of transistor components that can be placed on an integrated circuit, a number that has been doubling every two years since the integrated circuit was invented in 1958. What Moore (1965: np) actually said was that 'the complexity for minimum component costs has increased at a rate of roughly a factor of two per year'.

6. Bush (1945: various pages) in 'As We May Think'.

7. See Rheingold's (1993/2000) *The Virtual Community*.

8. Vinge (1993: 2) in 'Technological Singularity'.

9. As in the story *Blood Music* (Bear, 1985).

10. Kurzweil (2006: 8) in *The Singularity is Near*.

11. Rheingold (1993/2000: 353).

12. von Goethe's (1797) 'The Sorcerer's Apprentice'.

13. Rheingold (1993/2000: 403).

14. Castells (2001: 6, emphasis added) in *The Internet Galaxy*.

15. See, for example, de Kerckhove (2010), *The Augmented Mind*.

16. See Turkle's (1984/2005: 287) *The Second Self*.

17. See Bakardjieva's (2010) and Baym's (2010b) discussion of research on the 'Internet in Everyday Life' and on 'Social Networks 2.0', respectively.

18. There are exceptions to these weaknesses in research, with work on transnational mediations and on the challenges of cross-cultural comparative research, see, for example, Georgiou (2006), Livingstone (2003), and Madianou and Miller (2011).

19. Many studies are based on self-reports of social media use by university students, although some focus on large enterprises and community use in relation to social capital and self-esteem, see Bumgarner (2007), DiMicco et al. (2008), Ellison et al. (2007), Lampe et al. (2008), Raacke and Bonds-Raacke (2008), Skeels and Grudin (2009), and Subrahmanyam et al. (2008).

20. See Hartmann (2004), Hine (2000), Jones (1999), and Markham and Baym (2009) for discussions of methodological challenges for Internet researchers.

21. Veblen (1899/2008: 70) in *The Theory of the Leisure Class*.

22. Eco (1994: 141) in 'How not to use the mobile phone'.

23. See Wessels's (2010: 180) *Understanding the Internet*.

24. Diffusion theories build on Everett Roger's (1962, 1995) *Diffusion of Innovations*, whose central concern was to explain the rate and direction of adoption of new technologies.

25. A market analyst's study based on fourteen countries in 2010. See http://wallblog.co.uk/2010/05/20/average-number-of-social-networking-friends-195/, accessed 28/07/2011 and Golbeck (2007) and Oltmann (2010).

26. See Boyd and Ellison (2008) for research on social network sites.

27. More than seven out of ten people (71%) in the United Kingdom have access to a broadband connection at home (Ofcom, 2010: 1) and more than 77 per cent of the American population has access to the Internet, http://www.internetworldstats.com/am/us.htm, accessed 28/07/2011. For statistics on usage levels, see Livingstone et al. (2011) showing that 93 per cent of 9- to 16-year olds in Europe go online at least once a week; on mobiles, see Hoflich and Hartmann (2006); and Haddon (2004, 2011) on the role of ICTs in everyday life and on digital divides.

28. The term 'prosumer' was coined by Alvin Toffler (1980) in *The Third Wave*, and developed further in Toffler and Toffler (2006); Bruns (2010) writes about 'produsage'; and Benkler (2004) and Benkler and Nissenbaum (2006) write on 'commons based peer-production'. These terms imply the prominence and/or co-equal status of producers and users of goods. von Hippel (2005a, 2005b) focuses on user-led innovations in which the user is very prominent.

29. See Leadbeater's (2007) and Tapscott and Williams's (2007) *We-Think: Mass Innovation, Not Mass Production* and *Wikinomics*, respectively, and see Van Dijck and Nieborg (2009) for a critical assessment of their arguments.

30. Manovich (2009: 321) in 'the practice of everyday (media) life'.

31. Manovich compares the conventions of the Internet era with those of the earlier mass media era drawing analogies with the critical theory perspective on the workings of the ideological apparatus, see Adorno and Horkheimer's (1944/1972) *The Culture Industry*.

32. Wittgenstein (1951: 149–51) in *Tractatus Logico-Philosophicus*.

33. Waskul (2005: 55) on liminality and computer mediated communication.

34. See Feenberg (1991, 2010a) on affordances of technology, an idea that is applied in empirical research on social online communities (Wellman et al., 2003).

35. See Lesage (2009) on the careers of artists employing advanced networks.

36. Manovich (2009: 320) reports the lower figures based on 2007 data. Pew reports the higher figure for adults and for teenagers (Lenhart and Madden, 2005). See Burke et al. (2009), Daugherty et al. (2008), Huberman et al. (2009), and Manovich (2009) on contributions, motivations, attention and productivity, and conventions in online practices.

37. See Van Der Graaf (2009) for analysis of skill levels of contributors in Second Life.

38. See Nazir et al. (2008) on 'contributions to Facebook'.

39. See Sunstein's (2009) *Going to Extremes* and *Republic.com 2.0* (2001).

40. The term 'crowdsourcing' is attributed to Jeff Howe, writing in *Wired* magazine in 2006 (Letts, nd). See Organisciak (2010) for a review of motivations for crowdsourcing. The term is also used to refer to data mining techniques without user volition.

41. These websites are www.giffgaff.com and http://mvp.support.microsoft.com/, both accessed 21/07/2011.

42. See Letts (nd: np) for a corporate promotional website.

43. One study found a median wage of USD 1.38/hour (Horton and Chilton, 2010). See also McKercher and Mosco (2008) and Mosco (2008) on virtual labour.

44. The Extraordinaries, for example, has attracted more than 100,000 volunteers to work on projects in the developing world, see http://www.telegraph.co.uk/science/roger-highfield/8153252/Crowdsourcing-and-open-source-knowledge-is-a-gift.html, accessed 3/12/2010. See also Mullins (2010), Scott and Street (2001), and Van de Donk et al. (2004) on crowdsourcing aid in crisis situations, e-protests, and cyberprotests.

45. The perception of diversity is fostered by claims about the long tail phenomenon, a term popularized by Anderson (2006, 2009). The phenomenon of a 'long tail' refers to the efforts of retailers to attract users to large numbers of unique items in small quantities. Whether or not profits are generated depends on the expansibility (sharing of fixed costs) and replicability (adding units at constant costs) of the value-generating mechanism that is employed. If both apply, the companies depending on diversity in this way have a scalable model that is likely to be profitable (because unit costs decline), but this is a big 'if'.

46. See Rabby and Walther (2003) and Walther (2007) on relationship management and self-presentation.

47. See Danet and Herring (2003, 2007) on linguistics online.

48. See research by Baron (2008), Derks et al. (2008), Hargittai (2008), Hogan (2009), Holt (2004), Rettie (2009), Walther et al. (2008, 2009).

49. The European Commission's position on privacy is based on Article 8 of the Charter of Fundamental Rights of the European Union which states that everyone has the right to the protection of his or her own personal data (European Commission, 1995, 2000a), but the issue here is the capacity for enforcement.

50. See Debatin et al. (2009) on online privacy.

51. See Banks and Wu (2010) and Light and McGrath (2010), respectively, for behavioural approaches to online networking and privacy and on ethical issues raised by Facebook use.

52. For research on the implications for privacy, see Agre and Rotenberg (1997), Bennett and Raab (2003), and Lyon (2007, 2009).

53. See Cammaerts (2008a), Chadwick (2006), Fenton (2007), Keren (2006), Mossberger et al. (2008), and Toulouse and Luke (1998) for work on participatory potentials of the Internet.

54. For example, after the election of President Obama, an official report announced that 'for too long, the American people have experienced a culture of secrecy in Washington', calling for an emphasis on transparency, participation, and collaboration using online media platforms (The White House, 2009: 1).

55. See Makau (2011) on Internet ethics.

56. For example, Facebook can be transformed into a Denial-of-Service attack platform (Athanasopoulos et al., 2008) and Twitter accounts can be hacked, see Herwig (2009) and Johnson (2010).

57. See Morozov (2009, 2011) on the Twitter 'revolution' and *The Net Delusion* and Downing et al.'s (2001) *Radical Media* which argues that alternative media can be associated with both democratic and anti-democratic movements.

58. See Braman's (2006) 'tactical memory' advocating technological discretion. De Landa's (1991) *War in the Age of Intelligent Machines* developed the idea of the panspectron and Hookway et al.'s (1999) *Pandemonium* examines techniques of control in a digital culture. The panspectron is a situation in which it is impossible to hide physically due to sensors and other tracking devices. This can be contrasted with the panopticon where the watched know

that the watcher is present (Bentham, 1787/1995). See also Gandy Jr.'s (2009) *Coming to Terms with Chance.*

59. Shirky (2010: 211, emphasis added) in *Cognitive Surplus.*

60. See Gladwell and Shirky (2011) on social media and protest movements.

61. Turkle (2011: np e-book edition) in *Alone Together,* and *Life on the Screen* (1995).

62. See Dutton and Shepherd's (2005) analysis of confidence and risk on the Internet.

63. See Brautigan's (1970) short story 'The Library'.

64. Mateos-Garcia and Steinmueller (2008*b*) note that as in 'real world' museums, decisions are made by curators about what to represent, who to represent, and how identities and collective memories will be depicted, distancing these decisions from the individual contributor. In Brautigan's story, the author chooses where to display a work in the library, but still no-one finds it or reads it. Raymond (1999) differentiates between OSS development (or open content production) using a bazaar model in contrast to building conventional software following a master plan, as for building a cathedral, as earlier proposed by Brooks (1982).

65. See Brake (2009) on the imaginary audiences of bloggers.

66. Brautigan (1970: 20).

67. Rheingold (1993/2000: 57).

68. Licklider and Taylor (1968: 38) on 'the computer as a communication device' and using the term 'mediate'.

69. See O'Hara and Shadbolt (2005) and Sakata et al. (1997) on knowledge technologies and the Semantic Web, respectively.

70. See the Web science community, http://fuzzzy.com/, accessed 18/03/2011.

71. See Duman et al. (2009) on intelligent agents and visual information representation.

72. Park et al. (2008) and see http://www.cdc.gov/socialmedia/, accessed 15/03/2011.

73. To make sense of virtual worlds, Tim Berners-Lee et al. (2001: np) proposed the creation of the Semantic Web, 'to bring structure to the meaningful content of Web pages, creating an environment where software agents roaming from page to page can readily carry out sophisticated tasks for users'. A profligately used term in this connection is 'folksonomies' which are less formal systems of classification arising from collaborations that lead to the tagging and classification of digital content (Dotsika, 2009).

74. Pollock (2009: 1) on *The Semantic Web for Dummies.*

75. See Chen et al. (2009) and Kobilarov et al. (2009), and http://sig.biostr.washington.edu/projects/fm/AboutFM.html and http://sweet.jpl.nasa.gov/, both accessed 28/04/2011.

76. Ramshurn and Jennings (2005: 167, emphasis in original) on trust and agent-based software citing Dasgupta (1988) in 'Trust as a Commodity', in support of their definition.

77. Journalist and science fiction writer, Cory Doctorow, raises provocative issues, see blog at http://craphound.com/, accessed 28/07/2011, and there are criticisms by those working in the socio-technical studies field, see Bath (2009).

78. See Lachica and Karabeg (2008) on metadata and tagging. Ontologies are used in the social sciences and similarly involve assumptions about agency, causation, and choices, see, for example, Geels (2010). The issue in the context of software agents is that of the relative magnitude of dependence and the ability to challenge.

79. See van Eijk (2009) on search engines and information access. See also Van Couvering (2010) and Vanberg (2011) for scholarly treatments of search engine industry structure, potential biases, and dominance in the European market.
80. See Ciastellardi et al. (2011) on ontologies and folksonomies.
81. See Schmitz et al. (2009) on metadata and the importance of context.
82. See Benevenuto et al. (2009) and Thelwall (2008) on how user behaviours are characterized and MySpace member profiles, respectively.
83. See Gandy Jr. (2009), Lyon (2006, 2007), and Pierson and Heyman (2011) for scholarly treatments of surveillance issues, and Jowitt (2010), Judge (2010), and Reuters (2010) for press coverage.
84. See Alani et al. (2003), Golbeck et al. (2003), O'Hara (2004), Piper et al. (2005), and Richardson et al. (2003) on ontology network analysis, the dynamics of social networks, changing conceptions of online trust, identities and authentication, and trust management for the Semantic Web, respectively. See Bisogni et al. (2011) on private sector incentives to invest in cybersecurity. For a discussion of differences between Europe and the United States in the use of filtering technologies, see Elser (2005).
85. A data structure stored on a user's computer, which, if accepted, is available for query by the organization supplying it and, in certain cases, others as well, see Pierson and Heyman (2011).
86. See Fingar (2009) and Marinos and Briscoe (2009) on cloud computing. See also Willcocks et al. (2011) in 'Cloud and the Future of Business'.
87. See Dutton and Shepherd (2005) and this situation is not improving rapidly, see BBC News (2010).
88. Get Safe Online (2010) is a collaboration between the UK government, banks, software and telecommunication companies, payment and payment verification services.
89. Gunkel (2010: 137) on 'avatars and online social interaction'.
90. Žižek's (2006: 221) *The Parallax View*.
91. See Couldry's (2010) *Why Voice Matters*.
92. Veblen (1899/2008: 115, emphasis added) in *The Theory of the Leisure Class*.
93. See Ross (2011) 'Is there an expertise of production?' for a discussion of distinctions between expert and layperson's contributions to the production of new media technologies. For a longer treatment, see Ross (2005).

Chapter 6

1. Manuel De Landa's (2011) work in *Philosophy and Simulation* exemplifies attempts to employ computerization to explain emergent properties of systems on different scales including the social, integrating the works of scientists with that of Gilles Deleuze and Félix Guattari (1980/1987). He also develops the idea of self-organizing 'meshworks' as an alternative to hierarchy, see De Landa's (2000) *1,000 Years of Non-Linear History*.
2. Wetware is variously defined as referring to 'minds' or to people's involvement in software programming.
3. Taylor (2007: 171).
4. See Mansell and Steinmueller (2011 under review *b*) on the copyright paradox.
5. David (2004: 5) on 'the end of copyright history?'

6. See Bainbridge (1994), Bettig and Schiller (1997), David (1993), HM Treasury (2006), Liebowitz and Margolis (2005), Makeen (2000), Strategic Advisory Board for Intellectual Property Policy (2010), and Watt (2000) for discussion of the aims of copyright from economic, historical, cultural, and political economy perspectives.

7. The 1886 Berne Copyright Convention protects the expression of literary and artistic works that meet standards of originality (WIPO, 1886 as amended). In Europe and the United States, copyright on works created on or after 1 January 1978 endures for the life of the author plus 70 years after the author's death, which is longer than required by the Berne Convention (European Commission, 2006; US, 2009).

8. David (2004: 5).

9. See Hadfield (1992), Liebowitz (2006), and Liebowitz and Margolis (2005). Critical historical study demonstrates that the resolution of conflicts of interests between rights holders and others has changed through time, with the legal balance shifting in favour of rights holders, see Bannerman (2009, 2010), Bettig (1989), Drahos and Braithwaite (2003), Haunss and Shadlen (2009), Litman (2001), and May (2007).

10. See European Commission (2011) and reports cited therein and legislation proposed at the time of writing before the US Senate (US, 2011).

11. Samuelson (2007: 3) on 'prospects for copyright reform in the United States'.

12. In the United Kingdom, for example, see Hargreaves (2011).

13. For example, in the EU in 2008 it was estimated that the creative industries contributed 6.9 per cent, or approximately €860 billion, to total Gross Domestic Product. If no new efforts are made to curtail copyright infringement, cumulative revenue losses of some €240 billion were estimated by 2015 (TERA Consultants, 2010). Although growing from a small base, the value of the global market for digital music increased by 1,000 per cent between 2004 and 2010, representing some USD 4.6 billion (IFIP, 2009, 2010, 2011). See Cammaerts and Meng (2011) for a discussion of problems in evaluating the industry data sources on revenue losses.

14. 'The making available of files from a user's own computer for copying and transmission to other users over the Internet, and the receipt of files made available this way. File sharing thus involves uploading as well as downloading. File sharing takes place in networks of users. Third parties have developed the file-sharing services and technologies to connect users and enable them to carry out such transmission and copying activities in the third party's particular "peer-to-peer" (P2P) network' (Dixon, 2009: 13–14).

15. See discussions of trends in social practices online and specifically in the music industry in Baym (2010a) and Burnett (2010).

16. See, for example, Strategic Advisory Board for Intellectual Property Policy (2010).

17. See Jenkins's (2006) and Lessig's (2008) *Convergence Culture* and *Remix*, respectively.

18. See Burkart's (2010) *Music and Cyberliberties.*

19. Lessig (2003: 763) on the creative commons and Lessig (2001, 2006) in *The Future of Ideas* and *Code: Version 2.0.*

20. See http://creativecommons.org/, the website for this worldwide movement with affiliates in more than seventy jurisdictions established in 2002 and with supporters such as Google, and the Mozilla Foundation and Red Hat, both OSS organizations, accessed 28/07/2011. Notwithstanding its success, there are critics (Elkin-Koren, 2006) and disagreements about where the boundary between commercial and non-commercial use of works lies. By mid-

2011, there were more than 500 million pieces of work covered by Creative Commons licences.

21. See Benkler (2000, 2004, 2006), Benkler and Nissenbaum (2006), and Bettig and Schiller (1997) on the case for shifting the 'balance' in copyright protection.

22. The Office of Technology Assessment (OTA) report acknowledges that 'decisions about intellectual property law may be decisions about the *distribution of wealth and social status*' (OTA, 1986: 11, 14, emphasis added).

23. Pew Internet Survey data show that in 2009, in the United States, nearly four out of five (79%) teenagers owned an iPod or other MP3 player; three out of four adults reported online purchasing of products such as books, music, toys, and clothing; half of teenagers reported buying online (Lenhart et al., 2010). In the United Kingdom, the Oxford Internet Survey shows that the practice of downloading (any) music has been growing (54% of respondents reported downloading music in 2005; 59% in 2009) (Dutton et al., 2009).

24. See Boyle (2008: 248) who says 'in the middle of the most successful and exciting experiment in non-proprietary, distributed creativity in the history of the species, our policy makers can see only the threat from "piracy"'.

25. Industry associations such as RIAA, MPAA, and AACP are among those seeking to curtail online copyright infringement. The IIPA publishes an annual 'special 301' list estimating losses due to copyright infringement, and a 'watch list' of offending countries.

26. These include websites such as Baidu China, IsoHunt Canada, mp3fiesta Ukraine, RapidShare Germany, RMX4U Luxemburg, and The Pirate Bay Sweden (RIAA, 2010).

27. Efforts to counter copyright infringement are subject to the Digital Millennium Copyright Act (US, 1998, 2009).

28. In mid-2011, a voluntary agreement involving the five big US ISPs (AT&T, Cablevision, Comcast, Time Warner Cable, and Verizon) was put in place whereby ISPs would send six alerts to subscribers based on notifications received from content owners about potential copyright infringements, but would not release subscriber names or terminate subscriber accounts. Instead, 'mitigation measures' (temporary reductions in Internet speed, redirection to an educational landing page, or other measures determined by ISPs) will be used—the process of appeal was unclear at the time of writing, see Andersen (2011), Electronic Frontier Foundation (2011), and Lasar (2011).

29. See Mansell and Steinmueller's (2010) submission to the Judicial Review.

30. In France, initial drafts of the HADOPI legislation (France, 2009) made punishment an administrative decision. The final legislation made disconnection from the Internet a matter for the prosecutor attached to the high court, but left it to those accused to bear the costs of appealing decisions. The procedure is handled mainly electronically and the possibility of false positive identifications is deemed to be relatively high.

31. Fleming (2010: emphasis added).

32. The *Gowers Report* on Intellectual Property in the United Kingdom stated that 'copyright infringement through unauthorized copying and distribution of music and video across the Internet is likened to stealing by some, and to sharing by others' (HM Treasury, 2006: para 1.9). The *Digital Britain* report indicated the then Labour Government's alignment with the creative industry arguments (BIS and DCMS, 2009; UK, 2010). The Secretary of State was required to authorize actions taken by ISPs against individuals, in addition to sending warning letters to those suspected of infringing file-sharing.

33. High Court of Justice (2011). See also Mansell and Steinmueller (2011 under review *a*) for a discussion of this case.

34. High Court of Justice (2011: para 249, emphasis added).

35. The European Data Protection Supervisor suggested that disclosure of the identity of individual Internet users to the creative industries should be limited to those infringing on a commercial scale (Hustinx, 2010: para 43).

36. See Cammaerts (2011) on regulatory responses to file-sharing.

37. The European Parliament's draft Bono Report read 'criminalising consumers so as to combat digital piracy is not the right solution' (European Parliament, 2007: para 9). This was revised to read 'criminalising consumers who are not seeking to make a profit is not the right solution to combat digital piracy' (European Parliament, 2008: para 17).

38. See Breindl and Houghton (2010) for a discussion of 'techno-political activism'.

39. An 'Internet Freedom' provision was incorporated in the Telecom Reform Package as Annex 1, Article 1(3)a which makes reference to the fundamental rights and freedoms of natural persons, as guaranteed by the European Convention for the Protection of Human Rights and Fundamental Freedoms and general principles of Community law (Europa RAPID Press Releases, 2009). See Ryan and Heinl (2010) for a view supportive of the creative industries' position.

40. See Hampton and Gupta (2008) and Lindner et al. (2004) on wireless use in public places and business models for WiFi, respectively.

41. In France, prior to the controversial introduction of HADOPI, a study by Dejean et al. (2010) found a decline in P2P infringing activity, but an increase in the use of other technological means of accessing digital content following debate, but prior to charges under the law. In mid-2011, the Commission charged with receiving infringing notifications from rights holders was still considering whether to refer some ten people to the court, a figure the rights holders were claiming was not sufficiently high (Pichevin, 2011). There are ambiguous results on the impact of the legislation in Sweden (Lundstrom et al., 2010). Other studies based mainly on college student respondents find a wide range of factors likely to influence attitudes or behavioural change in the face of a legal threat of sanctions against infringing downloading, see Cox et al. (2010), David (2010), LaRose and Kim (2007), Liebowitz (2006), Oberholzer-Gee and Strumpf (2010), and Plowman and Goode (2009).

42. See Meyer and Van Audenhove (2010: 77, emphasis added) for an analysis of the graduated response strategy in Europe.

43. See Dutton and Shepherd (2005). As cases against ISP subscribers gain media attention they receive publicity, information is distributed across file-sharing networks, attracting the attention of those who might otherwise not have known that possibilities for infringing behaviour are available to them.

44. See Beebe (2008), Borgman (2007), Engle (2002), Hamelink (2002), and Klimkiewicz (2008), and the Electronic Frontier Foundation, Creative Commons (and its worldwide affiliates), Free Press and Public Knowledge in the United States, the Open Rights Group in the United Kingdom, Science Commons in the United States, and the P2P Foundation and the Open Knowledge Foundation in Europe, http://www.crisinfo.org/http://creativecommons.org/, http://www.eff.org/, http://blog.p2pfoundation.net/, http://www.openrightsgroup.org/, http://www.freepress.net/, http://www.publicknowledge.org/, http://okfn.org/, and http://sciencecommons.org/about/, all accessed 05/02/2011.

45. See Lehdonvirta and Virtanen (2010) on game player interests in virtual goods.

46. See Heeks (2010: 11) for an analysis of gamers' economic interests.

47. The initial offer of this service, iTunes Match, had a limit of 25,000 songs with iTunes purchases not counting against this limit, see http://www.apple.com/icloud/features/, accessed 24/07/2011.

48. See EBU (2010), Ernesto (2010), Quiring et al. (2008), and Regner et al. (2009). Spotify, for example, offers a premium and basic subscription service that is advertiser-supported and a 'free at the point of consumption', of 20 hours of music listening per month. This opportunity is not equivalent to downloading music from infringing sites: it is not replayed, but simply stored on a music enthusiast's computer, an example of overconsumption. The United Kingdom Treasury is using this technology to release public data on public spending, see http://data.gov.uk/dataset/coins, accessed 3/05/2011. See also Dubosson-Torbay et al. (nd) on new business models for music distribution.

49. Ofcom has a digital literacy programme, see http://www.imlrf.org/member/ofcom as does the European Commission, at http://ec.europa.eu/information_society/tl/edutra/skills/index_en. htm, part of the i2010 strategy aimed at inclusion and e-learning, accessed 1/07/2010.

50. Boyle (1996: 169) in *Shamans, Software & Spleens* on law and the information society. See also Boyle (2008) *The Public Domain* on enclosing the commons.

51. See Pilieci (2011).

52. See European Commission (2001, 2004, 2011) for relevant directives.

53. It is open to signature by the negotiating countries until March 2013 (ACTA, 2010).

54. ACTA (2010: Sec. 5, Art. 2.18.4, emphasis added).

55. WIPO (2011: 7).

56. See WIPO (1998).

57. See WIPO (2009).

58. WIPO (2009: 45). TRIPS forms Annex 1C of the Marrakesh Agreement Establishing the World Trade Organization (WTO, 1994). TRIPS is seen as offering 'an opportunity to use intellectual property protection to accelerate economic, social, and cultural development, as well as to increase awareness of intellectual property as a key natural resource in developing nations' (WIPO, 1998: 9).

59. WIPO (1998: 9).

60. WIPO (1998: 12).

61. See UNESCO (2005*a*, 2009).

62. See Meyer (2000) for a discussion of changing ideas about digital platforms.

63. The European Commission's Digital Agenda for Europe 2020 emphasizes the need for the development of open and interoperable solutions to create open platforms for new products and services (European Commission, 2010*b*: 2.5.3), in part, by working with stakeholders to develop a new generation Web-based applications and services. The case considered here was started earlier in the framework of European Commission supported enterprise systems projects. The European Commission adopted an Electronic Commerce Directive in 2000 to encourage the take up of ICTs within the single European market (European Commission, 2000*b*, 2010*d*).

64. This discussion is based on two European Commission-funded research projects: 'Digital Business Ecosystem' (DBE) (2003–2006) approx. €10.5m and 'Open Philosophies for Associative Autopoietic Digital Ecosystems' (OPAALS) (2007–2010) approx. €9m, which

aimed to develop a digital platform for small- and medium-sized enterprises, and in the latter case, for the research community. Dr Paolo Dini, Senior Research Fellow, London School of Economics and Political Science, was Scientific Coordinator of the DBE and Coordinator of the OPAALS projects, and Principal Investigator for LSE activities in both projects. I was a participant in both projects, contributing in various ways to the social science outputs of the projects. These projects were part of a large cluster of projects in areas such as Enterprise Software, Enterprise Interoperability and Collaboration to develop future Internet applications. See http://ec.europa.eu/information_society/activities/foi/research/index_en.htm, accessed 28/07/2011 for lists of the projects. Many of the references in this section are to deliverables for these projects. I am grateful to P. Dini for his compilation of the reports which eased my access to them. All DBE and OPAALS projects documentation was reviewed to develop the account given in this section.

65. Arthur (2009) acknowledges that it is necessary to bracket human activity to think in this way.

66. OPAALS (2010*b*) presentation on a new copyright model.

67. Nachira et al. (2007: xii) in *Digital Business Ecosystems*, a comprehensive statement on the ambitions that underpinned both projects.

68. Berdou (2007: 96) provides a critical view of the digital ecosystems project ambitions.

69. This separation has been criticized in the innovation literature, see, for example, Rosenberg (1982*a*) and von Hippel (2005*b*) on the logic of separating producers and users as innovators to obtain results through learning. The IBM project partner proposed a classification of the small- and medium-sized firms into 'drivers', 'discovers', 'implementers', and 'users', a more sophisticated segmentation, but still one that ignores insights from the innovation literature.

70. Nachira et al. (2007) provided an early definition while Nachira was serving as a project officer for this line of work in the European Commission. Moore (1997) is said to have coined the term 'business ecosystem' to indicate that organizations exist in dynamic interaction.

71. The technical challenge was to develop an open platform based on a decentralized Ecosystem Oriented Architecture (EOA), proposed by Ferronato (2007: 112) which would not be constrained by the limitations of the Service Oriented Architecture (SOA) which is managed via a centralized governance authority. The system for the digital ecosystem needed 'self-organizing capabilities' so that it could operate automatically without human intervention.

72. This involved an infrastructural and interaction model, interfaces, and Semantics of Business Vocabulary and Business Rules (SBVR), providing a metamodel for specification of a business context. The aim was to develop an information system with process-like behaviour without its processes being explicitly defined, see OPAALS (2010*a*).

73. It was claimed that, compared to the research community, where it was an issue, the absence of the decentralized data storage system was not an issue for those in small companies because they had different data storage needs in their 'ecosystem'.

74. See Dini (2007) on the scientific foundation for digital ecosystems.

75. Razavi Krause et al. (2010: 24) on the evolutionary and interaction framework.

76. See Darking (2007) on the role of governance.

77. Dini et al. (2010: 33). This form of computing is analogous to 'the ability of the biological cell to synthesize particular functional components such as enzymes in response to the needs of on-going metabolic processes or to signal transduction pathways from outside

the cell. The signals to initiate the synthesis of such components are somehow encoded in the metabolic processes themselves'.

78. See Desodt (2007) on demonstration of the OKS technical platform.

79. Brauer et al. (2007: 30) on principles, models, and processes for the OKS.

80. Shaikh and Berdou (2008: 8) reviewing open knowledge successes and failures.

81. See Brauer et al.'s (2010) report on improving the usability of the OKS.

82. See Bueso (2010), Lapteva (2010), and Nykänen (2010) on complexities of linguistic patterns in online environments, OKS visualization application and toolkit, and governance and regulatory strategies for the OKS.

83. Eder et al. (2007: 2) on design of the software for digital ecosystems.

84. Brauer et al. (2007) on principles, models, and processes for the OKS.

85. Personal communication with P. Dini 06/08/2011.

86. See Malone et al. (2010) and OPAALS (2010c) for case studies of partner networks in OSS value creation and on identity, trust, and accountability in the P2P network.

87. This is the Open Knowledge Society Association Internationale Sans But Lucratif (OKS AISBL), a Belgian legal entity.

88. Razavi et al. (2007: 116) on architecture for the P2P network.

89. Dini et al. (2008: 8–9) and see Dini et al. (2009) and Munro et al. (2008) on a biological and mathematical framework for interaction computing, biological design patterns of autopoietic behaviour, and foundations of the theory of associative autopoietic digital ecosystems.

90. See Brauer et al. (2010) and Lapteva (2010) on improving the usability of the OKS and on the complexities of linguistic patterns in online environments.

91. See OPAALS (2010b), Razavi Malone et al. (2010: 45), and Val (2010) on the impact of new intellectual property legislation on corporate behaviour, use of the P2P network with small- and medium-sized enterprises in Aragon, and identity, trust, and accountability in the transaction model.

92. Bueso et al. (2010: 48) on governance and sustainability, and see Botto (2010), Stanley (2010), and Van Egeraat and Curran (2010) on the experience of a living laboratory in Trentino, impact of changes in intellectual property legislation, and structures of knowledge flows in the Irish biotechnology industry. The issues included problems of the virtualization of information resources, technological turbulence, extraterritoriality, jurisdictional difficulties, and multiple information sources.

93. See Dini et al. (2011) in the '(Im)possibility of Interdisciplinarity'.

94. See Eder et al. (2007), Razavi Malone et al. (2010), and Razavi Moschoyiannis et al. (2010) on design of the software for digital ecosystems, the infrastructural and interaction model, and the integration of identity, trust, and accountability in the transaction model.

95. See Bueso (2010) on governance and sustainability.

96. See Briscoe et al. (2010) and Dini et al. (2010) on gene expression computing and operational closure of the ecosystem architecture.

97. Similar to an 'exit and voice' strategy as suggested by Hirschman (1970) in *Exit, Voice and Loyalty*.

98. Braman (1994: 362) in the 'autopoietic state'.

Chapter 7

1. See Mooney (2010).
2. Pfanner (2011) citing President Sarkozy's speech at the Summit.
3. See OECD (2011a). This communiqué sets out policy principles: promoting and protecting the global free flow of information; promoting the open, distributed, and interconnected nature of the Internet; promoting investment and competition in high-speed networks and services; promoting and enabling the cross-border delivery of services; encouraging multistakeholder cooperation in policy development processes; fostering voluntarily developed codes of conduct; developing capacities to bring publicly available, reliable data into the policy making process; ensuring transparent, fair process, and accountability; strengthening consistency and effectiveness in privacy protection at a global level; maximizing individual empowerment; and promoting creativity and innovation.
4. See OECD (2011b).
5. McQuail (2003: 91) and see Ó Siochrú and Girard's (2002) *Media Accountability and Global Media Governance*. The term 'network governance' has been coined to describe interactions among multiple public, semi-public, and private actors. It can be assumed that no single actor has the power to control the others, such that governance is 'self-regulating', that it is quasi-rational, or that it involves a struggle between conflicting interests and goals (Sörenson and Torfing, 2008). The self-regulating view is inspired in part by the claim that 'government is the historically constituted matrix within which are articulated all those dreams, schemes, strategies and manoeuvres of authorities that seek to shape the beliefs and conduct of others in desired directions by acting upon their will, their circumstances or their environment' (Rose and Miller, 1992: 175). The quasi-rational view is consistent with a reform approach, see Lindblom (1990) and Melody (1971). A conflictual view is consistent with persistent asymmetries of power, see Cammaerts (2005) and Carpentier (2011b) although these are non-exclusive categories.
6. See Kooiman (1993) and Puppis (2010) for a general discussion of theories of governance.
7. See Mansell and Raboy's (2011) 'Introduction' in *The Handbook of Global Media and Communication Policy*.
8. Waite (1877: np), the US Chief Justice who applied the concept based on the British jurist, Lord Chief Justice Hale's contributions written in 1676, but not published until 1787 in Hale (1787), see Hamilton (1930) for a discussion of the ruling.
9. See US Telecommunications Act 1996. The Communications Act was passed in 1934.
10. Hamilton (1930: 1104) in 'Affectation with Public Interest'.
11. In the United Kingdom, the regulator, Ofcom, is charged with furthering the interests of citizens and consumers in the 'public interest'. See UK Communications Act 2003. The British Broadcasting Corporation is regulated by a Trust, which replaced the Board of Governors in 2007, see http://www.bbc.co.uk/bbctrust/index.shtml, accessed 28/07/2011.
12. Hamilton (1930: 1109).
13. See Melody (1997) in *Telecom Reform*. Renda (2010) examines the history of the 'essential facility doctrine' in Europe where it was used to encourage 'open network provision', that is, access by competing operators to each other's networks. In the Internet era it is unclear which, if any, facilities should be deemed essential. The idea is traced to the earliest days of the postal service and telegraphy by Magder (2011).

14. For example, the UK Enterprise Act 2002, s.58 specifies a public interest in the press and broadcasting with respect to plurality and high quality. The UK Communications Act 2003 sets out requirements for public service broadcasting such as programming quotas, news and current affairs programming and production, and the role of the regulator Ofcom. The BBC's remit and purposes are provided for by its Charter and Agreement (DCMS, 2006). See also Feintuck and Varney (2006) on *Media Regulation, Public Interest and the Law*. In the United States, the media are regulated by the Federal Communications Commission (FCC) and the Telecommunications Act 1996. Websites providing information on the history of public interest decisions include www.benton.org and www.freepress.net, both accessed 28/07/2011.

15. See Donders and Pauwels (2010) and Tambini (2004) on the implications of new media for broadcast regulation and public service broadcasting.

16. The Internet can be defined as 'the global data communication capability realized by the interconnection of public and private telecommunication networks using Internet Protocol (IP), Transmission Control Protocol (TCP), and other protocols required to implement IP inter-networking on a global scale, such as DNS [domain name system] and packet routing protocols' (Mathiason, 2009: 11) citing Mueller et al. (2007). See also FCC (2005) for a policy statement.

17. See Chapter 1 for a discussion of the good society and see O'Hara (2004) on standards for policy with respect to ICTs and networks, and general standards for policy choice in Ackerman (1980), Rawls (1972), and Sen (2009), each of which differs in the way decisions are to be reached about the standard that should apply.

18. See Albagli and Maciel's (2010: 18) *Information, Power and Politics* and the United Nations Development Programme's (1990) warning about the folly of overemphasizing technology while neglecting people and their well-being.

19. de Sola Pool (1990: 101) commented that international satellite networks were 'often considered a mixed blessing by rulers' in *Technologies Without Boundaries*.

20. See Sparks's (2007) *Globalization, Development and the Mass Media* for an historical account.

21. See Arthur (2011). This is one example of the way states exercise power over the communication system. For other examples, see Gagliardone (2010), Ho et al. (2002), Ibrahim (2006), and Kalathil and Boas (2003).

22. Escobar (1995: 20) in *Encountering Development*.

23. See Johnson and Post (1998) for a widely cited early example of this position and Werbach (1997: 84) for an early paper published by the FCC Office of Plans and Policy, which though not a formal FCC position, takes a complex systems approach.

24. Barlow (1996: 1).

25. See David's (2001) historical analysis of the 'accidental information super-highway'. Solum (2009) provides a summary of models of Internet governance.

26. Sassen (2001: 28) in the 'Internet and Sovereignty'.

27. See, for example, Anheier et al. (2001), Brown (2001), and Cohen and Rai (2000) on social movements; and Cammaerts (2008*a*, 2011), Downing et al. (2001), and McCurdy (2008) on ICTs and social movements emphasizing that non-state and not-for-profit organizations can be advocates of positions across the political spectrum.

28. See Bygrave and Bing (2009) and Maclean (2011) for history and mandates, and see Mathiason (2009) and Mueller (2010*b*).

29. For discussion of the history and politics of this period, see Mansell and Nordenstreng (2006), Padovani and Nordenstreng (2005), and Samarajiva and Shields (1990).

30. See ICSCP (1980/2004).

31. Another report focused on the development of the communication infrastructure. The *Missing Links* was concerned with telecommunication networks and the implications of gaps in access to networks for the poor countries (ICWTD, 1984). The technology gap would later be labelled the 'digital divide'. There was a tendency to neglect the agency of active viewers of content and users of technology who would appropriate the tools of the communication system in their own interests. Some of the arguments especially with respect to a 'one way' flow of information promoted by the market-led model of the information society were contested and later modified, see Boyd-Barrett (1998) on media imperialism. Research on active audiences and on the emergence of a participatory culture (see Couldry et al., 2007; Jenkins et al., 2009) has helped to counter the earlier model, but arguably has done little to tackle the persistent asymmetries in the economic power of the dominant companies who are constructing the infrastructure and establishing online commercial sites on the Internet.

32. See the World Bank's (1999) *Knowledge for Development* annual report which put information and ICTs at the centre of its policy. See Soete (1985) for a discussion of technological leapfrogging and Abramovitz (1986) for factors that are said to enable countries to catch-up with the 'modernizing' leaders. Steinmueller (2001/2) discusses technological leapfrogging emphasizing the difficulties, though he ends on an optimistic note.

33. See Annan (1997). The United Nations General Assembly passed two resolutions on communication for development and encouraged decision-makers to include this as an integral component in developing programmes. This is not to suggest that Annan personally was persuaded by this view, but rather that as leader, he promoted it.

34. See UN (2001) for the resolution calling for the Summit.

35. World Bank (1999: 1).

36. This was evident in the texts produced by the WSIS, which had a strong technology-led orientation, despite concessions to a 'people-centred, inclusive and development-oriented Information Society', respecting human rights, see UN (2008: 48, 2010b), and UN/ITU (2003a, 2003b, 2005a, 2005b) for the documentation on the Summit. See also Adam (2005) and Stauffacher and Kleinwächter (2005) for reflections by participants.

37. UN (2010a, 2010b). MDG Goal 8, Target 5, includes: 'In cooperation with the private sector, make available benefits of new technologies, especially information and communications', see http://www.un.org/millenniumgoals/global.shtml, accessed 20/05/2010. Some argue that this was an afterthought. Indicators are used to monitor numbers of fixed telephone lines, mobile cellular subscriptions, and Internet users per 100 population as well as fixed and mobile broadband subscribers per 100 population.

38. See, for example, Cammaerts (2008b), Frau-Meigs (2011), Padovani and Nordenstreng (2005), Padovani and Pavan (2011), and Raboy et al. (2010).

39. See IGF (2010) and http://www.intgovforum.org/cms/dynamiccoalitions, accessed 02/02/2011. In 2010, the distribution of participants from 107 countries ($n = 1461$) was civil society 21%, government 24%, intergovernmental organizations 7%, media 3%, private sector 23%, and technical and academic 22% (Kleinwächter, 2010). For details, see Dakroury (2009) and Klang and Murray (2005) on the way human rights issues are considered; Livingstone (2011) on the case for and against regulating the

Internet in the interests of children; and Ghosh (2005) on open standards in the OSS environment.

40. Hofmann (2009) sees the forum as a positive force for change, while Malcolm (2008*a*, 2008*b*) sees it as a forum where traditional inequalities are replicated.

41. Drake and Wilson Jr. (2008: 11) in *Governing Global Electronic Networks*.

42. See Mueller's (2010*b*) *Networks and States*.

43. For the structure of ICANN, see http://www.icann.org/en/about/, accessed 20/03/2011. Board members are elected and specialize in law and intellectual property, competition, information systems, banking, politics, social science, computer science and software engineering, mathematics, media, software and network management, electrical and electronic engineering, physics, chemical engineering, and artificial intelligence, see http://www.icann.org/en/general/board.html, accessed 20/03/2011. The Internet Society also seeks to influence future developments as a non-profit society, see http://www.isoc.org/isoc/, accessed 20/03/2011.

44. See Mueller (2009) and Palfrey (2004) on ICANN. For commentary, see the Internet Governance Project website, www.internetgovernance.org. See Freedman (2011) on *The State of Internet Regulation* and Hofmann and Botzem (2010) and Stevenson and Clement (2010) for general overviews of the issues.

45. Mueller (2009: 3).

46. This raises issues around the question of deliberative democracy and the procedures consistent with multi-stakeholder participation when there is no consensus on the principles that should guide decision-making, see Gutmann and Thompson (2004), Guttman (2010), and Stirling (2008).

47. Wu is said to have introduced the term 'net neutrality' in 2003, in the United States.

48. Arthur and Halliday (2011).

49. See Denardis's (2009: 188) *Protocol Politics* for a detailed analysis of the contested transition from IPv4 to IPv6. As she argues 'Internet protocols and the resources they create are the least visible but arguably most critical component of the Internet's technical and legal architecture. The development of universal Internet protocols and the management of scarce resources are fundamental Internet governance responsibilities'.

50. Braman and Roberts (2003: Table 2) discuss the use of contracts for 'terms of service' and 'acceptable use policies' which perform a regulatory function based on a study of ISPs in 2002.

51. See Sandvig (2007) on 'network neutrality is the new common carriage'.

52. Including those offered by Blue Coat Systems, DtecNet Software, L7-filter, NetScreen-IDP, and NetScout Systems and the use of Packet Details Markup Language (PDML) (Sluijs, 2010). Bendrath and Mueller (2010: 25) in their review of cases of DPI use by ISPs for traffic management purposes and at the behest of copyright holders, argue that 'if there is no simple "technical fix" to the problems of the Internet, neither is there a one-way march into the Panopticon. Our findings suggest that the "end of the Internet" is not pre-determined, nor is its freedom secure; its future rests very much in our own hands'.

53. Civil liberties are at stake in cases such as that of the US law firm ACS which accidentally released many emails to the public, demonstrating the harm that can accompany wrongful accusations of illegal downloading, for example, a man wrongly accused of downloading gay porn movies and the collection of a fine from a women despite acknowledging that she was not the infringer, etc. (Enigmax, 2010).

54. In some countries, people have the right to decide whether to disclose information, but once it is given away, they have few rights to prevent its secondary use, even when legislation

requires their consent. For differences between Europe and the United States in the use of filtering technologies and perspectives on free speech, see Elser (2005). See Bing (2005) on the role of software agents and the techniques embedded in software code. T-Mobile is reported to be using DPI to manage video data traffic. The European Commission has brought charges against the UK government for allowing Phorm to employ DPI. There are reports of DPI use by governments to enhance security against cyber attacks, see http://www.commondreams.org/view/2011/01/28-12, accessed 07/02/2011.

55. Berners-Lee (2010: 4, 5, emphasis added). Sir Berners-Lee's co-inventor was Robert Cail-liau, a Belgian informatics engineer. Lessig emphasizes the threat to innovation of departures from network neutrality, arguing that deviation from the existing Internet Protocol, 'creates a tighter integration between the network and the content/applications that the network is carrying [and] would chill innovation by raising the danger that part of the value of any innovations might be captured by the network provider' (cited in Yoo, 2009: 4).

56. See Braman (2011).

57. Content distribution networks (CDN) are operated by firms that charge for reliability and quality of information transmission, and substitute data storage for long distance capacity by using local caches located close to users.

58. See Noam (2010: 5) on 'Regulation 3.0'.

59. Mueller (2010a) argues that the abundance and scarcity conditions with respect to this component of the system interact with those relating to the routing system whereby data packets move from point of origin to point of destination. The Council of Europe (2009: 6) considers critical resources to include the name root servers, the backbone structure, the domain name system, addresses, and the transmission protocols, arguing that 'the Internet's openness and accessibility have become preconditions for the enjoyment of fundamental human rights'.

60. The legal case of Comcast vs FCC sparked renewed debate on network neutrality, see US (2010). Comcast is a large cable operator and ISP.

61. See Lessig and McChesney (2006) in 'No Tolls on the Internet'.

62. The principle of common carriage is that operators may not 'make any unjust or unreasonable discrimination in charges, practices, classifications, regulations, facilities, or services.... or... make or give any undue or unreasonable preference to any particular person, class of persons, or locality' (US, 1996). See Lentz (2011) for changing definitions of 'information service' which emerged in the Computer Inquiries and Melody (1970) for regulation in the early days of data communication services.

63. See Donahue (2010: 4) for an assessment of the FCC's network neutrality enquiry. Fixed network operators are expected to adhere to a set of principles consistent with network neutrality and there is greater flexibility for mobile operators. See FCC (2010b: paras 1, 8, 35) for details. The policy does not apply to the treatment of illegal use of the Internet or to discrimination aimed at combating copyright infringement.

64. FCC (2010a: 1).

65. See Chandler (2007: np) for the United States. Rights derive from the United Nations Universal Declaration of Human Rights which states that 'Everyone has the right to freedom of opinion and expression; this right includes freedom to hold opinions without interference and to seek, receive and impart information and ideas through any media and regardless of frontiers' (UN, 1948: Art 19). See also Nordenstreng (2011).

66. See Wu's (2010) *The Master Switch*. See also Goldsmith and Wu (2006) and Wu (1999, 2003).

67. For example, in the United States there are symmetrical charges between the mobile and fixed network operators. In Europe, fixed network companies own many mobile operators and charges tend to be asymmetrical (Marsden, 2010, 2011). See also Powell and Cooper (2011) on the way the debate has been treated in the United States and the United Kingdom.

68. See Mansell and Steinmueller (2011, in press) on 'digital economies and public policies'.

69. See main elements of the reform, http://ec.europa.eu/information_society/policy/ecomm/tomorrow/reform/index_en.htm, accessed 26/11/2010 and Directive 2009/140/EC (Council of Europe, 2010; European Commission, 2009*a*).

70. Council of Europe (2010: para 6).

71. See http://europa.eu/rapid/pressReleasesAction.do?reference=SPEECH/10/153&format=HT%20ML&aged=0&language=EN&guiLanguage=en, accessed 26/11/2010.

72. European Commission (2010*e*: 1).

73. Ofcom in the United Kingdom framed its public consultation on Internet traffic management by suggesting that the aim is to balance a right to a neutral Internet with ensuring incentives are in place to promote competitiveness and economic growth. See Ofcom (2010) discussion paper on network neutrality. In 2011 Ofcom set out its policy indicating that it had no immediate concerns about the potential for 'managed services' to jeopardize 'best effort' services.

74. European Commission (2009*b*). National regulators have until 2012 (in some cases beyond that date). In March 2011, Ofcom announced a reduction in the wholesale charges that mobile operators make to other operators to connect calls to their networks, resulting in an 80 per cent reduction in termination rates by the operators 3, O2, Everything Everywhere, and Vodafone, over 4 years.

75. Marsden (2011: 64). Marsden's blog is a resource on the net neutrality issue, see http://chrismarsden.blogspot.com/, accessed 28/07/2011.

76. For a range of views, see Bauer (2007), Collins (2009), Dutton and Peltu (2005), Faulhaber (2007), Sidak (2007), Spulber and Yoo (2009), Yoo (2005), and Zittrain (2003).

77. Mueller (2010*b*: 269) labels the institutions that emerge as 'organically developed Internet institutions' (ODii).

78. Mueller (2010*b*: 209).

Chapter 8

* From 'Hope' or 'Hoffnung', 'Zu was Besserm sind wir geboren! Und was die innere Stimme spricht, Das täuscht die hoffende Seele nicht'. This poem opens Freeman's *The Economics of Hope* (1992).

1. Silverstone (2007: 26) in *Media and Morality* and quoted in Chapter 1.

2. See Williams (1990/2008: 51) in *Notes on the Underground*, building on Mumford's earlier work.

3. See Mumford's (1934) *Technics and Civilization*. Technics was based on the Greek *tekhne*. Dallas W. Smythe (1984) similarly insisted on a broad definition of technology and on the need to consider perspectives offered by the humanities, social sciences, and natural sciences.

4. Mumford's (1934: 4) *Technics and Civilization*. Needham (2004) addressed a similar issue in his magisterial, seven-volume work on science and technology in China, which aimed to

explain why China's lead did not establish the country's dominance in the world of science and technology.

5. Mumford (1934: 366, 367, emphasis added).

6. Turkle (1995: 46, emphasis added) in *Life on the Screen*.

7. Innis (1951/1991: 190) in *Bias of Communication*.

8. Innis (1951/1991: 34) in *Bias of Communication*. He pointed out also that 'a change in the type of medium implies a change in the type of appraisal and hence makes it difficult for one civilization to understand another' (Innis, 1950/2007: 29).

9. Melody (2003: 420) on 'policy implications of the new information economy'.

10. Taylor (2007: 176) in *A Secular Age*.

11. See Livingstone (2011).

12. Stirling (2008) discusses this notion of gradient.

13. Yeats (1926/1989: 219) in 'Among School Children'.

14. A paraphrasing of Bateson (1972: 463) 'I have experienced, as have many others, the disappearance of the division between self and the music to which I was listening'.

15. A 'bit tax' or Tobin tax was proposed by a group of European experts, but was met with strong resistance (Cordell et al., 1997; European Commission High Level Group of Experts, 1996; Soete and Kamp 1996). A digital tax was discussed in 2010 by the World Health Organization as a means of generating revenues. It has been debated in academic journals dealing with online commerce and financial and trade implications. Some countries are considering the introduction of some sort of 'Internet Tax', for example France which taxes online advertising. A European Tobin tax on financial transactions was proposed again in the context of the debt crisis in 2011 although at the time of writing was generally not being received favourably except in France.

16. Hardt and Negri (2001: 404) in *Empire*.

17. Hardt and Negri (2009: 381–2) in *Common Wealth*. This moment arises out of the dynamic of a biopolitical process.

18. Castells (2000: 16) in 'an exploratory theory of the network society'.

19. See Castells's (2009) *Communication Power*.

20. See Gutmann and Thompson (2004).

21. Mumford (1934: 434, 435, emphasis added).

22. It was first used in the 1920s in the United States, to refer to studies that bridged the boundaries of the branches of the natural sciences and, later, to describe studies that crossed the boundaries of branches of the social sciences. Other terms, such as multidisciplinarity, may refer to work conducted within generally accepted boundaries of a discipline, but with subsequent collaboration with those from other disciplines. The term cross-disciplinarity may refer to research based substantially on analyses and methods from more than one discipline, see Hulme and Toye (2006) for a useful discussion.

23. Streeten (1974: 26, emphasis added) on the use and transfer of 'intellectual technology'.

24. Neoclassical economic theory does lay claim to a theory of agency (economic agents seek to maximize some outcomes and are able to rank their preferences, represented by a utility function and behavioural economics seeks to take cognitive, social, and emotional factors into account) even if it is shunned by the humanities and other social science disciplines.

25. In addition, ideas such as autopoiesis in systems theory may not be widely accepted in the natural science because of the absence of a formal model to render it explanatory and predictive. The result of this is that 'in most substantive areas there is what to outsiders seems like an amazing lack of reciprocal knowledge' (Abbott, 2001: 142).

26. Plato (360BC) in 'Allegory of the Cave'.

27. Sen (2009: 18) in *The Idea of Justice*.

■ REFERENCES

Abbey, R. (ed.) (2004). *Charles Taylor*. Cambridge: Cambridge University Press.

Abbott, A. (2001). *Chaos of Disciplines*. Chicago, IL: University of Chicago Press.

Aboujaoude, E. (2011). *Virtually You: The Dangerous Powers of the E-Personality*. New York: W. W. Norton & Company.

Abramovitz, M. (1956). 'Resource and Output Trends in the United States Since 1870'. *American Economic Review, 46*(2): 5–23.

—— (1986). 'Catching Up, Forging Ahead and Falling Behind'. *Journal of Economic History, XLVI*(2): 385–406.

Ackerman, B. (1980). *Social Justice in the Liberal State*. New Haven, CT: Yale University Press.

ACTA. (2010). *Anti-Counterfeiting Trade Agreement*, 19 December, http://trade.ec.europa.eu/doclib/docs/2011/may/tradoc_147937.pdf accessed 28/07/2011.

Adam, L. (2005). 'Financing ICTs for Development with Focus on Poverty'. Document prepared for Instituto del Tercer Mundo (ITeM), WSIS Papers. Choike.org, July.

Adorno, T. and Horkheimer, M. (1944/1972). 'The Culture Industry: Enlightenment as Mass Deception', in M. Horkheimer and T. Adorno (eds), *Dialectic of Enlightenment*. New York: Seabury Press, pp. 120–67.

Aghion, P., David, P. A. and Foray, D. (2009). 'Science, Technology and Innovation for Economic Growth: Linking Policy Research and Practice in "STIG Systems"'. *Research Policy, 38*(4): 681–93.

Agre, P. E. (1998). 'Yesterday's Tomorrow'. *Times Literary Supplement*, 3 July, pp. 3–4.

—— Rotenberg, M. (eds) (1997). *Technology and Privacy: The New Landscape*. Cambridge, MA: The MIT Press.

Alani, H., Dasmahapatra, S., O'Hara, K. and Shadbolt, N. (2003). 'Identifying Communities of Practice through Ontology Network Analysis'. *IEEE Intelligent Systems*, March/April, pp. 18–25.

Albagli, S. and Maciel, M. L. (eds) (2010). *Information, Power and Politics: Technological and Institutional Mediations*. Lanham, MD: Lexington Books.

Albarran, A. B. (2002). *Media Economics: Understanding Markets, Industries and Concepts* (2nd edn). Ames, IO: Iowa State University Press.

Allen, P. M. and Torrens, P. M. (2005). 'Knowledge and Complexity'. *Futures, 37*(7): 581–4.

Althusser, L. (1971). 'Ideology and Ideological State Apparatuses', *Lenin and Philosophy and Other Essays*. London: New Left Books, pp. 79–87.

Amin, A. (ed.) (1994). *Post-Fordism: A Reader*. Oxford: Blackwell.

Andersen, N. (2011). 'Major ISPs Agree to "Six Strikes" Copyright Enforcement Plan'. *Arstechnica*, 5 July, http://arstechnicacom/tech-policy/news/2011/07/major-isps-agree-to-six-strikes-copyright-enforcement-planars accessed 28/07/2011.

Anderson, B. (1983). *Imagined Communities*. London: Verso.

Anderson, C. (2006). *The Long Tail: Why the Future of Business is Selling Less of More*. New York: Hyperion.

Anderson, C. (2009). *The Longer Tail: How Endless Choice is Creating Unlimited Demand*. New York: Random House Business.

—— (2010). 'The Web is Dead: Long Live the Internet—Who's to Blame: Us'. *Wired* September, pp. 1–17.

Andersson, K. P. and Ostrom, E. (2008). 'Analyzing Decentralized Resource Regimes from a Polycentric Perspective'. *Policy Sciences*, *41*(1): 71–93.

Anheier, H., Glasius, M. and Kaldor, M. (eds) (2001). *Global Civil Society 2001*. Oxford: Oxford University Press.

Annan, K. (1997). *Secretary General Stresses International Community's Objective of Harnessing Informatics Revolution for Benefit of Mankind*. Geneva. Commission on Science and Technology for Development 'Inter-Agency Project on Universal Access to Basic Communication and Information Services' 3rd Session, E/CN.16/1997/Misc.3.

Antonelli, C. (2003). 'The Digital Divide: Understanding the Economics of New Information and Communication Technology in the Global Economy'. *Information Economics and Policy*, *15*(2): 173–99.

—— (ed.) (2011). *Handbook on the Economic Complexity of Technological Change*. Cheltenham: Edward Elgar.

Argyris, C. and Schon, D. A. (1996). *Organisational Learning II: Theory, Method and Practice*. Reading, MA: Addison-Wesley.

Arnett, R. C. (1986). *Communication and Community: Implications of Martin Buber's Dialogue*. Carbondale, IL: Southern Illinois University Press.

Arrow, K. J. (1962). 'The Economic Implications of Learning by Doing'. *The Review of Economic Studies*, *29*(3): 155–73.

—— (1984). *The Economics of Information*. Oxford: Blackwell.

Arthur, C. (2011). 'Vodafone's Egypt Texts May Do Them Lasting Damage'. *The Guardian*, 3 February, http://www.guardian.co.uk/commentisfree/2011/feb/03/vodafone-egypt-text-messages accessed 28/07/2011.

—— Halliday, J. (2011). 'No Room at the Internet: Web Space Runs Out'. *The Guardian*, 2 February, p. 8.

Arthur, W. B. (1990). 'Positive Feedbacks in the Economy'. *Scientific American*, *262*: 92–9.

—— (2005). 'Complexity and the Economy: An Interview with W. Brian Arthur, interviewed by Robert Delorme and Geoffrey M. Hodgson of EAPE on 8 November in Aiz-en-Provence', in J. Finch and M. Orillard (eds), *Complexity and the Economy: Implications for Economic Policy*. Cheltenham: Edward Elgar, pp. 17–32.

—— (2009). *The Nature of Technology: What it Is and How it Evolves*. New York: Allen Lane.

Ashby, W. R. (1956). *An Introduction to Cybernetics*. London: Chapman and Hall.

Ashton, K. (2009). 'That "Internet of Things" Thing'. *RFID Journal*, 22 June, http://wwwrfidjournalcom/article/view/4986 accessed 28/07/2011.

Athanasopoulos, E., Makridakis, A., Antonatos, S., Antoniades, D., Ioannidis, S., Anagnostakis, K. and Markatos, E. (2008). 'Antisocial Networks: Turning a Social Network into a Botnet'. *Information Security*, *5222*: 146–60.

Atkinson, M. M. and Coleman, W. D. (1992). 'Policy Networks, Policy Communities and the Problems of Governance'. *Governance: An International Journal of Policy and Administration*, *5*(2): 154–80.

Avgerou, C. (2002a). *Information Systems and Global Diversity*. Oxford: Oxford University Press.

Avgerou, C. (2002b). 'The Socio Technical Nature of Information Systems Innovation', in C. Avgerou (ed.), *Information Systems and Global Diversity*. Oxford: Oxford University Press, pp. 50–71.

Bacon, F. (1597/1924). *Essayes. Religious Meditations, Pleaces of Perswasion & Disswasion (Of Heresies)*. London: The Haslewood Books.

Bailey, W. and Burgoon, M. (1992). 'PC at Last! PC at Last! Thank God Almighty, We Are PC at Last!'. *Journal of Communication*, 42(2): 95–104.

Bainbridge, D. I. (1994). *Intellectual Property* (2nd edn). London: Pitman Publishing.

Bakardjieva, M. (2010). 'The Internet in Everyday Life: Exploring the Tenets and Contributions of Diverse Approaches', in R. Burnett, M. Consalvo and C. Ess (eds), *The Handbook of Internet Studies*. New York: Wiley-Blackwell, np—e-book edition.

Banks, L. and Wu, S. (eds) (2010). *Toward a Behavioral Approach to Privacy for Online Social Networks*. Berlin: Springer.

Bannerman, S. (2009). 'Canada and the Berne Convention: 1886–1971'. Unpublished PhD Dissertation, Carleton University, Montreal.

—— (2010). 'Copyright: Characteristics of Canadian Reform', in M. Geist (ed.), *From 'Radical Extremism' to 'Balanced Copyright': Canadian Copyright and the Digital Agenda*. Ottawa: Irwin Law, pp. 17–44.

Barlow, J. P. (1996). *A Declaration of the Independence of Cyberspace*. Davos: Speech at Davos, Electronic Frontier Foundation at https://projects.eff.org/~barlow/Declaration-Final.html accessed 28/07/2011.

Barnett, C. (2003). *Culture and Democracy: Media, Space and Representation*. Edinburgh: Edinburgh University Press.

Baron, N. S. (2008). *Always On: Language in an Online and Mobile World*. Oxford: Oxford University Press.

Barry, A. and Slater, D. (2005). 'Introduction', in A. Barry and D. Slater (eds), *The Technological Economy*. London: Routledge, pp. 1–27.

Bateson, G. (1951a). 'Conventions of Communication: Where Validity Depends Upon Belief', in J. Ruesch and G. Bateson (eds), *Communication: The Social Matrix of Psychiatry*. New York: W. W. Norton & Co., pp. 213–27.

—— (1951b). 'Information and Codification: A Philosophical Approach', in J. Ruesch and G. Bateson (eds), *Communication: The Social Matrix of Psychiatry*. New York: W. W. Norton & Co., pp. 168–211.

—— (1970/1972). 'Form, Substance and Difference', *Proceedings of 19th Annual Korzybski Memorial Lecture for Institute of General Semantics in Steps to an Ecology of Mind: Collected Essays in Anthropology, Psychiatry, Evolution and Epistemology*. New York: Ballantine Books, pp. 448–66.

—— (1972). *Steps to an Ecology of the Mind: Collected Essays in Anthropology, Psychiatry, Evolution and Epistemology*. New York: Ballantine Books.

—— (1979). *Mind and Nature: A Necessary Unity*. New York: Bantam Books.

—— Bateson, M. C. (1987). *Angels Fear: Towards an Epistemology of the Sacred*. New York: Macmillan.

Bateson, M. C. (2005). 'The Double Bind: Pathology and Creativity'. *Cybernetics & Human Knowing*, 12(1–2): 11–21.

Bath, C. (2009). 'Gendered Orders of Knowledge in the Semantic Web'. Paper presented at the 4S (Society for Social Studies of Science) Annual Meeting, Crystal City, VA, 28 October.

Bauer, J. M. (2005). 'Bundling, Differentiation, Alliances and Mergers: Convergence Strategies in U.S. Communication Markets'. *Communications & Strategies, 60*(4): 59–83.

—— (2007). 'Dynamic Effects of Network Neutrality'. *International Journal of Communication, 1*: 531–47.

Baym, N. K. (2010a). *Personal Connection in the Digital Age: Digital Media and Society Series.* Cambridge: Polity Press.

—— (2010b). 'Social Networks 2.0', in R. Burnett, M. Consalvo and C. Ess (eds), *The Handbook of Internet Studies.* New York: Wiley-Blackwell, np—e-book edition.

BBC News. (2010). 'Warning Over Anti-Virus Cold-Calls to UK Internet Users'. *BBC OnLine,* 15 November, http://www.bbc.co.uk/news/uk-11754487 accessed 28/07/2011.

Bear, G. (1985). *Blood Music.* New York: Ace Books.

Beckett, C. and Mansell, R. (2008). 'Crossing Boundaries: New Media and Networked Journalism'. *Communication, Culture & Critique, 1*(1): 90–102.

Beebe, B. (2008). 'An Empirical Study of US Copyright Fair Use Opinions, 1978–2005'. *University of Pennsylvania Law Review, 156*(3): 549–625.

Beer, S. (1959/1964). *Cybernetics and Management.* New York: John Wiley & Sons.

—— (1966). *Decision and Control: The Meaning of Operational Research and Management Cybernetics.* London: John Wiley & Sons.

—— (1994). *Brain of the Firm* (2nd edn). New York: John Wiley & Sons.

Beinhocker, E. D. (2007). *The Origin of Wealth: Evolution, Complexity and the Radical Remaking of Economics.* New York: Random House Business Books.

Bell, D. (1962). *The End of Ideology: On the Exhaustion of Political Ideas in the Fifties* (Revised edn). New York: Free Press.

—— (1973). *The Coming of Post-Industrial Society: A Venture in Social Forecasting.* New York: Basic Books.

Bellamy, E. (1887/1960). *Looking Backward: 2000–1887.* New York: Ticknor and Company/ Signet.

Bendrath, R. and Mueller, M. L. (2010). 'The End of the Net as We Know It? Deep Packet Inspection and Internet Governance', 4 August, http://papers.ssrn.com/sol3/papers.cfm? abstract_id=1653259 accessed 28/07/2011.

Benevenuto, F., Rodrigues, T., Cha, M. and Almeida, V. (2009). 'Characterizing User Behavior in Online Social Networks', in *Proceedings of the 9th ACM SIGCOMM Conference on Internet Measurement.* New York: ACM, pp. 49–62.

Beniger, J. R. (1986). *The Control Revolution: Technological and Economic Origins of the Information Society.* Cambridge, MA: Harvard University Press.

Benkler, Y. (2000). 'From Consumers to Users: Shifting the Deeper Structures of Regulation Towards Sustainable Commons and User Access'. *Federal Communications Law Journal, 52*: 561–79.

—— (2004). 'Sharing Nicely: On Shareable Goods and the Emergence of Sharing as a Modality of Economic Production'. *Yale Law Journal, 114*(2): 273–58.

—— (2006). *The Wealth of Networks: How Social Production Transforms Markets and Freedom.* New Haven, CT: Yale University Press.

—— Nissenbaum, H. (2006). 'Commons-based Peer Production and Virtue'. *Journal of Political Philosophy, 14*(4): 394–419.

Bennett, W. L. (2003). 'New Media Power: The Internet and Global Activism', in N. Couldry and J. Curran (eds), *Contesting Media Power*. Lanham, MD: Rowman & Littlefield, pp. 17–37.

Bennett, C. J. and Raab, C. D. (2003). *The Governance of Privacy: Policy Instruments in Global Perspective*. Aldershot: Ashgate.

Bentham, J. (1787/1995). *Panopticon; or the Inspection-House*. London: Verso.

Berdou, E. (2007). 'A Critical, Inward and Outward View of Digital Ecosystems' Open, Collaborative Communities: Interdisciplinarity, Sustainability and Scalability at the Intersection of Gift and Exchange Economies', in F. Nachira, A. Nicolai, P. Dini, M. Le Louarn and L. Rivera Leon (eds), *Digital Business Ecosystems*. Brussels: European Commission, Directorate General Information Society and Media, pp. 92–7.

—— (2011). *Organization in Open Source Communities: At the Crossroads of the Gift and Market Economies*. New York: Routledge.

Berger, P. L. and Luckmann, T. (1966). *The Social Construction of Reality: A Treatise in the Sociology of Knowledge*. New York: Doubleday & Company.

Berger, J., with Blomberg, S., Fox, C., Bibb, M. and Hollis, R. (1972). *Ways of Seeing*. London: British Broadcasting Corporation and Penguin Books.

Bergquist, M. and Ljungberg, J. (2001). 'The Power of Gifts: Organizing Social Relationships in Open Source Communities'. *Information Systems Journal, 11*: 305–20.

Berners-Lee, T. (2010). 'Long Live the Web: A Call for Continued Open Standards and Neutrality'. *Scientific American*, 22 November, pp. 1–5.

—— Fischetti, M. (1999). *Weaving the Web: The Original Design and Ultimate Destiny of the World Wide Web*. London: Orion.

—— Hendler, J. and Lassila, O. (2001). 'The Semantic Web'. *Scientific American*, 17 May, http://www.scientificamerican.com/article.cfm?id=the-semantic-web accessed 28/07/2011.

Bettig, R. V. (1989). 'Critical Perspectives on the History and Philosophy of Copyright'. Paper presented at the 72nd Annual Meeting of the Association for Education in Journalism and Mass Communication, Washington, DC, 10–13 August.

—— Schiller, H. I. (eds) (1997). *Copyrighting Culture: The Political Economy of Intellectual Property*. Boulder, CO: Westview Press.

Bijker, W. E. and Law, J. (1992). *Shaping Technology/Building Society: Studies in Sociotechnological Change*. Cambridge, MA: MIT Press.

—— Hughes, T. and Pinch, T. (eds) (1987). *The Social Construction of Technological Systems: New Directions in the Sociology and History of Technology*. Cambridge, MA: MIT Press.

Billig, M., Condor, S., Edwards, D., Gane, M., Middleton, D. and Radley, A. (1990). *Ideological Dilemmas: A Social Psychology of Everyday Thinking*. London: Sage.

Bing, J. (2005). 'The Future of Digital Rights', in M. Klang and A. Murray (eds), *Human Rights in the Digital Age*. London: Glasshouse Press, pp. 203–18.

Bisogni, F., Calallini, S. and Di Trocchio, S. (2011). 'Cybersecurity at European Level: The Role of Information Availability'. *Communications & Strategies, 81*(1): 105–24.

Bloomfield, B. P., Coombs, R., Knights, D. and Littler, D. (eds) (1997). *Information Technology and Organizations: Strategies, Networks and Integration*. Oxford: Oxford University Press.

Boden, M. A. (ed.) (1996). *Artificial Intelligence: Handbook of Perception and Cognition* (2nd edn). San Diego, CA: Academic Press, Inc.

Bolter, J. D. and Grusin, R. (1999). *Remediation: Understanding New Media*. Cambridge, MA: MIT Press.

Borgman, C. L. (2007). *Scholarship in the Digital Age: Information, Infrastructure and the Internet*. Cambridge, MA: MIT Press.

Botto, F. (2010). 'Challenges and Results of the Trentino DCE Living Laboratory'. Deliverable 11.13, WP 11 Bridging Digital Ecosystems Research to Regional Development and Innovation in the Knowledge Economy, OPAALS Contract No. IST-034824, European Commission, August.

Bowker, G. C. (1996). 'How Things Change: The History of Sociotechnical Structures', Review Article. *Social Studies of Science, 26*(1): 173–82.

—— Star, S. L. (1999). *Sorting Things Out: Classification and its Consequences*. Cambridge, MA: MIT Press.

Bowles, S. (1998). 'Endogenous Preferences: The Cultural Consequences of Markets and Other Economic Institutions'. *Journal of Economic Literature, 36*(1): 75–111.

Boyd, D. M. and Ellison, N. B. (2008). 'Social Network Sites: Definition, History, and Scholarship'. *Journal of Computer-Mediated Communication, 13*(1): 210–30.

Boyd-Barrett, O. (1998). 'Media Imperialism Reformulated', in D. Thussu (ed.), *Electronic Empires: Global Media and Local Resistance*. London: Arnold, pp. 157–76.

Boyle, J. (1996). *Shamans, Software & Spleens: Law and the Construction of the Information Society*. Cambridge, MA: Harvard University Press.

—— (2008). *The Public Domain: Enclosing the Commons of the Mind*. New Haven, CT: Yale University Press.

Brake, D. (2009). 'As If Nobody's Reading: The Imagined Audience and Socio-technical Biases in Personal Blogging Practice in the UK'. Unpublished PhD Thesis, Department of Media and Communications. London School of Economics and Political Science.

Braman, S. (1994). 'The Autopoietic State: Communication and Democratic Potential in the Net'. *Journal of the American Society for Information Science, 45*(6): 358–68.

—— (1995). 'Alternative Conceptualizations of the Information Economy'. *Advances in Librarianship, 19*: 99–116.

—— (2006). 'Tactical Memory: The Politics of Openness in the Construction of Memory'. *First Monday, 11*(7): 1–21.

—— (2006). *Change of State: Information, Policy and Power*. Cambridge, MA: MIT Press.

—— (2011). 'The Framing Years: Policy Fundamentals in the Internet Design Process, 1969–1979'. *The Information Society, 27*(5): 295–310.

—— Roberts, S. (2003). 'Advantage ISP: Terms of Service as Media Law'. *New Media & Society, 5*(3): 422–48.

Brand, S. (1987). *The Media Lab: Inventing the Future at MIT*. New York: Viking Penguin.

Braudel, F. (1979/1992). *Civilization and Capitalism: 15th–18th Century: The Perspective of the World* (trans. S. Reynolds). Berkeley, CA: University of California Press.

Brauer, M., Dini, P., Dory, B., English, A., Iqani, M. and Zeller, F. (2007). 'Principles, Models and Processes for the Development of the Open Knowledge Space'. Deliverable 10.5, WP 10 on Sustainable Community Building, OPAALS Contract No. IST-034824, European Commission, July.

—— Steinicke, I. and Zeller, F. (2010). 'Report on Recommendations for Improving the Usability of the OKS'. Deliverable 10.21, WP 10 on Sustainable Community Building, OPAALS Contract No. IST-034824, European Commission, March.

Brautigan, R. (1968). 'All Watched Over by Machines of Loving Grace', *The Pill versus The Springhill Mine Disaster*. Boston, MA: Houghton Mifflin, p. 117.

—— (1970). 'The Library', in *The Abortion: An Historical Romance 1966*. New York: Simon and Schuster, pp. 11–17.

Breen, M. (2011). *Uprising: The Internet's Unintended Consequences*. Champaign, IL: Common Ground Publishing.

Breindl, Y. and Houghton, T. J. (2010). 'Techno-Political Activism as Counterpublic Spheres: Discursive Networking within Deliberative Transnational Politics?' Paper presented at the *ICA Conference*, Singapore, 22 June, http://canterbury-nz.academia.edu/TessaHoughton/Talks/24893/Techno-political_Activism_as_Counterpublic_Spheres_Discursive_Networking_Within_Deliberative_Transnational_Politics accessed 28/07/2011.

Bresnahan, T. F. and Trajtenberg, M. (1995). 'General Purpose Technologies "Engines of Growth?"'. *Journal of Econometrics*, 65(1): 83–108.

Bressand, A., Distler, C. and Nicolaidis, K. (1989). 'Networks at the Heart of the Service Economy', in A. Bressand and K. Nicolaidis (eds), *Strategic Trends in Services: An Inquiry into the Global Service Economy*. Grand Rapids, MI: Ballinger Publishers, pp. 17–32.

Briscoe, G., Dini, P., Nehaniv, C., Oros, N., Yinusa, A. and Buck, M. (2010). 'Integration of Gene Expression Computing and Operational Closure in the Software Ecosystem Architecture'. Deliverable 1.5, WP 1 on Cell Biology, Autopoiesis and Biological Design Patterns, OPAALS Contract No. IST-034824, European Commission. October.

British Broadcasting Corporation (2009). 'Electronic Tagging of Young People Shows Sharp Rise'. *BBC News*, 15 December, http://news.bbc.co.uk/1/hi/uk_politics/8413148.stm accessed 28/07/2011.

Brock, G. W. (1994). *Telecommunications Policy for the Information Age: From Monopoly to Competition*. Boston, MA: Harvard University Press.

Brooks, F. (1982). *The Mythical Man-Month*. London: Addison-Wesley Publishing Co.

Brown, C. (2001). 'Cosmopolitanism, World Citizenship and Global Civil Society'. *Critical Review of International Social and Political Philosophy*, 3(1): 7–27.

Brown, J. S. and Duguid, P. (1998). 'Organizing Knowledge'. *California Management Review*, 40(3): 90–112.

—— —— (2000). *The Social Life of Information*. Boston, MA: Harvard Business School Press.

Bruns, A. (2010). 'Distributed Creativity: Filesharing and Produsage', in S. Sonvilla-Weiss (ed.), *Mashup Cultures*. Vienna: Springer-Verlag, pp. 24–37.

Brusoni, S. and Prencipe, A. (2001). 'Unpacking the Black Box of Modularity: Technologies, Products and Organizations'. *Industrial and Corporate Change*, 10(1): 179–205.

Buckley, W. (1967). *Sociology and Modern Systems Theory*. Englewood Cliffs, CA: Prentice-Hall.

—— (1968). 'Society as a Complex Adaptive System', in W. Buckley (ed.), *Modern Systems Research for the Behavioural Scientist*. Chicago, IL: Aldine.

Bueso, P. (2010). 'Governance and Regulatory Strategies for DEs: OKS AISBL'. Deliverable 12.12, WP 12 on Open Source Software Innovation and Socio-economic Models for Digital Ecosystems, OPAALS Contract No. IST-034824, European Commission, October.

—— Oliver, D., Martin, T., Gomez, L. and Vollmer, D. (2010). 'Governance and Sustainability Strategies for DEs'. Deliverable 12.12, WP 12 on Open Source Software Innovation and Socio-economic Models for Digital Ecosystems, OPAALS Contract No. IST-034824, European Commission, July.

Bumgarner, B. A. (2007). 'You Have Been Poked: Exploring the Uses and Gratifications of Facebook Among Emerging Adults'. *First Monday, 12*(11): np.

Burkart, P. (2010). *Music and Cyberliberties*. Middletown, CT: Wesleyan University Press.

Burke, M., Marlow, C. and Lento, T. (2009). 'Feed Me: Motivating Newcomer Contribution in Social Network Sites', in *Proceedings of the 27th International Conference on Human Factors in Computing Systems*. New York: ACM, pp. 945–54.

Burnett, R. (2010). 'Internet and Music', in R. Burnett, M. Consalvo and C. Ess (eds), *The Handbook of Internet Studies*. New York: Wiley-Blackwell, p. np—e-book version.

Bush, V. (1945). 'As We May Think'. *The Atlantic Monthly, 176*(1): 101–8.

Bygrave, L. A. and Bing, J. (eds) (2009). *Internet Governance: Infrastructures and Institutions*. Oxford: Oxford University Press.

Byrne, D. (1998). *Complexity Theory and the Social Sciences*. London: Routledge.

Calabrese, A. and Sparks, C. (eds) (2004). *Toward a Political Economy of Culture, Capitalism and Communication in the 21st Century*. Lanham, MD: Rowman & Littlefield.

Calhoun, C. (1992). 'Introduction: Habermas and the Public Sphere', in C. Calhoun (ed.), *Habermas and the Public Sphere*. Cambridge, MA: MIT Press, pp. 1–48.

—— (2002). 'Imagining Solidarity: Cosmopolitanism, Constitutional Patriotism and the Public Sphere'. *Public Culture, 14*(1): 147–71.

Callon, M. (2001). 'Four Models for the Dynamics of Science', in S. Jasanoff, G. E. Markle, J. C. Peterson and T. Pinch (eds), *Handbook of Science and Technology Studies*. London: Sage, pp. 29–63.

Cammaerts, B. (2005). 'Through the Looking Glass: Civil Society Participation in the WSIS and the Dynamics between Online/Offline Interaction'. *Communications & Strategies, 60*(4): 151–74.

—— (2008a). 'Critiques on the Participatory Potentials of Web 2.0'. *Communication, Culture & Critique, 1*(3): 358–76.

—— (2008b). *Internet-Mediated Participation Beyond the Nation State*. Manchester: Manchester University Press.

—— (2011). 'Disruptive Sharing in a Digital Age: Rejecting Neoliberalism?'. *Continuum: Journal of Media & Cultural Studies, 25*(1): 47–62.

—— Meng, B. (2011). *Creative Destruction and Copyright Protection: Regulatory Responses to File-sharing*. Media Policy Brief 1. London: London School of Economics and Political Science, http://blogs.lse.ac.uk/mediapolicyproject/2011/03/21/media-policy-project-policy-brief-1-creative-destruction-and-copyright-protection/ accessed 28/07/2011.

—— Van Audenhove, L. (2005). 'Online Political Debate: Unbounded Citizenship and the Problematic Nature of a Transnational Public Sphere'. *Political Communication, 22*(2): 147–62.

Capra, F. (2002). *The Hidden Connections: A Science for Sustainable Living*. London: Harper Collins.

Carey, J. W. (1989/1992). 'A Cultural Approach to Communication', *Communication as Culture: Essays in Media and Society*. London: Routledge, pp. 13–36.

Carpentier, N. (2011a). *Media and Participation: A Site of Ideological-Democratic Struggle*. Bristol: Intellect.

—— (2011b). 'Policy's Hubris: Power, Fantasy, and the Limits of (Global) Media Policy Interventions', in R. Mansell and M. Raboy (eds), *Handbook of Global Media and Communication Policy*. Malden, MA: Wiley-Blackwell, pp. 113–28.

Carr, N. (2010). *The Shallows: What the Internet is Doing to Our Brains*. New York: W. W. Norton & Company.

Castells, M. (1996). *The Information Age: Economy, Society and Culture Volume I: The Rise of the Network Society*. Oxford: Blackwell.

—— (1997). *The Information Age: Economy, Society and Culture Volume II: The Power of Identity*. Oxford: Blackwell.

—— (1998). *The Information Age: Economy, Society and Culture Volume III: End of Millennium*. Oxford: Blackwell.

—— (2000). 'Materials for an Exploratory Theory of the Network Society'. *British Journal of Sociology, 51*(1): 5–24.

—— (2001). *The Internet Galaxy: Reflections on the Internet, Business and Society*. Oxford: Oxford University Press.

—— (2009). *Communication Power*. Oxford: Oxford University Press.

Castoriadis, C. (1987). *The Imaginary Institution of Society: Creativity and Autonomy in the Social Historical World* (trans. K. Blamey). Cambridge, MA: MIT Press.

Chadwick, A. (2006). *Internet Politics: States, Citizens, and New Communication Technologies*. Oxford: Oxford University Press.

Chandler, J. A. (2007). 'Reclaiming the First Amendment: Constitutional Theories of Media Reform: A Right to Reach and Audience, An Approach to Intermediary Bias on the Internet'. *Hofstra Law Review, 35*(3): 1095–138.

Charlton, N. G. (2008). *Understanding Gregory Bateson: Mind, Beauty, and the Sacred Earth*. New York: State University of New York Press.

Checkland, P. (1981). *Systems Thinking Systems Practice*. Chichester: Wiley.

Chen, H., Ding, L., Wu, Z., Yu, T., Dhanapalan, L. and Chen, J. Y. (2009). 'Semantic Web for Integrated Network Analysis in Biomedicine'. *Briefings in Bioinformatics, 10*(2): 177–92.

Chenail, R. J. and Morris, G. H. (1995). *The Talk of the Clinic: Explorations in the Analysis of Medical and Therapeutic Discourse*. Hillsdale, NJ: Lawrence Erlbaum Associates.

Chouliaraki, L. (2006). 'Towards an Analytics of Mediation'. *Critical Discourse Studies, 3*(2): 153–78.

Chroust, A.-H. (1946). 'The Origin and Meaning of the Social Compact Doctrine'. *Ethics, 57*(1): 38–56.

Ciastellardi, M., de Almeida, C. M. and de Kerckhove, D. (2011). 'From Ontologies to Folksonomies: A Design-driven Approach from Complex Information to Bottom-Up Knowledge'. Unpublished paper, IN3, Universitat Oberta de Catalunya, Barcelona.

Ciborra, C. (2004). 'Digital Technologies and the Duality of Risk'. London: ESRC Centre for Analysis of Risk and Regulation, Discussion Paper No. 27. London School of Economics and Political Science, October.

Clark, J. M. (1961). *Competition as a Dynamic Process*. New York: The Brookings Institution.

Cohen, S. (1980). *Folk Devils and Moral Panics*. New York: St. Martin's Press.

—— (2001). *States of Denial: Knowing about Atrocities and Suffering*. Cambridge: Polity Press.

Cohen, N. S. (2008). 'The Valorization of Surveillance: Towards a Political Economy of Facebook'. *Democratic Communique, 22*(1): 5–22.

Cohen, R. and Rai, S. (eds) (2000). *Global Social Movements*. London: Athlone.

Coleman, S. (2005). 'New Mediation and Direct Representation: Reconceptualizing Representation in the Digital Age'. *New Media & Society*, 7(2): 177–98.

Collins, R. (2009). *Three Myths of Internet Governance: Making Sense of Networks, Governance and Regulation.* Bristol: Intellect.

Comor, E. (1994). 'Introduction: The Global Political Economy of Communication and IPE', in E. Comor (ed.), *The Global Political Economy of Communication.* London: St. Martin's Press, pp. 1–18.

Conville, R. L. and Rogers, L. E. (1998). *The Meaning of 'Relationship' in Interpersonal Communication.* Westport, CT: Praeger Publishers.

Cordell, A. J., Ide, T. R., Soete, L. and Kamp, K. (1997). *The New Wealth of Nations: Taxing Cyberspace.* Toronto: Between the Lines.

Coriat, B., Petit, P. and Schméder, G. (eds) (2006). *The Hardship of Nations: Exploring the Paths of Modern Capitalism.* Cheltenham: Edward Elgar.

Coté, M. and Pybus, J. (2007). 'Learning to Immaterial Labour 2.0: MySpace and Social Networks'. *Ephemera: Theory & Politics in Organization*, 7(1): 88–106.

Couldry, N. (2003). 'Digital Divide or Discursive Design? On the Emerging Ethics of Information Space'. *Ethics and Information Technology*, 5(2): 89–97.

—— (2010). *Why Voice Matters: Culture and Politics after Neoliberalism.* London: Sage.

—— Livingstone, S. and Markham, T. (2007). *Media Consumption and Public Engagement: Beyond the Presumption of Attention.* Basingstoke: Palgrave Macmillan.

Council of Europe (2009). *Internet Governance and Critical Internet Resources.* Strasbourg: Media and Information Society Division, Directorate General of Human Rights and Legal Affairs, Council of Europe. http://www.coe.int/t/informationsociety/documents/internetcriticalresources_en.pdf accessed 28/07/2011.

—— (2010). *Declaration of the Committee of Ministers on Network Neutrality.* Strasbourg: Council of Europe.

Couts, A. (2011, 31 March). 'Microsoft Files Antitrust Lawsuit Against Google in EU'. *Digital Trends.* http://www.digitaltrends.com/computing/microsoft-files-antitrust-lawsuit-against-google-in-eu/ accessed 28/07/2011.

Cowan, R. and Foray, D. (1997). 'The Economics of Codification and the Diffusion of Knowledge'. *Industrial and Corporate Change*, 6(3): 595–622.

Cox, J., Collins, A. and Drinkwater, S. (2010). 'Seeders, Leechers and Social Norms: Evidence from the Market for Illicit Digital Downloading'. *Journal of Economics and Policy*, 22(4): 299–305.

Cusumano, M. A. (2010). *Staying Power: Six Enduring Principles for Managing Strategy and Innovation in an Uncertain World.* Oxford: Oxford University Press.

—— Yoffie, D. B. (1998). *Competing on Internet Time: Lessons from Netscape and its Battle with Microsoft.* New York: The Free Press.

Dakroury, A. (2009). *Communication and Human Rights.* Dubuque, IA: Kendall Hunt Publishing.

Dalle, J.-M., David, P. A., Ghosh, R. A. and Steinmueller, W. E. (2005). 'Advancing Economic Research on the Free and Open Source Software Mode of Production', in M. Wynants and J. Cornelis (eds), *How Open is the Future? Economic, Social & Cultural Scenarios inspired by Free & Open-Source Software.* Brussels: Vrjie Universiteit Brussels Press, pp. 395–426.

Damasio, A. (2003). *Looking for Spinoza: Joy, Sorrow, and the Feeling Brain.* Orlando, FL: Harcourt, Inc.

Damasio, A. and Meyer, K. (2008). 'Behind the Looking Glass'. *Nature, 454*(10): 167–8.

Danet, B. and Herring, S. C. (eds) (2003). 'The Multilingual Internet: Language, Culture and Communication in Instant Messaging, E-mail and Chat'. Special Issue, *Journal of Computer Mediated Communication, 9*(1): np.

—— —— (2007). *The Multilingual Internet: Language, Culture and Communication Online.* Oxford: Oxford University Press.

Darking, M. (2004). 'Integrating On-line Learning Technologies into Higher Education: A Case Study of Two UK Universities'. Unpublished PhD Thesis, Information Systems Group, London School of Economics and Political Science.

—— (2007). 'Understanding the Role of Governance in the Context of Digital Ecosystems', in F. Nachira, A. Nicolai, P. Dini, M. Le Louarn and L. Rivera Leon (eds), *Digital Business Ecosystems.* Brussels: European Commission Directorate General Information Society and Media, pp. 79–82.

Dasgupta, P. (1988). 'Trust as a Commodity', in D. Gambetta (ed.), *Trust: Making and Breaking Cooperative Relations.* Oxford: Blackwell, pp. 49–72.

Daugherty, T., Eastin, M. S. and Bright, L. (2008). 'Exploring Consumer Motivations for Creating User-Generated Content'. *Journal of Interactive Advertising, 8*(2): 16–25.

David, P. A. (1975). *Technical Change, Innovation and Economic Growth: Essays on American and British Experience in the 19th Century.* Cambridge: Cambridge University Press.

—— (1990). 'The Dynamo and the Computer: An Historical Perspective on the Modern Productivity Paradox'. *The American Economic Review, 80*(2): 355–61.

—— (1993). 'Intellectual Property Institutions and the Panda's Thumb: Patents, Copyrights, Trade Secrets in Economic Theory and History', in M. B. Wallerstein, M. E. Mogee and R. A. Schoen (eds), *Global Dimensions of Intellectual Property Rights in Science and Technology.* Washington, DC: National Academy Press, pp. 19–61.

—— (2001). 'The Evolving Accidental Information Super-Highway'. *Oxford Review of Economic Policy, 17*(2): 159–87.

—— (2004). 'The End of Copyright History?'. *Review of Economic Research on Copyright Issues, 1*(2): 5–10.

David, M. (2010). *Peer to Peer and the Music Industry: The Criminalization of Sharing.* London: Sage Publications.

David, P. A. and Bunn, J. A. (1988). 'The Economics of Gateway Technologies and Network Evolution: Lessons from the Electricity Supply Industry'. *Information Economics and Policy, 3*: 165–202.

—— Foray, D. (2003). 'Economic Fundamentals of the Knowledge Society'. *Policy Futures in Education, 1*(1): 20–49.

Davidow, W. H. (2011). *Overconnected: Where to Draw the Line at Being Online.* London: Headline Press.

—— Malone, M. S. (1992). *The Virtual Corporation: Structuring and Revitalizing the Corporation for the 21st Century.* New York: Harper Collins Publishers.

Davies, A. (1996). 'Innovation in Large Technical Systems: The Case of Telecommunications'. *Industrial and Corporate Change, 5*(4): 1143–80.

Dawkins, R. (1982). *The Extended Phenotype.* Oxford: Oxford University Press.

—— (1989). *The Selfish Gene* (2nd edn). Oxford: Oxford University Press.

de Kerckhove, D. (2010). *The Augmented Mind.* Milan: Digitpub.

De Landa, M. (1991). *War in the Age of Intelligent Machines*. New York: Zone Books.

—— (2000). *1,000 Years of Non-Linear History*. New York: Swerve Editions.

—— (2011). *Philosophy and Simulation: The Emergence of Synthetic Reason*. London: Continuum International Publishing Group.

de Sola Pool, I. (1990). *Technologies Without Boundaries: On Telecommunications in a Global Age* (ed. E. M. Noam). Cambridge, MA: Harvard University Press.

Dean, J. (2003). 'Why the Internet is not a Public Sphere'. *Constellations, 10*(1): 95–112.

Debatin, B., Lovejoy, J. P., Horn, A.-K. and Hughes, B. N. (2009). 'Facebook and Online Privacy: Attitudes, Behaviors, and Unintended Consequences'. *Journal of Computer-Mediated Communication, 15*(1): 83–108.

Dejean, S., Penard, T. and Suire, R. (2010). 'Une Premiere Evaluation des Effets de la Loi Hadopi sur les Pratiques des Internautes Francais'. Marsouin.org, Measure & Analyse des Usages Numeriques, CREM and University of Rennes 1, March.

Deleuze, G. and Guattari, F. (1980/1987). *A Thousand Plateaus: Captialism and Schizophrenia, Vol. 2* (trans. B. Massumi). Minneapolis, MN: University of Minnesota Press.

Delorme, R. (2010). *Deep Complexity and the Social Sciences*. Cheltenham: Edward Elgar.

Denardis, L. (2009). *Protocol Politics: The Globalization of Internet Governance*. Cambridge, MA: MIT Press.

Department of Business Innovation and Skills (BIS) and Department for Culture Media and Sport (DCMS). (2009). *Digital Britain: Final Report*. London: BIS and DCMS, June.

Department for Culture Media and Sport (2006). *Broadcasting: An Agreement Between Her Majesty's Secretary of State for Culture, Media and Sport and the British Broadcasting Corporation*. London: DCMS, July, http://www.bbc.co.uk/bbctrust/assets/files/pdf/about/how_we_govern/agreement.pdf accessed 28/07/2011.

Derks, D., Bos, A. E. R. and von Grumbkow, J. (2008). 'Emoticons in Computer-Mediated Communication: Social Motives and Social Context'. *CyberPsychology & Behavior, 11*(1): 99–101.

Desodt, T. (2007). 'Demonstration Implementation of the OKS Technical Platform'. Deliverable 10.4, WP 10 on Sustainable Community Building, OPAALS Contract No. IST-034824, European Commission, June.

DiMaggio, P., Hargittai, E., Neuman, W. R. and Robinson, J. P. (2001). 'Social Implications of the Internet'. *Annual Review of Sociology, 27*: 307–36.

DiMicco, J. M., Millen, D. R., Geyer, W., Dugan, C., Brownholtz, B. and Muller, M. (2008). 'Motivations for Social Networking at Work', *Proceedings of the 2008 ACM Conference on Computer Supported Cooperative Work*. New York: ACM, 711–20.

Dini, P. (2007). 'A Scientific Foundation for Digital Ecosystems', in F. Nachira, A. Nicolai, P. Dini, M. Le Louarn and L. Rivera Leon (eds), *Digital Business Ecosystems*. Brussels: European Commission Directorate General Information Society and Media, pp. 24–47.

—— Briscoe, G., Munro, A. and Lain, S. (2008). 'Towards a Biological and Mathematical Framework for Interaction Computing'. Deliverable 1.1, WP 1 on Automata Theory and Autopoiesis, OPAALS Contract No. IST-034824, European Commission, March.

—— Briscoe, G., Van Leeuwen, V., Munro, A. and Lain, S. (2009). 'Biological Design Patterns of Autopoietic Behaviour in Digital Ecosystems'. Deliverable 1.3, WP 1 on Cell Biology, Autopoiesis and Biological Design Patterns, OPAALS Contract No. IST-034824, European Commission, September.

Dini, P. Egri-Nagy, A., Nehaniv, C., Schilstra, M., Van Leeuwen, V., Munro, A. and Lain, S. (2010). 'Mathematical Models of Gene Expression Computing'. Deliverable 1.4, WP 1 on Cell biology, Autopoiesis and Biological Design Patterns, OPAALS Contract No. IST-034824, European Commission, October.

—— Iqani, M. and Mansell, R. (2011). 'The (Im)Possiblity of Interdisciplinarity: Lessons from Constructing a Theoretical Framework for Digital Ecosystems'. *Culture, Theory and Critique*, 52(1): 3–27.

Dixon, A. N. (2009). 'Liability of Users and Third Parties for Copyright Infringements on the Internet: Overview of International Developments', in A. Strowel (ed.), *Peer-to-Peer File Sharing and Secondary Liability in Copyright Law*. Cheltenham: Edward Elgar, pp. 12–42.

Donahue, H. C. (2010). 'The Network Neutrality Inquiry'. *Info, 12*(2): 3–8.

Donders, K. and Pauwels, C. (2010). 'The Introduction of an Ex Ante Evaluation for New Media Services: Is Europe Asking for It, or Does Public Service Broadcasting Need It?'. *International Journal of Media and Cultural Politics, 6*(2): 133–48.

Dopfer, K. and Potts, J. (2004). 'Evolutionary Foundations of Economics', in J. S. Metcalfe and J. Foster (eds), *Evolution and Economic Complexity*. Cheltenham: Edward Elgar, pp. 3–23.

Dosi, G. (1982). 'Technological Paradigms and Technological Trajectories: A Suggested Interpretation of the Determinants and Directions of Technical Change'. *Research Policy, 11*: 147–62.

Dotsika, F. (2009). 'Uniting Formal and Informal Descriptive Power: Reconciling Ontologies with Folksonomies'. *International Journal of Information Management, 29*(5): 407–15.

Downing, J. D. H., Ford, T. V., Gill, G. and Stein, L. (2001). *Radical Media: Rebellious Communication and Social Movements*. London: Sage.

Doyle, G. (2002). *Understanding Media Economics*. London: Sage.

Drahos, P. and Braithwaite, J. (2003). *Information Feudalism: Who Owns the Knowledge Economy?* New York: The New Press.

Drake, W. J. and Wilson, Jr., E. (2008). *Governing Global Electronic Networks: International Perspectives on Policy and Power*. Cambridge, MA: MIT Press.

Drucker, P. F. (1959). *The Landmarks of Tomorrow: A Report on the New 'Post-Modern' World*. New York: Transaction Publishers.

—— (1969). 'Knowledge Society'. *New Society, 13*(343): 629–31.

DuBoff, R. B. (1983). 'The Telegraph and the Structure of Markets in the United States, 1845–1890'. *Research in Economic History, 8*: 253–77.

Dubosson-Torbay, M., Pigneur, Y. and Usunier, J.-C. (nd). *Business Models for Music Distribution after the P2P Revolution*. Lausanne: University of Lausanne.

Ducatel, K., Bogdanowicz, M., Scapolo, F., Leijten, J. and Burgelman, J.-C. (2001). *Scenarios for Ambient Intelligence in 2010, Final Report*. Seville: Institute Prospective Technological Studies.

Duman, H., Healing, A. and Ghanea-Hercock, R. (2009,). 'An Intelligent Agent Approach for Visual Information Structure Generation', in *Proceedings of IEEE Symposium on Intelligent Agents 2009*, Nashville, TN, pp. 55–62.

Dutton, W. H. and Peltu, M. (2005). 'The Emerging Internet Governance Mosaic: Connecting the Pieces'. *Forum Discussion Paper No. 5*, Oxford: Oxford Internet Institute.

—— Shepherd, A. (2005). 'Confidence and Risk on the Internet', in R. Mansell and B. S. Collins (eds), *Trust and Crime in Information Societies*. Cheltenham: Edward Elgar, pp. 207–44.

Dutton, W. H., Helsper, E. J. and Gerber, M. M. (2009). *The Internet in Britain 2009*. Oxford: Oxford Internet Institute.

European Broadcasting Union (2010). *Peer-to-Peer (P2P) Technologies and Services*. Geneva: EBU. http://tech.ebu.ch/docs/techreports/tr009.pdf accessed 27/07/2011.

Eco, U. (1994). 'How Not to Use the Mobile Phone', in *How to Travel with a Salmon and Other Essays* (trans. W. Weaver). London: Secker & Warburg, pp. 139–42.

Economides, N. and Katsamakas, E. (2006). 'Two-Sided Competition of Proprietary vs. Open Source Technology Platforms and the Implications for the Software Industry'. *Management Science, 52*(7): 1057–71.

Eder, R., Kurz, T., Heistracher, T. J., Bayon, V., Russo, M. and Filieri, A. (2007). 'Design of Software Generation Prototype'. Deliverable 2.1, WP 2 on Automatic Code Generation from Models, OPAALS Contract No. IST-034824, European Commission, July.

Eicher-Catt, D. and Catt, I. E. (eds) (2010). *Communicology: The New Science of Embodied Discourse*. Madison, WI: Fairleigh Dickinson University Press.

Electronic Frontier Foundation. (2011). 'The Content Industry and ISPs Announce a "Common Framework for Copyright Alerts": What Does It Mean for Users?'. *Electronic Frontier Foundation*, 7 July, http://www.eff.org/deeplinks/2011/07/content-industry-and-isps-announce-common accessed 27/07/2011.

Eliot, T. S. (1936). 'Choruses from the Rock (1934)', in T. S. Eliot (ed.), *Collected Poems 1909–1935*. New York: Harcourt Brace, p. 179.

Elkin-Koren, N. (2006). 'Exploring Creative Commons: A Skeptical View of a Worthy Pursuit', in P. B. Hugenholtz and L. Guibault (eds), *The Future of the Public Domain*. Amsterdam: Kluwer Law International, pp. 325–45.

Ellison, N. B., Steinfield, C. and Lampe, C. (2007). 'The Benefits of Facebook "Friends": Social Capital and College Students' Use of Online Social Network Sites'. *Journal of Computer-Mediated Communication, 12*(4): 1143–68.

Ellul, J. (1990). *The Technological Bluff* (trans. G. W. Bromiley). Grand Rapids, MI: William B. Eerdmans Publishing.

Elser, B. W. (2005). 'Filtering, Blocking and Rating: Chaperones or Censorship?', in M. Klang and A. Murray (eds), *Human Rights in the Digital Age*. London: Glasshouse Press, pp. 99–110.

Engle, E. A. (2002). 'When is Fair Use Fair? A Comparison of EU and US Intellectual Property Law'. *Transnational Lawyer, 15*: 187–225.

Enigmax. (2010). 'ACS: Law (Gay) Porn Letters Target Pensioners, Married Men'. *TorrentFreak*, 25 September, http://torrentfreak.com/acslaw-gay-porn-letters-target-pensioners-married-men-100925/ accessed 28/07/2011.

Ernesto. (2010). 'Canadian Movie Pirate 'maVen' Sent to Jail'. TorrentFreak, 17 March, http://torrentfreak.com/canadian-movie-piracy-maven-sent-to-jail-100317/ accessed 28/07/2011.

Escobar, A. (1995). *Encountering Development: The Making and Unmaking of the Third World*. Princeton, NJ: Princeton University Press.

Etzioni, A. (2002). 'The Good Society'. *Seattle Journal for Social Justice, 1*(1): 93–6.

Europa RAPID Press Releases. (2009, 5 November). 'Agreement on EU Telecoms Reform Paves Way for Strong Consumer Rights, an Open Internet, a Single European Telecoms Market and High-Speed Internet Connections for All Citizens'. *Europa RAPID*. http://europa.eu/rapid/pressReleasesAction.do?reference=MEMO/09/491 accessed 28/07/2011.

European Commission (1994). *Europe and the Global Information Society: Recommendations to the European Council (Bangemann Report)*. Brussels: European Commission. http://www.epractice.eu/files/media/media_694.pdf accessed 28/07/2011.

—— (1995). *Directive 95/46/EC of the European Parliament and of the Council on the Protection of Individuals with Regard to the Processing of Personal Data and on the Free Movement of such Data*. Brussels: European Commission. http://ec.europa.eu/justice/policies/privacy/docs/95-46-ce/dir1995-46_part1_en.pdf accessed 28/07/2011.

—— (2000a). *Charter of Fundamental Rights of the European Union*. Brussels: European Commission, 2000/C 364/01. http://www.europarl.europa.eu/charter/pdf/text_en.pdf accessed 28/07/2011.

—— (2000b). *Directive 2000/31/EC of the European Parliament and of the Council of 8 June 2000 on Certain Legal Aspects of Information Society Services, in Particular Electronic Commerce, in the Internal Market (Directive on Electronic Commerce)*. Brussels: European Commission. http://eur-lex.europa.eu/LexUriServ/LexUriServ.do?uri=CELEX:32000L0031:EN:HTML accessed 28/07/2011.

—— (2001). *Directive 2001/29/EC of the European Parliament and of the Council of 22 May 2001 on the Harmonisation of Certain Aspects of Copyright and Related Rights in the Information Society*. Brussels: European Commission. http://eur-lex.europa.eu/LexUriServ/LexUriServ.do?uri=OJ:L:2001:167:0010:0019:EN:PDF accessed 28/07/2011.

—— (2004). *Directive 2004/48/EC of the European Parliament and of the Council of 29 April 2004 on the Enforcement of Intellectual Property Rights*. Brussels: European Commission. http://eur-lex.europa.eu/LexUriServ/LexUriServ.do?uri=OJ:L:2004:195:0016:0025:en:PDF accessed 28/07/2011.

—— (2006). *Directive 2006/116/EC of the European Parliament and of the Council of 12 December 2006 on the Term of Protection of Copyright and Certain Related Rights*. Brussels: European Commission. http://eur-lex.europa.eu/LexUriServ/LexUriServ.do?uri=OJ:L:2006:372:0012:0018:EN:PDF accessed 28/07/2011.

—— (2007). 'Antitrust: Commission Welcomes CFI Ruling Upholding Commission's Decision on Microsoft's Abuse of Dominant Position', 17 September, http://europa.eu/rapid/pressReleasesAction.do?reference=MEMO/07/359 accessed 28/07/2011.

—— (2008). *Consolidated Version of the Treaty on the Functioning of the European Union (TFEU)*. Brussels: European Commission OJ C115/47. http://eur-lex.europa.eu/LexUriServ/LexUriServ.do?uri=OJ:C:2010:083:0047:0200:en:PDF accessed 28/07/2011.

—— (2009a). *Directive 2009/140/EC of the European Parliament and the Council of 25 November 2009 Amending Directives 2002/21/EC on a Common Regulatory Framework for Electronic Communications Networks and Services, 2002/19/EC on Access to, and Interconnection of, Electronic Communications Networks and Associated Facilities, and 2002/20/EC on the Authorisation of Electronic Communications Networks and Services, OJEU L337/37*. Brussels: European Commission. http://eur-lex.europa.eu/LexUriServ/LexUriServ.do?uri=OJ:L:2009:337:0037:0069:EN:PDF accessed 28/07/2011.

—— (2009b). 'Telecoms: Commission Acts on Termination Rates to Boost Competition', 7 May, http://europa.eu/rapid/pressReleasesAction.do?reference=IP/09/710 accessed 28/07/2011.

—— (2010a). 'Antitrust: Commission Probes Allegations of Antitrust Violations by Google', 30 November, http://europa.eu/rapid/pressReleasesAction.do?reference=IP/10/1624&format=HTML&aged=0&language=EN&guiLanguage=en accessed 28/07/2011.

European Commission (2010b). *A Digital Agenda for Europe: Communication from the Commission to the European Parliament, the Council, the European Economic and Social Committee and the Committee of the Regions.* Brussels: European Commission COM(2010) 245 final. http:// eur-lex.europa.eu/LexUriServ/LexUriServ.do?uri=COM:2010:0245:FIN:EN:PDF accessed 28/07/2011.

—— (2010c). 'Digital Agenda for Europe: Key Initiatives'. *European Commission Memo/10/200,* 19 May, http://europa.eu/rapid/pressReleasesAction.do?reference=MEMO/10/200&format= HTML&aged=0&language=EN&guiLanguage=en accessed 28/07/2011.

—— (2010d). *Europe in Figures: Eurostat Yearbook 2010.* Luxembourg: Eurostat Statistical Books.

—— (2010e). *Report on the Public Consultation on 'The Open Internet and Net Neutrality in Europe'.* Brussels: European Commission. http://ec.europa.eu/information_society/policy/ ecomm/doc/library/public_consult/net_neutrality/report.pdf accessed 28/07/2011.

—— (2011). *Communication from the Commission to the European Parliament, the Council, the European Economic and Social Committee and the Committee of the Regions on a Single Market for Intellectual Property Rights—Boosting Creativity and Innovation to Provide Economic Growth, High Quality Jobs and First Class Products and Services in Europe.* Brussels: European Commission COM(2011)287 final. http://ec.europa.eu/internal_market/copyright/docs/ ipr_strategy/COM_2011_287_en.pdf accessed 28/07/2011.

European Commission High Level Group of Experts (1996). *Building the European Information Society for Us All—Interim Report, First Reflections of the High Level Group of Experts.* Luxembourg: Office for Official Publications of the European Communities. http://www. epractice.eu/files/media/media_688.pdf accessed 28/07/2011.

European Parliament (2007). *Draft Report on Cultural Industries in the Context of the Lisbon Strategy.* European Parliament Committee on Culture and Education, Rapporteur, Guy Bono, PR/684266EN. http://www.europarl.europa.eu/meetdocs/2004_2009/documents/pr/ 684/684266/684266en.pdf accessed 28/07/2011.

—— (2008). *Report on Cultural Industries in Europe (2007/2153(INI)).* European Parliament Committee on Culture and Education, Rapporteur, Guy Bono, A6-0063/2008. http://www. europarl.europa.eu/sides/getDoc.do?pubRef=-//EP//NONSGML+REPORT+A6-2008-0063 +0+DOC+PDF+V0//EN accessed 28/07/2011.

Evans, D. S., Hagiu, A. and Schmalensee, R. (2005). 'A Survey of the Economic Role of Software Platforms in Computer-based Industries'. *CESifo Economic Studies, 51*(2/3): 189–224.

Fairclough, N. (1992). *Discourse and Social Change.* Cambridge: Polity.

Faulhaber, G. R. (2007). 'Network Neutrality: The Debate Evolves'. *International Journal of Communication, 1*: 680–700.

Federal Communications Commission (2005). *Policy Statement.* Washington, DC: FCC, FCC 05-151. http://www.publicknowledge.org/pdf/FCC-05-151A1.pdf, accessed 28/07/2011.

—— (2010a). *Dissenting Statement of Commissioner Meredith Attwell Baker Re: Preserving the Open Internet, GN Docket No. 09-191, Broadband Industry Practices, WC Docket No. 07-52.* Washington, DC: FCC. http://transition.fcc.gov/Daily_Releases/Daily_Business/2010/db1221/ DOC-303746A5.pdf accessed 28/07/2011.

—— (2010b). *Report and Order in the Matter of Preserving the Open Internet, Broadband Industry Practices, GN Docket No. 09-191, WC Docket No. 07-52.* Washington, DC: FCC. http://www.scribd.com/doc/47905173/FCC-Report-and-Order-In-the-Matter-of- Preserving-the-Open-Internet-Broadband-Industry-Practices accessed 28/07/2011.

Feenberg, A. (1991). *Critical Theory of Technology.* Oxford: Oxford University Press.

—— (1992). 'Subversive Rationalization, Technology, Power, and Democracy'. *Inquiry—An Interdisciplinary Journal of Philosophy, 35*(3–4): 301–22.

—— (1999). *Questioning Technology.* New York: Routledge.

—— (2000). *Looking Backward, Looking Forward: Reflections on the 20th Century.* Burnaby, BC: Hitotsubashi University Conference on the 20th Century—Dreams and Realities. http://www-rohan.sdsu.edu/faculty/feenberg/hit1ck.htm accessed 20/10/2010.

—— (2010a). *Between Reason and Experience: Essays in Technology and Modernity.* Cambridge, MA: MIT Press.

—— (2010b). *Ten Paradoxes of Technology.* Burnaby, BC: Simon Fraser University, SFU Canada Chair Seminar Series, 11 February, http://www.youtube.com/watch?v=-HzJ_Jkqa2Q accessed 10/07/2011.

Fein, M. L. (1992). *Analyzing Psychotherapy: A Social Role Interpretation.* New York: Praeger.

Feintuck, M. and Varney, M. (2006). *Media Regulation, Public Interest and the Law* (2nd edn). Edinburgh: Edinburgh University Press.

Fenton, N. (2007). 'Contesting Global Capital, New Media, Solidarity, and the Role of a Social Imaginary', in B. Cammaerts and N. Carpentier (eds), *Reclaiming the Media: Communication Rights and Democratic Media Roles.* Bristol: Intellect Books, pp. 225–42.

Ferree, M., Gamson, W., Gerhrard, J. and Rucht, D. (2002). 'Four Models of the Public Sphere in Modern Democracies'. *Theory and Society, 31*(3): 289–324.

Ferronato, P. (2007). 'Ecosystem Oriented Architecture (EOA) vs SOA', in F. Nachira, A. Nicolai, P. Dini, M. Le Louarn and L. Rivera Leon (eds), *Digital Business Ecosystems.* Brussels: European Commission Directorate General Information Society and Media, pp. 111–18.

Fingar, P. (2009). *Dot Cloud: The 21st Century Business Platform Built on Cloud.* Tampa, FL: Meghan-Kiffer Press.

Fleming, M. (2010, 21 October). 'MPAA Urges Japan on Pic Pirate Issue'. *Deadline Hollywood.* http://www.deadline.com/tag/piracy-graduated-response/ accessed 28/07/2011.

Flichy, P. (2007) *The Internet Imaginaire.* Trans. L. Carey-Libbrecht, Cambridge, MA: MIT Press.

Foray, D. (2004). *The Economics of Knowledge.* Cambridge, MA: MIT Press.

—— (ed.) (2009). *The New Economics of Technology Policy.* Cheltenham: Edward Elgar.

—— Steinmueller, W. E. (2003). 'The Economics of Knowledge Reproduction by Inscription'. *Industrial and Corporate Change, 12*(2): 299–319.

Forge, S., Blackman, C., Bohlin, E. and Cave, M. (2009). 'A Green Knowledge Society: An ICT Policy Agenda to 2015 for Europe's Future Knowledge Society'. A Study for the Ministry of Enterprise, Energy and Communications, Government Offices of Sweden by SCF Associates, Ltd. Final Report.

Foucault, M. (1978). *The History of Sexuality. Vol. 1: An Introduction.* New York: Pantheon.

France. (2009). *LOI n° 2009-1311 du 28 octobre 2009 relative à la protection pénale de la propriété littéraire et artistique sur internet No. 2009-1311 of 28 October 2009.* Paris: Government of France. http://legifrance.gouv.fr/affichTexte.do?cidTexte=JORFTEXT000021208046&dateTexte= accessed 28/07/2011.

Fraser, I. (2007). *Dialectics of the Self: Transcending Charles Taylor.* New York: Academic Press.

Fraser, N. (1990). 'Rethinking the Public Sphere: A Contribution to the Critique of Actually Existing Democracy'. *Social Text, 25/26:* 56–80.

—— (2010). *Scales of Justice: Reimagining Political Space in a Globalizing World.* New York: Columbia University Press.

Frau-Meigs, D. (2011). *Media Matters in the Cultural Contradictions of the 'Information Society':
Towards a Human Rights-based Governance.* Strasbourg: Council of Europe Publishing.

Freedman, D. (2011). 'The State of Internet Regulation'. Paper presented at the IAMCR
Conference, Istanbul, 13–17 July.

Freeman, C. (1988). 'Introduction', in G. Dosi, C. Freeman, R. Nelson, G. Silverberg and L. Soete
(eds), *Technical Change and Economic Theory.* London: Pinter Publishers, pp. 1–8.

—— (1992). *The Economics of Hope: Essays on Technical Change, Economic Growth and the
Environment.* London: Pinter Publishers.

—— (1995). 'The "National System of Innovation" in Historical Perspective'. *Cambridge
Journal of Economics, 19*: 5–24.

—— (2007). 'The ICT Paradigm', in R. Mansell, C. Avgerou, D. Quah and R. Silverstone (eds),
The Oxford Handbook of Information and Communication Technologies. Oxford: Oxford
University Press, pp. 34–54.

—— Louçã, F. (2001). *As Time Goes By: From Industrial Revolutions to the Information
Revolution.* Oxford: Oxford University Press.

—— Perez, C. (1988). 'Structural Crises of Adjustment, Business Cycles and Investment
Behaviour', in G. Dosi, C. Freeman, R. Nelson, G. Silverberg and L. Soete (eds), *Technical
Change and Economic Theory.* London: Pinter, pp. 38–66.

Frenken, K. (2006). *Innovation, Evolution and Complexity Theory.* Cheltenham: Edward Elgar.

Fuchs, C. (2009). 'Information and Communication Technologies and Society: A Contribution
to the Critique of the Political Economy of the Internet'. *European Journal of Communication,
24*(1): 69–87.

Fukuyama, F. (1992). *The End of History and the Last Man.* New York: Avon Books, Inc.

Fuller, S. (2000). *Thomas Kuhn: A Philosophical History for Our Times.* Chicago, IL: University of
Chicago Press.

Functowicz, S. and Ravetz, J. R. (1994). 'Emergent Complex Systems'. *Futures, 26*(6): 568–82.

Gagliardone, I. (2010). 'Development and Destabilization: The Selective Adoption of ICTs in
Ethiopia'. Unpublished PhD Thesis, Department of Media and Communications, London
School of Economics and Political Science.

Galbraith, J. K. (1996). *The Good Society: The Humane Agenda.* New York: Houghton Mifflin.

Gandy, Jr., O. H. (2009). *Coming to Terms with Chance: Engaging Rational Discrimination and
Cumulative Disadvantage.* Burlington, VA: Ashgate.

Gaonkar, D. P. (2002). 'Toward New Imaginaries: An Introduction'. *Public Culture, 14*(1): 1–19.

Garnham, N. (1979). 'Contribution to a Political Economy of Mass-communication'. *Media,
Culture and Society, 1*(2): 123–46.

—— (1986). 'Contribution to a Political Economy of Mass-Communication', in R. Collins,
J. Curran, P. Scannell, P. Schlesinger and C. Sparks (eds), *Media, Culture and Society: A Critical
Reader.* London: Sage, pp. 9–32.

—— (1990). 'Media Theory and the Political Future of Mass Communication', in F. Inglis (ed.),
Capitalism and Communication: Global Culture and the Economics of Information. London:
Sage, pp. 1–19.

Gawer, A. and Henderson, R. M. (2007). 'Platform Owner Entry and Innovation in
Complementary Markets: Evidence from Intel'. *Journal of Economics and Management
Strategy, 16*(1): 1–34.

Geels, F. W. (2002). 'Technological Transitions as Evolutionary Reconfiguration Processes: A Multi-Level Perspective and a Case-Study'. *Research Policy, 31*: 1257–74.

—— (2010). 'Ontologies, Socio-technical Transitions (to Sustainability), and the Multi-level Perspective'. *Research Policy, 39*(4): 495–510.

—— Schot, J. (2007). 'Comment on "Techno Therapy or Nurtured Niches?"'. *Research Policy, 36*(7): 1100–1.

Georgiou, M. (2006). *Diaspora, Identity and the Media: Diasporic Transnationalism and Mediated Spatialities.* Cresskill, NJ: Hampton Press.

Gershuny, J. (1978). *After Industrial Society? The Emerging Self Service Economy.* London: Macmillan.

Get Safe Online. (2010). *UK Internet Security: State of the Nation, The Get Safe Online Report 2010.* London: Get Safe Online.

Ghosh, R. A. (2005). *Free/Libre/Open Source Software: Policy Support.* Maastricht: MERIT, University of Maastricht. http://flosspols.org/deliverables/FLOSSPOLS-D04-openstandards-v6.pdf accessed 28/07/2011.

Gibson, W. (1984). *Neuromancer.* New York: Ace Books.

Giddens, A. (1991). *Modernity and Self-Identity: Self and Society in the Late Modern Age.* Cambridge: Polity Press.

—— (1993). *New Rules of Sociological Method: A Positive Critique of Interpretative Sociologies* (2nd edn). Stanford, CA: University of Stanford Press.

—— Piersin, C. (1998: 77). *Conversations with Anthony Giddens: Making Sense of Modernity.* Stanford, CA: Stanford University Press.

Giusto, D., Iera, A., Morabito, G. and Atzori, L. (eds) (2010). *The Internet of Things: 20th Tyrrhenian Workshop on Digital Communications.* New York: Springer.

Gladwell, M. and Shirky, C. (2011). 'From Innovation to Revolution: Do Social Media Make Protests Possible?'. *Foreign Affairs,* March/April, np.

Goergen, M., Mallin, C., Mitleton-Kelly, E., Al-Hawamdeh, A. and Hse-Yu, I. (2010). *Corporate Governance and Complexity Theory.* Cheltenham: Edward Elgar.

Golbeck, J. (2007). 'The Dynamics of Web-based Social Networks: Membership, Relationships and Change'. *First Monday, 12*(11): np.

—— Hendler, J. and Parsia, B. (2003). 'Trust Networks on the Semantic Web', in M. Klusch, S. Ossowski, A. Omicini and H. Laamanen (eds), *Proceedings of Cooperative Information Agents VII (CIA 2003).* Berlin: Springer, pp. 238–49.

Golding, P. and Murdock, G. (2001). 'Digital Divides: Communications Policy and its Contradictions'. *New Economy, 8*: 110–15.

Goldsmith, J. L. and Wu, T. (2006). *Who Controls the Internet? Illusions of a Borderless World.* Oxford: Oxford University Press.

Gore, A. (1993). 'Remarks by Vice President Albert Gore at the National Press Club'. Washington, DC, 21 December.

Gould, S. J. (2007). *Punctuated Equilibrium.* Cambridge, MA: Belknap Press.

Graham, G. (1999). *The Internet://A Philosophical Inquiry.* London: Routledge.

Graham, P. (2007). 'Political Economy of Communication: A Critique'. *Critical Perspectives on International Business, 3*(3): 226–45.

Gramsci, A. (1971). *Selections From the Prison Notebooks* (ed. and trans. Q. Hoar and G. N. Smith). London: Lawrence and Wishart.

Grant, C. B. (2003). 'Destabilizing Social Communication Theory'. *Theory Culture & Society, 20*(6): 95–119.

Gras, A. (1993). *Grandeur et dépendance: sociologie des macro-systèmes technique.* Paris: Presses universitaires de France.

Griliches, Z. (1996). 'The Discovery of the Residual: A Historical Note'. *Journal of Economic Literature, 34*(3): 1324–30.

Grusin, R. (2010). *Premediation: Affect and Mediality After 9/11.* New York: Palgrave Macmillan.

Guimón, J. and Zac de Filc, S. (eds) (2001). *Challenges of Pscyhoanalysis in the 21st Century: Psychoanalysis, Health, and Psychosexuality in the Era of Virtual Reality.* New York: Kluwer Academic.

Gunkel, D. J. (2003). 'Second Thoughts: Toward a Critique of the Digital Divide'. *New Media & Society, 5*(4): 499–522.

—— (2010). 'The Real Problem: Avatars, Metaphysics and Online Social Interaction'. *New Media & Society, 12*(1): 127–41.

Gutmann, A. and Thompson, D. F. (2004). *Why Deliberative Democracy?* Princeton, NJ: Princeton University Press.

Guttman, N. (2010). 'Public Deliberation on Policy Issues: Normative Stipulations and Practical Resolutions', in C. T. Salmon (ed.), *Communications Yearbook No. 34.* New York: Routledge, pp. 169–212.

Haas, P. M. (1992). 'Introduction: Epistemic Communities and International Policy Coordination'. *International Organization, 46*(1): 1–36.

Habermas, J. (1962/1989). *The Structural Transformation of the Public Sphere: An Inquiry into a Category of Bourgeois Society.* Cambridge: Polity.

—— (1997). 'The Public Sphere', in S. E. Bonner (ed.), *20th Century Political Theory: A Reader.* London: Routledge.

Haddon, L. (2004). *Information and Communication Technologies in Everyday Life.* Cambridge: Berg.

—— (ed.) (2011). *The Contemporary Internet.* Frankfurt am Main: Peter Lang.

Hadfield, G. (1992). 'The Economics of Copyright: An Historical Perspective'. *ASCAP Copyright Law Symposium, 38*: 1–46.

Hagiu, A. and Yoffie, D. B. (2009). 'What's Your Google Strategy?'. *Harvard Business Review,* April, 1–7.

Hale, M. (1787). 'A Treatise, in Three Parts. "Pars Prima. De Jure Maris et Brachiorum ejufdem.—Pars Secunda. De Portibus Maris.—Pars Teria. Conserning the Custom of Goods Imported and Exported', in F. Hargrave (ed.), *A Collection of Tracts Relative to the Law of England from Manuscripts, Volume 1.* Dublin: E. Lynch et al., pp. 1–248.

Halloran, J. D. (1974). *Mass Media and Society: The Challenge of Research—An Inaugural Lecture delivered in the University of Leicester, 25 October 1973.* Leicester: Leicester University Press. http://www.asc.upenn.edu/gerbner/archive.aspx?sectionID=95&packageID=350 accessed 28/07/2011.

Hamelink, C. (2002). 'Social Development, Information and Knowledge: Whatever Happened to Communication?'. *Journal of Development, 45*(4): 4–9.

Hamilton, W. H. (1930). 'Affectation with Public Interest'. *Yale Law Journal, 39*(8): 1089–112.

Hampton, K. N. and Gupta, N. (2008). 'Community and Social Interaction in the Wireless City: Wi-Fi Use in Public and Semi-Public Places'. *New Media & Society*, *10*(6): 831–50.

Handy, C. (1994). *The Age of Paradox*. Boston, MA: Harvard Business School Press.

Haraway, D. (1985/1991). 'A Cyborg Manifesto: Science, Technology and Socialist-Feminism in the Late Twentieth Century', in D. Haraway (ed.), *Simians, Cyborgs and Women*. New York: Routledge, pp. 149–81.

Hardt, M. and Negri, A. (2001). *Empire*. Cambridge, MA: Harvard University Press.

—— —— (2009). *Common Wealth*. Cambridge, MA: Harvard University Press.

Hargittai, E. (2003). 'The Digital Divide and What to Do with It', in D. C. Jones (ed.), *The New Economy*. San Diego, CA: Academy Press, pp. 822–38.

—— (2004). 'Internet Access and Use in Context'. *New Media & Society*, *6*(1): 137–44.

—— (2008). 'Whose Space? Differences Among Users and Non-Users of Social Network Sites'. *Journal of Computer-Mediated Communication*, *13*(1): 276–97.

Hargreaves, I. (2011). 'Digital Opportunity: A Review of Intellectual Property and Growth'. London: An Independent Report Commissioned by the UK Prime Minister.

Harries-Jones, P. (2004). 'Revisiting Angels Fear: Recursion, Ecology and Aesthetics'. *SEED Journal*, *4*(1): 143–65.

Hartmann, M. (2004). *Technologies and Utopias: The Cyberflaneur and the Experience of 'Being Online'*. Munich: Verlag Reinhard Fischer.

Hassan, R. (2008). *The Information Society*. Cambridge: Polity.

Haunss, S. and Shadlen, K. C. (eds) (2009). *Politics of Intellectual Property: Contestation Over the Ownership, Use and Control of Knowledge and Information*. Cheltenham: Edward Elgar.

Hayles, N. K. (ed.) (1991). *Chaos and Order: Complex Dynamics in Literature and Science*. Chicago, IL: University of Chicago Press.

Healy, K. and Schussman, A. (2003). 'The Ecology of Open Source Software Development (Draft)'. Unpublished Working Paper, Department of Sociology, University of Arizona.

Heath, R. L. and Bryant, J. (2000). *Human Communication Theory and Research*. New York: Routledge.

Heeks, R. (2010). 'Understanding "Gold Farming" and Real-Money Trading as the Intersection of Real and Virtual Economies'. *Journal of Virtual Worlds Research*, *2*(4): 3–27.

Heidegger, M. (1993). 'Only a God Can Save Us' (trans. M. Alter and J. Caputo), in R. Wolin (ed.), *The Heidegger Controversy: A Critical Reader*. Cambridge, MA: MIT Press, pp. 91–115.

Henderson, R. M. and Clark, K. B. (1990). 'Architectural Innovation: The Reconfiguration of Existing Product Technologies and the Failure of Established Firms'. *Administrative Science Quarterly*, *35*: 9–30.

Henten, A., Samarajiva, R. and Melody, W. H. (2003). 'Designing Next Generation Telecom Regulation: ICT Convergence or Multi-Sector Utility'. *Info*, *5*(1): 26–33.

Herwig, J. (2009). 'Liminality and Communitas in Social Media: The Case of Twitter'. Paper presented at the Critical Internet Research 10.0 Conference, Milwaukee, 7–10 October.

Heylighen, F. and Joslyn, C. (2001). 'Cybernetics and Second-Order Cybernetics', in R. A. Meyers (ed.), *Encyclopedia of Physical Science & Technology* (3rd edn). New York: Academic Press, pp. 1–25.

High Court of Justice. (2011). *In the High Court of Justice Queen's Bench Division, Administrative Court, Case No. CO/7354/2010, between (1) British Telecommunications Plc (2) TalkTalk*

Telecom Group Plc and the Secretary of State for Business, Innovation and Skills. London: High Court of Justice Queen's Bench Division, Administrative Court.

Hine, C. (2000). *Virtual Ethnography*. London: Sage.

Hirschheim, R., Klein, H. K. and Lyytinen, K. (1996). 'Exploring the Intellectual Structures of Information Systems Development: A Social Action Theoretical Analysis'. *Accounting, Management & Information Technology*, 6(1/2): 1–63.

Hirschman, A. O. (1970). *Exit, Voice and Loyalty: Responses to Decline in Firms, Organizations and States*. Cambridge, MA: Harvard University Press.

HM Treasury. (2006). *Gowers Review of Intellectual Property*. London: HM Treasury.

Ho, K. C., Baber, Z. and Knondker, H. (2002). ' "Sites" of Resistance: Alternative Websites and State-Society Relations'. *British Journal of Sociology*, 53(1): 127–48.

Hobday, M. (1998). 'Product Complexity, Innovation and Industrial Organisation'. *Research Policy*, 26: 689–710.

Hodgson, G. M. (2006). *Economics in the Shadows of Darwin and Marx: Essays on Institutional and Evolutionary Themes*. Cheltenham: Edward Elgar.

Hoflich, J. R. and Hartmann, M. (eds) (2006). *Mobile Communication in Everyday Life: Ethnographic Views, Observations and Reflections*. Berlin: Frank & Timme.

Hofmann, J. (2009). 'Critical Internet Resources: Coping with the Elephant in the Room', in W. J. Drake (ed.), *Internet Governance: Creating Opportunities for All*. Sharm el Sheikh, Egypt: United Nations Committee for Economic and Social Affairs, pp. 1–14.

—— Botzem, S. (2010). 'Transnational Governance Spirals: The Transformation of Rule-making Authority in Internet Regulation and Corporate Financial Reporting'. *Critical Policy Studies*, 4(1): 18–37.

Hogan, B. J. (2009). 'Networking in Everyday Life'. Unpublished PhD Dissertation. University of Toronto.

Holmes, C. A. V. (1998). *There Is No Such Thing as a Therapist: An Introduction to the Therapeutic Process*. London: Karnac Books.

Holt, R. (2004). *Dialogue on the Internet: Language, Civic Identity, and Computer-Mediated Communication*. Westport, CT: Greenwood Publishing Group.

Hookway, B., Kwinter, S. and Mau, B. (1999). *Pandemonium: The Rise of Predatory Locales in the Postwar World*. Princeton, NJ: Princeton Architectural Press.

Horton, J. J. and Chilton, L. B. (2010). 'The Labor Economics of Paid Crowdsourcing', in *Proceedings of the 11th ACM Conference on Electronic Commerce*. New York: ACM, pp. 209–18.

Howard, P. N. (2010). *The Digital Origins of Dictatorship and Democracy: Information Technology and Political Islam*. Oxford: Oxford University Press.

Huberman, B. A., Romero, D. M. and Wu, F. (2009). 'Crowdsourcing, Attention and Productivity'. *Journal of Information Science*, 35(6): 758–65.

Hughes, T. P. (1987). 'The Evolution of Large Technological Systems', in W. E. Bijker, T. P. Hughes and T. Pinch (eds), *The Social Construction of Technological Systems*. Cambridge, MA: MIT Press, pp. 51–82.

Hulme, D. and Toye, J. (2006). 'The Case for Cross-Disciplinary Social Science Research on Poverty, Inequality and Well-Being'. *Journal of Development Studies*, 42(7): 1085–107.

Hustinx, P. (2010). *Opinion of the European Data Protection Supervisor on the Current Negotiations by the European Union of an Anti-Counterfeiting Trade Agreement (ACTA)*. Brussels: Official Journal of the European Union, 2010/C 147. http://www.edps.europa.eu/

EDPSWEB/webdav/site/mySite/shared/Documents/Consultation/Opinions/2010/10-02-22_ACTA_EN.pdf accessed 28/07/2011.

Ibrahim, Y. (2006). 'The Role of Regulations and Social Norms in Mediating Online Political Discourse'. Unpublished PhD Thesis, Department of Media and Communications, London School of Economics and Political Science.

Ibrus, I. (2010). 'Evolutionary Dynamics of New Media Forms: The Case of Open Mobile Web'. Unpublished PhD Thesis, Department of Media and Communications, London School of Economics and Political Science.

IDATE (2010). *DigiWorld Yearbook 2010: The Digital World's Challenges.* Montpellier: IDATE.

Independent Commission for World-wide Telecommunication Development (ICWTD) (1984). *The Missing Link: Report of the Independent Commission for World-wide Telecommunication Development.* Geneva: International Telecommunication Union.

Innis, H. A. (1950/2007). *Empire and Communication.* Toronto: University of Toronto Press, republished by Lanham, MD: Rowman & Littlefield.

—— (1951/1991). *The Bias of Communication.* Toronto: University of Toronto Press.

International Commission for the Study of Communication Problems (ICSCP) (1980/2004). *Many Voices, One World: Report of the International Commission for the Study of Communication Problems.* Lanham, MD: Rowman & Littlefield/International Commission for the Study of Communication Problems.

International Federation for Information Processing (IFIP) (2009). *Digital Music Report 2009.* London: IFIP.

—— (2010). *Digital Music Report 2010.* London: IFIP.

—— (2011). *Digital Music Report 2011.* London: IFIP.

International Telecommunication Union (ITU) (2006). *Digital Life: ITU Internet Report 2006.* Geneva: ITU.

Internet Governance Forum (IGF) (2010). *Fifth Meeting of the Internet Governance Forum, Chairman's Summary (Expanded Version).* Vilnius: IGF.

Internet World Stats. (2011). *Internet World Stats—Usage and Population Statistics*: Internet World Stats. http://www.internetworldstats.com/stats.htm accessed 1/06/2011.

Introna, L. D. (1997). *Management, Information and Power: A Narrative of the Involved Manager.* Basingstoke: Macmillan.

Ito, Y. (1991). 'Johoka as a Driving Force of Social Change'. *KEIO Communication Review, 12*: 33–58.

Jaeger, P. T. and Burnett, G. (2010). *Information Worlds.* New York: Routledge.

Jefferson, T. (1813). 'Letter of 1813 to Isaac McPherson' *Thomas Jefferson: Writings.* New York: The Library of America.

Jenkins, H. (2006). *Convergence Culture: Where Old and New Media Collide.* New York: New York University Press.

—— Purushotma, R., Weigel, M., Clinton, K. and Robison, A. J. (2009). *Confronting the Challenges of Participatory Culture: Media Education for the 21st Century.* Cambridge, MA: MIT Press for John D. and Catherine T. MacArthur Foundation Reports on Digital Media and Learning.

Jessop, B. (2005). 'Cultural Political Economy, the Knowledge-based Economy and the State', in A. Barry and D. Slater (eds), *The Technological Economy.* London: Routledge, pp. 142–64.

Johansen, H. P. M. (2009). 'Re-Conceptualising Party-Centred Politics in Terms of 'Market': A Relationship Marketing Approach'. Unpublished PhD Thesis, Department of Media and Communications, London School of Economics and Political Science.

Johnson, J. (2010). 'Hacked Twitter Account Leads to Panic for Millions'. *The Blog Herald*, 26 November, http://www.blogherald.com/2010/11/26/hacked-twitter-account-leads-to-panic-for-millions/ accessed 28/07//2011.

Johnson, D. R. and Post, D. G. (1998). 'The New 'Civic Virtue' of the Net: A Complex Systems Model for the Governance of Cyberspace', in C. Firestone (ed.), *The Emerging Internet: 1998 (Annual Review of the Institute for Information Studies)*. Denver, CO: The Aspen Institute, pp. 81–108.

Johnson, B., Lorenz, E. and Lundvall, B.-Å (2002). 'Why All This Fuss about Codified and Tacit Knowledge?'. *Industrial and Corporate Change*, 11(2): 245–62.

Jones, S. (1999). *Doing Internet Research: Critical Issues and Methods for Examining the Net.* London: Sage Publications.

Jowitt, T. (2010). 'Google Street View Cars Broke Canadian Privacy Laws'. *eweekeurope*, 20 October, http://www.eweekeurope.co.uk/news/google-street-view-cars-violated-canadian-privacy-laws-10773 accessed 28/07/2011.

Judge, P. (2010). 'Privacy Group Says Google Broke the Law'. *eweekeurope*, 10 June, http://www.eweekeurope.co.uk/news/privacy-group-threatens-legal-action-on-google-7628 accessed 28/07/2011.

Juneau, P. (1980). 'Concluding Statement by the Chairman Mr. Pierre Juneau, Deputy Minister of Communications, Canada', in OECD (ed.), *High Level Conference on Information Computer and Communications Policies for the 80s, 6–8 October*. Paris: OECD.

Jussawalla, M. and Edenfield, H. (eds) (1984). *Communication and Information Economics.* Amsterdam: North Holland.

Kahin, B. (2004). 'Codification in Context', in S. Braman (ed.), *The Emergent Global Information Policy Regime*. New York: Palgrave Macmillan, pp. 39–61.

Kalathil, S. and Boas, T. C. (2003). *Open Networks, Closed Regimes: The Impact of the Internet on Authoritarian Rule*. Washington, DC: Carnegie Endowment for International Peace.

Katz, J. E. and Aakhus, M. (eds) (2002). *Perpetual Contact: Mobile Communication, Private Talk, Public Performance*. Cambridge: Cambridge University Press.

Keane, J. (1995). 'Structural Transformations of the Public Sphere'. *The Communications Review*, 1(1): 8–22.

Kelly, K. (1995). *Out of Control: The New Biology of Machines*. London: Fourth Estate.

Kenis, P. and Schneider, V. (1991). 'Policy Networks and Policy Analysis: Scrutinizing a New Analytical Toolbox', in B. Marin and R. Mayntz (eds), *Policy Networks Empirical Evidence and Theoretical Considerations*. Frankfurt and Boulder, CO: Campus Verlag and Westview Press, pp. 25–62.

Keren, M. (2006). *Blogosphere: The New Political Arena*. Lanham, MD: Lexington Books.

Kettell, S. (2008). 'The Political Economy of Open-Source in the United Kingdom'. *Bulletin of Science, Technology & Society*, 28(4): 306–15.

Klang, M. (2006). *Disruptive Technology: Effects of Technology Regulation on Democracy*. PhD Dissertation, Department of Applied Information Technology, Göteborg University, Göteborg.

Klang, M. and Murray, A. (eds) (2005). *Human Rights in the Digital Age*. London: Glasshouse Press/Cavendish Publishing.

Kleinwächter, W. (2010). 'Latest Developments in IGF, ICANN and WSIS'. IAMCR Note, http://iamcr.org/news/642-internet-governance-2010 accessed 19/11/2010.

Klimkiewicz, B. (2008). 'Media Pluralism and Enlargement: The Limits and Potential for Media Policy Change', in D. Ward (ed.), *The European Union and the Culture Industries: Regulation and the Public Interest*. Aldershot: Ashgate, pp. 81–104.

Kobilarov, G., Scott, T., Raimond, Y., Oliver, S., Sizemore, C., Smethurst, M., Bizer, C. and Lee, R. (2009). 'Media Meets Semantic Web—How the BBC Uses DBpedia and Linked Data to Make Connections'. *The Semantic Web: Research and Applications: Lecture Notes in Computer Science, 5554*: 723–37.

Kollock, P. (1999). 'The Economies of Online Cooperation: Gifts and Public Goods in Cyberspace', in M. A. Smith and P. Kollock (eds), *Communities in Cyberspace*. London: Routledge, pp. 220–42.

Kooiman, J. (1993). 'Governance and Governability: Using Complexity, Dynamics and Diversity', in J. Kooiman (ed.), *Modern Governance: New Government-Society Interactions*. London: Sage, pp. 35–48.

Korzybski, A. (1933/1994). *Science & Sanity: An Introduction to Non-Aristotelian Systems and General Semantics* (5th edn). Englewood, NJ: Institute of General Semantics.

Kraut, R. E., Patterson, M., Lundmark, V., Kiesler, S., Mukhopadhyay, T. and Scherlis, W. (1998). 'Internet Paradox: A Social Technology that Reduces Social Involvement and Psychological Well-being?'. *American Psychologist, 53*(9): 1017–32.

—— Kiesler, S., Boneva, B., Cummings, J., Helgeson, V. and Crawford, A. (2002). 'Internet Paradox Revisited'. *Journal of Social Issues, 58*(1): 49–74.

Krippendorff, K. (1984). 'An Epistemological Foundation for Communication'. *Journal of Communication, 34*(2): 21–36.

—— (1989). 'The Power of Communication and the Communication of Power: Toward an Emancipatory Theory of Communication'. *Communication, 12*(3): 175–96.

—— (1995). 'Undoing Power'. *Critical Studies in Mass Communication, 12*(2): 101–32.

Krotz, F. (2007). 'The Meta-process of "Mediatization" as a Conceptual Frame'. *Global Media and Communication, 3*(3): 256–60.

Krugman, P. (1996). *The Self-Organising Economy*. New York: Blackwell.

Kuhn, T. S. (1962). *The Structure of Scientific Revolutions*. Chicago, IL: University of Chicago Press.

—— (2000). *The Road Since Structure: Philosophical Essays, 1970–1993, with an Autobiographical Interview* (ed. James Conant and John Haugeland). Chicago, IL: University of Chicago Press.

Küng, L., Picard, R. G. and Towse, R. (2008). *The Internet and the Mass Media*. London: Sage.

Kurzweil, R. (2006). *The Singularity is Near: When Humans Transcend Biology*. London: Gerald Duckworth & Co Ltd.

Lacan, J. (ed.) (1994). *Le séminaire. Livre IV: La relation d'objet*. Paris: Seuil.

Lachica, R. and Karabeg, D. (2008). 'Metadata Creation in Socio-semantic Tagging Systems: Towards Holistic Knowledge Creation and Interchange', in L. Maicher and L. Garshol (eds), *Scaling Topic Maps*. Berln: Springer, pp. 160–71.

Laclau, E. (1990). *New Reflections on the Revolution of Our Time*. London: Verso.

Laclau, E., Mouffe, C. (1985). *Hegemony and Socialist Strategy: Towards a Radical Democratic Politics.* London: Verso.

Lahlou, S. (2008). 'Cognitive Technologies, Social Science and the Three-Layered Leopardskin of Change'. *Social Science Information, 47*(3): 227–51.

Lakhani, K. R. and von Hippel, E. (2003). 'How Open Source Software Works: "Free" User-to-user Assistance'. *Research Policy, 32*(6): 923–43.

Lamberton, D. M. (ed.) (1971). *The Economics of Information and Knowledge: Selected Readings.* Harmondsworth: Penguin.

Lampe, C., Ellison, N. B. and Steinfield, C. (2008). 'Changes in Use and Perception of Facebook', in *Proceedings of the 2008 ACM Conference on Computer Supported Cooperative Work.* New York: ACM, pp. 721–30.

Langlois, R. N. (2002). 'Modularity in Technology and Organization'. *Journal of Economic Behavior & Organization, 49*(1): 19–37.

Lapteva, O. (2010). 'Complexities and Frequencies of Linguistic Patterns (Natural and Formal) in Online Environments'. Deliverable 6.13, WP 6 on Socio-construction of Language, OPAALS Contract No. IST-034824, European Commission, July.

LaRose, R. and Kim, J. (2007). 'Share, Steal, or Buy? A Social Cognitive Perspective of Music Downloading'. *Journal of Cyberpsychology & Behavior, 10*(2): 267–77.

Lasar, M. (2011). 'Big Content, ISPs Nearing Agreement on Piracy Crackdown System'. *Ars Technica*, June, http://arstechnica.com/tech-policy/news/2011/06/big-content-isps-nearing-agreement-on-piracy-crackdown-system.ars accessed 28/07/2011.

Lasswell, H. D. (1951). 'Educational Broadcasters as Social Scientists'. Paper presented at the *NAEB Annual Convention*, Biloxi, Mississippi, 2–5 November.

—— (1972). 'Communications Research and Public Policy'. *The Public Opinion Quarterly, 36*(3): 301–10.

Latour, B. (1994). 'On Technical Mediation—Philosophy, Sociology, Genealogy'. *Common Knowledge, 3*: 29–64.

—— (2005). *Reassembling the Social: An Introduction to Actor-Network-Theory.* Oxford: Oxford University Press.

—— Woolgar, S. (1986). *Laboratory Life: The Construction of Scientific Facts* (Revised edn). Princeton, NJ: Princeton University Press.

Law, J. (1999). 'After ANT: Complexity, Naming and Topology', in J. Law and J. Hassard (eds), *Actor Network Theory and After.* Oxford: Oxford University Press, pp. 1–14.

Layard, R. (2005). *Happiness: Lessons from a New Science.* New York: Penguin.

Lazarsfeld, P. F. (1941/2004). 'Administrative and Critical Communications Research', in J. D. Peters and P. Simonson (eds), *Mass Communication and American Social Thought: Key Texts 1919–1968.* Lanham, MD: Rowman & Littlefield, pp. 166–73.

Lazzarato, M. (1996). *Immaterial Labour* (Trans. P. Colilli and E. Emery). Generation-Online. org. http://www.generation-online.org/c/fcimmateriallabour3.htm accessed 28/07/2011.

—— (2004). *Towards an Inquiry into Immaterial Labour.* Makeworlds.org. http://www.makeworlds.org/node/141 accessed 28/07/2011.

Leadbeater, C. (2007). *We-Think: Mass Innovation, Not Mass Production.* London: Profile Books.

Leghorn, R. S. (2011). *Richard S Leghorn Biography:* RichardLeghorn.com. http://richardleghorn.com/index.html accessed 28/07/2011.

Lehdonvirta, V. and Virtanen, P. (2010). 'A New Frontier in Digital Content Policy: Case Studies in the Regulation of Virtual Goods and Artificial Scarcity'. *Policy & Internet, 2*(2): 7–29.

Lenhart, A. and Madden, M. (2005). *Teen Content Creators and Consumers.* Washington, DC: Pew Internet & American Life Project.

—— Purcell, K., Smith, A. and Zickuhr, K. (2010). *Social Media & Mobile Internet Use Among Teens and Young Adults.* Washington, DC: Pew Internet & American Life Project.

Lentz, R. G. (2011). 'Regulation as Linguistic Engineering', in R. Mansell and M. Raboy (eds), *The Handbook of Global Media and Communication Policy.* Malden, MA: Wiley-Blackwell, pp. 432–48.

Leonard-Barton, D. (1992). 'Core Capabilities and Core Rigidities: A Paradox in Managing New Product Development'. *Strategic Management Journal, 13*: 111–25.

Lerner, J. and Tirole, J. (2000). 'Some Simple Economics of Open Source Software'. *Journal of Industrial Economics, 50*(2): 197–234.

Lesage, F. (2009). 'Networks for Art Work: An Analysis of Artistic Creative Engagements with New Media Standards'. Unpublished PhD Thesis, Department of Media and Communications, London School of Economics and Political Science.

Lessig, L. (1999). *Code and Other Laws of Cyberspace.* New York: Basic Books.

—— (2001). *The Future of Ideas: The Fate of the Commons in a Connected World.* New York: Random House.

—— (2003). 'The Creative Commons'. *Florida Law Review, 55*(3): 736–77.

—— (2006). *Code: Version 2.0.* New York: Basic Books.

—— (2008). *Remix: Making Art and Commerce Thrive in the Hybrid Economy.* London: Bloomsbury Academic.

—— McChesney, R. (2006). 'No Tolls on the Internet'. *The Washington Post,* 8 June.

Letts, P. (nd). 'The Rise of and Future of Crowdsourcing'. *Blurgroup.* http://www.internetworld.co.uk/page.cfm/Link=196/nocache=true accessed 27/07/2011.

Lévy, P. (1997). *Collective Intelligence: Mankind's Emerging World in Cyberspace* (trans. R. Bononno). New York: Helix Books—Perseus Books.

Lewis, M. W. (2000). 'Exploring Paradox: Toward a More Comprehensive Guide'. *Academy of Management Review, 25*(4): 760–76.

Licklider, J. C. R. and Taylor, R. W. (1968). 'The Computer as a Communication Device'. *International Science and Technology, 76*(April): 21–31.

Liebowitz, S. J. (2006). 'File Sharing: Creative Destruction or Just Plain Destruction?'. *The Journal of Law and Economics, 49*(1): 1–28.

—— Margolis, S. E. (2005). 'Seventeen Famous Economists Weigh in on Copyright: The Role of Theory, Empirics, and Network Effects'. *Harvard Journal of Law and Technology, 18*(2): 435–57.

Lievrouw, L. A. (2009). 'New Media, Mediation, and Communication Study'. *Information, Communication & Society, 12*(3): 303–25.

Light, B. and McGrath, K. (2010). 'Ethics and Social Networking Sites: A Disclosive Analysis of Facebook'. *Information Technology and People, 23*(4): 290–311.

Lilly, J. C. (1972). *Programming and Metaprogramming in the Human Biocomputer.* New York: The Julian Press.

Lindblom, C. E. (1990). *Inquiry and Change: The Troubled Attempt to Understand & Shape Society.* New Haven, CT: Yale University Press.

Lindner, T., Fritsch, L., Plank, K. and Rannenberg, K. (2004). 'Exploitation of Public and Private WiFi Coverage for New Business Models', in W. Lamersdorf, V. Tschammer and S. Amarger (eds), *Building the E-Service Society: E-Commerce, E-Business, and E-Government*. Dordrecht: Springer, pp. 131–48.

Litman, J. (2001). *Digital Copyright*. New York: Prometheus Books.

Livingstone, S. (1996). 'On the Continuing Problem of Media Effects', in J. Curran and M. Gurevitch (eds), *Mass Media and Society*. London: Edward Arnold, pp. 305–24.

—— (2003). 'On the Challenges of Cross-National Comparative Media Research'. *European Journal of Communication, 18*(4): 477–500.

—— (2009). 'On the Mediation of Everything. ICA Presidential Address'. *Journal of Communication, 59*(1): 1–18.

—— (2011). 'Regulating the Internet in the Interests of Children: Emerging European and International Approaches', in R. Mansell and M. Raboy (eds), *Handbook on Global Media and Communication Policy*. Malden, MA: Wiley-Blackwell, pp. 505–24.

—— Haddon, L., Görzig, A. and Ólafsson, K. (2011). *Risks and Safety on the Internet: The Perspective of European Children. Full Findings*. London: LSE, EU Kids Online. http://www.edukidsonline.net accessed 28/07/2011.

Ljundgberg, J. (2000). 'Open Source Movements as a Model of Organizing'. *European Journal of Information Systems, 9*(4): 208–16.

Luhmann, N. (1985). *A Sociological Theory of Law*. London: Routledge and Kegan Paul.

—— (1992). 'Autopoiesis: What is Communication?'. *Communication Theory, 2*: 251–59.

—— (1995). *Social Systems* (trans. John Bednarz and Dirk Baecker). Paolo Alto, CA: Stanford University Press.

—— (1996/2000). *The Reality of the Mass Media* (trans. K. Cross). Paolo Alto, CA: Stanford University Press.

Lukes, S. (1974/2005). *Power: A Radical View* (2nd edn). London: Macmillan.

Lundgren, A. (1995). *Technological Innovation and Network Evolution*. London: Routledge.

Lundstrom, J., Widriksson, J. and Zaunders, V. (2010). 'Changes in Media Consumption and File Sharing: The Impact of Legislation and New Digital Media Services'. Jönköping International Business School, May.

Lundvall, B.-Å. (ed.) (1992). *National Systems of Innovation: Towards a Theory of Innovation and Interactive Learning*. London: Pinter.

—— Johnson, B. (1994). 'The Learning Economy'. *Journal of Industry Studies, 1*(2): 23–42.

Lyon, D. (2006). *Theorizing Surveillance: The Panopticon and Beyond*. Uffcolm Devon: Willan Publishing.

—— (2007). *Surveillance Studies: An Overview*. Cambridge: Polity Press.

—— (2009). *ID Cards as Surveillance*. Cambridge: Polity Press.

Macdonald, S. (1998). *Information for Innovation: Managing Change from an Information Perspective*. Oxford: Oxford University Press.

Machlup, F. B. (1962). *The Production and Distribution of Knowledge in the US Economy*. Princeton, NJ: Princeton University Press.

MacKenzie, D. (1996). *Knowing Machines: Essays on Technical Change*. Cambridge MA: The MIT Press.

MacKenzie, D. and Wajcman, J. (eds) (1985). *The Social Shaping of Technology.* Milton Keynes: Open University Press.

Maclean, D. (2011). 'The Evolution of GMCP Institutions', in R. Mansell and M. Raboy (eds), *Handbook of Global Media and Communication Policy.* Malden, MA: Wiley-Blackwell, pp. 40–57.

Madianou, M. and Miller, D. (2011). *Migration and New Media: Transnational Families and Polymedia.* London: Routledge.

Magder, T. (2011). 'The Origins of International Agreements and Global Media: The Post, the Telegraph, and Wireless Communication Before World War I', in R. Mansell and M. Raboy (eds), *Handbook of Global Media and Communication Policy.* Malden, MA: Wiley-Blackwell, pp. 23–39.

Makau, J. M. (2011). 'Response and Conclusion: A Vision of Applied Ethics for Communication Studies', in G. Cheney, S. May and D. Munshi (eds), *The Handbook of Communication Ethics.* New York: Routledge, pp. 494–515.

Makeen, M. F. (2000). *Copyright in a Global Information Society: The Scope of Copyright Protection under International, US, UK and French Law.* The Hague: Kluwer Law International.

Malcolm, J. (2008a). 'Appraising the Success of the Internet Governance Forum'. *Internet Governance Project,* 21 November, http://internetgovernance.org accessed 28/07/2011.

—— (2008b). *Multi-Stakeholder Governance and the Internet Governance Forum.* Wembley, WA: Terminus Press.

Malone, P., Mcloughlin, M. and Finnegan, J. (2010). 'Integration of Identity, Trust and Accountability into P2P Network'. Deliverable 5.5, WP 5 on Integration with the Digital Ecosystem Platform, OPAALS Contract No. IST-034824, European Commission, Project Review, October.

Maniadaki, K. (2011). 'The Application of Competition Law to Questions of Access to Platforms for the Distribution of Online Content: The Case of Network Neutrality'. Paper presented at the *EuroCPR Conference,* Ghent, 26–28 March.

Manovich, L. (2009). 'The Practice of Everyday (Media) Life: From Mass Consumption to Mass Cultural Production'. *Critical Inquiry, 35*(2): 319–31.

Mansell, R. (1994). 'A Networked Economy: Unmasking the 'Globalisation' Thesis'. *Telematics and Informatics, II*(1): 25–43.

—— (1995). 'Standards, Industrial Policy and Innovation', in R. Hawkins, R. Mansell and J. Skea (eds), *Standards, Innovation and Competitiveness: The Politics and Economics of Standards in Natural and Technical Environments.* Cheltenham: Edward Elgar, pp. 213–27.

—— (1996). 'Information Highways: Controls, Signals, Congestion and Tolls', in C. Scott and O. Audeoud (eds), *The Future of EC Telecommunications Law: Series of Publications by the Academy of European Law in Trier,* Vol. 19. Cologne: Bundesanzeiger, pp. 41–50.

—— (2004). 'Political Economy, Power and New Media'. *New Media & Society, 6*(1): 74–83.

—— (ed.) (2009). *The Information Society (Critical Concepts in Sociology),* Four Volumes. London: Routledge.

Mansell, R. (2011). 'New Visions, Old Practices: Policy and Regulation in the Internet Era'. *Continuum: Journal of Media & Cultural Studies, 25*(1): 19–32.

—— (2011). 'Power and Interests in Information and Communication Technologies and Development: Exogenous and Endogenous Discourses in Contention'. *Journal of International Development,* pre-publication on Web.

Mansell, R. and Nordenstreng, K. (2006). 'Great Media and Communications Debates—An Assessment of the MacBride Report after 25 Years'. *Information Technologies and International Development*, 3(4): 15–36.

Mansell, R. and Raboy, M. (2011). 'Introduction: Foundations of the Theory and Practice of Global Media and Communication Policy', in R. Mansell and M. Raboy (eds), *The Handbook of Global Media and Communication Policy*. Malden, MA: Wiley-Blackwell, pp. 1–20.

—— Steinmueller, W. E. (2000). *Mobilizing the Information Society: Strategies for Growth and Opportunity*. Oxford: Oxford University Press.

—— —— (2010). 'British Telecommunications plc ("BT") and TalkTalk Telecom Group Limited v Secretary of State for Business, Innovation and Skills ("BIS") in the Matter of an Intended Claim'. Report prepared for Judicial Review of the Digital Economy Act 2010. LSE Enterprise, London.

—— —— (2011). 'Digital Economies and Public Policies: Contending Rationales and Outcome Assessment Strategies', in W. H. Dutton (ed.), *Oxford Handbook of Internet Studies*. Oxford: Oxford University Press.

—— —— (2011 under review-a). 'Copyright Infringement Online: The Case of the Digital Economy Act Judicial Review in the United Kingdom'. *New Media & Society*.

—— —— (2011 under review-b). 'The Copyright Paradox: Creative Destruction, under review Re-publication and the Impact of New Technologies'. *Industrial and Corporate Change*.

Marinos, A. and Briscoe, G. (2009). 'Community Cloud Computing'. *Cloud Computing: Lecture Notes in Computer Science, 5931*: 472–84.

Marion, R. (1999). *The Edge of Organization: Chaos, Complexity Theories and Formal Social Systems*. Newbury Park, CA: Sage.

Markham, A. N. and Baym, N. K. (eds) (2009). *Internet Inquiry: Conversations about Method*. London: Sage Publications.

Marsden, C. T. (2010). 'European Law and Regulation of Mobile Net Neutrality'. *European Journal of Law and Technology, 1*(2): np. http://ejlt.org//article/view/32/52 accessed 28/07/2011.

—— (2011). 'Network Neutrality and Internet Service Provider Liability Regulation: Are the Wise Monkeys of Cyberspace Becoming Stupid?'. *Global Policy Journal, 2*(1): 53–64.

Martin-Barbero, J. (1993). *Communication, Culture and Hegemony: From the Media to Mediations*. London: Sage.

Masuda, Y. (1980). 'Computopia: Rebirth of Theological Synergism', in Y. Masuda (ed.), *The Information Society as Post-Industrial Society*. Tokyo: Institute for the Information Society, pp. 146–54.

Mateos-Garcia, J. and Steinmueller, W. E. (2008a). 'The Institutions of Open Source Software: Examining the Debian Community'. *Information Economics and Policy, 20*(4): 333–44.

—— —— (2008b). 'Open, But How Much? Growth, Conflict, and Institutional Evolution in Open-Source Communities', in A. Amin and J. Roberts (eds), *Community, Economic Creativity, and Organization*. Oxford: Oxford University Press, pp. 254–82.

Mathiason, J. (2009). *Internet Governance: The New Frontiers of Global Institutions*. London: Routledge.

Mathur, P. (2003). 'Theorizing "Ecological Communication"'. Unpublished PhD Dissertation in Science and Technology Studies, Virginia Polytechnic Institute and State University, Blacksburg, VA.

Mattelart, A. (1996/2000). *Networking the World: 1794–2000* (trans. J. A. Cohen). Minneapolis, MN: University of Minnesota Press.

Mattelart, A. and Mattelart, M. (1998). *Theories of Communication: A Short Introduction* (trans. S. G. Taponier). London: Sage.

Maturana, H. R. (1997). *Metadesign in Articulos y Conferences*. Santiago: Instituto de Terpia Cognitiva. http://www.inteco.cl/articulos/006/doc_ing1.htm accessed 28/07/2011.

—— Varela, F. J. (1987). *Tree of Knowledge: The Biological Roots of Human Understanding* (trans. R. Paolucci). Boston, MA: Shambhala.

Mauss, M. (1954/1969). *The Gift: Forms and Functions of Exchange in Archaic Societies*. London: Routledge and Kegan Paul.

Maxwell, R. and Miller, T. (2011). 'The Environment and Global Media and Communication Policy', in R. Mansell and M. Raboy (eds), *Handbook of Global Media and Communication Policy*. Malden, MA: Wiley-Blackwell, pp. 467–86.

May, C. (2007). *The World Intellectual Property Organization: Resurgence and the Development Agenda*. New York: Routledge.

Mayntz, R. and Hughes, T. P. (eds) (1988). *The Development of Large Technical Systems*. Frankfurt and Boulder, CO: Campus Verlag and Westview Press.

McCaffery, L. (2000). 'An Interview with William Gibson'. *Project Cyberpunk*. http://project.cyberpunk.ru/idb/gibson_interview.html accessed 28/07/2011.

McChesney, R. W. (2008). *The Political Economy of Media: Enduring Issues, Emerging Dilemmas*. New York: Monthly Review Press.

McCulloch, W. S. (1945). 'A Heterarchy of Values Determined by the Topology of Nervous Nets'. *Bulleting of Mathematical Biophysics*, 7(December): 89–93.

McCurdy, P. M. (2008). 'Inside the Media Event: Examining the Media Practices of Dissent! at the Hori-Zone Eco-Village at the 2005 G8 Gleneagles Summit'. *Communications*, *33*(3): 293–311.

McKercher, C. and Mosco, V. (eds) (2008). *Knowledge Workers in the Information Society*. Lanham, MD: Lexington Books.

McLuhan, H. M. (1964). *Understanding Media: The Extensions of Man*. New York: McGraw-Hill Publishers.

McQuail, D. (2003). *Media Accountability and Freedom of Publication*. Oxford: Oxford University Press.

McWhinney, W. (2005). 'The White Horse: A Reformulation of Bateson's Typology of Learning'. *Cybernetics & Human Knowing*, *12*(1/2): 22–35.

Medina, J. E. M. (2005). 'The State Machine: Politics, Ideology and Computing in Chile, 1964–1973'. Unpublished PhD in History and Social Study of Science and Technology, Program in Science, Technology and Society, MIT, Cambridge, MA.

Meier, R. L. (1962). *A Communications Theory of Urban Growth*. Cambridge, MA: MIT Press.

Melody, W. H. (1970). 'Regulation and Competition in Data Communications in the United States: A Redirection of Public Policy'. Paper presented at the Panel on Policy Issues of Computer/Telecommunications Interaction, Group of Experts on Computer Utilisation, Paris, 19 October.

—— (1971). 'Technological Determinism and Monopoly Power in Communications'. Paper presented at the 84th Annual Meeting of the American Economic Association, Jung Hotel, New Orleans, Louisiana, 28 December.

Melody, W. H. (1973). 'The Role of Advocacy in Public Policy Planning', in G. Gerbner, L. Gross and W. H. Melody (eds), *Communication Technology and Social Policy*. New York: John Wiley & Sons, pp. 165–81.

—— (1985). 'The Information Society: Implications for Economic Institutions and Market Theory'. *Journal of Economic Issues, XIX*(2): 523–39.

—— (ed.) (1997). *Telecom Reform: Principles, Policies and Regulatory Practices*. Lyngby: Technical University of Denmark.

—— (1999). 'Review of "Marshall McLuhan: The Medium and the Messenger" by P. Marchand'. *Information, Communication & Society, 2*(3): 374–7.

—— (2003). 'Policy Implications of the New Information Economy', in M. Tool and P. Bush (eds), *Institutional Analysis and Economic Policy*. Dordrecht: Kluwer, pp. 411–32.

—— Mansell, R. (1983). 'The Debate over Critical vs. Administrative Research: Circularity or Challenge'. *Journal of Communication, 33*(3): 103–16.

Metcalfe, J. S. and Foster, J. (2004). 'Introduction and Overview', in J. S. Metcalfe and J. Foster (eds), *Evolution and Economic Complexity*. Cheltenham: Edward Elgar, pp. ix–xix.

—— Ramlogan, R. (2005). 'Limits to the Economy of Knowledge and Knowledge of the Economy'. *Futures, 37*(7): 655–74.

Meyer, L. (2000). 'Digital Platforms: Definition and Strategic Value'. *Communications & Strategies, 38*(2): 127–51.

Meyer, T. and Van Audenhove, L. (2010). 'Graduated Response and the Emergence of a European Surveillance Society'. *Info, 12*(6): 69–79.

Meyrowitz, J. (1985). *No Sense of Place: The Impact of Electronic Media on Social Behaviour*. Oxford: Oxford University Press.

Mill, J. S. (1829/1874/2000). *Essays on Some Unsettled Questions of Political Economy by John Stuart Mill*, 2nd edn. London: Longmans, Green, Reader and Dyer.

Mills, C. W. (1959/2000). *The Sociological Imagination*. Oxford: Oxford University Press.

Mingers, J. C. (1995). *Self-producing Systems: Implications and Applications of Autopoiesis*. New York: Plenum Press.

Ministry of International Trade and Industry (MITI). (1994). *Program for Advanced Information Infrastructure*. Tokyo: MITI.

Mintzberg, H. (1989). 'Five Ps for Strategy', in H. Mintzberg, J. B. Quinn and S. Ghoshal (eds), *The Strategy Process: Revised European Edition*. New York: Prentice-Hall, pp. 13–21.

Mirowski, P. (2002). *Machine Dreams: Economics Becomes a Cyborg Science*. Cambridge: Cambridge University Press.

Mitchell, R. W. (1991). 'Bateson Concept of Metacommunication in Play'. *New Ideas in Psychology, 9*(1): 73–87.

Möller, K. and Wilson, D. (eds) (1995). *Business Marketing: An Interaction and Network Perspective*. Boston, MA: Kluwer Academic Publishers.

Monge, P. R. and Contractor, N. S. (2003). *Theories of Communication Networks*. Oxford: Oxford University Press.

Moon, Y.-J. and Sproull, L. (2002). 'Essence of Distributed Work: The Case of the Linux Kernel', in P. Hinds and S. Kiesler (eds), *Distributed Work*. Cambridge, MA: MIT Press, pp. 381–404.

Mooney, A. (2010). 'Internet Regulation Proposal Sets Off Political Firestorm'. *CNN Politics*, 21 December, http://politicalticker.blogs.cnn.com/2010/12/21/internet-regulation-proposal-sets-off-political-firestorm/ accessed 28/07/2011.

Moore, G. E. (1965). 'Cramming More Components onto Integrated Circuits'. *Electronics Magazine, 38*(8): np.

Moore, J. F. (1997). *The Death of Competition: Leadership and Strategy in the Age of Business Ecosystems.* New York: Harper Paperbacks.

Moreno, J. L. (1934). *Who Shall Survive?* Washington, DC: Nervous and Mental Disease Publishing Company.

Morozov, E. (2009). 'Iran: Downside to the 'Twitter Revolution''. *Dissent, 56*(4): 10–14.

—— (2011). *The Net Delusion: How Not to Liberate the World.* New York: Allen Lane.

Morrison, C. M. and Gore, H. (2010). 'The Relationship between Excessive Internet Use and Depression: A Questionnaire-Based Study of 1,319 Young People and Adults'. *Psychopathology, 43*(2): 121–6.

Mosco, V. (1996). *The Political Economy of Communication.* London: Sage Publications.

—— (2008). 'Knowledge Workers of the World! Unite?'. *Communication, Culture & Critique, 1*(1): 105–15.

—— (2009). *The Political Economy of Communication* (2nd edn). London: Sage.

Mossberger, K., Tolbert, C. J. and McNeal, R. S. (2008). *Digital Citizenship: The Internet, Society, and Participation.* Cambridge, MA: MIT Press.

Mouffe, C. (1999). 'Deliberative Democracy or Agonistic Pluralism?'. *Social Research, 66*(3): 746–58.

—— (2005). *On the Political.* London: Routledge.

Mowery, D. C. (2009). 'What Does Economic Theory Tell Us About Mission-Oriented R&D?', in D. Foray (ed.), *The New Economics of Technology Policy.* Cheltenham: Edward Elgar, pp. 131–47.

Mowles, C. (2011). *Rethinking Management: Radical Insights from the Complexity Sciences.* Farnham: Gower.

Mueller, M. L. (2009, 16 November). 'ICANN, Inc.: Accountability and Participation in the Governance of Critical Internet Resources'. *Internet Governance Project.* http://www.internetgovernance.org/pdf/ICANNInc.pdf accessed 28/07/2011.

—— (2010a). 'Critical Resource: An Institutional Economics of the Internet Addressing-Routing Space'. *Telecommunications Policy, 34*(8): 405–16.

—— (2010b). *Networks and States: The Global Politics of Internet Governance.* Cambridge, MA: MIT Press.

—— Mathiason, J. and Klein, H. K. (2007). 'The Internet and Global Governance: Principles and Norms for a New Regime'. *Global Governance, 13*(2): 237–54.

Mullins, J. (2010). 'How Crowd-sourcing Has Helped in Haiti'. *The New Scientist, 205*(2745): 8–9.

Mumford, L. (1934). *Technics and Civilization.* New York: Harcourt Brace & Company.

Mumford, E. (2000). 'Socio-technical Design: An Unfulfilled Promise or a Future Opportunity', in R. Baskerville, J. Stage and J. DeGross (eds), *Organizational and Social Perspectives on Information Technology.* Amsterdam: North-Holland, pp. 33–46.

Munro, A., Iqani, M., Moschoyiannis, S., Zeller, F., Gabaldon, J., Colugnati, F. and Bueso, P. (2008). 'Foundations of the Theory of Associative Autopoetic Digital Ecosystems: Part 1'. Deliverable 1.2, WP 1 on Automata Theory and Autopoiesis, OPAALS Contract No. IST-034824, European Commission, July.

Murdock, G. (1978). 'Blindspots about Western Marxism: A Reply to Dallas Smythe'. *Journal of Political and Social Theory, 2*: 109–19.

Murdock, G. and Golding, P. (2004). 'Dismantling the Digital Divide: Rethinking the Dynamics of Participation and Exclusion', in A. Calabrese and C. Sparks (eds), *Toward a Political Economy of Culture: Capitalism and Communication in the Twenty-first Century*. Lanham, MD: Rowman & Littlefield, pp. 244–60.

Nachira, F., Nicolai, A., Dini, P., Le Louarn, M. and Rivera Leon, L. (eds) (2007). *Digital Business Ecosystems*. Brussels: European Commission Directorate General Information Society and Media.

Napoli, P. M. (2011). *Audience Evolution: New Technologies and the Transformation of Media Audiences*. New York: Columbia University Press.

Nazir, A., Raza, S. and Chuah, C.-N. (2008). 'Unveiling Facebook: A Measurement Study of Social Network Based Applications', *Proceedings of the 8th ACM SIGCOMM Conference on Internet Measurement*. New York: ACM, pp. 43–56.

Needham, J. (2004). *Science and Civilisation in China, Vol 7, The Social Background and Part 2, General Conclusions and Reflections* (edited by K. G. Robinson). Cambridge: Cambridge University Press.

Negroponte, N. (1995). *Being Digital*. London: Hodder and Stoughton.

Nelson, R. R. (ed.) (1993). *National Innovation Systems: A Comparative Analysis*. New York: Oxford University Press.

——(1994). 'The Co-evolution of Technology, Industrial Structure, and Supporting Institutions'. *Industrial and Corporate Change*, 3(1): 47–63.

—— Winter, S. G. (1977). 'In Search of a Useful Theory of Innovation'. *Research Policy*, 6: 36–76.

—— —— (1982). *An Evolutionary Theory of Economic Change*. Cambridge, MA: Harvard University Press.

Neogi, P. K. and Cordell, A. J. (2010). 'The Internet and the Need for Governance: Learning from the Past, Coping with the Future'. *Journal of Internet Banking and Commerce*, 15(2): 1–30.

Nightingale, P., Brady, T., Davies, A. and Hall, J. (2003). 'Capacity Utilization Revisited: Software, Control and Growth of Large Technical Systems'. *Industrial and Corporate Change*, 12(3): 477–517.

Noam, E. M. (2010). 'Regulation 3.0 for Telecom 3.0'. *Telecommunications Policy*, 34(1–2): 4–10.

Noble, D. F. (1998). *The Religion of Technology: The Divinity of Man and the Spirit of Invention*. New York: Alfred A. Knopf.

Nordenstreng, K. (2011). 'Free Flow Doctrine in Global Media Policy', in R. Mansell and M. Raboy (eds), *Handbook of Global Media and Communication Policy*. Malden, MA: Wiley-Blackwell, pp. 79–94.

Norris, P. (2001). *Digital Divide: Civic Engagement, Information Poverty, and the Internet Worldwide*. Cambridge: Cambridge University Press.

Nussbaum, M. C. (2000). *Woman and Human Development: The Capabilities Approach*. Cambridge: Cambridge University Press.

—— (2006). *Frontiers of Justice: Disability, Nationality, Species Membership*. Cambridge, MA: Belknap Press.

Nykänen, O. (2010). 'Wille Visualisation Toolkit for Developers with a Concise OKS Visualisation Application Catalogue for End-Users'. Deliverable 10.18, WP 10 on Sustainable Community Building, OPAALS Contract No. IST-034824, European Commission, Project Review, October.

Oberholzer-Gee, F. and Strumpf, K. (2010). *File-sharing and Copyright*: Music Business Research Files, World Press.com. http://musicbusinessresearch.files.wordpress.com/2010/06/paper-felix-oberholzer-gee.pdf accessed 28/07/2011.

Office of Communication (Ofcom) (2010). *Traffic Management and 'Net Neutrality': A Discussion Document*. London: Ofcom.

Office of Technology Assessment (OTA). (1986). *Intellectual Property Rights in an Age of Electronics and Information*. Washington, DC: OTA.

O'Hara, K. (2004). *Trust: From Socrates to Spin*. Cambridge: Icon Books.

—— Shadbolt, N. (2005). 'Knowledge Technologies and the Semantic Web', in R. Mansell and B. S. Collins (eds), *Trust and Crime in Information Societies*. Cheltenham: Edward Elgar, pp. 113–64.

Oltmann, S. M. (2010). 'Katz Out of the Bag: The Broader Privacy Ramifications of Using Facebook'. Paper presented at the *ASIST 2010 Conference*, Pittsburgh, PA, 22–27 October.

O'Mahony, S. and Ferraro, F. (2003). 'Managing the Boundary of an "Open Source" Project'. Prepared for the *Santa Fe Institute Workshop on the Network Construction of Markets*, Santa Fe, NM.

One Laptop Per Child (OLPC) (2010). 'Nicholas Negroponte on Success of One Laptop Per Child'. *OLPC//News*, 20 September, http://www.olpcnews.com/people/negroponte/nicholas_negroponte_on_success.html accessed 28/07/2011.

—— (2011). 'Who is to Blame for OLPC Peru's Failure? An OLPC Intern Viewpoint'. *OLPC//News*, 24 January, http://www.olpcnews.com/countries/peru/who_is_to_blame_for_olpc_peru.html accessed 28/07/2011.

OPAALS. (2010a). 'Finalised Infrastructural and Interaction Model, Interfaces and SBVR'. Based on D. 3.15 P. Krause and S. Moschoyiannis, WP 3 on Autopoietic P2P Networks, OPAALS Contract No. IST-034824, European Commission . Project Review, October.

—— (2010b). 'The Impact of New IP Legislation on Corporate Behaviour, SME Opportunities and Global Markets for Protected Innovations and the Presentation of a Formal Copyright Model'. Based on D 11.12 J. Stanley, WP 11 on Bridging Digital Ecosystems Research to Regional Development and Innovation in the Knowledge Economy, OPAALS Contract No. IST-034824, European Commission, Project Review, October.

—— (2010c). 'Case Studies on the Role of Partner Networks in OSS Value Creation and Capture Process'. Based on D 12.13 F. Botto, WP 11 on Socio-economic Models for Digital Ecosystems, OPAALS Contract No. IST-034824, European Commission, Project Review, October.

Ophir, E., Nass, C. and Wagner, A. D. (2009). 'Cognitive Control in Media Multitaskers', in *Proceedings of the National Academy of Sciences, PNAS Early Edition*, pp. 1–5.

Oppy, G. and Dowe, D. (2011). 'The Turing Test', in E. N. Zalta (ed.), *The Stanford Encyclopedia of Philosophy*, (Spring 2011 edn.) Stanford, CA: Stanford University. http://plato.stanford.edu/archives/spr2011/entries/turing-test/ accessed 28/07/2011.

Orgad, S. (2005). *Storytelling Online: Talking Breast Cancer on the Internet*. New York: Peter Lang.

Organisation for Economic Cooperation and Development (OECD) (1988). *New Technologies in the 1990s: A Socio-Economic Strategy*. Paris: OECD.

—— (2010). *OECD Information Technology Outlook 2010*. Paris: OECD.

—— (2011a). 'Communique on Principles for Internet Policy-Making' OECD High Level Meeting on The Internet Economy: Generating Innovation and Growth, Paris, 28–29 June, http://www.oecd.org/dataoecd/40/21/48289796.pdf accessed 28/04/2011.

Organisation for Economic Co-operation and Development (OECD) (2011b). *Shaping Polices for the Future of the Internet Economy.* Paris: OECD. http://www.oecd.org/dataoecd/1/29/40821707.pdf accessed 28/07/2011.

Organisciak, P. (2010). 'Why Bother? Examining the Motivations of Users of Large-Scale Crowd-Powered Online Initiatives'. Unpublished MA Thesis, Humanities Computing—Library and Information Studies, University of Alberta, Edmonton. http://repository.library.ualberta.ca/dspace/bitstream/10048/1370/1/ThesisOrganisciak-08-2010v2.pdf accessed 28/07/2011.

Orlikowski, W. J. (1992). 'The Duality of Technology: Rethinking the Concept of Technology in Organizations'. *Organization Science, 3*(3): 398–427.

Osborne, A. (1979). *Running Wild: The Next Industrial Revolution.* Berkeley, CA: McGraw-Hill Inc.

Ó Siochrú, S. and Girard, B. (2002). *Global Media Governance: A Beginners' Guide.* Lanham, MD: Rowman & Littlefield.

Ostrom, E. (2005). *Understanding Institutional Diversity.* Princeton, NJ: Princeton University Press.

Otlet, P. (1934). *Traite de documentation: Le livre sur le livre, theorie et pratique.* Brusells: Editiones Mundaneum, Palais Mondial.

Padovani, C. and Nordenstreng, K. (2005). 'From NWICO to WSIS: Another World Information and Communication Order?' *Global Media and Communication, 1*(3): 264–72.

—— Pavan, E. (2011). 'Actors and Interactions in Global Communication Governance: The Heuristic Potential of a Network Approach', in R. Mansell and M. Raboy (eds), *Handbook on Global Media and Communication Policy.* Malden, MA: Wiley-Blackwell, pp. 543–63.

Palfrey, J. G. (2004). 'The End of the Experiment: How ICANN's Foray into Global Internet Democracy Failed'. *Harvard Journal of Law & Technology, 17*(2): 410–73.

Papert, S. (1980). *Mindstorms: Children, Computers, and Powerful Ideas.* New York: Basic Books.

Park, E. G., Mitchell, C. and de Lange, N. (2008). 'Social Uses of Digitisation within the Context of HIV/AIDS: Metadata as Engagement'. *Online Information Review, 32*(6): 716–25.

Parsons, T. (1951/1991). *The Social System.* London: Routledge.

Pearson, I. (2010). 'Mad Scientists'. *Futurizon.* http://www.futurizon.com/articles/madscientists.pdf accessed 28/07/2011.

Perez, C. (1983). 'Structural Change and the Assimilation of New Technologies in the Economic and Social System'. *Futures, 15*(4): 357–75.

—— (2002). *Technological Revolution and Financial Capital: The Dynamics of Bubbles and Golden Ages.* Cheltenham: Edward Elgar.

Pfanner, E. (2011). 'G-8 Leaders to Call for Tighter Internet Regulation'. *New York Times,* 24 May, http://www.nytimes.com/2011/05/25/technology/25tech.html accessed 28/07/2011.

Picard, R. G. (1996). 'The Rise and Fall of Communications Empires'. *Journal of Media Economics, 9*(4): 23–40.

Pichevin, A. (2011). 'France's HADOPI Sends Out Final Copyright Infringement Notices, But Many are Critical'. *Billboardbiz,* 19 July, http://www.billboard.biz/bbbiz/industry/digital-and-mobile/france-s-hadopi-sends-out-final-copyright-1005282382.story accessed 28/07/2011.

Pierce, C. S. (1931/1935). 'Collected Papers of Charles Sanders Peirce, Vols. I–VI', in C. Hartshorne and P. Weiss (eds), *Collected Papers.* Cambridge, MA: Harvard University Press.

Pierce, J. R. (1956). *Electrons, Waves and Messages.* New York: Hanover House.

Pierson, J. and Heyman, R. (2011). 'Dataveillance and Privacy in Social Computing: Conceptual Exploration and Analysis of Corporate Profiling Techniques'. Paper presented at the *EuroCPR Conference,* Ghent, 26–28 March.

Pierson, J. and Heyman, R. (2011). 'Social Media and Cookies: Challenges for Online Privacy'. *Info* 13(6): 30–42.

Pilieci, V. (2011). 'Canadian Songwriters Propose $10 Fee for Music-sharing'. *The Gazette*, 5 March, http://www.montrealgazette.com/entertainment/Songwriters+propose+music+sharing/4387146/story.html accessed 28/07/2011.

Piper, F., Robshaw, M. J. B. and Schwiderski-Grosche, S. (2005). 'Identities and Authentication', in R. Mansell and B. S. Collins (eds), *Trust and Crime in Information Societies*. Cheltenham: Edward Elgar, pp. 91–112.

Plato (360BC). 'The Allegory of the Cave'. *The Republic, Book VII* (trans. B. Jowett). Cambridge, MA. http://classics.mit.edu/Plato/republic.8.vii.html accessed 10/07/2011.

Plowman, S. and Goode, S. (2009). 'Factors Affecting the Intention to Download Music: Quality Perceptions and Downloading Intensity'. *Journal of Computer Information Systems* 49(4): 84–97.

Polanyi, K. (1944/2001). *The Great Transformation: The Political and Economic Origins of Our Time*. Boston, MA: Beacon Press.

Polanyi, M. (1966). *The Tacit Dimension*. London: Routledge and Kegan Paul.

Pollock, J. T. (2009). *Semantic Web for Dummies*. Hoboken, NJ: Wiley Publishing.

Porat, M. U. and Rubin, M. R. (1977). *The Information Economy, Nine Volumes*. Washington, DC: Department of Commerce Government Printing Office.

Poteete, A. R., Janssen, M. A. and Ostrom, E. (2010). *Working Together: Collective Action, the Commons, and Multiple Methods in Practice*. Princeton, NJ: Princeton University Press.

Powell, A. and Cooper, A. (2011). 'Net Neutrality Discourses: Comparing Advocacy and Regulatory Arguments in the United States and the United Kingdom'. *The Information Society*, 27(5): 311–25.

Prencipe, A., Davies, A. and Hobday, M. (eds) (2003). *The Business of Systems Integration*. Cheltenham: Edward Elgar.

Price, D. (2011). *Technical Report: An Estimate of Infringing Use of the Internet*. Cambridge: Envisional Ltd. http://documents.envisional.com/docs/Envisional-Internet_Usage-Jan2011.pdf accessed 28/07/2011.

Prigogine, I. (1997). *The End of Certainty*. New York: Free Press.

Puppis, M. (2010). 'Media Governance: A New Concept for the Analysis of Media Policy and Regulation'. *Communication, Culture & Critique*, 3(2): 134–49.

Quiring, O., Von Walter, B. and Atterer, R. (2008). 'Can Filesharers be Triggered by Economic Incentives? Results of an Experiment'. *New Media & Society*, 10(3): 433–53.

Raacke, J. and Bonds-Raacke, J. (2008). 'MySpace and Facebook: Applying the Uses and Gratifications Theory to Exploring Friend-Networking Sites'. *CyberPsychology & Behavior*, 11(2): 169–74.

Rabby, M. K. and Walther, J. B. (2003). 'Computer-Mediated Communication Effects on Relationship Formation and Maintenance', in D. J. Canary and M. Dainton (eds), *Maintaining Relationships through Communication: Relational, Contextual and Cultural Variations*. London: Routledge, pp. 141–62.

Raboy, M., Shtern, J., with McIver, W. J., Murray, L. J. O., Siochru, S. and Shade, L. R. (2010). *Media Divides: Communication Rights and the Right to Communicate in Canada*. Vancouver: University of British Columbia Press.

Ramage, M. and Shipp, K. (2009). *Systems Thinkers*. London: Springer.

Ramshurn, S. D. and Jennings, N. R. (2005). 'Trust in Agent-based Software', in R. Mansell and B. S. Collins (eds), *Trust and Crime in Information Societies*. Cheltenham: Edward Elgar, pp. 165–204.

Rapport, N. (1999). 'Context as an Act of Personal Externalisation, Gregory Bateson and the Harvey Family in the English Village of Wanet', in R. Dilley (ed.), *The Problem of Context*. New York: Berghahn Books, pp. 187–212.

Rawls, J. (1972). *A Theory of Justice*. Oxford: Oxford University Press.

Raymond, E. S. (1999). *The Cathedral and the Bazaar: Musings on Linux and Open Source by an Accidental Revolutionary*. Sebastopol, CA: O'Reilly and Associates.

Rayward, W. B. (ed.) (1990). *International Organisation and Dissemination of Knowledge: Selected Essays of Paul Otlet, Translated and Edited with an Introduction*. Amsterdam: Elsevier Science Publishers.

Razavi, A., Moschoyiannis, S. and Krause, P. (2007). 'Preliminary Architecture for P2P Network Focusing on Hierarchical Virtual Super-Peers, Birth and Growth Models'. Deliverable 3.1, WP 3 on Autopoietic P2P Networks, OPAALS Contract No. IST-034824, European Commission, June.

—— Krause, P., Munro, A., Gilbert, N., Hoyle, R. and McFadden, J. (2010). 'Paper on 'Evolutionary and Interaction Framework'. Deliverable 3.13, WP on Autopoietic P2P Networks OPAALS Contract No. IST-034824, European Commission, September.

—— Malone, P., Siqueira, P. and Serra, F. (2010). 'Infrastructure Integration, Distributed Identity, Trust, Accountability and RESTful Transaction Model'. Deliverable 3.12, WP 3 on Autopoietic P2P Networks, OPAALS Contract No. IST-034824, European Commission, September.

—— Moschoyiannis, S., Malone, P., Finnegan, J., Agrawa, A., Margarito, A., Wilson Souza Rosa, D., Heistracher, T. J. and Marinos, A. (2010). 'Finalised Infrastructural and Interaction Model, Interfaces and SBVR Part 1'. Deliverable 3.15, WP 3 onAutopoietic P2P Networks, OPAALS Contract No. IST-034824, European Commission, September.

Recording Industry Association of America (RIAA) (2010). 'RIAA Joins Congressional Caucus in Unveiling First-Ever List of Notorious Illegal Sites'. *RIAA*, 19 May, http://www.riaa.com/newsitem.php?id=58185AFD-5525-19D4-FFD2-4233518393AD accessed 28/07/2011.

Regner, T., Barria, J., Pitt, J. and Neville, B. (2009). 'An Artist Life Cycle Model for Digital Media Content: Strategies for the Light Web and the Dark Web'. *Electronic Commerce Research and Applications*, 8(6): 334–42.

Renda, A. (2010). 'Competition-Regulation Interface in Telecommunications: What's Left of the Essential Facility Doctrine'. *Telecommunications Policy*, 34(1–2): 23–35.

Rettie, R. (2009). 'Mobile Phone Communication: Extending Goffman to Mediated Interaction'. *Sociology*, 43(3): 421–38.

Reuters (2010). 'FTC Ends Probe of Google Street View Controversy', 27 October. *CNBC*. http://www.cnbc.com/id/39870448/FTC_Ends_Probe_of_Google_Street_View_Controversy accessed 28/07/2011.

Rheingold, H. (1993/2000). *The Virtual Community: Homesteading on the Electronic Frontier* (Revised edn). Cambridge, MA: MIT Press.

—— (2002). *Smart Mobs: The Next Social Revolution*. New York: Perseus Press.

Richardson, M., Agrawal, R. and Domingos, P. (2003). 'Trust Management for the Semantic Web', in D. Fensel, K. P. Sycara and J. Mylopoulos (eds), *The Semantic Web—ISWC 2003, Second International Semantic Web Conference*. Berlin: Springer, pp. 351–68.

Rieber, R. W. and Green, M. (1989). 'The Psychopathy of Everyday Life: Antisocial Behavior and Social Distress', in R. W. Rieber (ed.), *The Individual, Communication and Society: Essays in Memory of Gregory Bateson*. Cambridge: Cambridge University Press, pp. 48–89.

Rihani, S. (2002). *Complex Systems Theory and Development Practice*. London: Zed Books.

Robins, K. and Webster, A. (1999). *Times of Technoculture: From the Information Society to the Virtual Life*. London: Routledge.

Rogers, E. M. (1962). *The Diffusion of Innovations* New York: Free Press.

—— (1987). 'Progress, Problems and Prospects for Network Research: Investigating Relationships in the Age of Electronic Communication Technologies'. *Social Networks, 9*: 285–310.

—— (1994/1997). *A History of Communication Study: A Biographical Approach*. New York: Free Press.

—— (1995). *The Diffusion of Innovations*. (4th edn). New York: The Free Press.

Romer, P. (1990). 'Endogenous Technological Change'. *Journal of Political Economy, 98*(5, Pt. 2): 71–102.

Rooney, D. and Schneider, U. (2005). 'The Material, Mental, Historical and Social Character of Knowledge', in D. Rooney, G. Hearn and A. Ninan (eds), *Handbook on the Knowledge Economy*. Cheltenham: Edward Elgar, pp. 19–36.

Rose, N. (1999). *Governing the Soul: The Shaping of the Private Self*. London: Free Association Books.

—— Miller, P. (1992). 'Political Power Beyond the State: Problematics of Government'. *British Journal of Sociology, 43*(2): 173–205.

Rosen, R. (1991). *Life Itself: A Comprehensive Inquiry into the Nature, Origin and Fabrication of Life*. New York: Columbia University Press.

Rosen, L. (2004). *Open Source Licensing: Software Freedom and Intellectual Property Law*. Upper Saddle River, NJ: Prentice-Hall.

Rosenberg, N. (1976). *Perspectives on Technology*. Cambridge: Cambridge University Press.

—— (1982a). *Inside the Black Box: Technology and Economics*. Cambridge: Cambridge University Press.

—— (1982b). 'Learning by Using' *Inside the Black Box: Technology and Economics*. Cambridge: Cambridge University Press, pp. 120–40.

—— (1994). *Exploring the Black Box: Technology, Economics and History*. Cambridge: Cambridge University Press.

Ross, P. (2005). 'Mediation in New Media Production: Representation and Involvement of Audiences/Users at NESTA Futurelab'. Unpublished PhD Thesis, Department of Media and Communications, London School of Economics and Political Science.

—— (2011). 'Is There an Expertise of Production? The Case of New Media Producers'. *New Media & Society, 13*(6): 912–28.

Rosser, J. B. (ed.) (2009). *Handbook of Research on Complexity*. Cheltenham: Edward Elgar.

Roszak, T. (1994). *The Cult of Information: A Neo-Luddite Treatise on High-tech, Artificial Intelligence, and the True Art of Thinking* (2nd edn). Berkeley, CA: University of California Press.

Ruesch, J. and Bateson, G. (1951). *Communication, The Social Matrix of Psychiatry*. New York: Norton.

Russell, S. J. and Norvig, P. (2010). *Artificial Intelligence: A Modern Approach* (3rd edn). New York: Prentice-Hall.

Ryan, J. and Heinl, C. (2010). 'Internet Access Controls: Three Strikes 'Graduated Response' Initiatives'. Note for Comment by The Institute of International and European Affairs (IIEA), Dublin, May.

Rycroft, R. and Kash, D. (1999). *The Complexity Challenge*. London: Pinter.

Sadowski, B. M., Sadowski-Rasters, G. and Duysters, G. (2008). 'Transition of Governance in a Mature Open Software Source Community: Evidence from the Debian Case'. *Information Economics and Policy, 20*(4): 323–32.

Sakata, T., Tada, H. and Ohtake, T. (1997). 'Metadata Mediation: Representation and Protocol', in P. H. Enslow, M. Genesereth and A. Patterson (eds), *Selected Papers from the Sixth International Conference on the World Wide Web*. Amsterdam: Elsevier Science Publishers, pp. 1137–46.

Samarajiva, R. and Shields, P. (1990). 'Integration, Telecommunication, and Development: Power in the Paradigms'. *Journal of Communication, 40*(3): 84–105.

Samuelson, P. (2007). 'Preliminary Thoughts on Copyright Reform'. *Utah Law Review, 2007*(3): 551–71.

Sandvig, C. (2007). 'Network Neutrality is the New Common Carriage'. *Info, 9*(2/3): 136–47.

Santucci, G. (2011). 'The Internet of Things: A Window to Our Future'. *The Internet of Things Council*, February. http://wwwtheinternetofthingseu/content/gérald-santucci-internet-things-window-our-future accessed 28/07/2011.

Sassen, S. (2001). 'On the Internet and Sovereignty'. *Indiana Journal of Global Legal Studies, 5*(2): 545–59.

Schiller, H. I. (1974). 'Waiting for Orders—Some Current Trends in Mass Communications Research in the United States'. *Gazette, 1*(1): 11–21.

—— (1981). *Who Knows? Information in the Age of the Fortune 500*. Norwood, NJ: Ablex.

Schiller, D. (1996). *Theorizing Communication: A History*. New York: Oxford University Press.

—— (2007). *How to Think about Information*. Urbana, IL: University of Illinois Press.

Schmitz, H.-C., Wolpers, M. and Kirschenmann, U. (2009). *Contextualized Attention Metadata*: CAPLE-Group, Fraunhofer FIT.

Schumpeter, J. A. (1934/1961). *The Theory of Economic Development: An Inquiry into Profits, Capital, Credit, Interest and the Business Cycle*. Oxford: Oxford University Press.

Scott, A. and Street, J. (2001). 'From Media Politics to E-protest? The Use of Popular Culture and New Media in Parties and Social Movements', in F. Webster (ed.), *Culture and Politics in the Information Age: A New Politics?* London: Routledge.

Sen, A. (1985). 'Rights as Goals', in S. Guest and A. Milne (eds), *Equality and Discrimination: Essays in Freedom and Justice*. Stuttgart: Franz Steiner, pp. 12–26.

—— (1999). *Development as Freedom*. Oxford: Oxford University Press.

—— (2009). *The Idea of Justice*. New York: Allen Lane.

Sennett, R. (2006). *The Culture of the New Capitalism*. New Haven, CT: Yale University Press.

Shaikh, M. and Berdou, E. (2008). 'Review of Open Knowledge Initiatives Successes and Failures Evolving Characterization of the OSS 2.0 Phenomenon'. Deliverable 8.3, WP 8 on Open Source and Open Knowledge, OPAALS Contract No. IST-034824, European Commission, May.

Shannon, C. E. (1948). 'The Mathematical Theory of Communication'. *Bell System Technical Journal, 27*: 379–423 and 623–56.

Shannon, C. E. and Weaver, W. (1949). *Mathematical Theory of Communication*. Urbana, IL: University of Illinois Press.

Shapiro, A. L. (1999). *The Control Revolution: How the Internet is Putting Individuals in Charge and Changing the World We Know* (1st edn). New York: Public Affairs.

Shapiro, C. and Varian, H. R. (1998). *Information Rules: A Strategic Guide to the Network Economy*. Cambridge, MA: Harvard Business School Press.

Shirky, C. (2010). *Cognitive Surplus: Creativity and Generosity in a Connected Age*. New York: Allen Lane.

Sidak, J. G. (2007). 'What is the Network Neutrality Debate Really About?'. *International Journal of Communication, 1*: 377–88.

Silverstone, R. (1994). *Television and Everyday Life*. London: Routledge.

—— (1999). *Why Study the Media?* London: Sage Publications.

—— (2002). 'Complicity and Collusion in the Mediation of Everyday Life'. *New Literary History, 33*(4): 761–80.

—— (2007). *Media and Morality: On the Rise of the Mediapolis*. Cambridge: Polity Press.

—— Hirsch, E. (eds) (1992). *Consuming Technologies: Media and Information in Domestic Spaces*. London: Routledge.

Simmel, G. (1946). *The Web of Group-Affiliations* (trans. R. Bendix). New York: Free Press.

Sinclair, L. (2010). 'Surfing the Web Can Make You Depressed'. *Sky News Online*, 3 February, http://news.sky.com/skynews/Home/Technology/Internet-Surfing-Linked-To-Depression-According-To-New-Research-In-Psychopathology/Article/201002115540691 accessed 28/07/2011.

Skeels, M. M. and Grudin, J. (2009). 'When Social Networks Cross Boundaries: A Case Study of Workplace Use of Facebook and LinkedIn', *Proceedings of the ACM 2009 International Conference on Supporting Group Work*. New York: ACM, pp. 95–104.

Sluijs, J. P. (2010). 'Network Neutrality Between False Positives and False Negatives: Introducing a European Approach to American Broadband Markets'. *Federal Communications Law Journal, 62*(1): 77–117.

Smythe, D. W. (1977). 'Communications: Blindspot of Western Marxism'. *Canadian Journal of Political and Social Theory, 1*(3): 1–27.

—— (1981). *Dependency Road: Communications, Capitalism, Consciousness and Canada*. Norwood, NJ: Ablex.

—— (1984). 'New Directions for Critical Communications Research'. *Media Culture and Society, 6*(3): 205–17.

Soete, L. (1985). 'International Diffusion of Technology, Industrial Development and Technological Leapfrogging'. *World Development, 13*(3): 409–22.

—— Kamp, K. (1996). 'The "Bit Tax": The Case for Further Research'. Draft Paper, MERIT, University of Maastricht, 12 August.

Solow, R. M. (1956). 'A Contribution to the Theory of Economic Growth'. *Quarterly Journal of Economics, 70*(1): 65–94.

Solum, L. B. (2009). 'Models of Internet Governance', in L. A. Bygrave and J. Bing (eds), *Internet Governance: Infrastructures and Institutions*. Oxford: Oxford University Press, pp. 48–91.

Sörenson, E. and Torfing, J. (eds) (2008). *Theories of Democratic Network Governance*. Basingstoke: Palgrave Macmillan.

Sparks, C. (2007). *Globalization, Development and the Mass Media*. London: Sage.

Spulber, D. F. and Yoo, C. S. (2009). *Networks in Telecommunications Economics and Law.* Cambridge: Cambridge University Press.

Stacey, R., Griffin, D. and Shaw, P. (2000). *Complexity and Management: Fad or Radical Challenge to Systems Thinking?* London: Routledge.

Stallman, R. (2009). 'Viewpoint: Why "Open Source" Misses the Point of Free Software'. *Communications of the ACM, 52:* 31.

Stanley, J. (2010). 'The Impact of New IP Legislation on Corporate Behaviour, SME Opportunities and Global Markets for Protected Innovations and the Presentation of a Formal Copyright Model'. Deliverable 11.12, WP 11 on Bridging Digital Ecosystems Research to Regional Development and Innovation in the Knowledge Economy, OPAALS Contract No. IST-034824, European Commission, September.

Star, S. L. and Griesemer, J. R. (1989). 'Institutional Ecology, "Translations" and Boundary Objects: Amateurs and Professionals in Merkeley's museum of Vertebrate Zoology, 1907–1939'. *Social Studies of Science, 19*(3): 387–420.

—— Ruhleder, K. (1994). 'Steps Towards an Ecology of Infrastructure: Complex Problems in Design and Access for Large-Scale Collaborative Systems', in *Proceedings of the ACM Conference on Computer Supported Cooperative Work.* New York: ACM, pp. 253–64.

Stauffacher, D. and Kleinwächter, W. (eds) (2005). *The World Summit on the Information Society: Moving from the Past into the Future.* New York: United Nations Task Force on ICTs.

Steier, F. (2005). 'Exercising Frame Flexibility'. *Cybernetics & Human Knowing, 12*(1–2): 36–49.

Steinmueller, W. E. (2000). 'Will New Information and Communication Technologies Improve the "Codification" of Knowledge'. *Industrial and Corporate Change, 9*(2): 361–76.

—— (2001/2). 'ICTs and the Possibilities for Leapfrogging by Developing Countries'. *International Labour Review, 140*(2): 193–211.

—— (2006). 'Learning in the Knowledge-based Economy: The Future as Viewed from the Past', in C. Antonelli, D. Foray, B. H. Hall and W. E. Steinmueller (eds), *New Frontiers in the Economics of Innovation and New Technology.* Cheltenham: Edward Elgar, pp. 207–38.

Stevenson, J. H. and Clement, A. (2010). 'Regulatory Lessons for Internet Traffic Management from Japan, the European Union, and the United States: Toward Equity, Neutrality, and Transparency'. *Global Media Journal—Canadian Edition, 3*(1): 9–29.

Stigler, G. J. (1961). 'The Economics of Information'. *Journal of Political Economy, 69*(3): 213–25.

Stiglitz, J. E., Sen, A. and Fitoussi, J.-P. (2010). *Report by the Commission on the Measurement of Economic Performance and Social Progress.* Paris: Commission on the Measurement of Economic Performance and Social Progress.

Stiglitz, J. E. (2010). *Freefall: Free Markets and the Sinking of the Global Economy.* London: Allen Lane.

Stirling, A. (2008). ' "Opening Up" and "Closing Down": Power, Participation, and Pluralism in the Social Appraisal of Technology'. *Science, Technology & Human Values, 33*(2): 262–94.

Strategic Advisory Board for Intellectual Property Policy. (2010). *The Economics of Copyright and Digitisation: A Report on the Literature and the Need for Further Research,* Prepared by C. Hanke, Erasmus University for the Strategic Advisory Board for Intellectual Property Policy, Rotterdam.

Streeten, P. P. (1974). *Some Problems in the Use and Transfer of an Intellectual Technology: The Social Sciences and Development.* Washington, DC: World Bank.

Streeten, P. P. (1982). 'Approaches to a New International Economic Order'. *World Development*, *10*(1): 1–17.

Strickland, J. (2011). 'How Web 3.0 Will Work'. *HowStuffWorks*. http://computer. howstuffworks.com/web-305.htm accessed 28/07/2011.

Subrahmanyam, K., Reich, S. M., Waechter, N. and Espinoza, G. (2008). 'Online and offline Social Networks: Use of Social Networking Sites by Emerging Adults'. *Journal of Applied Developmental Psychology*, *29*(6): 420–33.

Summerton, J. (ed.) (1994). *Changing Large Technical Systems*. Boulder, CO: Westwiew Press.

Sunstein, C. R. (2001). *Republic.com*. Princeton, NJ: Princeton University Press.

—— (2009). *Going to Extremes: How Like Minds Unite and Divide*. Oxford: Oxford University Press.

Surowiecki, J. (2004). *The Wisdom of Crowds: Why the Many are Smarter than the Few and How Collective Wisdom Shapes Business, Economies, Societies and Nations*. New York: Doubleday.

Swanson, E. B. and Ramiller, N. C. (1997). 'The Organizing Vision in Information Systems Innovation'. *Organization Science*, *8*(5): 458–74.

Tambini, D. (2004). 'The Passing of Paternalism: Public Service Television and Increasing Channel Choice', in D. Tambini and J. Cowling (eds), *From Public Service Broadcasting to Public Service Communications*. London: Institute for Public Policy Research, pp. 46–60.

Tapscott, D. (1995). *The Digital Economy: Promise and Peril in the Age of Networked Intelligence*. New York: McGraw-Hill.

—— (2010). 'ClimateSpark—A New Venture Capital Context'. *Don Tapscott Blog*, 3 November, http://dontapscott.com/2010/11/03/climatespark-a-new-venture-capital-contest/ accessed 28/07/2011.

—— Williams, A. D. (2007). *Wikinomics: How Mass Collaboration Changes Everything*. New York: Tantor Media.

Taylor, C. (2002a). 'Modern Social Imaginaries'. *Public Culture*, *14*(1): 91–124.

—— (2002b). *Understanding the Other: A Gadamerian View on Conceptual Schemes*. Cambridge, MA: MIT Press.

—— (2004). *Modern Social Imaginaries*. Durham, NC: Duke University Press.

—— (2007). *A Secular Age*. Cambridge, MA: Belknap Press.

TERA Consultants. (2010). *Building the Digital Economy: The Importance of Saving Jobs in the EU's Creative Industries*. Paris: TERA Consultants, Commissioned by the International Chamber of Commerce/BASCAP Initiative. http://www.teraconsultants.fr/assets/publications/PDF/2010-Mars-Etude_Piratage_TERA_full_report-En.pdf accessed 28/07/2011.

The Economist. (2011). 'Not Just Talk: Clever Services on Cheap Mobile Phones Make a Powerful Combination—Especially in Poor Countries'. *The Economist*, pp. 1–4.

The Guardian. (2010). 'Britain Logs On To a World-beating £100bn Internet Economy'. *The Guardian*. http://www.guardian.co.uk/technology/2010/oct/28/net-worth-100bn-uk accessed 28/07/2011.

Thelwall, M. (2008). 'Social Networks, Gender, and Friending: An Analysis of MySpace Member Profiles'. *Journal of the American Society for Information Science and Technology*, *59*(8): 1321–30.

The White House. (2009). *Open Government: A Progress Report to the American People*. Washington, DC: United States Government White House, December.

Thompson, E. P. (1971). 'The Moral Economy of the English Crowd in the Eighteenth Century'. *Past and Present*, *50*: 78–136.

Thompson, J. B. (1982). 'Ideology and the Social Imaginary: An Appraisal of Castoriadis and Lefort'. *Theory and Society, 11*(5): 659–81.

Thompson, J. B. (1993). 'The Theory of the Public Sphere'. *Theory, Culture & Society, 10*(3): 173–89.

—— (1995). *The Media and Modernity: A Social Theory of the Media.* Cambridge: Polity.

Time Magazine (1993). 'The Info Highway: Bringing a Revolution in Entertainment, News, and Communication'. *Time Magazine,* 12 April, http://www.atlanticfinancial.com/about-atlantic-financial/time_magazine_information_highway.htm accessed 09/09/2011.

Titelman, G. Y. (1996). *Random House Dictionary of Popular Proverbs and Sayings.* New York: Random House.

Toffler, A. (1980). *The Third Wave.* New York: Pan Books.

—— Toffler, H. (2006). *Revolutionary Wealth: How It Will Be Created and How It Will Change Our Lives.* New York: Currency.

Toulouse, C. and Luke, T. W. (eds) (1998). *The Politics of Cyberspace.* London: Routledge.

Touré, H. I. (2008). *ITU Secretary-General's Declaration on Cybersecurity and Climate Change.* Geneva: High-Level Segment of Council, International Telecommunication Union. http://www.itu.int/council/C2008/hls/statements/closing/sg-declaration.html accessed 28/07/2011.

Trivers, R. (1985). *Social Evolution.* Menlo Park, CA: Benjamin Cummings.

Turing, A. (1950). 'Computing Machinery and Intelligence: Can Machines Think?'. *Mind, 59* (236): 433–60.

Turkle, S. (1984/2005). *The Second Self: Computers and the Human Spirit.* Cambridge, MA: MIT Press.

—— (1995). *Life on the Screen: Identity in the Age of the Internet.* New York: Simon & Schuster.

—— (2011). *Alone Together: Why We Expect More from Technology and Less from Each Other.* New York: Basic Books.

United Kingdom Government (2002). *Enterprise Act 2002 c.40.* London: Government of the United Kingdom. http://www.legislation.gov.uk/ukpga/2002/40/section/58 accessed 28/07/2011.

—— (2003). *Communications Act 2003 c.21.* London: Government of the United Kingdom. thttp://www.legislation.gov.uk/ukpga/2003/21/contents accessed 28/07/2011.

—— (2010). *Digital Economy Act 2010 c.24.* London: Government of the United Kingdom. http://www.legislation.gov.uk/ukpga/2010/24/contents accessed 28/07/2011.

United Nations (1948). *The Universal Declaration of Human Rights.* Geneva: United Nations at http://www.un.org/en/documents/udhr/index.shtml accessed 28/07/2011.

—— (2001). *United Nations General Assembly Resolution on the World Summit on the Information Society.* New York: United Nations General Assembly, Resolution A/RES/56/183. http://unpan1.un.org/intradoc/groups/public/documents/un/unpan014250.pdf accessed 28/07/2011.

—— (2008). *The Millennium Development Goals Report 2008.* New York: United Nations. http://www.un.org/millenniumgoals/pdf/The%20Millennium%20Development%20Goals%20Report%202008.pdf accessed 28/07/2011.

—— (2010a). *The Global Partnership for Development at a Critical Juncture: Millennium Development Goal 8.* New York: United Nations MDG Gap Task Force Report 2010. http://www.un.org/millenniumgoals/pdf/10-43282_MDG_2010%20(E)%20WEBv2.pdf accessed 28/07/2011.

United Nations (2010b). *The Millennium Development Goals Report 2010.* New York: United Nations. http://www.un.org/millenniumgoals/pdf/MDG%20Report%202010%20En%20r15%20-low%20res%2020100615%20-.pdf accessed 28/07/2011.

United Nations Conference on Trade and Development (UNCTAD) (2010a). *Creative Economy Report 2010.* Geneva: UNCTAD. http://www.unctad.org/Templates/WebFlyer.asp?intItemID=5763&lang=1 accessed 28/07/2011.

—— (2010b). *Information Economy Report 2010: ICTs, Enterprises and Poverty Alleviation.* Geneva: United Nations Conference on Trade and Development.

United Nations Development Programme (UNDP) (1990). *Human Development Report 1990.* New York: United Nations Development Programme.

—— (1999). *Human Development Report 1999.* New York: United Nations Development Programme and Oxford University Press.

United Nations Educational, Scientific and Cultural Organization (UNESCO) (2005a). *Convention on the Protection and Promotion of the Diversity of Cultural Expressions.* Paris: UNESCO Publishing.

—— (2005b). *Towards Knowledge Societies—UNESCO World Report.* Paris: UNESCO Publishing.

—— (2009). *Investing in Cultural Diversity and Intercultural Dialogue: UNESCO World Report.* Paris: UNESCO Publishing.

United Nations/International Telecommunication Union (2003a). *Declaration of Principles: Building the Information Society: A Global Challenge in the New Millennium.* Geneva: United Nations and International Telecommunication Union, WSIS-03/Geneva/Doc/4-E, 12 December.

—— (2003b). *Plan of Action: WSIS.* Geneva: United Nations and International Telecommunication Union, WSIS-03/Geneva/Doc/5-E, 12 December.

—— (2005a). *Tunis Agenda for the Information Society.* Tunis: United Nations and International Telecommunication Union, WSIS-05/Tunis/Doc/6(Rev.1)-E, 18 November.

—— (2005b). *Tunis Commitment.* Tunis: United Nations and International Telecommunication Union, WSIS-05/Tunis/Doc/7-E, 18 November.

United States Government. (1958). *USA v Western Electric Company, Inc and American Telephone and Telegraph Co., Report Regarding Equipment Manufactured by Western for the Bell System, Hearings before the Antitrust Subcommittee of the Committee of the Judiciary House of Representatives, 85th Congress, Second Session, Part II, Volume III, Consent Decree Programme of the Department of Justice.* Washington, DC: United States Department of Justice.

—— (1996). *Telecommunications Act of 1996, Pub. LA. No. 104-104, 110 Stat. 56 (1996).* Washington, DC: United States Government. http://www.fcc.gov/Reports/tcom1996.pdf accessed 28/07/2011.

—— (1998). *Digital Millennium Copyright Act.* United States: United States Government. http://frwebgate.access.gpo.gov/cgi-bin/getdoc.cgi?dbname=105_cong_public_laws&docid=f:publ304.105.pdf accessed 28/07/2011.

—— (2009). *Copyright Law of the United States and Related Laws Contained in Title 17 of the United States Code.* Washington, DC: United States Government. http://www.copyright.gov/title17/circ92.pdf accessed 28/07/2011.

—— (2010). *Comcast Corp. v. FCC, Case No. 08-1291.* Washington, DC: United States District of Columbia Circuit, Court of Appeals for the District of Columbia Circuit. http://pacer.cadc.uscourts.gov/common/opinions/201004/08-1291-1238302.pdf accessed 22/11/2010.

United States Government. (2011). *S.968: Protect IP Act—Preventing Real Online Threats to Economic Creativity and Theft of Intellectual Property Act of 2011*. Washington, DC: United States Government, 12 May, http://leahy.senate.gov/imo/media/doc/BillText-PROTECTIPAct.pdf accessed 28/07/2011.

Universities-National Bureau Staff (ed.) (1962). *The Rate and Direction of Inventive Activity: Economic and Social Factors* (ed. R. R. Nelson). Washington, DC: National Bureau of Economic Research Inc.

Urry, J. (2004). 'Small Worlds and the New "Social Physics"'. *Global Networks*, 4(2): 109–30.

Val, J. (2010). 'A Complete Use Case Integration with Aragon SMEs'. Deliverable 5.10, WP on Integration with the Digital Ecosystem Platform, OPAALS Contract No. IST-034824, European Commission Project Review, October.

Vanberg, A. D. (2011). 'Search Engine Dominance in the European Digital Economy'. Paper presented at the EuroCPR Conference, Ghent, 26–28 March.

Van Couvering, E. J. (2010). 'Search Engine Bias: The Structuration of Traffic on the World-Wide Web'. Unpublished PhD Thesis, London School of Economics and Political Science.

Van de Donk, W., Loader, B. D., Nixon, P. G. and Rucht, D. (eds) (2004). *Cyberprotest: New Media, Citizens and Social Movements*. London: Routledge.

Van Der Graaf, A. A. C. G. (2009). 'Designing for Mod Development: User Creativity as Product Development Strategy on the Firm-hosted 3D Software Platform'. Unpublished PhD Thesis, Department of Media and Communications, London School of Economics and Political Science.

Vanderstraeten, R. (2000). 'Autopoiesis and Socialization: On Luhmann's Reconceptualization of Communication and Socialization'. *British Journal of Sociology*, 51(3): 581–98.

Van Dijck, J. and Nieborg, D. (2009). 'Wikinomics and its Discontents: A Critical Analysis of Web 2.0 Business Manifestos'. *New Media & Society*, 11(5): 855–74.

van Dijk, J. A. G. M. (2006a). 'Digital Divide Research, Achievements and Shortcomings'. *Poetics*, 34(4–5): 221–35.

—— (2006b). *The Network Society* (2nd edn). London: Sage Publications.

Van Egeraat, C. and Curran, D. (2010). 'Structures of Knowledge Flow and Innovation in the Irish Biotechnology Industry'. Deliverable 11.11, WP 11 Bridging Digital Ecosystems Research to Regional Development and Innovation in the Knowledge Economy, OPAALS Contract No. IST-034824, European Commission, June.

van Eijk, N. (2009). 'Search Engines, the New Bottleneck for Content Access' in J. Haucap and B. Preissl (eds), *Telecommunication Markets: Drivers and Impediments*. Heidelberg: Springer Physica-Verlag, pp. 141–56.

Veblen, T. (1899/2008). *The Theory of the Leisure Class*. Charleston, SC: Forgotten Books.

Vinge, V. (1993). 'Technological Singularity'. *Whole Earth Review* (Spring): np. Original version presented at the VISION-21 Symposium, NASA Leis Research Center and Ohio Aerospace Institute, 30–31 March 1993, Winter.

von Bertalanffy, L. (1950). 'An Outline of General System Theory'. *British Journal of the Philosophy of Science*, 1(2): 134–65.

—— (1956). 'General System Theory'. *General Systems Yearbook*, 1: 1–10.

—— (1968). *General Systems Theory: Foundations, Development, Applications*. New York: Braziller.

von Goethe, J. W. (1797). *Der Zauberlehrling (The Sorcerer's Apprentice)* (trans. E. Zeydel). http://www.margotserowyfineart.com/socapppoem.html accessed 28/07/2011.

von Hippel, E. (2002). 'Shifting Innovation to Users via Toolkits'. *Management Science, 48*(7): 821–33.

—— (2005a). *Democratizing Innovation*. Cambridge, MA: MIT Press.

—— (2005b). 'Open Source Software Projects as "User Innovation Networks"', in J. Feller, B. Fitzgerald, S. Hissam and K. R. Lakhani (eds), *Perspectives on Free and Open Source Software*. Cambridge, MA: MIT Press, pp. 267–78.

von Schiller, F. (1797). *Hope* (Trans. E. Ezust). Die Horen. http://www.recmusic.org/lieder/ get_text.html?TextId=14499 accessed 28/07/2011.

Wade, R. H. (2002). 'Bridging the Digital Divide: New Route to Development or New Form of Dependency?'. *Global Governance, 8*(4): 365–88.

Wagner, R. K. and Sternberg, R. J. (1985). 'Practical Intelligence in Real World Pursuits—The Role of Tacit Knowledge'. *Journal of Personality and Social Psychology, 49*(2): 436–58.

Waite, C. J. (1877). *Opinion of the Court*. Supreme Court of the United States, 94 US 113 Munn v. Illinois. http://www.law.cornell.edu/supct/html/historics/USSC_CR_0094_0113_ZO.html accessed 28/07/2011.

Wall, D. S. (ed.) (2001). *Crime and the Internet*. London: Routledge.

Walsham, G. (1993). *Interpreting Information Systems in Organizations*. Chichester: John Wiley.

Walther, J. B. (2007). 'Selective Self-presentation in Computer-mediated Communication: Hyperpersonal Dimensions of Technology, Language, and Cognition'. *Computers in Human Behavior, 23*(5): 2538–57.

—— Van Der Heide, B., Kim, S.-Y., Westerman, D. and Tong, S. T. (2008). '"The Role of Friends" Appearance and Behavior on Evaluations of Individuals on Facebook: Are We Known by the Company We Keep?'. *Human Communication Research, 34*(1): 28–49.

—— —— Hamel, L. M. and Shulman, H. C. (2009). 'Self-Generated Versus Other-Generated Statements and Impressions in Computer-Mediated Communication'. *Communication Research, 36*(2): 229–53.

Warner, M. (2002). 'Publics and Counterpublics'. *Public Culture, 14*(1): 49–90.

Warschauer, M. (2003). *Technology and Social Inclusion: Rethinking the Digital Divide*. Cambridge, MA: MIT Press.

Wasko, J., Murdock, G. and Sousa, H. (eds) (2011). *The Handbook of Political Economy of Communications*. Malden, MA: Wiley-Blackwell.

Waskul, D. D. (2005). 'Ekstasis and the Internet: Liminality and Computer-mediated Communication'. *New Media & Society, 7*(1): 47–63.

Watt, R. (2000). *Copyright and Economic Theory: Friends or Foes?* Cheltenham: Edward Elgar.

Watts, A. W. (1961). *Psychotherapy, East and West*. New York: Pantheon Books.

Watzlawick, P., Jackson, D. and Beavin, J. (1967). *Pragmatics of Human Communication: A Study of Interaction Patterns, Pathologies, and Paradoxes*. New York: W. W. Norton.

Weber, S. (2004). *The Success of Open Source*. Cambridge, MA: Harvard University Press.

Webster, F. (1999). 'Media Technology and Society, a History: From the Telegraph to the Internet'. *European Journal of Communication, 14*(3): 417–18.

—— (2006). *Theories of the Information Society* (3rd edn). London: Routledge.

Weick, K. E. (2001). *Making Sense of the Organization*. Oxford: Blackwell.

Wellman, B. (1983). 'Network Analysis: Some Basic Principles', in R. Collins (ed.), *Sociological Theory*. San Francisco, CA: Jossey-Bass, pp. 155–200.

Wellman, B., Quan-Haase, A., Boase, J., Chen, W., Hampton, K. N., Diaz, I. and Miyata, K. (2003). 'The Social Affordances of the Internet for Networked Individualism'. *Journal of Computer Mediated Communication, 8*(3): np.

Wenger, E. (1998). *Communities of Practice: Learning, Meaning and Identity.* Cambridge: Cambridge University Press.

Werbach, K. (1997). 'Digital Tornado: The Internet and Telecommunications Policy'. *FCC Office of Plans and Policy Working Paper Series No. 29*, Washington, DC, March.

Wessels, B. (2010). *Understanding the Internet: A Socio-Cultural Perspective.* Basingstoke: Palgrave Macmillan.

White, H. (1992). *Identity and Control.* Princeton, NJ: Princeton University Press.

Whitehead, A. N. and Russell, B. (1910). *Principia Mathematica.* Cambridge: Cambridge University Press.

Whitley, E. A. (1997). 'In Cyberspace All They See Is Your Words: A Review of the Relationship between Body, Behaviour and Identity Drawn from the Sociology of Knowledge'. *Information Technology and People, 10*(2): 147–63.

—— Hosein, G. (2009). *Global Challenges for Identity Policies.* Basingstoke: Palgrave Macmillan.

Wiener, N. (1948/1961). *Cybernetics: Or Control and Communication in the Animal and Machine.* Cambridge, MA: MIT Press.

—— (1950). *The Human Use of Human Beings: Cybernetics and Society.* New York: Houghton Mifflin.

Wilden, A. (1972/2001). *System and Structure: Essays in Communication and Exchange* (2nd edn). London: Tavistock Publications and Routledge.

—— Hammer, R. (1987). *The Rules are No Game: The Strategy of Communication.* London: Routledge & Kegan Paul.

Willcocks, L., Venters, W. and Whitley, E. A. (2011). 'Cloud and the Future of Business: From Costs to Innovation, Part Three: Impacts'. Report prepared for Accenture in association with The Outsourcing Unit, Department of Management, London School of Economics and Political Science.

Williams, R. (1990/2008). *Notes on the Underground: An Essay on Technology, Society and the Imagination,* (New edn). Cambridge, MA: MIT Press.

Williams, R. (1996). *Communications.* London: Chatto & Windus.

Williamson, J. (1990). *Latin American Adjustment: How Much Has Happened.* Washington, DC: Institute for International Economics.

Wilson, D. S. (2008). *Evolution for Everyone: How Darwin's Theory Can Change the Way We Think about Our Selves.* New York: Delta Trade Paperbacks.

Winner, L. (1977). *Autonomous Technology: Technology Out of Control as a Theme in Political Thought.* Cambridge, MA: MIT Press.

Winston, B. (1998). *Media, Technology and Society: From the Telegraph to the Internet.* London: Routledge.

Wittgenstein, L. (1951). *Tractatus Logico-Philosophicus.* New York: Humanities Press.

World Bank. (1999). *World Development Report—Knowledge for Development.* Washington, DC: The World Bank.

World Intellectual Property Organization (WIPO) (1886). *Berne Convention for the Protection of Literary and Artistic Works.* Geneva: World Intellectual Property Organization. http://www.wipo.int/treaties/en/ip/berne/trtdocs_wo001.html accessed 28/07/2011.

World Intellectual Property Organization (WIPO) (1998). *WIPO Annual Report*. Geneva: WIPO.

—— (2009). *World Intellectual Property Organization: An Overview*. Geneva: WIPO.

—— (2011). *WIPO Summer School Reading Material*. Geneva: WIPO. http://www.wipo.int/export/sites/www/academy/en/courses/summer_school/summer_school_textbook.pdf accessed 28/07/2011.

World Trade Organization (WTO) (1994). *Marrakesh Declaration of 15 April 1994*. Marrakesh: WTO. http://www.wto.org/english/docs_e/legal_e/marrakesh_decl_e.pdf accessed 28/07/2011.

Wright, A. (2003). 'Forgotten Forefather: Paul Otlet'. *Boxes and Arrows*. http://www.boxesandarrows.com/view/forgotten_forefather_paul_otlet accessed 28/07/2011.

Wu, T. (1999). 'Application-Centered Internet Analysis'. *Virginia Law Review, 85*(6): 1163–204.

—— (2003). 'Network Neutrality, Broadband Discrimination'. *Journal of Telecommunications and High Technology Law, 2*: 141–79.

—— (2010). *The Master Switch: The Rise and Fall of Information Empires*. New York: Alfred A. Knopf.

Yeats, W. B. (1926/1989). 'Among School Children', in R. J. Finneran (ed.), *The Collected Poems of W. B. Yeats, Vol 1: The Poems*, (2nd edn). New York: Scribner, pp. 219–21.

Yoo, C. S. (2005). 'Beyond Network Neutrality'. *Harvard Journal of Law & Technology, 19*(1): 1–77.

—— (2009). 'Network Neutrality after Comcast: Toward a Case-by-Case Approach to Reasonable Network Management'. *Scholarship at Penn. Law Paper 298*, University of Pennsylvania Law School, Philadelphia.

Zack, M. H. (1999). 'Managing Codified Knowledge'. *MIT Sloan Management Review, 40*(4): 45–58.

Zeleny, M. and Hufford, K. D. (1992). 'The Application of Autopoiesis in Systems Analysis: Are Autopoietic Systems also Social Systems?'. *International Journal of General Systems, 21*(4): 145–59.

Zittrain, J. (2003). 'Internet Points of Control'. *Boston College Law Review, 44*(2): 653–88.

—— (2008). *The Future of the Internet and How to Stop It*. New York: Allen Lane.

Žižek, S. (2006). *The Parallax View*. Cambridge, MA: MIT Press.

Zohar, D. and Marshall, I. (1994). *The Quantum Society*. New York: William Morrow.

■ INDEX